Introduction to Behavioral Research Methods

2nd Edition

Introduction to Behavioral Research Methods
2nd Edition

Mark R. Leary
Wake Forest University

Brooks/Cole Publishing Company

I(T)P ™An International Thomson Publishing Company

Pacific Grove • Albany • Bonn • Boston • Cincinnati • Detroit • London • Madrid • Melbourne
Mexico City • New York • Paris • San Francisco • Singapore • Tokyo • Toronto • Washington

Sponsoring Editor: *Jim Brace-Thompson*
Marketing Team: *Carolyn Crockett and Margaret Parks*
Marketing Representative: *Tom Orsi*
Editorial Associate: *Patsy Vienneau*
Production Editor: *Kirk Bomont*
Manuscript Editor: *Barbara Kimmel*
Permissions Editor: *Elaine Jones*

Interior Design: *Detta Penna*
Interior Illustration: *Laurie Albrecht*
Cover Design: *Mark Swindle*
Art Coordinator: *Susan H. Horovitz*
Typesetting: *Bi-Comp, Inc.*
Cover Printing: *Color Dot Graphics, Inc.*
Printing and Binding: *Quebecor Printing Fairfield*

For more information, contact:

BROOKS/COLE PUBLISHING COMPANY
511 Forest Lodge Road
Pacific Grove, CA 93950
USA

International Thomson Publishing Europe
Berkshire House 168-173
High Holborn
London WC1V 7AA
England

Thomas Nelson Australia
102 Dodds Street
South Melbourne, 3205
Victoria, Australia

Nelson Canada
1120 Birchmount Road
Scarborough, Ontario
Canada M1K 5G4

International Thomson Editores
Campos Eliseos 385, Piso 7
Col. Polanco
11560 México D. F. México

International Thomson Publishing GmbH
Königswinterer Strasse 418
53227 Bonn
Germany

International Thomson Publishing Asia
221 Henderson Road
#05-10 Henderson Building
Singapore 0315

International Thomson Publishing Japan
Hirakawacho Kyowa Building, 3F
2-2-1 Hirakawacho
Chiyoda-ku, Tokyo 102
Japan

Printed in the United States of America

10   9   8   7   6   5   4   3   2

Library of Congress Cataloging-in-Publication Data

Leary, Mark R.
    Introduction to behavioral research methods / Mark R. Leary. —
2nd ed.
        p.   cm.
    Includes bibliographical references and index.
    ISBN 0-534-20490-2
    1. Psychology—Research—Methodology. I. Title. II. Title:
Behavioral research methods.
8F76.5.L39   1995
150′,72—dc20
                                                    94-32272
                                                    CIP

To Ed, Eleanor, and Dale

Regardless of how good a particular class is, the students' enthusiasm for the course material is rarely, if ever, as great as the professor's. No matter how interesting the material, how motivated the students, or how skillful the professor, those who take a course are seldom as enthralled with the content as are those who teach it. In some courses, the discrepancy between student and professor attitudes is slight, whereas in others, the schism is large. But the difference virtually always exists. We've all taken many courses in which an animated, nearly zealous professor faced a classroom of only mildly interested students.

In departments founded on the principles of behavioral science—psychology, communication, human development, education, marketing, social work, and the like—this student–professor discrepancy is perhaps most pronounced in courses that deal with research design and analysis. On one hand, the individuals who teach courses in research methods are usually quite enthused about research. They typically enjoy the research process, some have contributed to the research literature in their own areas of expertise, and many are highly regarded researchers within their fields. On the other hand, despite these instructors' best efforts to bring the course alive, students often dread taking methods courses, find such courses dry and difficult, and wonder why such courses are required as part of their curriculum. Thus, the enthused, involved instructor is often confronted by a class of disinterested, even hostile students who begrudge the fact that they must study research methods at all.

These attitudes are, in many ways, understandable. After all, students who choose to study psychology, education, human development, and other areas that rely on behavioral research usually do so either because they plan to enter a profession in which knowledge of behavior is relevant (such as professional psychology, social work, teaching, or public relations) or because they are intrinsically interested in the subject matter. In either case, few students initially decide to study these areas because they are enamored with research. Although some students eventually come to appreciate the value of research to behavioral science, to the helping professions, and to society, others continue to view it as an unnecessary curricular diversion imposed by misguided academicians. For many students, being required to take courses in methodology and statistics supplants other courses in which they are more interested.

In addition, the concepts, principles, analyses, and ways of thinking central to methodology are new to most students and, thus, require extra effort to comprehend, learn, and retain. Add to that the fact that the topics covered in research methods courses are, on the whole, inherently less interesting than most other courses in psychology and related fields. If the instructor and textbook do not make a special effort to make the material interesting and relevant, students are unlikely to derive much enjoyment from studying research methods.

I wrote *Introduction to Behavioral Research Methods* because, as a teacher and as a researcher, I wanted a book that would help counteract students' natural tendencies to dislike and shy away from research—a book that would make research methodology as understandable, palatable, useful, and interesting for my students as it was for me.

My primary goal was to write a text that was *readable*. Students should be able to understand most of the material in a book such as this without the course instructor having to serve as an interpreter. Enhancing comprehensibility can be achieved in two ways. The less preferred way is simply to dilute the material by omitting complex topics. The alternative, which I chose in this text, is to present the material with sufficient elaboration, explanation, and examples to render it understandable.

A second goal was to integrate the various topics covered in the book to a greater extent than is done in most methods texts, using the concept of variability as a unifying theme. From the development of a research idea, through measurement issues, to design and analysis, the entire research process is an attempt to understand variability in behavior. Because the concept of variability is woven throughout the research process, I've used it as a framework to provide coherence to the various topics in the book.

Third, I tried to write a book that is interesting—that presents ideas in an engaging fashion and uses provocative examples of real and hypothetical research. (Unfortunately, a few topics defied my best attempts.) Like most researchers, I am enthusiastic about the research process, and I hope that some of my fervor will be contagious.

Courses in research methods differ widely in the degree to which statistics are incorporated into the course. My personal view is that statistics *are* research methods and that students' understanding of research methodology is enhanced by an elementary understanding of statistical principles. Students design better studies when they understand what will become of the data they collect. Furthermore, students find it difficult to understand the research articles they read without an elementary grasp of statistical concepts. Thus, although this book is decidedly about research methodology and design, I've sprinkled essential statistical topics here and there throughout the book.

Because I think it is more important for students in a methods course to develop a conceptual understanding of statistics than to learn to perform a wide array of analyses, I emphasize the conceptual foundations of statistics and provide calculation procedures for only a few basic analyses. Furthermore, knowing that instructors differ widely in the degree to which they incorporate statistics into their methods courses, I have made it easy for individual instructors to choose whether or not students will deal with the calculational aspects of the analyses that appear. For the most part, presentation of statistical calculations are confined to a few within-chapter boxes, Chapters 11 and 12, and Appendix B.

This edition of *Introduction to Behavioral Research Methods* differs from the first edition in four primary ways. First, the new edition has added a second chapter that focuses on measurement. Following Chapter 3, which deals with basic measurement issues, Chapter 4 focuses in detail on observational and self-report approaches to measurement. A second change in this edition involves inclusion of a chapter on advanced correlational research strategies. Given the pervasiveness of approaches such as partial correlation, regression, path analysis, and factor analysis in the research literature, today's students need at least a conceptual introduction to these kinds of procedures. Although these topics were included in the first edition, combining them into a single chapter provides an additional degree of coherence to the material.

A third change in this edition involves a reorganizing of the material on the design and analysis of experiments. In this edition, two full chapters are devoted to experimental methodology and design (Chapters 9 and 10), followed by two chapters on the logic of hypothesis testing and inferential statistics (Chapters 11 and 12). Instructors who wish to de-emphasize the statistical aspects of the material will find it easier to do so now than with the first edition. Finally, the chapter on single-case research (Chapter 14) has been expanded to include a section on case study methodology.

Many people contributed their time and effort to this book. Thanks especially to the following reviewers: Michael Berzonsky, SUNY-Cortland; Clarke Burnham, University of Texas at Austin; Valerie Greaud Folk, Educational Testing Service; Elizabeth Glisky, University of Arizona; David Hogan, Northern Kentucky University; Robin Kowalski, Western Carolina University; Frederick Meeker, California State Polytechnic University at Pomona; Peter Mikulka, Old Dominion University; Jessie Namikas, Madonna University; Padraig O'Seaghdha, Lehigh University; Theron Stimmel, Southwest Texas State University; Margaret Thomas, University of Central Florida; Paul Toro, Wayne State University; Toni

Wegner, University of Virginia; and Shuqiang, Zhang, University of Hawaii at Manoa.

As a teacher and author, I know that there will always be some discrepancy between professors' and students' interest in research methods. I hope this book will help narrow the gap.

Mark R. Leary
Winston-Salem, NC

CHAPTER I **Research in the Behavioral Sciences**   *I*

CHAPTER 5   *Describing and Presenting Data*   **94**

CHAPTER 6   *Sampling in Behavioral Research*   *118*

CHAPTER 9   *Basic Issues in Experimental Research*   **175**

CHAPTER 13 Quasi-Experimental Designs   268

CHAPTER 16 *Scientific Writing*   **334**

APPENDIX A *Statistical Tables*   372

APPENDIX B *Computational Formulas for ANOVA*   377

CHAPTER 1

Research in the Behavioral Sciences

S top for a moment and imagine, as vividly as you can, a scientist at work. Let your imagination fill in as many details as possible regarding this scene. What does the imagined scientist look like? Where is the person working? What is the scientist doing? When I asked a group of undergraduate students to imagine a scientist and to tell me what they imagined, their answers were quite enlightening. First, virtually every student said that the imagined scientist was male. This in itself is interesting given that a high percentage of scientists are, of course, women.

Second, a great majority reported that they imagined the scientist wearing a white lab coat and working indoors in some kind of laboratory. The details of this laboratory differed from student to student, but the lab almost always contained specialized scientific equipment of some kind. Some students imagined a chemist surrounded by substances in test tubes and beakers. Other students thought of a biologist peering into a microscope. Still others conjured up a physicist working with sophisticated electronic equipment. One or two students even imagined an astronomer peering through a telescope. Most interesting to me was that although these students were members of a psychology class (in fact, most were psychology majors), not one of them thought of any kind of a *behavioral scientist* when I asked them to imagine a scientist.

The students' responses were probably typical of what most people would say if asked to imagine a scientist. For most people, the prototypic scientist is a man wearing a white lab coat working in a laboratory filled with technical equipment. Most people do not think of psychologists and other behavioral researchers as scientists in the same way they think of physicists, chemists, and biologists as scientists. People tend to think of psychologists only in their roles as mental health professionals. If I had asked you to imagine a psychologist, you probably would have thought of a counselor talking with a client about his or her problems. You probably would not have imagined a behavioral researcher, such as a physiological

1

psychologist studying startle responses, a social psychologist conducting an experiment on aggression, or an industrial psychologist interviewing the line supervisors at an automobile assembly plant.

Psychology, however, is not only a profession that promotes human welfare through counseling, education, and other activities; it is also a scientific discipline that studies behavior and mental processes. Just as biologists study living organisms and astronomers study the stars, behavioral scientists conduct research involving behavior and mental processes.

Goals of Behavioral Research

Research holds an important place in the behavioral sciences, as well as in society in general. A large number of people devote part or all of their working lives to the scientific study of human and animal behavior. This group includes not only research psychologists but also researchers in areas as diverse as education, social work, family studies, communication, management, health and sport science, marketing, and a number of medical fields (such as nursing, neurology, psychiatry, and geriatrics). What researchers in all areas of behavioral science have in common is that they apply scientific methodologies to the study of behavior, thought, and emotion.

Roughly speaking, behavioral research fulfills four interrelated functions: describing behavior, understanding behavior, predicting behavior, and solving applied problems.

Describing Behavior

Some behavioral researchers are interested primarily in describing behavior. Marketing researchers, for example, study consumers' preferences and buying practices. Public opinion polls, such as those that dominate the news during election years, attempt to describe people's attitudes. Similarly, developmental psychologists have conducted a great deal of research that describes how patterns of behavior and thought change with age; psychophysiological psychologists have described the structure and workings of the nervous system; and industrial–organizational psychologists have described the behavior of effective managers.

Understanding Behavior

Throughout written history, people have asked questions about the causes of behavior. Aristotle was perhaps the first to systematically address basic questions about the nature of humans and why they behave as they do. For centuries, however, the approach to answering these questions was entirely speculative. People would simply concoct explanations of behavior based on everyday observation, creative insight, or religious doctrine.

For several centuries, people who wrote about behavior tended to be philosophers or theologians, and their approach was not scientific. Even so, many of these early insights into behavior were, of course, quite accurate. On the other hand, many of their explanations of behavior were completely wrong. They shouldn't be faulted for having made mistakes, for even modern researchers sometimes draw incorrect conclusions. But, unlike behavioral scientists today, these early "psychologists" (to use the term loosely) did not rely on scientific research to provide answers about behavior. As a result, they had no way to test the validity of their explanations and, thus, no way to discover whether their interpretations were accurate.

Scientific psychology (and thus, more broadly, behavioral science) was born during the last quarter of the 19th century. Through the influence of such early researchers as Wilhelm Wundt, William James, John Watson, G. Stanley Hall, and others, people began to realize that basic questions about behavior could be addressed using many of the same approaches that were used in the more established sciences, such as biology, chemistry, and physics.

Today, a great deal of behavioral research is devoted to providing a better understanding of behavior. **Basic research**, as it is often called, is aimed toward understanding behavior without regard for the immediate application of this knowledge. A great deal of behavioral research is designed to advance our knowledge of psychological processes—to help us build and test theories of behavior, thought, and emotion. This is not to say that basic researchers are not interested in the applicability of their findings; they often are. However, the immediate goal of basic research is to advance knowledge rather than solve a particular problem.

Predicting Behavior

Many behavioral researchers are interested in predicting people's behavior. Personnel psychologists try to predict employees' job performance on the basis of employment tests and interviews. Educational psychologists develop ways to predict academic performance from scores on standardized tests, to identify students who might have learning difficulties in school. Some forensic psychologists are interested in predicting which criminals are likely to be dangerous if released from prison.

Developing ways to predict job performance, school grades, or violent tendencies requires considerable research. The tests used (such as employment or achievement tests) must be administered, analyzed, and refined to meet certain statistical criteria. Data are then collected and analyzed to identify the best predictors of the target behavior. Prediction equations are calculated and validated on other samples of subjects to be sure they predict the target behavior well enough to be used. In brief, the scientific prediction of behavior involves behavioral research methods.

Solving Applied Problems

The goal of **applied research** is to provide solutions for current problems rather than to study basic psychological processes. For example, industrial–organizational psychologists are hired by businesses to study and solve problems related to employee morale, satisfaction, and productivity. Community psychologists are sometimes asked to investigate social problems such as racial tension, littering, and violence. Researchers in human development and social work study problems like child abuse and teenage pregnancy. Such behavioral researchers use scientific approaches to understand and solve some problem of immediate concern (such as employee morale or prejudice).

One category of applied research involves **evaluation research** (also called **program evaluation**), which uses behavioral research methods to assess the effects of social or institutional programs on behavior. When new programs are implemented—such as when new educational programs are introduced into the schools, new laws are passed, or new employee policies are started in a business organization—program evaluators are sometimes called in to determine whether the new program is effective in achieving its intended purpose. If so, the evaluator often tries to determine precisely why the program works; if not, the evaluator tries to uncover why the program was unsuccessful.

These four goals of behavioral research—description, understanding, prediction, and solving problems—overlap considerably. Much basic research is immediately applicable, often in ways that were not anticipated by the researchers themselves. For example, basic research involving brain function led to the development of drugs that control some symptoms of mental illness, and basic research on cognitive development in children led to educational innovations in schools. At the same time, much applied research provides information regarding basic psychological processes. Description and basic research often provide the foundation on which predictive and applied research rests, and applied research often provides questions for basic researchers. Regardless of whether their goal is to describe, understand, predict, or change behavior, researchers largely rely on the same general research strategies. Thus, you should regard these goals as four primary reasons that behavioral scientists conduct research, rather than as four distinct types of research.

The Value of Research to the Student

Aside from the important role that research plays in psychology and other behavioral sciences, a firm grasp of basic research methodology has advantages for students in many fields. After all, most students who take courses in research methods have no intention of becoming researchers. Such students understandably wonder how studying research can benefit them.

A solid background in research has at least four important outcomes. First, knowledge about research methods is important because it allows people to understand research that is relevant to their professions. Many professionals who deal with people—not only psychologists but also those in social work, nursing, education, management, public relations, communication, advertising, and the ministry—must keep up with advances in their fields. For example, counselors and therapists are obligated to stay abreast of the research literature that deals with therapy and related topics, and teachers try to stay informed about current research that might help improve their teaching. Most such information is published in professional research journals, but, as you may have already learned from personal experience, journal articles are often incomprehensible unless the reader knows something about research methodology and statistics. Thus, a background in research will provide you with knowledge and skills that you may find useful in professional life.

A second outcome of becoming involved in research activities is that it helps one become an authority not only on research procedures but also in particular fields. In the process of reading about previous studies, wrestling with issues involving research strategy, collecting data, and interpreting the results, researchers grow increasingly familiar with their topics. For this reason, the faculty at many colleges urges students to become involved in independent or class research projects or to assist with a faculty member's research. This is also one reason many colleges and universities insist that their faculty maintain ongoing research programs. By remaining active as researchers, professors engage in a continual learning process that keeps them at the forefront of their fields.

A third outcome of research training involves the development of critical thinking. Scientists are a critical lot, always asking questions, considering alternative explanations, insisting on hard evidence, refining their methods, and critiquing their own and others' conclusions. Many people have found that a critical, scientific approach to solving problems is useful in areas other than research. For example, the surgeon general of the United States and the tobacco industry have long been engaged in a debate regarding the dangers of cigarette smoking. The surgeon general maintains that cigarettes are hazardous to your health, whereas cigarette manufacturers claim that no conclusive evidence exists that cigarette smoking causes lung cancer and other diseases in humans. Furthermore, both sides present scientific data to support their arguments. Who is right? As you'll see later in the book, even a basic knowledge of research methods will allow you to resolve this controversy; we'll return to this debate in Chapter 7.

Related to this third practical outcome is a fourth: a knowledge of research methodology makes one a more intelligent and effective "research consumer." Increasingly, we are asked to make everyday decisions on the basis of scientific research findings. When we try to decide which new car to buy, how much we should exercise, which weight-loss program to select, whether to enter our children in public or private schools, whether to get a flu shot, or whether we should follow the latest fad to improve our happiness or prolong our life, we are often confronted with research findings that argue one way or the other. Similarly, many decisions that executives and managers make in the workplace must be based on the outcomes of research studies. How do we evaluate the merits of these findings? How do we spot shoddy studies, questionable statistics, and unjustified conclusions? People who have a basic knowledge of research design and analysis are in a better position than those who don't to evaluate the scientific evidence they encounter in everyday life.

Many years ago, science fiction writer H. G. Wells predicted that "statistical thinking will one day be as necessary for efficient citizenship as the ability to read and write." Although we are not at the point where the ability to think like a scientist is as important as reading or writing, knowledge of research methods and statistics is becoming increasingly important for successful living.

CONTRIBUTORS TO BEHAVIORAL RESEARCH

WILHELM WUNDT AND THE FOUNDING OF SCIENTIFIC PSYCHOLOGY

Wilhelm Wundt (1832–1920) was the first bona fide research psychologist. Most of those before him who were interested in behavior identified themselves primarily as philosophers, theologians, biologists, physicians, or physiologists. Wundt, on the other hand, was the first to view himself as a research psychologist.

Wundt, who was born near Heidelberg, Germany, began studying medicine but switched to physiology after working with Johannes Müller, perhaps the leading physiologist of the time. His early research, then, was not in psychology but in physiology. Wundt, however, became interested in applying the methods of physiology to the study of psychology. In 1874, Wundt published a landmark text, *Principles of Physiological Psychology*, in which he boldly stated his plan to "mark out a new domain of science." Wundt's interests were far ranging, but his research centered on processes involved in sensation, perception, attention, and association.

In 1875, Wundt established one of the first two psychology laboratories in the world at the University of Leipzig. Although it has been customary to cite 1879 as the year in which his lab was founded, Wundt was actually given laboratory space by the university for his laboratory equipment in 1875 (Watson, 1978). William James established a laboratory at Harvard University at about the same time, thus establishing the first psychological laboratory in the United States (Bringmann, 1979).

Beyond establishing the Leipzig laboratory, Wundt made numerous other contributions to behavioral science. He founded a journal in 1881 for the publication of research in experimental psychology; this was the first journal to devote more space to psychology than to philosophy. (At the time, psychology was viewed as an area of philosophy.) He also conducted a great deal of research on a variety of psychological processes, including sensation, perception, reaction time, attention, emotion, and introspection. Importantly, he also trained many students who went on to make their own contributions to early psychology: G. Stanley Hall (who founded the American Psychological Association and is considered the founder of child psychology), Witmer Lightner (who established the first psychological clinic), Edward Titchener (who brought Wundt's ideas to the United States), and Hugo Münsterberg (a pioneer in applied psychology). Also among Wundt's students was James McKeen Cattell who, in addition to conducting early research on mental tests, was the first to integrate the study of experimental methods into the undergraduate psychology curriculum (Watson, 1978). In part, we have Cattell to thank for the importance colleges and universities place on courses in research methods.

The Scientific Approach

I noted earlier that it is more difficult for people to think of psychology and other behavioral sciences as sciences than it is to think of chemistry, biology, or astronomy as sciences. In part, this difficulty occurs because many people misunderstand what science is. Most people appreciate that scientific knowledge is somehow special, but they judge whether a discipline is scientific on the basis of the topics it studies. Research involving molecules, chromosomes, and sunspots, for example, seems more scientific than research involving emotions, memories, or social interactions. Whether an area is scientific has little to do with the topics it studies; rather, science is defined in terms of the approaches used to study the topic. Specifically, three criteria must be met for an investigation to be regarded as scientific: systematic empiricism, public verification, and testability.

Systematic Empiricism

Empiricism refers to the practice of relying on observation to draw conclusions. The phenomena studied in science must be objective and observable and not the product of one person's imagination. Although most people today would agree that the best way to find out about something is to observe it directly, this was not always the case. Until the late 16th century, experts relied more heavily on reason, intuition, and religious doctrine than on observation to answer questions about the world.

But observation alone does not make something a science. After all, everyone draws conclusions about human nature from observing people in everyday life. Scientific observation is *systematic*. Scientists structure their observations in systematic ways so that they can draw conclusions about the nature of the world from them. For example, a behavioral researcher who is interested in the effects of exercise on stress is unlikely simply to chat with people who exercise about how much stress they feel. Rather, the researcher is likely to design a carefully controlled study in which people are randomly assigned to different exercise programs, and then measure their stress using well-validated techniques. Data obtained through systematic empiricism allow researchers to draw more confident conclusions than they can draw from casual observation alone.

The criterion of systematic empiricism does not require that scientists study only those things that are *directly* observable. Many of the constructs in any science cannot be observed directly. As a result, scientists must often rely on indirect observation—observing and measuring things that are assumed to be related to the phenomenon of interest. Just as physical scientists rely on indirect observations of gravity, magnetism, or quarks (none of which can be directly observed), behavioral scientists use indirect means of assessing constructs such as anxiety, satiation, fluid intelligence, and drive.

Public Verification

The second criterion for scientific investigation is that it be *publicly verifiable*. In other words, research must be conducted in such a way that the findings of one researcher can be observed, replicated, and verified by others.

There are two reasons for this requirement. First, it ensures that the phenomena scientists study are real, and not one person's fabrications. Scientists disregard claims that cannot be verified by others. For example, a person's claim that he or she was captured by Bigfoot makes interesting reading, but it is not scientific because it cannot be publicly verified. Second, public verification makes science self-correcting. When research is open to public scrutiny, errors in methodology and interpretation can be discovered and corrected by other researchers.

Public verification requires that researchers report both their methods and their findings to the scientific community. Scientific reporting usually occurs in the form of journal articles or presentations at professional meetings. In this way, the methods, results, and conclusions of a study can be examined and, possibly, challenged by others. As long as the researcher reports his or her methods in full detail, other researchers can attempt to repeat, or replicate, the research. This replication not only catches errors but also allows researchers to build on and extend the work of others.

Testability

The third criterion for scientific investigation is *testability*. Scientific research must deal only with questions that can be tested (in an empirical and publicly verifiable manner) given current knowledge and research techniques. This means that many questions are out of the realm of science. For example, the question, "Are there angels?" is not scientific: no one has yet devised a way of testing whether angels exist that is empirical, systematic, and publicly verifiable. This does not necessarily imply that angels do not exist or that the question is unimportant. It simply means that this question is beyond the scope of scientific investigation.

PSEUDOSCIENCE: BELIEVING THE UNBELIEVABLE

Many people are willing to believe in things for which there is little, if any, empirical proof. They readily defend their belief that extraterrestrials have visited Earth; that some people can read others' minds; that they have been visited by the dead; or that Bigfoot, the Abominable Snowman, and Elvis Presley have all been sighted recently.

From the perspective of science, such beliefs present a problem because the evidence that is marshalled to support them is nearly always pseudoscientific. Pseudo-scientific evidence involves claims that masquerade as science but that in fact violate the basic assumptions of scientific investigation (Radner & Radner, 1982). It is not so much that people believe things that have not been confirmed; even scientists do that. Rather, it is that the evidence that pseudoscientists offer in support of such ideas pretends to be scientific but usually is not. **Pseudoscience** is easy to recognize because it violates the basic criteria of science discussed above: systematic empiricism, public verification, and testability.

Nonempirical Evidence

To test their hypotheses, scientists rely on observation. Pseudoscientific evidence, however, often is not based on observation but consists of myths, opinions, and hearsay. Some pseudoscientific belief systems are based in part on evidence provided by unsubstantiated myths. For example, in *Chariots of the Gods?*, von Daniken (1970) used biblical references to "chariots of fire" as evidence for ancient spacecrafts. Because biblical evidence is neither systematic nor verifiable, it cannot be considered scientific. This is not to say that such evidence is necessarily inaccurate; it is simply not permissible in scientific investigation because its veracity cannot be determined conclusively.

Furthermore, unlike science, pseudoscience tends to use highly biased evidence to support its case. For example, those who believe in precognition (telling the future) point to specific episodes in which people seemed to know in advance that something was going to happen. A few years ago, the *National Enquirer* invited its readers to send in their predictions of what would happen during the next year. When the 1500 submissions were opened a year later, one contestant was correct in all 5 of her predictions. The *Enquirer* called this a "stunning display of psychic ability." Was it? Isn't it just as likely that, out of 1500 entries, some people would make correct predictions simply by chance? Scientific logic requires that the misses be considered as evidence along with the hits. Pseudoscientific logic, on the other hand, is satisfied with a single (perhaps random) occurrence.

Unverifiability

Much pseudoscience is based on individuals' accounts of what they have experienced, which are essentially unverifiable reports. If Mr. Smith claims to have spent last Thursday in an alien spacecraft, how do we know whether he is telling the truth? If Ms. Brown says she "knew" beforehand that her uncle had been hurt in an accident, who's to refute her? Of course, Mr. Smith and Ms. Brown might be telling the truth. On the other hand, they might be either playing a prank, mentally disturbed, trying to cash in on the publicity, or sincerely confused. Regardless, because they are unverifiable, their claims cannot be used as scientific evidence.

Untestable Hypotheses

As we discuss in detail later, to be testable, scientific hypotheses must be potentially falsifiable. If a hypothesis cannot be shown to be false by empirical data, we have no way to determine its validity. Pseudoscientific beliefs, on the other hand, are often stated in such a way that they can never be disconfirmed. Those who believe in extrasensory perception (ESP), for example, sometimes argue that ESP cannot be tested empirically because the conditions necessary for the occurrence of ESP are violated under controlled laboratory conditions. Thus, even though "not a single individual has been found who can demonstrate ESP to the satisfaction of independent investigators" (Hansel, 1980, p. 314), adherents continue to believe. Similarly, some advocates of creationism claim that the Earth is much younger than it appears from geological evidence. When the Earth was created in the relatively recent past, they argue, God included in the ground fossils and geological formations that only make it *appear* to be millions of years old. In both examples, the hypothesis is irrefutable and untestable, and thus pseudoscientific.

The Role of Theory in Science

As we saw earlier, one primary purpose of scientific research is to advance our understanding of the world. Theories play an important role in this process. One primary purpose of science is to generate and test theories.

When you hear the word *theory*, you probably think of theories such as Darwin's theory of evolution or Einstein's theory of relativity. However, nothing in the concept of theory requires that it be as grand or all-encompassing as evolution or relativity. Most theories, both in psychology and other sciences, are much less ambitious, attempting to explain only a small and circumscribed range of phenomena.

A **theory** is a set of propositions that attempts to specify the interrelationships among a set of concepts. For example, Fiedler's (1967) contingency theory of leadership specifies the conditions under which certain kinds of leaders will be more

THE UNKNOWN SCIENTIST (WHO DID SOME VERY IMPORTANT GROUNDWORK)

© 1990 by Sidney Harris, *American Scientist* Magazine.

effective than others in group settings. Some leaders are predominately task-oriented; they keep the group focused on its purpose, discourage socializing, and demand participation by members. Other leaders are predominately relationship-oriented; these leaders are more concerned with fostering positive relations among group members and with group satisfaction. The contingency theory proposes that whether a task-oriented or relationship-oriented leader will be more effective depends on three factors: the quality of the relationship between the leader and group members, the degree to which the group's task is structured, and the leader's power within the group. In fact, the theory specifies quite precisely the conditions under which certain leaders are more effective than others. The contingency theory of leadership fits our definition of a theory because it attempts to specify the interrelationships among a set of concepts (the concepts of leadership effectiveness, task versus interpersonal leaders, leader–member relations, task structure, and leader power).

Occasionally, people use the word *theory* in everyday language to refer to hunches or unsubstantiated ideas. For example, in the debate on whether to teach creationism in public schools, creationists dismiss evolution because it's "only a theory." This use of the term *theory* is misleading: scientific theories are not wild guesses or unsupported hunches. On the contrary, theories are accepted as valid only to the extent that they are *supported by empirical findings*. Science insists that theories be consistent with the facts as they are currently known. Theories that are not supported by data are usually replaced by other theories.

You might imagine that scientific theories are discovered by diligent scientists poring over reams of data. On the contrary, theories are constructed rather than discovered. Behavioral scientists construct theories to explain patterns of behavior they observe. Theory construction is very much a creative exercise, and ideas for theories can come from virtually anywhere. Sometimes, researchers immerse themselves in the research literature and purposefully work toward developing a theory. In other instances, researchers construct theories to explain patterns they observe in data they have collected. Some theories are developed on the basis of case studies or everyday observation; others spring to a scientist's mind fully developed at a time when he or she is not even working on research. (A friend of mine gets his best ideas during his daily 5-mile run; I seem to get good ideas in the shower.) Researchers are not constrained in terms of where they get their theoretical ideas; there is no single way to formulate a theory.

Research Hypotheses

On the whole, scientists are a skeptical bunch, and they are seldom inclined to accept theories that have not been supported by research. Thus, a great deal of their time is spent testing theories to determine their usefulness in explaining and predicting behavior. Although theoretical ideas may come from anywhere, scientists are much more constrained in the procedures they use to *test* their theories.

The process of testing theories is an indirect one. Theories themselves are not tested directly because the propositions in the theory are usually too broad and complex to be tested directly in a particular study. Rather, when researchers set about to test a theory, they do so indirectly by testing one or more hypotheses that are derived from the theory.

Hypotheses are specific propositions that follow logically from the theory. Deriving hypotheses from a theory involves **deduction**, a process of reasoning from a general proposition (the theory) to specific implications of that proposition (the hypotheses). Hypotheses, then, can be thought of as the logical implications of the theory. When deriving a hypothesis, the researcher asks, "If the theory is true, what would we expect to observe?" For example, one hypothesis that can be derived from the contingency model of leadership is that relationship-oriented leaders will be more effective when the group's task is moderately structured than when it is unstructured. If we do an experiment to test the validity of this hypothesis, we are testing part—but only part—of the contingency theory of leadership.

You can think of hypotheses as if-then statements of the general form, "If *a*, then *b*." On the basis of the theory, the researcher hypothesizes that *if* certain conditions occur, *then* certain consequences should follow. Although not all hypotheses are actually expressed in this manner, virtually all hypotheses are reducible to an if-then statement.

Not all hypotheses are derived deductively from theory. Often, scientists arrive at hypotheses through **induction**—abstracting a hypothesis from a collection of facts. A researcher may develop hypotheses, for example, after puzzling over apparently contradictory findings, by thinking about what a group of behaviors may have in common, or by casually observing patterns of behavior in everyday life. Whereas deduction involves working from broad principles to specific testable hypotheses, induction involves developing hypotheses by piecing together various bits of information.

To understand the difference in how scientists develop hypotheses through deduction versus induction, imagine that you are interested in determining whether depressed people differ from nondepressed people in how they think about their successes and failures in life. How would you go about generating testable hypotheses about the relationship between these kinds of thoughts and depression?

On one hand, you could develop your hypotheses *deductively*, deriving them from an existing theory of depression. For example, based on the attributional theory of depression (Abramson, Seligman, & Teasdale, 1978), you could deduce several hypotheses about ways in which depressed and nondepressed people should differ in how they think about their successes and failures. For example, this theory would lead us to predict that depressed people would attribute their failures to their own shortcomings more strongly than nondepressed people would, and that depressed people would see the causes of their failures as less likely to change in the future. Thus, you could design a study that tested hypotheses you deduced from the theory.

Alternatively, you could develop your hypotheses *inductively* by collecting information that would allow you to formulate a hypothesis about the link between thought and depression. For example, you could interview several depressed people with an eye toward how they talk about their successes and failures. You could also examine published research that deals with depressive cognition or ask practicing psychologists for their opinions about how depressed people differ from nondepressed people. Pulling together the pieces of information available to you, you could generate hypotheses about depression and thought that could then be tested in a study.

Whether derived deductively from theory or inductively from observed facts, hypotheses must be formulated very precisely to be testable. Specifically, hypotheses must be stated in such a way that they are **falsifiable**. A hypothesis is of little use unless it has the potential to be found false (Popper, 1959). One criticism of Freud's psychoanalytic theory, for example, is that researchers have found it difficult to generate hypotheses that can be falsified by research. Although psychoanalytic theory can explain virtually any behavior after it has occurred, researchers have found it difficult to derive specific falsifiable hypotheses from the theory that will predict how people will behave under certain circumstances. Because parts of the theory do not easily generate falsifiable hypotheses, most behavioral scientists regard aspects of psychoanalytic theory as inherently nonscientific.

Some have suggested that empirical falsification is the hallmark of science—the characteristic that distinguishes it from other ways of seeking knowledge, such as philosophical argument, personal experience, casual observation, or religious insight. In fact, one loose definition of science is that science is "knowledge about the universe on the basis of explanatory principles subject to the possibility of empirical falsification" (Ayala & Black, 1993).

A Priori Predictions and Post Hoc Explanations

Most people can find reasons for almost anything that happens. In fact, we often find it equally easy to explain completely opposite occurrences. Consider Jim and Marie, a married couple I know. If I hear in 5 years that Jim and Marie are happily married, I'll be able to look back and find clear-cut reasons why their relationship worked out so well. If, on the other hand, I learn in 5 years that they're getting divorced, I'll undoubtedly be able to recall indications that all was not well even from the beginning. As the saying goes, hindsight is 20/20; nearly everything makes sense after it happens.

The ease with which we can retrospectively explain even opposite occurrences leads scientists to be skeptical of **post hoc explanations**—explanations made after the fact. In light of our ability to generate such explanations, a theory's ability to explain occurrences in a post hoc fashion provides little evidence of its accuracy or usefulness. More telling is the degree to which a theory can successfully *predict* what will happen. Theories that accurately predict the outcomes of research are regarded more positively than those that can only explain the outcomes after the research or after the event.

This is one reason researchers seldom conduct studies just "to see what happens." If they have no preconceptions about what should happen in their study, they can easily explain whatever pattern of results they obtain in a post hoc fashion. To provide a more convincing test of the theory, researchers usually make specific research hypotheses **a priori**—before collecting the data. By making specific predictions about what will occur in a study, researchers avoid the pitfalls associated with purely post hoc explanations.

Conceptual and Operational Definitions

We noted earlier that scientific hypotheses must be potentially falsifiable by empirical data. For a hypothesis to be falsifiable, the terms used in the hypothesis must be clearly defined. In everyday language, we usually don't worry about precisely how we define the terms we use. If I tell you "the baby is hungry," you understand what I mean without my specifying the criteria I'm using to conclude that the baby is indeed hungry. You are unlikely to ask detailed questions about exactly what I mean; you understand well enough for practical purposes.

More precision is required of the definitions we use in research, however. If the terms used in research are not defined precisely, we may be unable to determine whether the hypothesis was supported. Suppose that we are interested in studying the effects of hunger on attention. Our hypothesis is that people's ability to pay attention decreases as they become more hungry. We can study this topic only if we define very clearly what we mean by *hunger* and *attention*. Without clear definitions, we won't know whether the hypothesis has been supported.

Researchers use two distinct kinds of definitions: conceptual and operational. **Conceptual definitions** are more or less like the definitions we might find in a dictionary. For example, we might define *hunger* as "having a desire for food." Although conceptual definitions are necessary, they are seldom specific enough for research purposes. **Operational definitions** define a concept by specifying precisely how the concept is measured or manipulated in a particular study. For example, we could operationally define *hunger* in our study as "being deprived of food for 12 hours." An operational definition converts an abstract conceptual definition into concrete, situation-specific terms.

There are potentially many operational definitions of a single construct. As noted, we could operationally define *hunger* in terms of hours of food deprivation, or, we could define hunger in terms of responses to the question, "How hungry are you at this moment?" given the options (1) not at all, (2) slightly, (3) moderately, (4) very. We could classify a person as "hungry" if he or she indicated that he or she was either moderately or very hungry on this scale. A recent study of the incidence of hunger in America defined hungry people as those who were eligible for food stamps but who didn't get them. This particular operational definition is a poor one, however. Many people with low income living in a farming area would be classified as "hungry" no matter how much food they raised on their own.

Operational definitions are essential so that researchers can replicate one another's studies. Without knowing precisely how hunger was measured or manipulated in a particular study, other researchers have no way of replicating the study in precisely the same manner that it was originally conducted. Using operational definitions also forces the researcher to clarify his or her concepts very precisely (Underwood, 1957), thereby allowing scientists to communicate clearly and unambiguously.

Occasionally, you will hear people criticize the use of operational definitions. In most cases, they are not criticizing operational definitions per se but rather a perspective known as **operationism**. Proponents of operationism argue that operational definitions are the only legitimate definitions in science. According to this view, concepts can be defined *only* in terms of specific measures and operations. Conceptual definitions, they argue, are far too vague to serve the needs of a precise science. Most contemporary behavioral scientists reject the assumptions of strict operationism; Conceptual definitions do have their uses, even though they are admittedly vague and often refer to unobservable phenomena.

DEVELOPING YOUR RESEARCH SKILLS

GETTING IDEAS FOR RESEARCH

Researchers get their ideas from almost everywhere. Sometimes the ideas come easily, but other times they are slow to emerge. Following are some suggestions to stimulate ideas for research.

Read the research literature in an area that interests you. Be on the lookout for unanswered questions and conflicting findings. Often, the authors of research articles offer their personal suggestions for future research.

Deduce hypotheses from an existing theory. Read about a theory and ask yourself, "If this theory is true, what are some implications for behavior?" State your hypotheses in an if-then fashion. Traditionally, this has been the most common way for behavioral researchers to develop ideas for research.

Apply an old theory to a new phenomenon. Often, a theory that was developed originally to explain one kind of behavior can be applied to an entirely different topic.

Perform an intensive case study of a particular animal, person, group, or event. Such case studies invariably raise interesting questions about behavior. For example, Irving Janis's study of the Kennedy administration's ill-fated Bay of Pigs invasion led to his theory of Groupthink (Janis, 1982). Similarly, when trying to solve an applied problem, researchers often talk to people who are directly familiar with the problem.

Reverse the direction of causality for a commonsense hypothesis. Think of some behavioral principle that you take for granted. Then, reverse the direction of causality to see whether you can construct a plausible new hypothesis. For example, most people think that people daydream when they are bored. Is it possible that people become bored when they daydream?

Break down a process into its subcomponents. What are the steps involved in the process by which people learn to ride a bicycle? decide to end a romantic relationship? choose a career? identify a sound?

Think about variables that might mediate a known cause-and-effect relationship. Behavioral researchers are interested in knowing more than that a particular effect occurs; they also want to understand the psychological processes that mediate the connection between the cause and the behavior. For example, we know that people are more likely to be attracted to others who are similar to them, but why? What mediating variables are involved?

Analyze a puzzling behavioral phenomenon in terms of its functions. Look around at all the seemingly incomprehensible things people do. Instead of studying, John got drunk the night before the exam. Gwen continues to date a guy who always treats her like dirt. The family dog keeps running into the street even though he's punished each time he does. Why do these behaviors occur? What function might they have?

Imagine what would happen if a particular factor were reduced to zero in a given situation. What if nobody ever cared what other people thought of them? What if there were no leaders? What if people had no leisure time? Such questions often raise provocative insights and questions about behavior.

Proof and Disproof in Science

Given that much, if not most, research in behavioral science is designed to test the validity of hypotheses that are derived from more general theories, I suspect you will be surprised to learn that no theory can be proved or disproved by the data from research. In fact, scientists virtually never speak of *proving* a theory, although they often talk of theories being *confirmed* or *supported* by research.

The claim that theories cannot be proved may strike you as bizarre; what's the use of testing theories if we can't actually prove or disprove them anyway? Before answering this question, let me explain why theories cannot be proved or disproved.

The Logical Impossibility of Proof

Theories cannot be proved because obtaining empirical support for a hypothesis does not necessarily mean that the theory from which it was derived is true. For example, imagine that we want to test Theory A. To do so, we logically deduce an implication of the theory that we'll call Hypothesis H. We then collect data to see whether Hypothesis H is, in fact, correct. If we find that Hypothesis H is supported by the data, can we conclude that Theory A is true? The answer is no. Hypothesis H may be supported even if the theory is completely wrong. In logical terminology, it is invalid to prove the antecedent of an argument (the theory) by affirming the consequent (the hypothesis).

To show that this is true, imagine we are detectives trying to solve a murder that occurred at a large party. In essence, we're trying to develop and test "theories" about the identity of the murderer. I propose the theory that Jake is the murderer. One hypothesis that can be deduced from this "theory" is that, if Jake is the murderer, then Jake must have been at the party. (Remember the *if-then* nature of hypotheses.) We check on Jake's whereabouts on the night in question and, sure enough, he was at the party! Given that my hypothesis was supported, would you conclude that this proves my theory that Jake is, in fact, the murderer? Of course not. Why not? Because we can't logically prove a theory by affirming hypotheses that are derived from it.

This state of affairs is one reason we sometimes find that several theories appear to do an equally good job of explaining a particular behavior. Hypotheses derived from each of the theories have been empirically supported in research studies, yet this support does not *prove* that any one of the theories is better than the others. For example, during the 1970s, a great deal of research was conducted to test explanations of attitude change provided by cognitive dissonance theory versus self-perception theory. By and large, researchers found that the data supported the hypotheses derived from both theories. Yet, for the reasons we discussed above, this support did not prove either theory.

The Practical Impossibility of Disproof

Unlike proof, disproof is a *logically* valid operation. If I deduce Hypothesis H from Theory A and then find that Hypothesis H is not supported by the data, Theory A must be false by logical inference. If I hypothesize that, if Jake is the murderer, then Jake must have been at the party and then find that Jake was *not* at the party, my "theory" that Jake was the murderer is logically disconfirmed.

However, testing hypotheses in real-world research involves a number of practical difficulties that may lead to disconfirmation of a hypothesis even if the theory is true. Failure to find empirical support for a hypothesis can be attributed to a number of factors other than the fact that the theory is incorrect. For example, using poor measuring techniques may result in apparent disconfirmation of a hypothesis, even though the theory is actually valid. (Maybe Jake slipped into the party, undetected, for only long enough to commit the murder.) Similarly, obtaining an inappropriate or biased sample of subjects, failing to account for or control extraneous variables, and using improper research designs or statistical analyses can produce negative findings. Much of this book focuses on ways to eliminate problems that hamper a researcher's ability to produce strong, convincing evidence regarding the accuracy of a hypothesis.

Because there are many ways a research study can go wrong, a study's failure to support a particular hypothesis seldom, if ever, means the death of a theory (Hempel, 1966). There are simply too many possible reasons that a study might fail to support a theory. This is one reason scientific journals are reluctant to publish the results of studies that fail to support a theory (see the box, "Publishing Null Findings"). The failure to confirm one's research hypotheses can occur for many reasons.

If Not Proof or Disproof, Then What?

If proof is logically impossible and disproof is practically impossible, how does science advance? How do we ever decide which theories are good ones and which are not? This question has provoked considerable interest among philosophers and scientists alike (Feyerabend, 1965; Kuhn, 1962; Popper, 1959).

In practice, the merit of theories is judged not on the basis of a single research study but on the accumulated evidence of several studies. Although any particular piece of research that fails to support a theory may be disregarded, the failure to obtain support in many studies provides evidence that the theory has problems. Similarly, a theory whose hypotheses are repeatedly corroborated by research is regarded as *supported* by the data.

Importantly, the degree of support for a theory or hypothesis depends not only on the number of times it has been supported but on the stringency of the tests it has survived. Some studies provide more convincing support for a theory than other studies (Ayala & Black, 1993; Stanovich, 1992). Not surprisingly, seasoned researchers try to design studies that will provide the strongest, most stringent tests of their hypotheses. The findings of tightly conceptualized and well-designed studies are simply more convincing than the findings of poorly conceptualized and weakly designed ones.

Some of the most compelling evidence in science is obtained from studies that directly pit the predictions of one theory against the predictions of another theory. Rather than simply testing whether or not the predictions of a particular theory are supported, researchers often design studies to test the opposing predictions of two theories simultaneously. Such studies are designed so that, depending on how the results turn out, the data will confirm one of the theories while disconfirming the other. This head-to-head approach to research is sometimes called the **strategy of strong inference**, because the findings of such studies allow researchers to draw stronger conclusions about the relative merits of competing theories than studies that test a single theory (Platt, 1964).

An example of the strategy of strong inference comes from recent research on self-evaluation. For many years, researchers have disagreed regarding the primary motive that affects people's perceptions and evaluations of themselves: self-enhancement (the motive to evaluate oneself favorably), self-assessment (the motive to see oneself accurately), and self-verification (the motive to maintain one's existing self-image). And, over the years, a certain amount of empirical support has been obtained for each of these motives and for the theories on which they are based.

Sedikides (1993) conducted six experiments that directly opposed each of these theories against one another. In these studies, subjects indicated the kinds of questions they would ask themselves if they wanted to know whether they possessed a particular characteristic (such as whether they were open-minded, greedy, or selfish). Subjects could choose among various questions, which varied according to the degree to which the question would lead to information about themselves that was (1) favorable (reflecting a self-enhancement motive), (2) accurate (reflecting a desire for accurate self-assessment), or (3) consistent with their current self-views (reflecting a motive for self-verification). Results of the six studies provided overwhelming support for the precedence of the self-enhancement motive. When given the choice, people tend to ask themselves questions that allow them to evaluate themselves positively rather than choosing questions that would either support how they already perceived themselves or lead to accurate self-knowledge. By using the strategy of strong inference, Sedikides was able to provide a stronger test of these three theories than would have been obtained from research that focused on any one of them alone.

Throughout this process of scientific investigation, theory and research interact to advance science. Research is often conducted explicitly to test theoretical propositions, and then the findings obtained in that research are used to further develop, elaborate, qualify, or fine-tune the theory. Then more research is conducted to test hypotheses derived from the refined theory, and the theory is further modified on the basis of new data. This process typically continues until researchers tire of the theory (usually because most of the interesting and important issues seem to have been addressed) or until a new theory, with the potential to explain the phenomenon more fully, gains support.

Science advances most rapidly when researchers work on the fringes of what is already known about a phenomenon. Not much is likely to come of devoting oneself to continual research on topics that are already reasonably well understood. As a result, researchers tend to gravitate toward areas in which we have more questions than answers. As Horner (1990), a paleontologist who first discovered evidence that some dinosaurs cared for their young, observed, "In some ways, scientific research is like taking a tangled ball of twine and trying to unravel it. You look for loose ends. When you find one, you tug on it to see if it leads to the heart of the tangle."

This is one reason researchers often talk more about what they *don't* know rather than what is already known (Stanovich, 1992). Because they live in a world of "tangles" and "loose ends," scientists sometimes seem uncertain and indecisive, if not downright incompetent, to the lay public. However, as McCall (1988) noted, we must realize that

> by definition, professionals on the edge of knowledge do *not* know what causes what. Scientists, however, are privileged to be able to say so, whereas business executives, politicians, and judges, for example, sometimes make decisions in audacious ignorance while appearing certain and confident. (p. 88)

IN DEPTH

PUBLISHING NULL FINDINGS

Students are often surprised to learn that scientific journals are reluctant, if not actually unwilling, to publish studies that fail to obtain effects. You might think that such **null findings** tell us that certain variables are *not* related to behavior. After all, if we predict that certain psychological variables are related, but our data show that they are not, haven't we learned something important?

The answer is no, for as we have seen, data may fail to support our research hypotheses for reasons that have nothing to do with the truth of a particular hypothesis. As a result, null findings are usually uninformative regarding the hypothesis being tested. Was the hypothesis disconfirmed, or did we simply design a lousy study? Because we can never know for certain, journals generally will not publish studies that fail to obtain effects.

Strategies of Behavioral Research

Roughly speaking, behavioral research can be classified into four broad categories: descriptive, correlational, experimental, and quasi-experimental. Although we will return to each of these research strategies in later chapters, it will be helpful for you initially to understand the differences among them.

Descriptive Research

Descriptive research describes the behavior, thoughts, or feelings of a particular group of subjects. Perhaps the most common example of purely descriptive research is public opinion polls that describe the attitudes of a particular group of people. Similarly, in developmental psychology, the purpose of some studies is to describe the typical behavior of children of a certain age, and naturalistic observation describes the behavior of animals or humans in their natural habitats. In descriptive research, there is little attempt to relate the behavior under study to other variables or to study its causes systematically. Rather, the purpose is, as the term indicates, to describe.

Some research in clinical psychology, for example, is conducted to describe the prevalence, severity, or symptoms of certain psychological problems. In a descriptive study of the incidence of emotional and behavioral problems among high school students (Lewinsohn, Hops, Roberts, Seeley, & Andrews, 1993), researchers obtained a representative sample of students from high schools in Oregon. Through personal interviews and the administration of standard measures of psychopathology, the researchers found that nearly 10% of the students had a recognized psychiatric disorder at the time of the study—most commonly, depression. Furthermore, 33% of the respondents had experienced a disorder at some time in their lives. Female respondents were more likely than male respondents to experience unipolar depression, anxiety disorders, and eating disorders, whereas males had higher rates of problems related to disruptive behavior.

Correlational Research

If behavioral researchers only described how people and animals think, feel, and behave, they would provide us with little insight into the complexities of psychological processes. Thus, most research goes beyond mere description to an examination of factors associated with behavior. **Correlational research** investigates the relationships among various psychological variables. Is there a relationship between self-esteem and shyness? Does parental neglect in infancy relate to particular problems in adolescence? Do certain personality characteristics predispose people to abuse drugs? Is a person's ability to cope with stress related to his or her physical health? Each of these questions asks whether there is a relationship—a *correlation*—between two variables.

Health psychologists have known for many years that people who have Type A personalities—are highly achievement-oriented and hard-driving—have an exceptionally high risk of heart disease. More recently, research has suggested that Type A people are most likely to develop coronary heart disease if they have a tendency to become hostile when their goals are blocked. In a correlational study designed to explore this issue, Kneip and his associates (1993) asked the spouses of 185 cardiac patients to rate their mates' tendency to become hostile and angry. They also conducted scans of the patients' hearts to measure the extent of their heart disease. The data showed not only that spouses' ratings of the patients' hostility correlated with heart disease but also that hostility predicted heart disease above and beyond traditional risk factors such as age, whether the patient smoked, and high blood pressure. Thus, the data supported the hypothesis that hostility is correlated with coronary heart disease.

Correlational studies such as this provide valuable information regarding the relationships between variables. However, although correlational research can establish that certain variables are related to one another, it cannot tell us whether one variable actually *causes* the other. We'll return to a full discussion of correlational research strategies in Chapters 7 and 8.

Experimental Research

When researchers are interested in identifying variables that *cause* changes in behavior, thought, or emotion, they turn to **experimental research**. In an experiment, the researcher manipulates or changes one or more *independent variables* to see whether changes in behavior (the *dependent variable*) occur as a consequence. If behavioral changes do occur when the independent variable is manipulated, we can conclude that the independent variable caused changes in the dependent variable (assuming certain conditions are met).

For example, Terkel and Rosenblatt (1968) were interested in whether maternal behavior in rats is caused by hormones in the bloodstream. They injected virgin female rats with blood plasma from rats who either had just given birth or were not new mothers. They found that the rats who were injected with the blood of mother rats showed more maternal behavior toward rat pups than did those who were injected with the blood of nonmothers, suggesting that the presence of hormones in the blood of mother rats is partly responsible for maternal behavior. In this study, the nature of the injection (blood from mothers versus blood from non-mothers) was the independent variable and maternal behavior was the dependent variable. (Four subsequent chapters will examine the design and analysis of experiments such as these.)

Note that the term *experiment* applies to only one kind of research—that in which the researcher controls an independent variable to assess its effects on behavior. Thus, it is incorrect to use *experiment* as a synonym for *research* or *study*.

Quasi-Experimental Research

When behavioral researchers are interested in understanding cause-and-effect relationships, they prefer to use experimental designs. However, as we've already noted, experimental research requires that the researcher vary an independent variable to assess its effects on the dependent variable. Often when researchers are not able to vary the independent variable, they use **quasi-experimental designs**. In a quasi-experimental design, the researcher studies the effects of some variable or event that occurs naturally.

Many parents and teachers worry that students' schoolwork will suffer if students work at a job each day after school. Indeed, previous research has shown that part-time employment in adolescence is associated with a number of problems, including lower academic achievement. What is unclear, however, is whether employment causes these problems, or whether the students who choose to have an after-school job tend to be those who are already doing poorly in school. Researchers would find it difficult to conduct a true experiment on this question because they would have to manipulate the independent variable of employment by requiring certain students to work after school while prohibiting other students from having a job.

Because a true experiment was not feasible, Steinberg, Fegley, and Dornbusch (1993) conducted a quasi-experiment. They tested high school students during the 1987–88 school year and then tested the same students again in 1988–89. They then compared those students who had started working during that time to those who did not take a job. As they expected, even before starting to work, students who later became employed earned lower grades and had lower academic expectations than those who did not later work. Even so, the researchers found clear effects of working above and beyond these preexisting differences. Compared to students who did not work, those who took a job subsequently spent less time on homework, cut class more frequently, and had lower academic expectations. Although quasi-experiments do not allow the same degree of confidence in interpretation as do true experiments, the data from this study appear to show that after-school employment can have deleterious effects on high school students.

Each of these basic research strategies—descriptive, correlational, experimental, and quasi-experimental—has its uses. One task of the behavioral researcher is to select the strategy that will best address his or her research question, given the limitations imposed by practical concerns (such as time, money, and control over the situation) as well as ethical issues (the manipulation of certain independent variables would be ethically indefensible). By the time you reach the end of this book, you will have the background to make informed decisions regarding how to choose the best strategy for a particular research question.

Behavioral Science and Common Sense

Unlike research in the physical and natural sciences, research in the behavioral sciences often deals with topics that are familiar to most people. For example, although few of us would claim to have much personal knowledge of subatomic particles, cellular structure, or chloroplasts, we all have a great deal of direct experience with memory, prejudice, sleep, and emotion. Because of their personal experience with many of the topics of behavioral science, people sometimes maintain that the findings of behavioral researchers are mostly common sense—things that we all knew already.

In some instances, this is undoubtedly true. It would be a strange science indeed whose findings contradicted everything that the layperson believed about behavior, thought, and emotion. Even so, the fact that a large percentage of the population believes something is no proof of its accuracy. After all, most people once believed that the sun revolved around the Earth, that flies generated spontaneously from decaying meat, and that epilepsy was brought about by demonic possession—all formerly "commonsense" beliefs that were disconfirmed through scientific investigation.

Likewise, behavioral scientists have discredited many widely held beliefs about behavior; for example, that parents should not respond too quickly to a crying infant because doing so will make it spoiled and difficult (greater parental responsiveness actually leads to less demanding babies), that geniuses are more likely to be crazy or strange than people of normal intelligence (on the contrary, exceptionally intelligent people tend to be more emotionally and socially adjusted), that paying people a great deal of money to do a job increases their motivation to do it (high rewards can undermine intrinsic motivation), and that most differences between men and women are purely biological (only in the past 40 years have we begun to fully understand the profound effects of socialization on gender-related behavior). Only through scientific investigation can we test popular beliefs to see which are accurate and which are myths.

Furthermore, as we have seen, science involves a great deal more than gathering facts. One goal of behavioral science is to construct broad theories that help us understand the complex interplay of factors that affect behavior, thought, and emotion. Everyday commonsense views of behavior do not take us very far down the road toward a comprehensive understanding of psychological processes. Finally, behavioral research takes us beyond common sense to uncover processes that people are unlikely to detect in the course of everyday life. Although we are sometimes quite accurate in understanding the factors that affect our everyday behavior, we are just as often inaccurate (Nisbett & Wilson, 1977). Not only are we sometimes simply wrong in our assumptions about the causes of our or others' behavior, often we are not even aware of the factors that affect us. Only through carefully designed research can such processes be detected and studied.

Thus, although behavioral researchers have verified many facts about behavior that are known by laypeople, it is a gross simplification to suggest that behavioral science is nothing but common sense.

A Preview

The research process is a complex one. In every study researchers must address many questions such as these:

- How should I measure subjects' behavior in this study?
- How do I obtain a sample of subjects for my research?
- Given my research question, what is the most appropriate research strategy?
- How can I be sure my study is as well designed as possible?
- What are the most appropriate and useful ways of analyzing the data?
- How should my findings be reported?
- What are the ethical issues involved in conducting this research?

Each chapter in this book deals with an aspect of the research process. Chapter 2 sets the stage by discussing what is perhaps the central concept in research design and analysis—variability. Armed with an understanding of behavioral variability, you will be better equipped to understand many of the issues we'll address in later chapters.

The topics in Chapters 1 through 6 are relevant to all behavioral research. Chapters 3 and 4 deal with the issues one must consider when measuring behavior and psychological processes. Chapter 5 covers ways of describing and presenting data, and Chapter 6 addresses issues that are involved in obtaining samples of subjects for research. After covering these basic topics, we'll turn to specific research strategies. In Chapters 7 and 8, you'll learn about correlation and regression techniques, procedures that are used to investigate whether two variables are related and, if so, to describe the nature of their relationship.

Chapter 9 will introduce you to the basics of experimentation, research that looks for causal relationships among variables, and Chapter 10 will go into greater detail regarding the design of experiments. In Chapters 11 and 12, you'll go beyond learning how to design experiments to learning how to analyze experimental data. Chapter 13 deals with quasi-experimental designs, and Chapter 14 with single-subject designs, including case studies. The complex ethical issues involved in conducting behavioral research are discussed in Chapter 15. Finally, in Chapter 16, we'll take a close look at how to write research reports.

At the end of the book are two appendixes containing statistical tables and formulas, along with a glossary and a list of references.

Summary

1. Behavioral scientists conduct research to describe, understand, and predict behavior, as well as to solve applied problems.

2. Scientific psychology emerged in the late 1800s, stimulated in part by the laboratories established by Wundt in Germany and by James in the United States.

3. To be considered scientific, observations must be systematic and empirical, research must be conducted in a manner that is publicly verifiable, and the questions addressed must be testable given current knowledge.

4. Pseudoscience involves evidence that masquerades as science but that fails to meet one or more of the three criteria listed in item 3.

5. Much research is designed to test the validity of theories. A theory is a set of propositions that attempts to specify the interrelationships among a set of concepts.

6. Researchers assess the usefulness of a theory by testing hypotheses— propositions that are deduced logically from the theory. To be tested, hypotheses must be stated in a manner that is potentially falsifiable.

7. By stating their hypotheses a priori, researchers avoid the risks associated with post hoc explanations.

8. Researchers use two distinct kinds of definitions in their work. Conceptual definitions are much like dictionary definitions. Operational definitions, on the other hand, define concepts by specifying precisely how they are measured or manipulated in the context of a particular study. Operational definitions are essential for replication as well as for nonambiguous communication among scientists.

9. Strictly speaking, theories can never be proved or disproved by research. Proof is logically impossible because it is invalid to prove the antecedent of an argument by showing that the consequent is true. Disproof, though logically possible, is impossible in a practical sense; failure to obtain support for a theory may reflect more on the research procedure than on the accuracy of the hypothesis. Because of this, the failure to obtain

hypothesized findings (null effects) are often uninformative regarding the validity of a hypothesis.

10. Behavioral research falls into roughly four categories: descriptive, correlational, experimental, and quasi-experimental.

Key Terms

basic research	post hoc explanation
applied research	a priori prediction
evaluation research	conceptual definition
program evaluation	operational definition
empiricism	operationism
public verification	strategy of strong inference
pseudoscience	null finding
theory	descriptive research
hypothesis	correlational research
deduction	experimental research
induction	quasi-experimental design
falsifiability	

Review Questions

1. In what sense is psychology both a science and a profession?
2. What are the four basic purposes of behavioral research?
3. What was Wilhelm Wundt's primary contribution to behavioral research?
4. Briefly discuss the importance of systematic empiricism, public verification, and testability to the scientific method.
5. In what ways does pseudoscience differ from true science?
6. Describe briefly the process by which hypotheses are developed and tested.
7. Why must hypotheses be falsifiable?
8. One theory suggests that people feel socially anxious or shy in social situations when two conditions are met: (1) they are highly motivated to make a favorable impression on others who are present, but (2) doubt that they will be able to do so. Suggest at least three research hypotheses that can be derived from this theory. Be sure your hypotheses are falsifiable.
9. Why are scientists skeptical of post hoc explanations?
10. Briefly discuss the importance of operational definitions in research.

11. Suggest three operational definitions for each of the following constructs:
    a. aggression
    b. patience
    c. test anxiety
    d. memory

12. What are some ways in which scientists get ideas for their research?

13. Why can theories not be proved or disproved by research? Given that proof and disproof are impossible in science, how does scientific knowledge advance?

14. Explain the strategy of strong inference.

15. Distinguish among descriptive, correlational, experimental, and quasi-experimental research.

16. For each of the research questions below, indicate which kind of research—descriptive, correlational, experimental, or quasi-experimental—would be most appropriate.
    a. What percentage of Americans label themselves feminists?
    b. Does the artificial sweetener aspartame cause dizziness and confusion in some people?
    c. What personality variables are related to depression?
    d. What is the effect of a manager's style on employees' morale and performance?
    e. Do SAT scores predict college performance?
    f. Do state laws mandating that drivers wear seat belts reduce traffic fatalities?

Questions for Thought and Discussion

1. Why do you think behavioral sciences, such as psychology, developed later than other sciences, such as chemistry, physics, astronomy, and biology?

2. Why do you think many people have difficulty seeing psychologists and other behavioral researchers as scientists?

3. How would today's world be different if the behavioral sciences had not developed?

4. Come up with your own idea for research. If you have trouble thinking of a research idea, use one of the tactics described in the box, "Getting Ideas for Research."

5. After a researcher comes up with an idea, he or she must evaluate its quality to decide whether the idea is really worthwhile to pursue. Evaluate the research idea you developed in Question 4 using the four criteria below. If your idea fails to meet one or more of these criteria, think of another idea.

a. *Does the idea have the potential to advance our understanding of behavior?* Assuming that the study is conducted and the expected patterns of results are obtained, will we have learned something new about behavior?

b. *Is the knowledge that may be gained potentially important?* Importance is, of course, in the eye of the beholder. A study can be important in many ways: (1) it tests hypotheses derived from a theory (thereby providing evidence for or against the theory); (2) it identifies a qualification to a previously demonstrated finding; (3) it demonstrates a weakness in a previously used research method or technique; (4) it documents the effectiveness of procedures for modifying a behavioral problem (such as in counseling, education, or industry, for example); (5) it demonstrates the existence of a phenomenon or effect that had not been previously recognized. Rarely does a single study provide earthshaking information that revolutionizes the field, so don't expect too much. Just ask yourself whether this idea is likely to provide information that other behavioral researchers or practitioners (such as practicing psychologists) would find interesting or useful.

c. *Do I find the idea interesting?* No matter how important an idea might be, it is difficult to do research that one finds boring. This doesn't mean that you have to be fascinated by the topic, but if you really don't care about the area and aren't interested in the answer to the research question, consider getting a different topic.

d. *Is the idea researchable?* Many research ideas are not viable because they are ethically questionable or because they require resources that the researcher cannot possibly obtain.

CHAPTER 2

Behavioral Variability and Research

Psychologists use the word *schema* to refer to a cognitive generalization that organizes and guides the processing of information. You have schemas about many categories of events, people, and other stimuli that you have encountered in life. For example, you probably have a schema for "leadership." Through your experiences with leaders of various sorts, you have developed a generalization of what a good leader is like. Similarly, you probably have a schema for big cities. What do you think of when I say "New York, Los Angeles, and Atlanta?" Some people's schemas of large cities include generalizations such as "crowded and dangerous," whereas other people's schemas include attributes such as "interesting and exciting." We all hold schemas about many categories of stimuli.

Researchers have found that people's reactions to particular stimuli are strongly affected by the schemas they possess. For example, if you were a business executive, your decisions about whom to promote to a managerial position would be affected by your schema for "leadership." You would promote a very different kind of employee if your schema for leadership included attributes such as caring, involved, and people-oriented than if you saw effective leaders as autocratic, critical, and aloof. Similarly, your schema for large cities would affect your reaction to receiving a job offer in Miami or Dallas.

Importantly, when people have a schema, they more easily process and organize information relevant to that schema. Schemas provide us with frameworks for organizing, remembering, and acting upon the information we receive. It would be difficult for an executive to decide whom to promote to manager if the executive didn't have a a schema for "leadership," for example. Although schemas that are not rooted in reality sometimes lead us to wrong conclusions (as when our stereotypes about a particular group bias our perceptions of a member of a particular group), they are essential for effective information processing. If we could not rely on the generalizations of our schemas, we would have to painstakingly consider every new piece of information when processing information and making decisions.

By now, you are probably wondering how schemas relate to research methods. Having taught courses in research methods and statistics for several years, I have come to the conclusion that, for most students, the biggest stumbling block in the road toward understanding behavioral research involves the failure to develop a schema for the material. Many students have little difficulty mastering specific concepts and procedures, yet leave their first course in research methods without seeing the "big picture." They have learned many concepts, facts, principles, designs, and analyses, but they have not developed an overarching framework for integrating and organizing all of the information they have learned. Their lack of a schema impedes their ability to organize, process, remember, and use information about research methods. In contrast, seasoned researchers have a well-articulated schema for the research process that facilitates their research activities and helps them make methodological decisions.

The purpose of this chapter is to provide you with a schema for thinking about the research process. By giving you a framework for thinking about research, I hope that you will find the rest of the book easier to comprehend and remember. In essence, this chapter will give you pegs on which to hang the various things that you learn. Rather than dumping all of the new information you learn in a big heap on the floor, we'll put schematic hooks on the wall for you to use in organizing the incoming information.

The essence of this schema is that, at the most basic level, all behavioral research attempts to answer questions about behavioral variability—that is, how and why behavior varies across situations, differs among individuals, and changes over time. The concept of variability underlies many of the topics we will discuss in later chapters and provides the foundation on which much of this book rests. The better you understand this basic concept now, the more easily you will grasp many of the topics we will discuss later.

Variability and the Research Process

All aspects of the research process revolve around the concept of **variability**. The concept of variability runs through the entire enterprise of designing and analyzing research. To demonstrate, the following five propositions illustrate the relationship between variability and behavioral research.

Proposition I. *Psychology and other behavioral sciences involve the study of behavioral variability.* Psychology is often defined as the study of behavior and mental processes. In other words, psychologists and other behavioral researchers want to understand behavioral variability, or why behavior varies—why it varies across situations, why it varies among people, and why it varies over time.

Think about the people you interact with each day and about the variation you see in their behavior. First, their behavior varies *across situations*. People act differently at a party than they do in class. College students are often more nervous when interacting with a person of the other sex than when interacting with a person of their own sex. Children behave more aggressively after watching violent TV shows than they did before watching them. A hungry pigeon who has been reinforced for pecking when a green light is on pecks more in the presence of a green light than a red light. In brief, people and animals behave differently in different situations. Behavioral researchers are interested in how and why situational factors cause this variability in behavior.

Second, behavior varies *among individuals*. Even in similar situations, not everyone acts the same. At a lively party, some people are talkative and outgoing, whereas others are quiet and shy. Some people are more conscientious and responsible than others. Some individuals appear generally confident and calm, whereas others seem nervous. And certain animals, such as dogs, display marked differences in behavior depending on their breed. Thus, because of differences in their biological makeup and previous experience, different people and different animals behave differently. A great deal of behavioral research focuses on understanding this variability across individuals.

Third, behavior also varies *over time*. A baby who could barely walk a few months ago can run today. An adolescent girl who two years ago thought boys were "gross" now has romantic fantasies about them. A task that was interesting an hour ago has become boring. Even when the situation remains constant, behavior may change as time passes. Some of these changes, such as developmental changes that occur with age, are permanent; other changes, such as boredom or sexual drive, are temporary. Many behavioral researchers are interested in understanding how and why behavior varies over time.

Proposition 2.   *Research questions in all behavioral sciences are questions about behavioral variability.* Whenever behavioral scientists design research, they are interested in answering questions about behavioral variability. For example, suppose we want to know the extent to which sleep deprivation affects performance on cognitive tasks (such as deciding whether a blip on a radar screen is a flock of geese or an incoming enemy aircraft). In essence, we are asking how the amount of sleep people get causes their performance to change or vary. Or, imagine that we're interested in whether a particular form of counseling reduces family conflict. Our research centers on the question of whether counseling causes changes or variation in a family's interactions. Any specific research question we might develop can be phrased in terms of behavioral variability.

Proposition 3.   *Research should be designed in a manner that best allows the researcher to answer questions about behavioral variability.* Given that all behavioral research involves understanding variability, research must be designed in a way that allows us to identify, as unambiguously as possible, factors related to behavioral variability. A well-designed study is one that permits the researcher to describe and account accurately for the variability in the behavior of his or her research subjects. A poorly designed study is one in which the researcher has difficulty answering questions about the variability he or she observes.

As we'll see in later chapters, flaws in the design of a study can make it impossible for a researcher to determine why subjects behaved as they did. At each step of the design and execution of a study, researchers must be sure that their research will permit them to answer their questions about behavioral variability.

Proposition 4. *The measurement of behavior involves the assessment of behavioral variability.* All behavioral research involves the measurement of some behavior, thought, emotion, or physiological process. Our measures may involve the number of times a rat presses a bar, a subject's heart rate, the score a child obtains on an intelligence test, or a person's rating of how tired he or she feels on a scale of 1 to 7. In each case, we're assigning a number to a person's or animal's behavior: 15 bar presses, 65 heartbeats per minute, an IQ score of 127, a tiredness rating of 5.

No matter what is being measured, we want the number we assign to a subject's behavior to correspond in a meaningful way to the behavior being measured. That is, we would like the variability *in the numbers we assign* to correspond to the variability *in subjects' behaviors*. We must have confidence that the scores we use to capture subjects' behaviors reflect the true variability in the behavior we are measuring. If the scores do not correspond, at least roughly, to the attribute we are measuring, the measurement technique is worthless and our research is doomed.

Proposition 5. *Statistical analyses are used to describe and account for the observed variability in the behavioral data.* No matter what topic is being investigated or what research strategy is being used, one phase of the research process always involves the analysis of the data that are collected. Thus, the study of research methods necessarily involves an introduction to statistics. Unfortunately, many students are initially intimidated by statistics and sometimes wonder why they are so important. The reason is that statistics are necessary for us to understand behavioral variability.

After a study is completed, all we have is a set of numbers that represent the responses of our research subjects. The purpose of statistics is to summarize and answer questions about the behavioral variability we observe in our research. Assuming that the research was competently designed and conducted, statistics help us account for or explain the behavioral variability we observed. Does a new treatment for depression cause an improvement in mood? Does a particular drug enhance memory in mice? Is self-esteem related to the variability we observe in how hard people try when working on difficult tasks? We use statistics to answer questions about the variability in our data.

As we'll see in greater detail in later chapters, statistics serve two general purposes for researchers. **Descriptive statistics** are used to summarize and describe the behavior of subjects in a study. They are ways of reducing a large number of scores or observations down to interpretable numbers such as averages and percentages. **Inferential statistics**, on the other hand, are used to draw conclusions about the reliability and generalizability of one's findings. They are used to help answer questions such as: "How likely is it that my findings are due to random extraneous factors rather than to the variables of central interest in my study?" "How representative are my findings of the larger population from which my subjects came?"

Descriptive and inferential statistics are simply tools that researchers use to interpret the behavioral data they collect. Beyond that, however, understanding statistics provides insight into what makes some research studies better than others. As you learn about how statistical analyses are used to study behavioral variability, you'll develop a keener sense of how to design powerful, well-controlled studies.

In brief, the concept of variability follows us through the entire research process: Our research questions are about the causes and correlates of behavioral variability. We try to design studies that best let us describe and understand variability in a particular behavior. The measures we use attempt to capture numerically the variability we observe in subjects' behavior. And our statistics help us analyze the variability in our data to answer the questions we began with. Variability is truly the thread that runs through the research process. Understanding variability will provide you with a schema for understanding, remembering, and using what you learn about behavioral research. For this reason, we'll return to it repeatedly throughout the book.

Variance: An Index of Variability

Given the importance of the concept of variability in designing and analyzing behavioral research, researchers need a way of expressing how much variability there is in a set of data. Not only are researchers interested simply in knowing the amount of variability in their data, but they need a numerical index of the variability in their data to conduct certain statistical analyses that we'll examine in later chapters. Researchers use a statistic known as **variance** to indicate the amount of observed variability in subjects' behavior. We will confront variance in a variety of guises throughout this book, so we need to understand it well.

Let's imagine that you conducted a very simple study in which you asked 6 subjects to give their attitudes about capital punishment on a scale of 1 to 5 (where 1 indicates strong opposition and 5 indicates strong support for capital punishment). Suppose you obtained these responses:

Subject	Response
1	4
2	1
3	2
4	2
5	4
6	3

For a variety of reasons (that we'll discuss later), you may need to know how much variability there is in these data. Can you think of a way of expressing how much these responses, or scores, vary from one person to the next?

A Conceptual Explanation of Variance

One possible solution is simply to take the difference between the largest and the smallest scores. In fact, this number, the **range**, is sometimes used to express variability. If we subtract the smallest from the largest score in our list, we find that the range of these data is 3 ($4 - 1 = 3$). Unfortunately, the range has limitations as an indicator of the variability in our data. The problem is that the range tells us only how much the largest and smallest scores vary; it does not take into account the other scores and how much they vary from one another.

Consider the two distributions of data in Figure 2.1. These two sets of data have the same range. That is, the difference between the largest and smallest scores is the same in each set. However, the variability in the data in Figure 2.1(a) is much smaller than the variability in Figure 2.1(b), where the scores are more spread out. What we need is a way of expressing variability that includes information about all of the scores.

When we talk about things varying, we usually do so in reference to some standard. A useful standard for this purpose is the average, or **mean**, of the scores in our data set. Researchers use the term *mean* as a synonym for what you probably call the average—the sum of a set of scores divided by the number of scores you have.

The mean stands as a fulcrum around which all of the other scores balance. So, we can express the variability in our data in terms of how much the scores vary *around the mean*. If most of the scores in a set of data are tightly clustered around the mean [as in Figure 2.1(a)], then the variance of the data will be small. If, however, our scores are more spread out [as in Figure 2.1(b)], they will vary a great deal around the mean, and the variance will be large. So, the variance is nothing more than an indication of how tightly or loosely a set of scores clusters around the mean of the scores. As we will see, this provides a very useful indication of the amount of variability in a set of data.

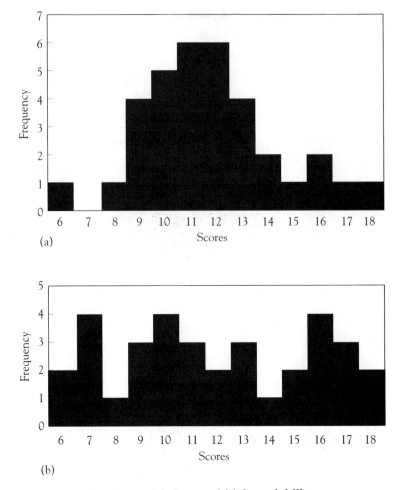

(a)

(b)

Figure 2.1   Distributions with low and high variability

Explanation: The two sets of data shown in these graphs contain the same
number of scores and have the same range. However, the variability in the scores
in (a) is less than the variability in (b). Overall, most of the subjects' scores are
more tightly clustered together in (a)—that is, they vary less among themselves. By
itself, the range fails to reflect the difference in variability in these two sets of
scores.

A Statistical Explanation of Variance

You'll understand more precisely what the variance tells us about our data if you look now at how variance is expressed statistically. My goal in showing how the variance is calculated is to help you better understand what variance is from a *conceptual* standpoint rather than to teach you how to calculate it statistically. Use the statistical description below to help you get a clear picture of what variance tells us but *not* to learn how to calculate it.

 We can see what the variance is by going through five simple steps. We will refer here to the scores or observations obtained in our study of attitudes toward capital punishment.

Step 1. Remember, variance refers to how much the scores are spread out around the mean of the data. So, first we need to calculate the mean of our data. Just sum the numbers (4 + 1 + 2 + 2 + 4 + 3 = 16) and divide by the number of scores you have (16/6 = 2.67). Note that statisticians use the symbol $\bar{y}$ (or $\bar{x}$) to represent the mean of a set of data. In short, all we do on the first step is calculate the mean of the six scores.

Step 2. Now we need a way of expressing how much the scores vary around the mean. We do this by subtracting the mean from each score. This difference is called a *deviation score*.

 Let's do this calculation for our data involving people's attitudes toward capital punishment:

Subject	Deviation Score
1	4 − 2.67 = 1.33
2	1 − 2.67 = −1.67
3	2 − 2.67 = −0.67
4	2 − 2.67 = −0.67
5	4 − 2.67 = 1.33
6	3 − 2.67 = 0.33

Step 3. By looking at these deviation scores, we can see how much each score varies or deviates from the mean. Subject 2's score falls furthest from the mean (1.67 units below the mean), whereas Subject 6's falls closest to the mean (0.33 unit above it). Note that a positive number indicates that the person's score fell above the mean, whereas a negative sign (−) indicates a score below the mean. (What would a deviation score of zero indicate?)

 You might think we could add these six deviation scores to get a total variability score for the sample. However, if we sum the deviation scores for all of the subjects in a set of data, they always add to zero. So we need to get rid of the negative signs. We do this by squaring each of the deviation scores.

Subject	Deviation Score	Deviation Score Squared
1	1.33	1.77
2	−1.67	2.79
3	−0.67	0.45
4	−0.67	0.45
5	1.33	1.77
6	0.33	0.11

Step 4.   Now we add the squared deviation scores. If we add all of the squared deviation scores obtained in Step 3 above, we get

$$1.77 + 2.79 + 0.45 + 0.45 + 1.77 + 0.11 = 7.34$$

As we'll see later, this number—the sum of the squared deviations of the scores from the mean—is central to the analysis of much research data. We have a shorthand way of referring to this important quantity; we call it the **total sum of squares**.

Step 5.   In Step 4 we obtained an index of the total variability in our data—the total sum of squares. However, this quantity is affected by the number of scores we have; the more subjects in our sample, the larger the total sum of squares will be. However, just because we have a larger number of subjects does not necessarily mean that the variability of our data will be greater.

Because we do not want our index of variability to be affected by the size of the sample, we divide the sum of squares by a function of the number of subjects in our sample. Although you might suspect that we would divide by the actual number of subjects from whom we obtained data, we usually divide by one less than the number of subjects. (Don't concern yourself with why this is the case.) This gives us the variance of our data, which is indicated by the symbol s^2. If we do this calculation for our data, the variance (s^2) is 1.47.

To review, to calculate the variance, we (1) calculate the mean of the data, (2) subtract the mean from each score, (3) square these differences or deviation scores, (4) sum these squared deviation scores (this, remember, is the total sum of squares), and (5) divide by the number of scores minus 1. By following these steps, you should be able to see precisely what the variance is; it is an index of the average amount of variability in a set of data expressed in terms of how much the scores differ from the mean in squared units. Again, the variance is important because virtually every aspect of the research process will lead toward the analysis of behavioral variability as expressed in the statistic known as the variance.

DEVELOPING YOUR RESEARCH SKILLS

STATISTICAL NOTATION

Statistical formulas are typically written using **statistical notation**. Just as we commonly use symbols such as a plus sign to indicate *add* and an equal sign to indicate *is equal to*, researchers use special symbols—such as Σ and s^2—to indicate statistical terms and operations. Although some of these symbols may be new to you, they are nothing more than symbolic representations of variables or mathematical operations, all of which are elementary.

For example, the formula for the mean, expressed in statistical notation, is

$$\bar{y} = \Sigma y_i / n$$

The uppercase Greek letter sigma (Σ) is the statistical symbol for summation and tells us to add what follows. The symbol y_i is the symbol for each individual subject's score. So the operation Σy_i simply tells us to add up all of the scores in our data. That is,

$$\Sigma y_i = y_1 + y_2 + y_3 + \cdots + y_n$$

where n is the number of subjects. Then, the formula for the mean tells us to divide Σy_i by n, the number of subjects. Thus, the formula $\bar{y} = \Sigma y_i / n$ indicates that we should add all of the scores and divide by the number of subjects.

Similarly, the variance can be expressed in statistical notation as

$$s^2 = \Sigma \, (y_i - \bar{y})^2 / (n - 1)$$

Look back at the steps for calculating variance on the preceding pages and see whether you can interpret this formula for s^2.

Step 1. Calculate the mean, $\bar{y}$

Step 2. Subtract the mean from each subject's score to obtain the deviation scores, $(y_i - \bar{y})$

Step 3. Square each subject's deviation score, $(y_i - \bar{y})^2$

Step 4. Sum the squared deviation scores, $\Sigma \, (y_i - \bar{y})^2$

Step 5. Divide by the number of scores minus 1 $(n - 1)$

As we will see throughout the book, statistical notation will allow us to express certain statistical constructs in a shorthand and unambiguous manner.

Systematic and Error Variance

So far, our discussion of variance has dealt with the **total variance** in the responses of subjects in a research study. However, the total variance in a set of data can be split into two parts:

$$\text{Total variance} = \text{Systematic variance} + \text{Error variance}$$

The distinction between systematic and error variance will follow us through all the chapters of this book. Because systematic and error variance are important to the research process, developing a grasp of the concepts now will allow us to use them as needed throughout the book. We'll explore them in greater detail in later chapters.

Systematic Variance

Most research is designed to test the hypothesis that there is a relationship between two or more variables. For example, a researcher may wish to test the hypothesis that self-esteem is related to drug use, or that changes in office illumination cause systematic changes in on-the-job performance. Put differently, researchers are usually interested in whether the variability in one variable (self-esteem, illumination) is related *in a systematic fashion* to variability in other variables (drug use, on-the-job performance).

Systematic variance is that part of the total variability in subjects' behavior that is related in an orderly, predictable fashion to the variables the researcher is investigating. If the subjects' behavior varies in a systematic way as certain other variables change, the researcher has evidence that those variables are related to behavior. That is, when some of the total variance in subjects' behavior is found to be associated with certain variables in an orderly, systematic fashion, we can conclude that those variables are related to subjects' behavior. Two examples may help clarify the concept of systematic variance.

Temperature and aggression. In an experiment that examined the effects of temperature on aggression, Baron and Bell (1976) led subjects to believe that they would administer electric shocks to another person. (In reality, that other person was an accomplice of the experimenter and was not actually shocked.) Subjects performed this task in a room in which the ambient temperature was either 73°, 85°, or 95°F. To determine whether temperature did, in fact, affect aggression, the researchers had to determine how much of the variability in subjects' aggression was related to temperature. That is, they needed to know how much of the total variance in the aggression scores was systematic variance due to temperature. We wouldn't expect all of the variability in subjects' aggression to be a function of temperature. After all, subjects entered the experiment already differing in their tendencies to respond aggressively. In addition, other factors in the experimental setting may have affected aggressiveness. What the researchers wanted to know was whether *any* of the variance in aggression was due to differences in the temperatures in the three experimental conditions (cool, warm, and hot). If systematic variance related to temperature was obtained, they could conclude that changes in temperature affected aggressive behavior. Indeed, this and other research has shown that the likelihood of aggression is greater when the temperature is moderately hot than when it is cool, but that aggression decreases under extremely high temperatures (Anderson, 1989).

Optimism and health. In a correlational study of the relationship between optimism and health (Scheier & Carver, 1985), subjects completed a measure of optimism. Four weeks later, the same subjects completed a checklist on which they indicated the degree to which they were bothered by each of 39 physical symptoms. Of course, there was considerable variability in the number of symptoms that subjects reported experiencing. Some indicated that they were quite healthy, whereas others reported many symptoms. Interestingly, subjects who scored high on the optimism scale reported fewer symptoms than less optimistic subjects; that is, there was a correlation between optimism scores and the number of symptoms that subjects reported. In fact, approximately 7% of the total variance in reported symptoms was related to optimism; in other words, 7% of the variance in symptoms was *systematic variance* related to subjects' optimism scores. Note, however, that 7% is not a great deal of variance, indicating that although optimism and physical symptoms were related in an orderly, systematic fashion, optimism accounts for only a small portion of the variance in symptoms.

As we'll see in detail in later chapters, researchers must design their studies so that they can tell how much of the total variance in subjects' behavior is systematic variance associated with the variables they are investigating. If they don't, the study will fail to detect relationships among variables that, in fact, exist. Poorly designed studies do not permit researchers to conclude confidently which variables were responsible for the systematic variance they obtained. We'll return to this important point in later chapters as we learn how to design good studies.

Error Variance

Not all of the total variability in subjects' behavior is systematic variance. Factors that the researcher is *not* investigating may also be related to subjects' behavior. In the Baron and Bell experiment, not all of the variability in aggression across subjects was due to temperature, for example. And, in the Scheier and Carver study, only 7% of the variance in the symptoms that subjects reported was related to optimism; the remaining 93% of the variance in symptoms was due to other factors.

Clearly, then, other factors are at work. Much of the variance in these studies was not associated with the primary variables of interest. For example, in the experiment on aggression, some subjects may have been in a worse mood than others, leading them to behave aggressively for reasons that had nothing to do with room temperature. Some may have come from aggressive homes, whereas others may have been raised by parents who were pacifists. The experimenter may have unconsciously treated some subjects more politely than others, thereby lowering their aggressiveness. A few subjects may have been unusually hostile because they had just failed an exam. Each of these factors may have contributed to the total variability in subjects' aggression, but none is related to the variable of interest in the study—temperature.

Even after a researcher has determined how much of the total variance is systematic variance, some of the total variance remains unaccounted for. Variance that remains unaccounted for is called **error variance**. Error variance is that portion of the total variance that remains after systematic variance is identified.

Do not think of the term *error* as indicating errors or mistakes in the usual sense of the word. Although error variance may be due to mistakes in recording or coding the data, most often it is simply the result of factors that remain unidentified in a study. No single study can investigate every factor that is related to the behavior of interest. Rather, a researcher chooses to investigate the impact of only one or a few variables on the target behavior. Baron and Bell chose to study temperature, for example, and ignored other variables that might influence aggression. Carver and Scheier focused on optimism but not on the myriad of other variables related to physical symptoms.

Error variance tends to mask or obscure the effects of the variables in which researchers are primarily interested. The more error variance there is, the more difficult it is to determine whether certain variables cause or predict behavior. For

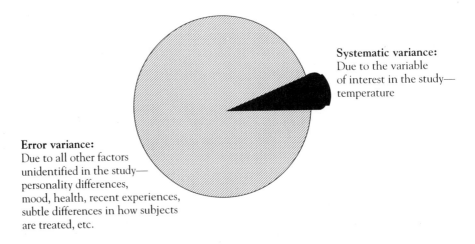

Systematic variance: Due to the variable of interest in the study—temperature

Error variance: Due to all other factors unidentified in the study—personality differences, mood, health, recent experiences, subtle differences in how subjects are treated, etc.

Figure 2.2   Variability in aggression scores

Explanation: If we draw a circle to represent the total variability in subjects' aggression scores, systematic variance is that portion of the total variability that is related to the variable under investigation in the study. Error variance is that portion of the total variability that is not related to the variables being studied.

example, the more that subjects' aggression is affected by extraneous factors such as mood and weather, the more difficult it is to see whether temperature affects aggression. As we'll see later, a good research design is one that allows researchers to minimize error variance.

Assessing the Strength of Relationships

From the standpoint of variability, the questions behavioral researchers most often address involve whether any of the total variability in the data they collect is related in a systematic fashion to the variables they are investigating. If the subjects' behavior varies in a systematic way as certain other variables change, systematic variance is present, providing evidence that those variables are related to the behavior under study.

Typically, researchers are interested not only in whether certain variables are related to subjects' responses but also in *how strongly* they are related. Sometimes, variables are associated only weakly with particular cognitive, emotional, behavioral, or physiological responses, whereas other variables are strongly related to thoughts, emotions, and behavior. For example, in a study of variables that predict workers' reactions to losing their jobs, Prussia, Kinicki, and Bracker (1993) found that the degree to which respondents were emotionally upset about losing their jobs was moderately related to how much effort they expected they would have to exert to find a new job, but only weakly related to their expectations of actually finding a new job.

Researchers assess the strength of the empirical relationships they discover by determining the proportion of the total variability in subjects' responses that is systematic variance related to the variables under study. As we saw, the total variance of a set of data is composed of systematic variance and error variance. Once we calculate these types of variance, we can easily determine the *proportion* of the total variance that is systematic variance:

$$\text{Proportion of total variance that is systematic variance} = \text{Systematic variance/total variance}$$

How researchers calculate these types of variance is a topic for later chapters. For now, simply understand that this proportion tells us about the strength of the relationships between the variables we study. The statistics that express the strength of relationships are sometimes called **measures of strength of association** (Maxwell, Camp, & Arvey, 1981).

At one extreme, if the proportion of the total variance that is systematic variance is .00, *none* of the variance in subjects' responses in a study is systematic variance. When this is the case, we know there is absolutely no relationship between the variables under study and subjects' responses. At the other extreme, if *all* of the variance in subjects' responses is systematic variance (that is, if systematic variance/total variance = 1.00), then all of the variability in the data can be attributed to the variables under study. When this is the case, the variables are as strongly related as they possibly can be (in fact, this is called a "perfect" relationship.) When the measure of strength of association is between .00 and 1.00, the larger the proportion of the total variance that is systematic variance, the stronger the relationship between the variables.

Because measures of the strength of association are proportions, we can compare the strength of relationships directly. For example, in the study of reactions to job loss described earlier, 26% of the total variance in emotional upset was related to how much effort respondents expected they would have to exert to find a new job. In contrast, only 5% of the variance in emotional upset was related to their expectations of finding a new job. Taken together, these findings suggest that, for people who lose their jobs, it is not the possibility of being forever unemployed that is most responsible for their upset, but rather their expectations of how difficult things are going to be in the short run as they seek reemployment.

The strength of the relationships studied by behavioral researchers varies a great deal across areas of research. In some studies, as little as 1% of the total variance may be systematic variance, whereas in other contexts, the proportion of the total variance that is systematic variance may exceed .40 or .50. Although researchers differ in the standards they use to interpret the strength of relationships, Cohen's (1977) criteria are often used: the association between two variables should be regarded as *small* if the proportion of systematic to total variance is around .01, *medium* if the proportion is around .06, and *large* if the proportion of systematic to total variance exceeds .15 (keep in mind that these are just rules of thumb that differ across research areas). (See Keppel, 1982.)

If you are surprised that researchers regard .15 as indicating a relatively strong relationship (after all, only 15% of the total variance is systematic variance, and 85% of the variance is error variance that remains unaccounted for), keep in mind that most behaviors are determined by a large number of factors. Thus, we should not be surprised to find that *any single variable* investigated in a particular study is systematically related to only a small portion of the total variance in the behavior.

Meta-Analysis: Systematic Variance Across Studies

As we've seen, researchers are often interested in the strength of the relationships they uncover in a particular study. However, any particular piece of research can provide only a rough estimate of the "true" proportion of the total variance in a particular behavior that is systematically related to other variables. This limitation exists because the strength of the relationship obtained in a particular study is affected not only by the relationship between the variables but also by the characteristics of the study itself—the sample of subjects who participated, the measures used, and the research procedures, for example. Thus, although Prussia and others (1993) found that 26% of the variance in their respondents' emotional upset was related to their expectations of how much effort they would exert to find a new job, the strength of the relationship between expectations and emotional upset in this study may have been affected by the particular subjects, measures, and procedures the researchers used. We may find a somewhat stronger or weaker relationship if we conducted a similar study using different participants or methods.

For this reason, behavioral scientists have become increasingly interested in examining the strength of relationships between particular variables *across many studies*. Although any given study provides only a rough estimate of the strength of a particular relationship, averaging these estimates over many studies that use different subjects, measures, and procedures should provide a more accurate indication of how strongly the variables are "really" related.

A procedure known as **meta-analysis** is used to analyze and integrate the results from a large set of individual studies (Cooper, 1990; Glass, 1976). When researchers conduct a meta-analysis, they examine every study that has been conducted on a particular topic to assess the relationship between whatever variables are the focus of their analysis. Using information provided in the journal article or report of each study, the researcher calculates an index of the strength of the relationship between the variables (this is often called the **effect size**). These data are then statistically integrated to obtain a general estimate of the strength of the relationship between the variables. By combining information from many individual studies, researchers assume that the resulting estimate of the average strength of the relationship will be more accurate than the estimate provided by any particular study.

In many meta-analyses, researchers not only determine the degree to which certain variables are related but also explore the effects of factors that affect their relationship. For example, in looking across many studies, they may find that the relationship was generally stronger for male than for female subjects, that it was stronger when certain kinds of measures were used, or that it was weaker when particular experimental conditions were present. Thus, not only is meta-analysis used to document relationships across studies, but it can be used to explore factors that affect those relationships.

BEHAVIORAL RESEARCH CASE STUDY

META-ANALYSES OF GENDER DIFFERENCES

In recent years, meta-analyses have been conducted on studies in many areas of research, including expectancy effects, mood and helping, factors that influence the effectiveness of psychotherapy, gender differences in sexuality, and employees' commitment to work organizations. However, by far the most popular topic for meta-analysis has been gender differences.

Although many studies have found that men and women differ on a variety of cognitive, emotional, and behavioral variables, researchers have been quick to point out that the differences obtained in these studies are often quite small, and typically smaller than popular stereotypes of men and women assume. Researchers have conducted meta-analyses of research on gender differences to answer the question of whether men and women really differ in regard to certain behaviors and, if so, to document the strength of the relationship between gender and these behaviors. Using the concepts we have learned in this chapter, we can rephrase these questions as follows: "Is any of the total variability in people's behavior related to their gender, and, if so, what proportion of the total variance is systematic variance due to gender?"

For example, Hyde, Fennema, and Lamon (1990) conducted a meta-analysis to examine gender differences in mathematical performance. Based on analyses of 100 individual studies (that involved over 3 million participants), these researchers concluded that, overall, the relationship between gender and mathematical performance is very weak. Analyses showed that girls slightly outperformed boys in mathematical computation in elementary and middle school, but that boys tended to outperform girls in mathematical problem solving in high school. By looking at studies that were conducted before and after 1974, they also found that the relationship between gender and mathematical ability has weakened over the past 20 years.

In another meta-analysis, Eagly and Johnson (1990) reviewed previous research on male–female differences in leadership style. Contrary to the stereotype that women adopt a relationship-oriented leadership style whereas men are more task-oriented, their analysis found that men and women did not differ in leadership style in studies conducted in actual business organizations. That is, none of the variability in managers' leadership styles was systematic variance due to gender. However, in laboratory studies of leadership, some variance in leadership style was associated with gender, with men being more task-oriented and women being more relationship-oriented. Although men and women managers in real organizations do not differ with respect to their task or relationship orientation, the meta-analysis showed that female leaders tend to adopt a more democratic style than male leaders.

Summary

1. Psychology and other behavioral sciences involve the study of behavioral variability. Most aspects of behavioral research are aimed at explaining variability in behavior: research questions are about the causes and correlates of behavioral variability; researchers try to design studies that will best explain the variability in a particular behavior; the measures used by researchers attempt to capture numerically the variability in subjects' behavior; and statistics are used to analyze the variability in our data.

2. Variance is a statistical index of variability. Variance is calculated by subtracting the mean of the data from each subject's score, squaring these differences, summing the squared difference scores, and dividing this sum by the number of subjects minus 1.

3. The total variance in a set of data can be broken into two components. Systematic variance is that part of the total variance that is related to the variables under investigation in a particular study. Error variance is variance that is due to unidentified sources.

4. To examine the strength of the relationships they study, researchers determine the proportion of the total variability in behavior that is systematic variance associated with the variables under study. The larger the proportion of the total variance that is systematic variance, the stronger the relationship between the variables.

5. Meta-analysis is used to examine the nature and strength of relationships between variables across many individual studies.

Key Terms

variability	statistical notation
descriptive statistics	total variance
inferential statistics	systematic variance
variance	error variance
range	measures of strength of association
mean	meta-analysis
total sum of squares	effect size

Review Questions

1. Discuss how the concept of behavioral variability relates to
   a. the research questions that interest behavioral researchers
   b. the design of research studies
   c. the measurement of behavior
   d. the analysis of behavioral data.

2. Conceptually, what does the variance tell us about a set of data?

3. Statistically, explain how you would calculate the variance.

4. The total variance in a set of scores can be partitioned into two components. What are they, and how do they differ?

5. What are some factors that contribute to error variance in a set of data?

6. Why are researchers often interested in the proportion of the total variance that is systematic variance?

7. What would it indicate if the proportion of the total variance that is systematic variance is .25? .00? .98?

8. Why do researchers use meta-analysis?

Questions for Thought and Discussion

1. Restate each of the following research questions as a question about behavioral variability.
    a. Does eating too much sugar increase children's activity level?
    b. Do continuous reinforcement schedules result in faster learning than intermittent reinforcement schedules?
    c. Do people who are depressed sleep more or less than those who are not depressed?

2. Several years ago, Mischel (1968) observed that the typical relationship obtained in much psychological research is rather weak. Specifically, Mischel pointed out that, on average, only about 10% of the total variability in a particular behavior is systematic variance associated with another variable being studied. Reactions to Mischel's observation were of two varieties. On one hand, some researchers concluded that the theories and methods of behavioral science must somehow be flawed; surely, if our theories and methods were better we would obtain stronger relationships. However, others argued that, given that any particular behavior is affected by many different factors, accounting for 10% of the variability in a behavior with any single variable is not a bad track record at all. Where do you stand on this issue? How much of the total variability in a particular phenomenon should we expect to explain with some other variable?

CHAPTER 3

The Measurement of Behavior

*I*n 1904, the French minister of public education decided that children of lower intelligence required special education, and he hired Alfred Binet to design a procedure to identify children in the Paris school system who needed special attention. Binet faced a complicated task. Previous attempts to measure intelligence had been notably unsuccessful. Earlier in his career, Binet had experimented with craniometry, which involved estimating intelligence (as well as personality characteristics) from the size and shape of people's heads. Craniometry was an accepted practice at the time, but Binet was skeptical about its usefulness as a measure of intelligence. He wrote in 1900, "The idea of measuring intelligence by measuring heads seemed ridiculous" (p. 403). Other researchers had tried using other aspects of physical appearance, such as facial features, to measure intelligence, but these attempts were also unsuccessful. Still others had used tests of reaction time under the assumption that more-intelligent people would show faster reaction times than less-intelligent people. However, evidence for a link between intelligence and reaction time was also weak.

Thus, Binet rejected the previous methods and set about designing a new approach for measuring intelligence. The technique he developed involved a series of short tasks that utilized basic cognitive processes such as comprehension and reasoning. For example, children would be asked to name objects, answer commonsense questions, and interpret pictures. Binet published the first version of his intelligence test in 1905 in collaboration with one of his students, Theodore Simon.

When he revised the test three years later, Binet proposed a new index of intelligence based on the age level of each task on the test. The various tasks were arranged sequentially in the order in which a child of average intelligence could successfully pass them. For example, an average 4-year-old knows his or her sex, can indicate which of two lines is longer, and can name familiar objects (such as a key), but cannot give differences between pairs of abstract terms (such as *pride* and *pretension*). By seeing which tasks a child could and could not complete, one could estimate the "mental age" of a child—the intellectual level at which the child is able to perform. Later, the German psychologist William Stern recommended dividing a child's mental age (as measured by Binet's test) by his or her chronological age to create the intelligence quotient, or IQ.

Binet's work provided the first useful measure of intelligence and set the stage for the widespread use of tests in psychology and education. Furthermore, it gave behavioral researchers the measurement tools they needed to conduct research on intelligence, a topic that continues to attract a great deal of research attention today. Although contemporary intelligence tests still have their critics, development of adequate measures was a prerequisite to the scientific study of intelligence.

All behavioral research involves the measurement of some behavioral, cognitive, emotional, or physiological response. It would be inconceivable to conduct a study in which nothing is measured. Importantly, the success of a particular piece of research depends heavily on the quality of the measures used. Measures of behavior that are flawed in some way can distort our results and lead us to draw erroneous conclusions about the data. Because measurement is so important to the research process, an entire specialty known as **psychometrics** is devoted to the study of psychological measurement. Psychometricians investigate the properties of the measures used in behavioral research and work toward improving psychological measurement.

In this and the following chapter, we will look at how researchers measure behavioral and mental events. Along the way, we will examine the types of measures that behavioral researchers commonly use, discuss the numerical properties of such measures, highlight the characteristics that distinguish good measures from bad ones, and consider ways to develop the best possible measures for research purposes.

Measures Used in Behavioral Research

The measures used in behavioral research fall roughly into three categories: behavioral measures, physiological measures, and self-reports.

Behavioral Measures

Behavioral measures involve the direct observation of behavior. Behavioral measures can therefore be used to measure anything an animal or person does that researchers can observe—a rat pressing a bar, eye contact between people in conversation, fidgeting by a person giving a speech, aggression in children on the playground, the time it takes a worker to complete a task. In each case, researchers observe and record the subject's behavior either directly or from audio- or videotape recordings.

To measure behaviors such as these, researchers often use a **behavioral coding system** to record the behaviors they observe. A coding system is used to convert observed behavior to numerical data for purposes of analysis. In a very simple coding system, a researcher may simply count the number of times a particular behavior occurs (such as bar presses or head nods) or measure the duration of certain behaviors (such as how long it takes to complete a task). In more complex coding systems, researchers classify behaviors into categories. For example, a researcher interested in decision making in groups might classify subjects' comments during a group discussion into one of several categories, such as *gives opinion, agrees, disagrees, asks for information, seems unfriendly,* and so on (Bales, 1970). Many standardized behavioral coding systems have been developed, although researchers often must create their own coding systems for use in a particular study. In Chapter 4, we'll discuss in greater detail how researchers develop and use behavioral coding strategies.

Occasionally, researchers recruit **knowledgeable informants**—people who know the subjects well—to observe and rate subjects' behavior (Moscowitz, 1986). Typically, these individuals are people who play a significant role in the subjects' lives, such as best friends, parents, romantic partners, co-workers, or teachers. For example, in a study of factors that affect the degree to which people's perceptions of themselves are consistent with others' perceptions of them, Cheek (1982) obtained ratings of 85 college men given by three of their fraternity brothers.

Because people often behave unnaturally when they know they are being watched, researchers sometimes measure behavior indirectly rather than through direct observation. For example, because he was concerned that people might lie about how much alcohol they drink, Sawyer (1961) counted the number of empty liquor bottles in neighborhood garbage cans rather than directly asking residents to report on their alcohol consumption. **Unobtrusive measures** such as this are useful when direct observation would lead to unnatural behavior.

Physiological Measures

Many behavioral researchers are interested in the relationships between bodily processes and behavior. Most such internal processes are not directly observable but can be measured with sophisticated equipment. Other physiological processes, such as certain reflexes, can be observed with the naked eye but cannot be measured accurately without specialized equipment. **Physiological measures** can be classified into three general types.

First, some physiological measures are used to investigate activity within the nervous system. For example, researchers who study sleep, dreaming, and other states of consciousness use the electroencephalogram (EEG) to measure brain wave activity. Electrodes are attached to the outside of the head to record the brain's patterns of electrical activity. Other researchers implant electrodes directly into areas of the nervous system to measure the activity of specific neurons or groups of neurons. Physiological techniques are also used to measure activity in the autonomic nervous system, that portion of the nervous system that controls involuntary responses of the visceral muscles and glands. For example, measures of heart rate, respiration, blood pressure, skin temperature, and electrodermal response all reflect activity in the autonomic nervous system.

Second, some researchers study physiological processes by drawing and analyzing blood samples. For example, certain hormones such as adrenaline and cortisol are released in response to stress, and other hormones such as testosterone are related to activity level and aggression. In their research on the beneficial effects of writing about personally traumatic experiences, Pennebaker, Kiecolt-Glaser, and Glaser (1988) analyzed white blood cells to to assess the functioning of subjects' immune system (see the case study, "Converging Operations in Measurement"). Of course, analyzing blood samples requires sophisticated equipment and extensive technical knowledge.

Finally, other physiological measures are used to precisely measure bodily reactions that, though observable, require specialized equipment for quantification. For example, electromyographs are used to measure muscular reactions such as reflexes. To measure sexual arousal, researchers use a plethysmograph (for women) and a penile strain gauge (for men).

Self-Reports

Self-report measures involve the replies subjects give in response to questionnaires and interviews. The information that self-reports provide may involve cognitive, affective, or behavioral events.

Cognitive self-reports measure what subjects *think* about something. For example, a developmental psychologist may ask a child which of two chunks of clay is larger—one rolled into a ball or one formed in the shape of a hot dog. Or, a political pollster may ask voters about their preferences regarding candidates for president. As we'll see, researchers cannot always trust people's statements about what they think; a man who is prejudiced toward those of another race may be reluctant to admit it, for example. Even so, self-report measures are the only direct way to access a person's thoughts.

Affective self-reports involve subjects' responses regarding how they *feel*. Many behavioral researchers are interested in emotional reactions such as depression, anxiety, stress, grief, and happiness and in people's evaluations of themselves and others. The most straightforward way of assessing these kinds of reactions is to ask subjects to report on them.

Behavioral self-reports involve subjects' reports of how they *act*. Subjects may be asked how often they read the newspaper, go to the dentist, or have sex, for example. Similarly, many personality inventories ask subjects to indicate how frequently they engage in certain behaviors. Like other self-report measures, behavioral self-reports are open to reporting bias. When possible, researchers prefer to observe subjects' behaviors directly rather than relying on subjects' reports about how they behave. However, self-reports are sometime necessary because direct observation is often not practically or ethically possible.

BEHAVIORAL RESEARCH CASE STUDY

CONVERGING OPERATIONS IN MEASUREMENT

Because any particular measurement procedure may provide only a rough and imperfect measure of a given construct, researchers sometimes measure a given construct in several different ways. By taking several types of measures—each approaching the construct from a different angle—researchers can more accurately assess the construct under study. This approach to measurement is called **converging operations** or **triangulation**. (In the vernacular of navigation and land surveying, *triangulation* is a technique for determining the position of an object based on its relationship to points whose positions are known.)

A case in point involves Pennebaker, Kiecolt-Glaser, and Glaser's (1988) research on the effects that writing about one's experiences has on health. On the basis of previous studies, these researchers hypothesized that people who wrote about the personally traumatic events they had experienced would show an improvement in their physical health. To test this idea, they conducted an experiment in which 50 university students were instructed to write for 20 minutes a day for 4 days about either a traumatic event they had experienced (such as death of a loved one, child abuse, rape, or intense family conflict) or about superficial topics.

Rather than relying on any single measure of physical health—which is a complex and multifaceted construct—Pennebaker and his colleagues used converging operations to assess the effects of writing on subjects' healthfulness. First, they obtained *behavioral measures* involving subjects' visits to the university health center. Second, they used *physiological measures* to assess the functioning of subjects' immune systems directly. Specifically, they collected samples of subjects' blood three times during the study and tested the lymphocytes, or white blood cells. Third, they used *self-report measures* to assess how distressed subjects later felt—1 hour, 6 weeks, and 3 months after the experiment.

Together, these triangulating data supported the experimental hypothesis. Compared to subjects who wrote about superficial topics, those who wrote about traumatic experiences visited the health center less frequently, showed better functioning of their immune systems (as indicated by the action of the lymphocytes), and reported they felt better. This and other studies by Pennebaker and his colleagues were among the first to demonstrate empirically the beneficial effects of expressing one's thoughts and feelings about troubling events. Pennebaker (1990) provides a fascinating summary of his work in this area in *Opening Up: The Healing Power of Confiding in Others.*

Contemporaneous Versus Archival Research

In most studies, measurement is *contemporaneous*—it occurs at the time the research is conducted. A researcher designs a study, recruits subjects, and then collects data about those subjects using a predesigned behavioral, physiological, or self-report measure.

However, some research is conducted using data that were collected *prior to the time* the research was designed. In **archival research**, researchers analyze data pulled from existing records, such as census data, court records, personal letters, newspaper reports, government documents, and so on. In most instances, archival data were collected for purposes other than research. Like contemporaneous measures, archival data may involve information about behavior (such as immigration records, school records, and marriage statistics), physiological processes (such as hospital records), or self-reports (such as personal letters and diaries).

For example, Simonton (1988) used archival data to study the leadership styles of American presidents. Simonton gathered biographical information about all U.S. presidents on dimensions such as family background, formal education, personal characteristics, occupational experiences, and political accomplishments. He also obtained data on each president's performance in office using criteria such as the number of bills he got passed and the number of times his vetoes were overridden by Congress. Researchers also rated each president on 82 descriptive items. From these data, Simonton was able to classify each president according to five styles of leadership, which he called interpersonal, charismatic, deliberative, creative, and neurotic. George Washington's leadership style, for example, can be characterized as high on the interpersonal and deliberative dimensions, whereas Thomas Jefferson was deliberative and creative, and Ronald Reagan was predominately charismatic and creative. In contrast, Ulysses . S. Grant's style of leadership was low in deliberation and charisma but highly neurotic. Furthermore, Simonton was able to identify variables that predicted the style a president was likely to adopt, as well as consequences of each style for the administration's success. Because the data were obtained from existing records and biographies, this research can be classified as archival.

Scales of Measurement

Regardless of what kind of measure is used—behavioral, physiological, or self-report—the goal of measurement is to assign numbers to subjects' responses so that they can be summarized and analyzed. For example, a researcher may convert subjects' marks on a questionnaire to a set of numbers (from 1 to 5, perhaps) that meaningfully represent the subjects' responses. These numbers are then used to describe and analyze subjects' answers.

However, in analyzing and interpreting research data, not all numbers can be treated the same way. As we'll see, some numbers used to represent subjects' behaviors are, in fact, "real" numbers that can be added, subtracted, multiplied, and divided. Other numbers have special characteristics and require special treatment.

Researchers distinguish between four different levels, or scales, of measurement. These scales differ in the degree to which the numbers being used to represent subjects' behaviors correspond to the real number system. Differences between these scales of measurement are important because they have implications for what a particular number indicates about a subject and how one's data may be analyzed.

The simplest type of scale is a **nominal scale**. With a nominal scale, the numbers assigned to subjects' behaviors or characteristics are really just labels. For example, for purposes of analysis, we may assign all boys in a study the number 1 and all girls the number 2. Or, we may indicate whether a student was late to class by giving punctual students a 0 and tardy students a 1. Numbers on a nominal scale indicate things about our subjects, but they are labels, or names (nominal means *name*), rather than real numbers. Thus, it usually makes no sense to perform mathematical operations on these numbers.

An **ordinal scale** involves the rank ordering of a set of behaviors or characteristics, and it conveys more information than a nominal scale does. Measures that use ordinal scales tell us the relative order of our subjects on a particular dimension but do not indicate the distance between subjects on the dimension being measured. Imagine being at a talent contest where the winner is the contestant who receives the loudest applause. Although we may be able to rank the contestants by the applause they receive, we would find it difficult to judge precisely *how much* the audience liked one contestant more than another.

When an **interval scale** of measurement is used, equal differences between the numbers reflect equal differences between subjects in the characteristic being measured. On an IQ test, for example, the difference between scores of 90 and 100 is the same as the difference between scores of 130 and 140 (10 points). However, an interval scale does not have a true zero point that indicates the absence of the quality being measured. An IQ score of 0 does not necessarily indicate that no intelligence is present, just as on the Fahrenheit thermometer (which is an interval scale) a temperature of zero degrees does not indicate the absence of temperature. Because it has no true zero point, numbers on an interval scale can not be multiplied or divided. It makes no sense to say that a temperature of 100 degrees is twice as hot as a temperature of 50 degrees, or that a person with an IQ of 60 is one third as intelligent as one with an IQ of 180.

The highest level of measurement is the **ratio scale**. Because a ratio scale has a true zero point, ratio measurement involves real numbers that can be added, subtracted, multiplied, and divided. Many measures of physical characteristics, such as weight, are on a ratio scale. As weight has a true zero point (indicating no weight), it makes sense to talk about 100 pounds being twice as heavy as 50 pounds.

Scales of measurement are important to the researcher for two reasons. First, the measurement scale used determines the amount of information provided by a particular measure. Nominal scales provide less information than ordinal, interval, or ratio scales. When asking people about their opinions, for example, simply asking whether they agree or disagree with particular statements (which is a nominal scale) does not capture as much information as an interval scale that asks *how much* they agree or disagree. In many cases, choice of a measurement scale is determined by the characteristic being measured; it would be difficult to measure gender, for example, on anything other than a nominal scale. However, given a choice, researchers prefer to use measures that are at a higher level of measurement because they provide more information about subjects' responses or characteristics.

The second important implication of scales of measurement involves the kinds of statistical analyses that can be performed on the data. Certain mathematical operations can be performed only on numbers that conform to the properties of a particular measurement scale. The more useful and powerful statistical analyses, such as t-tests and F-tests (which we'll discuss in later chapters), generally require numbers on interval or ratio scales. As a result, researchers try to use scales that allow them to use the most informative statistical tests.

Now that we've learned about the kinds of measures that behavioral researchers use, we'll turn our attention to characteristics that distinguish good from bad measures.

Estimating the Reliability of a Measure

The goal of measurement is to assign numbers to objects or events (such as behaviors) in such a way that the numbers correspond in some meaningful way to the attribute we are trying to measure. From the standpoint of variability, researchers want the variability in the numbers assigned to reflect, as accurately as possible, the variability in the attribute being measured. A perfect measure would be one for which the variability in the numbers provided by the measure perfectly matched the true variability in the event being assessed. But how do we know whether a particular measurement technique does, in fact, give us scores that are meaningful and useful reflections of what we want to measure?

The first characteristic any good measure must possess is reliability. **Reliability** refers to the consistency or dependability of a measuring technique. If you weigh yourself on a bathroom scale three times in a row, you expect to obtain the same weight each time. If, however, you weigh 140 pounds the first time, 98 pounds the second time, and 167 pounds the third time, then the scales are *unreliable*—they can't be trusted to provide consistent weights. Similarly, measures used in research must be reliable. When they aren't, we can't trust them to provide meaningful data regarding the behavior of our subjects.

Measurement Error

A subject's score on a particular measure consists of two components: the true score and measurement error. We can portray this by the equation

Observed score = True score + Measurement error

The **true score** is the score that the subject would have obtained if our measure were perfect and we were able to measure without error. If researchers were omniscient beings, they would know exactly what a subject's score should be—that Susan's IQ was *exactly* 138 or that the rat pressed the bar *precisely* 52 times, for example.

However, the measures used in research are never that precise. Virtually all measures contain **measurement error**. This component of the subject's observed score is the result of factors that distort the score so that it isn't precisely what it should be (that is, it doesn't perfectly equal the subject's true score). If Susan were anxious and preoccupied when she took the IQ test, for example, her observed IQ score might be lower than 138. If the counter on the bar in a Skinner box malfunctioned, it might record only 50 bar presses instead of 52.

Although many factors can contribute to measurement error, they can be broken down into five categories. First, measurement error is affected by *transient states* of the subject. For example, the subject's mood, health, level of fatigue, and anxiety level can all contribute to measurement error.

Second, *stable attributes* of the subject can lead to measurement error. For instance, paranoid or suspicious subjects may distort their answers, and less intelligent subjects may misunderstand certain questions. Individual differences in motivation can also affect test scores; on tests of ability, motivated subjects will score more highly than unmotivated subjects, regardless of their real level of ability. Both transient and stable characteristics can give us observed scores that are lower or higher than subjects' true scores would be.

Third, *situational factors* in the research setting can create measurement error. If the researcher is particularly friendly, a subject might try harder; if the researcher is stern and aloof, subjects may be intimidated, angered, or unmotivated. Rough handling of animals can introduce changes in their behavior. Room temperature, lighting, and crowding can also artificially affect scores.

Fourth, *characteristics of the measure* itself can create measurement error. For example, ambiguous questions create error because they can be interpreted in more than one way. And measures that induce fatigue (such as tests that are too long) or fear (such as intrusive or painful physiological measures) can also affect scores.

Finally, actual *mistakes* in recording subjects' responses can make the observed score different from the true score. If a researcher sneezes while counting the number of times a rat presses a bar, he may lose count; a careless researcher may write 3s that look like 5s.

Whatever its source, measurement error undermines the reliability of the measures researchers use. In fact, the reliability of a measure is an inverse function of measurement error: the more measurement error present in a measuring technique, the less reliable the measure is. Anything that increases measurement error decreases the consistency and dependability of the measure.

Reliability as Systematic Variance

Unfortunately, researchers never know for certain precisely how much measurement error is contained in a particular subject's score or what the subject's true score really is. In fact, in many instances, researchers have no way of knowing for sure whether their measure is reliable and, if so, how reliable it is.

However, for certain kinds of measures, researchers have ways of *estimating* the reliability of the measures they use. If they find that a measure is not acceptably reliable, they can take steps to increase its reliability. If that doesn't work, they may decide not to use it at all.

Assessing a measure's reliability involves an analysis of the variability in a set of scores. We saw earlier that each subject's observed score is composed of a true-score component and a measurement-error component. If we combine the scores of several subjects and calculate the variance, the total variance of the *set of scores* is composed of the same two components:

$$\begin{array}{ccc} \text{Total} & & \text{Variance due} & & \text{Variance due} \\ \text{variance in} & = & \text{to true scores} & + & \text{to measurement} \\ \text{a set of scores} & & & & \text{error} \end{array}$$

Stated differently, the portion of the total variance in a set of scores that is associated with subjects' true scores is **systematic variance**, and the variance due to measurement error is **error variance**. (See Chapter 2 for a review of systematic and error variance.) To assess the reliability of a measure, researchers estimate the proportion of the total variance in the data that is true-score (systematic) variance versus measurement error. Statistically,

$$\text{Reliability} = \text{True-score variance/Total variance}$$

Thus, reliability is the proportion of the total variance in a set of scores that is systematic variance associated with subjects' true scores.

The reliability of a measure can range from .00 (indicating no reliability) to 1.00 (indicating perfect reliability). As the equation shows, the reliability is .00 when none of the total variance is true-score variance. When the reliability is zero, the scores reflect nothing but measurement error and the measure is totally worthless. At the other extreme, a reliability of 1.00 would be obtained if all the total variance is true-score variance. A measure is perfectly reliable if there is no measurement error. As a rule of thumb, a measure is considered sufficiently reliable if at least 50% of the total variance in scores is systematic, true-score variance.

Assessing Reliability

Researchers use three ways to estimate the reliability of their measures: test–retest reliability, interitem reliability, and interrater reliability. All three methods are based on the same general logic. To the extent that two measurements of the same behavior, object, or event yield similar scores, we can assume that both measurements are tapping into the same true score. However, if two measurements of the same thing yield very different scores, the measures must contain a high degree of measurement error. Thus, by statistically testing the degree to which the two measurements yield similar scores, we can estimate the proportion of the total variance that is systematic (true-score) variance versus measurement-error variance, thereby estimating the reliability of the measure.

Most estimates of reliability are obtained by examining the **correlation** between what are supposed to be two measures of the same behavior, attribute, or event. We'll discuss correlation in considerable detail in Chapters 7 and 8. For now, all you need to know is that a **correlation coefficient** is a statistic that expresses the strength of the relationship between two measures on a scale from .00 (no relationship between the two measures) to 1.00 (a perfect relationship between the two measures). Correlation coefficients can be positive, indicating a direct relationship between the measures, or negative, indicating an inverse relationship.

If we square a correlation coefficient, we obtain the proportion of the total variance in one set of scores that is systematic variance related to another set of scores. As we saw in Chapter 2, the proportion of systematic variance to total variance (that is, systematic variance/total variance) is an index of the strength of the relationship between two variables. Thus, the higher the correlation (and its square), the more closely two variables are related. In light of this relationship, correlation is a useful tool in estimating reliability because it tells us about the degree to which two measurements yield similar scores.

Test–retest reliability. **Test–retest reliability** refers to the consistency of subjects' responses on a measure over time. Assuming that the characteristic being measured is relatively stable, subjects should obtain approximately the same score each time they are measured. If a person takes an intelligence test twice, we would expect his or her two test scores to be similar. Because there is some measurement error in even well-designed tests, the scores won't be exactly the same, but they should be close.

Test–retest reliability is determined by measuring subjects on two occasions, usually separated by a few weeks. Then the two sets of scores are correlated to see how closely related the second set of scores is to the first. If the scores correlate highly (at least .70), the measure has good test–retest reliability. If they do not correlate highly, the measure contains too much measurement error, is unreliable, and should not be used. Researchers generally require that a test–retest correlation exceed .70 because a correlation coefficient of .70 indicates that approximately 50% of the total variance in the scores is systematic variance due to subjects' true scores. We saw earlier that squaring a correlation coefficient tells us the proportion of the total variance that is systematic variance; thus, when the correlation is .70, $.70^2 = .49$, indicating that nearly 50% of the variance is systematic. Low and high test–retest reliability is shown in Figure 3.1.

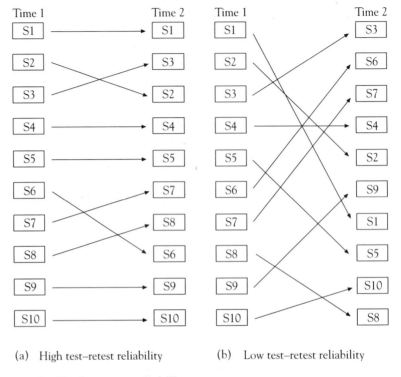

(a) High test–retest reliability   (b) Low test–retest reliability

Figure 3.1   Test–retest reliability

Explanation: High test–retest reliablity indicates that subjects' scores are consistent across time. In (a), for example, subjects' scores were relatively consistent from Time 1 to Time 2. If they are not consistent across time, as in (b), test–retest reliability is low.

Assessing test–retest reliability makes sense only if the attribute being measured would not be expected to change between the two measurements. We would generally expect high test–retest reliability on a measure of intelligence, attitudes, or personality, for example, but not on a measure of hunger or fatigue.

Interitem reliability.   A second kind of reliability is relevant only for measures that consist of more than one item. Personality inventories are measures that typically consist of several questions that are summed to provide a single score. For example, the most commonly used measure of self-esteem consists of ten statements on which respondents rate themselves (Rosenberg, 1965). Similarly, on a scale used to measure depression, subjects may be asked to rate themselves on several mood-related items (sad, unhappy, blue, helpless) that are then added together to provide a single depression score.

When several questions or items are summed to provide a single score, researchers are interested in interitem reliability. **Interitem reliability** refers to consistency among the items on a scale. Ideally, we would like all of the questions on a particular scale to measure the same construct (such as a personality trait or mood). On an inventory to measure extraversion, for example, we want all of the items to measure some aspect of extraversion. Including items in a test score that don't measure the construct of interest increases measurement error.

Researchers examine interitem reliability by looking at item-total correlations, split-half reliability, and by computing Cronbach's alpha coefficient. First, researchers look at the **item-total correlation** for each question or item on the scale. Does each item correlate with the sum of all other items? If a particular item measures the same construct as the rest of the items, it should correlate with them. If not, the item adds only measurement error to the observed score and doesn't belong on the scale. Generally, the correlation between each item on a questionnaire and the sum of the other items should exceed .30.

Researchers also use **split-half reliability** as an index of interitem reliability. With split-half reliability, the researcher divides the items on the scale into two sets. Sometimes the first and second halves of the scale are used; sometimes the odd-numbered items form one set and even-numbered items form the other; sometimes items are randomly put into one set or the other. A total score is obtained for *each set* by adding the items within each set, and the correlation between these two sets of scores is then calculated. If the items on the scale hang together well and estimate the true score consistently, scores obtained on the two halves of the test should correlate highly (> .70). If the split-half correlation is small, however, it indicates that the total score contains a great deal of measurement error.

There is one drawback to the use of split-half reliability; the reliability one obtains depends on how the items are split. Using a first-half-second-half split is likely to provide a slightly different estimate of reliability than an even-odd split. What, then, is the *real* interitem reliability? To get around this ambiguity, researchers often use **Cronbach's alpha coefficient** (Cronbach, 1970). Cronbach's alpha is equivalent to the average of all possible split-half reliabilities. As a rule of thumb, researchers consider a measure to have adequate interitem reliability if Cronbach's alpha coefficient exceeds .70. As with test–retest reliability, an alpha coefficient of greater than .70 indicates that at least 50% of the total variance is systematic, true-score variance.

Interrater reliability. **Interrater reliability** (also called interjudge or interobserver reliability) involves the consistency among two or more researchers who observe and record subjects' behavior. Obviously, when we have two or more observers, we would like them to be consistent among themselves. If one observer records 15 bar presses and another observer records 18 bar presses, the difference between their observations represents measurement error.

For example, Gottschalk, Uliana, and Gilbert (1988) analyzed recent presidential debates for evidence that the candidates were cognitively impaired at the time of the debates. They coded what the candidates said during the debates using the Cognitive Impairment Scale. In their report of the study, the authors presented data to support the interrater reliability of their procedure. The reliability analysis demonstrated that the raters agreed sufficiently among themselves and that measurement error was acceptably low. (By the way, their results showed that Ronald Reagan exhibited significantly more evidence of impairment than either Jimmy Carter in 1980 or Walter Mondale in 1984 and that Reagan showed more impairment during the 1984 debates than he did four years earlier.)

Researchers use two general ways of assessing interrater reliability. If the raters are simply recording whether a behavior occurred, we can calculate the percentage of times they agreed. Alternatively, if the raters are rating the subjects' behavior along a scale (an anxiety rating from 1 to 5, for example), we can correlate their ratings across subjects. If the observers are making similar ratings, we should obtain a relatively high correlation (at least .70) between them.

DEVELOPING YOUR RESEARCH SKILLS

INCREASING THE RELIABILITY OF MEASURES

Unfortunately, it is not always possible to assess the reliability of measures used in research. For example, if we ask a person to rate how happy he or she feels at the moment on a scale of 1 to 7, we have no direct way of testing the reliability of the response. Test–retest reliability is inappropriate because the state we are measuring changes over time; interitem reliability is irrelevant because there is only one item; and, because others cannot observe and rate the subject's feelings of happiness, we cannot assess interrater reliability. Even though researchers assess the reliability of their techniques whenever possible, the reliability of some measures cannot be determined.

In light of this fact, often the best a researcher can do is to make every effort to maximize the reliability of his or her measures by eliminating possible sources of measurement error. A few ways of increasing the reliability of behavioral measures are listed below.

- *Standardize administration of the measure.* Ideally, every subject should be tested under precisely the same conditions. Differences in how the measure is taken can contribute to measurement error. If possible, have the same researcher administer the measure to all subjects in precisely the same setting.

- *Clarify instructions and questions.* Measurement error results when some subjects do not fully understand the instructions or questions. When possible, questions to be used in interviews or questionnaires should be pilot tested to be sure they are understood properly.

- *Train observers.* If subjects' behavior is being observed and rated, train the observers carefully. Observers should also be given the opportunity to practice using the rating technique.
- *Minimize errors in coding data.* No matter how reliable a measuring technique is, error is introduced if researchers make mistakes in recording, coding, tabulating, or computing the data.

In summary, reliable measures are a prerequisite of good research. A reliable measure is one that is relatively unaffected by sources of measurement error and thus is consistent and dependable. More specifically, reliability reflects the proportion of the total variance in a set of scores that is systematic, true-score variance. The reliability of measures is estimated in three ways: test–retest reliability, inter-item reliability, and interrater reliability. Even in instances in which the reliability of a technique cannot be determined, steps should be taken to minimize sources of measurement error.

Estimating the Validity of a Measure

The measures used in research must not only be reliable, they must also be valid. **Validity** refers to the extent to which a measurement procedure actually measures what it is intended to measure, rather than measuring something else. Validity is the degree to which variability in subjects' scores on a particular measure reflects variability in the characteristic we want to measure. Do scores on the measure relate to the attribute of interest? Are we measuring what we think we are measuring? If a researcher is interested in the effects of a new drug on obsessive–compulsive disorder, the measure of obsession–compulsion used must reflect actual differences in the degree to which subjects actually have the disorder. That is, the measure must actually measure obsession–compulsion and not something else (or nothing at all).

It is important to note that a measure can be highly reliable but not valid. For example, the cranial measurements that early psychologists such as Binet used to assess intelligence were very reliable. When measuring a person's skull, two researchers would arrive at similar, though not always identical, measurements—that is, interrater reliability was quite high. Skull size also demonstrates high test–retest reliability; it can be measured consistently over time with little measurement error. However, no matter how reliable skull measurements may be, they are not a *valid* measure of intelligence. They are not valid because they do not measure the construct of intelligence. Thus, researchers need to know whether measures are reliable *and* whether they assess what they're supposed to measure.

Assessing Validity

When researchers refer to a measure as valid, they do so in terms of a particular scientific or practical purpose. Validity is not a property of a measuring technique per se, but an indication of the degree to which the technique measures a particular entity *in a particular context*. Thus, a measure may be valid for one purpose but not for another. Cranial measurements, for example, are valid measures of hat size, but they are not valid measures of intelligence.

Researchers often refer to three different types of validity: face validity, construct validity, and criterion-related validity.

Face validity.   **Face validity** refers to the extent to which a measure *appears* to measure what it's supposed to measure. Rather than being a technical or statistical procedure, face validation involves the judgment of the researcher or of subjects recruited by the researcher.

In general, a researcher is likely to have more faith in an instrument whose content obviously taps into the construct he or she is interested in measuring than in a measure that is not face valid. Furthermore, if a measuring technique, such as a test, does not have face validity, subjects, clients, job applicants, and other lay-people are likely to doubt its relevance and importance (Cronbach, 1970). They are even likely to feel resentful if they are affected by the results of a test whose validity they doubt. Thus, all other things being equal, it is usually better to have a measure that is face valid than one that is not; it simply engenders greater confidence by the public at large.

Although face validity is often desirable, three qualifications must be kept in mind. First, just because a measure has face validity doesn't necessarily mean that it is actually valid. There are many cases of face-valid measures that did not measure what they appeared to measure. To researchers of the 19th century, skull size was a face-valid measure of intelligence.

Second, there are many measures that lack face validity that are, in fact, valid. Many items from the Minnesota Multiphasic Personality Inventory (MMPI)—a measure of personality used in both practice and research—do not appear face valid, yet they predict various psychological problems. For example, expressing a preference for Washington over Lincoln as president, or for corn over peas, is a valid indicator of certain attributes, although these items are by no means face valid.

Third, researchers sometimes want to disguise the purpose of their tests. If they think that respondents will be hesitant to answer sensitive questions honestly, they may design instruments that lack face validity and thereby conceal the purpose of the test.

Construct validity.   Much behavioral research involves the measurement of **hypothetical constructs**—entities that cannot be directly observed but are inferred on the basis of empirical evidence. Behavioral science abounds with hypothetical constructs such as anxiety, intelligence, satiation, attraction, status, schema, self-concept, moral maturity, motivation, learning, and so on. None of these entities can be observed directly, but they are hypothesized to exist on the basis of indirect evidence. In studying these kinds of constructs, researchers must use valid measures. But how does one go about validating the measure of a hypothetical (and invisible) construct?

In an important article, Cronbach and Meehl (1955) suggested that the validity of measures of such constructs can be assessed by studying the relationship between the measure of the construct and scores on other measures. For any measure, we can specify what the scores on the measure should be related to if the measure is valid. For example, scores on a measure of self-esteem should be positively related to scores on measures of confidence and optimism but negatively related to measures of insecurity and anxiety. Thus, we can assess **construct validity** by seeing whether a particular measure is related as it should be to other measures.

When Hart, Leary, and Rejeski (1989) developed a measure of physique anxiety—the tendency to become apprehensive when others scrutinize one's body (at the beach, for example)—the researchers needed to know whether the scale actually measured people's concerns about others' evaluations of their physiques. To examine construct validity, the researchers asked themselves what physique anxiety should be associated with. They reasoned that physique anxiety should be related to negative ratings of one's bodily attractiveness, with weight and skin-fold measurements (heavier and fatter people should be more physique-anxious), with a fear of being negatively evaluated by others, and with self-consciousness. Indeed, their data showed that, compared to people who scored low in physique anxiety, people who scored high on the physique anxiety scale judged their attractiveness lower, weighed more, had a higher percentage of body fat, scored higher in fear of negative evaluation, and were more self-conscious. These data supported the construct validity of the physique anxiety measure. If some of the predicted relationships with other measures had not been obtained, the validity of the scale would have been questioned.

Researchers typically examine construct validity by calculating correlations between the measure they wish to validate and other measures. Because correlation coefficients describe the strength and direction of relationships between variables, they can tell us whether a particular measure is related to other measures as it should be. Sometimes we expect the correlations between one measure and measures of other constructs to be high, whereas in other instances we expect only moderate or weak relationships, or none at all. Thus, unlike in the case of reliability (where we want correlations to exceed .70), no general criteria can be specified for evaluating the size of correlations when assessing validity. The size of each correlation coefficient must be considered relative to the correlation we would expect to find if our measure were valid and measured what it was intended to measure.

To have construct validity, a measure must both correlate with other measures that it should correlate with (**convergent validity**) and *not* correlate with measures that it should not correlate with (**discriminant validity**). When measures correlate highly with measures they should correlate with, we have evidence of convergent validity. When measures correlate weakly (or not at all) with conceptually unrelated measures, we have evidence of discriminant validity. Thus, we can examine the correlations between scores on a test and scores from other measures to see whether the relationships converge and diverge as predicted. In brief, evidence that the measure is related to other measures as it should be supports its construct validity.

Criterion-related validity.   A third type of validity is criterion-related validity. **Criterion-related validity** refers to the extent to which a measure allows researchers to distinguish among subjects on the basis of some behavioral criterion. For example, do scores on the Scholastic Aptitude Test (SAT) permit us to distinguish people who will do well in college from those who will not? Note that the issue is not one of assessing the link between the measure and other constructs (as in construct validity) but of assessing the relationship between the measure and a relevant *behavioral criterion.*

Researchers distinguish between two kinds of criterion validity: concurrent and predictive validity. A measure that allows a researcher to distinguish between people at the present time is said to have **concurrent validity**. In the study of physique anxiety described above, women who scored high on the physique anxiety scale showed significantly higher increases in heart rate when their physiques were being examined than did women who scored low (Hart et al., 1989). Thus, the scale successfully distinguished among high and low physique-anxious women at the present time.

Predictive validity refers to a measure's ability to distinguish between people on a relevant behavioral criterion at some time in the future. Does the measure predict future behavior? For the SAT, for example, the issue is one of predictive validity. No one really cares whether high school seniors who score high on the SAT are better prepared for college than low scorers are *at the time they take the test* (concurrent validity). Instead, college admissions officers want to know whether SAT scores predict academic performance one to four years later (predictive validity).

Criterion-related validity is most often of interest to researchers in applied research settings. In educational research, for example, researchers are often interested in the degree to which tests predict academic performance. Similarly, before using tests to select new employees, personnel psychologists must demonstrate that the tests predict future on-the-job performance.

"You can't build a hut, you don't known how to find edible roots, and you know nothing about predicting the weather. In other words, you do terribly on our IQ test."

© 1990 by Sidney Harris, *American Scientist* Magazine.

IN DEPTH

THE RELIABILITY AND VALIDITY OF COLLEGE ADMISSION EXAMS

Most colleges and universities use applicants' scores on one or more entrance examinations as one criterion for making admissions decisions. By far the most frequently used exam for this purpose is the Scholastic Aptitude Test (SAT), developed by the Educational Testing Service.

Many students are skeptical of the SAT and similar exams. Many claim, for example, that they don't perform well on standardized tests and that their scores indicate little, if anything, about their ability to do well in college. No doubt, there are many people for whom the SAT does not predict performance well. Like all tests, the SAT contains measurement error and thus underestimates and overestimates some people's true aptitude scores. (Interestingly, I've never heard anyone derogate the SAT because they scored *higher* on it than they should have. From a statistical perspective, measurement error should lead as many people to obtain scores that are higher than their true ability as to obtain scores lower than their ability.) However, a large amount of data attests to the overall reliability and validity of the SAT. The psychometric data regarding the SAT are extensive, based on tens of thousands of scores over a span of many years.

The reliability of the SAT is impressive in comparison with most psychological tests. The SAT possesses high test–retest reliability, as well as high interitem reliability. Reliability coefficients average around .90 (Kaplan, 1982), easily exceeding the standard criterion of .70. In fact, over 80% of the total variance in SAT scores is systematic, true-score variance.

In the case of the SAT, *predictive validity* is of paramount importance. Many studies have examined the relationship between SAT scores and college grades. These studies have shown that the criterion-related validity of the SAT depends, in part, on one's major in college; SAT scores predict college performance better for some majors than for others. In general, however, the predictive validity of the SAT is fairly good. On the average, about 16% of the total variance in first-year college grades is systematic variance accounted for by SAT scores (Kaplan, 1982). Sixteen percent may not sound like a great deal until one considers all the other factors that contribute to variability in college grades, such as motivation, health, personal problems, the difficulty of one's courses, the academic ability of the student body, and so on. Given everything that affects performance in college, it is not too surprising that a single test score does not predict with greater accuracy.

Of course, most colleges and universities also use criteria other than entrance exams in the admissions decision. The Educational Testing Service advises admissions offices to consider high school grades, activities, and awards, as well as SAT scores. Using these other criteria further increases the validity of the selection process.

This is not to suggest that the SAT and other college entrance exams are infallible or that certain people do not obtain inflated or deflated scores. But such tests are not as unreliable or as invalid as many students suppose.

To sum up, validity refers to the degree to which a measuring technique measures what it's intended to measure. Although face-valid measures are often desirable, construct and criterion validity are much more important. Construct validity is assessed by seeing whether scores on a measure are related to other measures as they should be. A measure has criterion-related validity if it correctly distinguishes between people on the basis of a relevant behavioral criterion either at present (concurrent validity) or in the future (predictive validity).

Summary

1. Measurement lies at the heart of all research. Behavioral researchers have a wide array of measures at their disposal, including behavioral measures, physiological measures, and self-report measures. Some measures are administered at the time of the study (contemporaneous), whereas others are based on existing records (archival).

2. Whatever type of measure they use, researchers must consider whether the measure is on a nominal, ordinal, interval, or ratio scale of measurement. A measure's scale of measurement has implications for the kind of information the instrument provides as well as for the statistical analyses that can be performed.

3. Reliability refers to the consistency or dependability of a measuring technique.

4. All observed scores consist of two components: the true score and measurement error. The true-score component reflects the score that would have been obtained if the measure were perfect; measurement error reflects the effects of factors that distort the true score. The more measurement error, the less reliable the measure.

5. Three types of reliability can be assessed: test–retest reliability (consistency of the measure across time), interitem reliability (consistency among a set of items intended to assess the same construct), and interrater reliability (consistency between two or more researchers who have observed and recorded the subject's behavior).

6. Reliability is tested by examining correlations between either two administrations of the same measure (test–retest), items on a questionnaire (interitem), or the ratings of two or more observers (interrater).

7. Reliability can be enhanced by standardizing the administration of the measure, clarifying instructions and questions, training observers, and minimizing errors in coding and analyzing data.

8. Validity refers to the extent to which a measurement procedure measures what it's supposed to measure.

9. Three types of validity were discussed: face validity (does the measure appear to measure the construct of interest?), construct validity (does the measure correlate with measures of other constructs as it should?), and criterion-related validity (does the measure correlate with measures of current or future behavior as it should?).

Key Terms

psychometrics	correlation coefficient
behavioral measure	test–retest reliability
behavioral coding system	interitem reliability
knowledgeable informant	item-total correlation
unobtrusive measure	split-half reliability
physiological measure	Cronbach's alpha coefficient
self-report measure	interrater reliability
converging operations	validity
archival research	face validity
nominal scale	hypothetical construct
ordinal scale	construct validity
interval scale	convergent validity
ratio scale	discriminant validity
reliability	criterion-related validity
true score	concurrent validity
measurement error	predictive validity

Review Questions

1. Distinguish between behavioral, physiological, and self-report measures.

2. Distinguish between nominal, ordinal, interval, and ratio scales of measurement. Why do researchers prefer to use interval and ratio scales whenever possible?

3. What is the relationship between the reliability of a measure and the degree of measurement error it contains?

4. What factors can contribute to measurement error?

5. What are the three primary ways in which researchers assess the reliability of their measures?

6. Distinguish between item-total correlation, split-half reliability, and Cronbach's alpha coefficient as ways to assess interitem reliability.

7. What steps can a researcher take to increase the reliability of his or her measuring techniques?

8. Distinguish between face validity, construct validity, and criterion-related validity. In general, which kind of validity is least important to researchers?

9. Can a measurement procedure be valid but not reliable? reliable but not valid? Explain.

Questions for Thought and Discussion

1. Many students experience a great deal of anxiety whenever they take tests. Imagine that you are conducting a study involving test anxiety. Suggest three behavioral measures, three physiological measures, and three self-report measures you might use in such a study.

2. Hypochondriacs are obsessed with their health. They often talk about their real and imagined health problems, and visit their physician frequently. Imagine that you developed a self-report measure of hypochondriacal tendencies.

   a. Describe how you would examine the test–retest and interitem reliability of your measure.

   b. Describe how you would test the construct and criterion-related validity of the measure.

CHAPTER 4

Observational and Self-Report Measurement Strategies

Evidence suggests that certain schizophrenics (though, by no means all) *want* other people to view them as psychologically disturbed because being perceived as "crazy" has benefits for them. Being regarded as mentally incompetent frees people from normal responsibilities at home and at work, provides a ready-made excuse for their failures, and may even allow people living in poverty to improve their living conditions by being admitted to a mental institution. Indeed, Braginsky, Braginsky, and Ring (1982) suggest that some very poor people use mental institutions as "resorts" where they can rest, relax, and escape the stresses of everyday life. This is not to say that people who display symptoms of schizophrenia are not psychologically troubled, but it suggests that psychotic symptoms sometimes reflect patients' attempts to manage the impressions other have of them rather than underlying psychopathology per se (Leary & Miller, 1986).

Imagine that you are a member of a research team investigating the hypothesis that some patients use psychotic symptoms as an impression-management strategy. Think for a moment about how you would measure the patients' behavior to test your hypothesis. What behaviors could you focus on that would reflect psychotic symptoms? Would you directly observe the patients, use self-report measures, or rely on others' reports of the patients' behavior? If you observed the patients directly, how could you be sure that your presence alone would not affect their behavior? Would it be worthwhile simply to *ask* subjects whether they wanted others to perceive them as disturbed? Could you obtain useful information by examining the content of what the patients talked about during psychotherapy sessions?

We learned in Chapter 3 that behavioral researchers use a diverse array of measuring techniques to assess behavior, thought, and emotion. Some of these techniques are highly specialized and are used by only those few researchers who study a particular phenomenon. In contrast, other measurement strategies are used at one time or another by nearly every researcher who studies human behavior. In this chapter, we will go into detail regarding two of the approaches to measurement introduced in the previous chapter that the vast majority of behavioral scientists use at least occasionally: observational methods (in which subjects' overt behaviors are observed and recorded) and self-report measures (in which subjects report their own behavior, feelings, or thoughts on questionnaires or in interviews).

Observational Methods

A great deal of behavioral research involves the direct observation of human or nonhuman behavior. Behavioral researchers have been known to observe and record behaviors as diverse as eating, arguing, bar pressing, smiling, helping, food salting, hand clapping, eye blinking, mating, yawning, conversing, and even urinating. Roughly speaking, researchers who use **observational methods** must make three decisions about the approach they will take in a particular study: (1) Will the observation occur in a natural or contrived setting? (2) Will the participants know they are being observed? (3) How will subjects' behavior be recorded?

Naturalistic Versus Contrived Settings

Researchers sometimes observe and record behavior in real-world settings. **Naturalistic observation** involves the observation of ongoing behavior as it occurs naturally with no intrusion or intervention by the researcher. In naturalistic studies, the subjects are observed as they engage in ordinary activities in settings that have not been arranged specifically for research purposes. For example, researchers have used naturalistic observation to study behavior during riots and other mob events, nonverbal behavior, littering, and parent–child interactions on the playground.

Researchers interested in the behavior of nonhuman animals in their natural habitats—ethologists and comparative psychologists—also use naturalistic observation methods. Animal researchers have studied a wide array of behaviors under naturalistic conditions, including tool use by elephants, mating among iguana lizards, foraging in squirrels, and aggression among monkeys (see, for example, Chevalier-Skolnikoff & Liska, 1993). Jane Goodall and Dianne Fossey used naturalistic observation of chimpanzees and gorillas, respectively, in their well-known field studies.

Participant observation is one special type of observation in natural settings. In participant observation, the researcher engages in the same activities as the people he or she is observing. In a classic example of participant observation, social psychologists infiltrated a doomsday group that prophesied that much of the world would soon be destroyed (Festinger, Reicken, & Schachter, 1956). The researchers, who were interested in how such groups react when their prophecies are disconfirmed (as the researchers assumed they would be in this case), concocted ficticious identities to gain admittance to the group and then observed and recorded the group members' behavior as the time for the cataclysm came and went. In other studies involving participant observation, researchers have posed as cult members, homeless people, devil worshippers, homosexuals, blacks (in this case, a white researcher tinted his skin and passed as black for several weeks), salespeople, and street gang members.

Participating in the events being studied can raise special problems for a researcher who uses participant observation. To the extent that researchers become immersed in the group's activities and come to identify with the people they study, they may lose their ability to observe and record others' behavior objectively. In addition, in all participant observation studies, the researcher runs the risk of influencing the behavior of the individuals being studied. To the extent that the researcher interacts with other participants, helps to make decisions that affect the group, and otherwise participates in the group's activities, he or she may unwittingly affect subjects' behavior in ways that make it unnatural.

In contrast to naturalistic observation, **contrived observation** involves the observation of behavior in settings that are arranged specifically for observing and recording behavior. Often such studies are conducted in laboratory settings in which subjects know they are being observed, although the observers are usually concealed, such as behind a one-way mirror. For example, to study parent–child relationships, researchers often observe parents interacting with their children in laboratory settings. In one such study (Rosen & Rothbaum, 1993), parents brought their children to an laboratory "playroom." Both parent and child behaviors were videotaped as the child explored the new environment with the parent present, as the parent left the child alone in the lab for a few minutes, and again when the parent and child were reunited. In addition, parents and their children were videotaped playing, reading, cleaning up the toys in the lab, and solving easy and difficult problems. Analyses of the videotapes provided a wealth of information about the relationship between the quality of the care parents provided their children and the nature of the parent–child relationship.

This study utilized contrived observation that occurred in a setting specifically designed for research purposes, and the parents (if not the children) knew that they were being videotaped and observed. In some cases, researchers conceal the fact that subjects are being observed, even in laboratory settings (see the case study, "Disguised Observation in Laboratory settings").

In other cases, researchers conduct contrived observational studies in the "real world." In these studies, the researcher sets up situations outside the laboratory to observe people's reactions. Several field experiments on determinants of helping behavior have been conducted in everyday settings. In one such study, researchers interested in factors that affect helping staged an "emergency" on a New York City subway (Piliavin, Rodin, & Piliavin, 1969). Over more than two months, researchers staged 103 accidents in which a research confederate would stagger and collapse on a moving subway car. Sometimes the confederate carried a cane and acted as if he we injured or infirm; at other times he carried a bottle in a paper bag and pretended to be drunk. Two observers then recorded bystanders' reactions to the "emergency."

Disguised Versus Nondisguised Observation

The second decision a researcher must make when using behavioral observation is whether to let participants know they are being observed. Sometimes the individuals who are being studied know that that the researcher is observing their behavior (**undisguised observation**). As you might guess, the problem with undisguised observation is that people often do not respond naturally when they know they are being scrutinized. Researchers refer to behaviors that are affected by observation as **reactive**.

When they are concerned about reactivity, researchers may conceal the fact that they are observing and recording subjects' behavior (**disguised observation**). Festinger and his colleagues (1956) used disguised observation when studying the doomsday group because they undoubtedly would not have been allowed to observe the group otherwise. Similarly, the subway passengers studied by Piliavin, Rodin, and Piliavin (1969) did not know that their reactions to the staged emergency were being observed.

However, disguised observation may raise ethical issues because researchers may invade subjects' privacy as well as violate subjects' right to decide whether to participate in the research (the right of *informed consent*). As long as the behaviors under observation occur in public and the researcher does not unnecessarily inconvenience or upset the subjects, the ethical considerations are small. However, if the behaviors are not public or the researcher intrudes uninvited into subjects' everyday lives, then disguised observation may be problematic.

In some instances, researchers compromise by letting subjects know they are being observed, but withholding information regarding precisely what aspects of the subject's behavior are being recorded. This *partial concealment* strategy (Weick, 1968) lowers (but does not eliminate) the problem of reactivity while avoiding ethical questions involving invasion of privacy and informed consent. We'll return to these ethical issues in Chapter 15.

BEHAVIORAL RESEARCH CASE STUDY

DISGUISED OBSERVATION IN LABORATORY SETTINGS

Researchers who use observation to measure subjects' behavior face a dilemma. On one hand, they are most likely to obtain accurate, unbiased data if subjects do not know they are being observed. In studies of interpersonal interaction, for example, subjects have a great deal of difficulty acting naturally when they know their behavior is being observed or videotaped for analysis. On the other hand, failing to obtain subjects' prior approval to be observed violates their right to consent to participate in the research and, possibly, their right to privacy.

Researcher William Ickes has devised an ingenious solution to this dilemma (Ickes, 1982). His approach has been used most often to study dyadic, or two-person, social interactions (hence, it is known as the *dyadic interaction paradigm*), but it could be used to study other behavior as well. Pairs of subjects reporting for an experiment are escorted to a waiting room and seated on a couch. The researcher excuses him- or herself to complete preparations for the experiment and leaves the two subjects alone. Unknown to the subjects, their behavior is then recorded by means of a concealed videotape recorder in a darkened room across the hall and a microphone hidden under a table in the waiting room.

But how does this subterfuge avoid the ethical issues we just posed? Haven't we observed subjects' behavior without their consent and thereby invaded their privacy? The answer is no because, although the subjects' behavior was recorded, *no one has observed their behavior or seen the videotape*. Their conversation in the waiting room is still as private and confidential as if it hadn't been recorded at all.

After a few minutes, the researcher returns and explains to the subjects that their behavior was videotaped. The purpose of the study is explained, and the researcher asks the subjects for permission to code and analyze the tape. However, subjects are free to deny their permission, in which case the tape is erased in the subjects' presence or, if they want, given to them. Ickes reports that most subjects are willing to let the researcher analyze their behavior.

This observational paradigm has been successfully used in studies of sex role behavior, empathy, shyness, Machiavellianism, interracial relations, social cognition, and birth-order effects. Importantly, this approach to diguised observation in laboratory settings can be used to study not only overt social behavior but also covert processes involving thoughts and feelings. In some studies, researchers have shown subjects the videotapes of their own behavior and asked them to indicate the thoughts or feelings they had at certain points during their interaction in the waiting room (see Ickes, Bissonnette, Garcia, & Stinson, 1990).

Behavioral Recording

The third decision facing the researcher who uses observational strategies involves precisely how the subjects' behavior will be recorded. Whenever researchers observe subjects' behavior, they must devise ways of recording what they see and hear.

Sometimes the behaviors being observed are relatively simple and easily recorded, such as the number of times a pigeon pecks a key or the number of M&Ms eaten by a subject (which might be done in a study of social influences on eating).

In other cases, the behaviors are more complex. When observing complex, multifaceted reactions such as embarrassment, group discussion, or union–management negotiations, researchers must spend a great deal of time designing and pretesting the system they will use to record their observations. Although the specific techniques used to observe and record behavioral data are nearly endless, most fall into four general categories: narrative records, checklists, temporal measures, and rating scales.

Narratives. Although used only rarely in psychological research, **narrative records** (sometimes called *specimen records*) have long been commonplace in other social and behavioral sciences. A narrative or specimen record is a full description of a subject's behavior. The intent is to capture, as completely as possible, everything the subject said and did during a specified period of time. Although researchers once wrote handwritten notes as they observed subjects in person, researchers today are more likely to produce written narratives from audio- or videotapes, or to record a spoken narrative into a tape recorder as they observe subjects' behavior; the taped narrative is then transcribed.

One of the best known uses of narrative records is Piaget's ground-breaking studies of children's cognitive development. As he observed a child, Piaget kept a running account of precisely what the child said and did. For example, in a study of Jacqueline, who was about to have her first birthday, Piaget (1951) wrote,

> when I seized a lock of my hair and moved it about on my temple, she succeeded for the first time in imitating me. She suddenly took her hand from her eyebrow, which she was touching, felt above it, found her hair and took hold of it, quite deliberately. (p. 55)

Narrative records differ in their explicitness and completeness. Sometimes researchers try to record verbatim virtually everything the subject says or does. More commonly, researchers take **field notes** that include summary descriptions of the subject's behaviors, but with no attempt to record behavior verbatim.

Although narrative records provide the most complete description of a researcher's observations, they cannot be analyzed quantitatively until they are *content analyzed*. As we'll discuss later in this chapter, content analysis involves classifying or rating behavior so that it can be analyzed.

Checklists. Narrative records are often called *unstructured* observation methods because of their open-ended nature. In contrast, most observation methods used by behavioral researchers are *structured*. A structured observation method is one in which the observer records, measures, or rates behavior on dimensions that have been decided upon in advance.

The simplest structured observation technique is a **checklist** (or tally sheet) on which the researcher records attributes of the subjects (such as sex, age, and race) and whether particular behaviors were observed. In some cases, researchers are interested only in whether a single particular behavior occurred. For example, in a study of helping, Bryan and Test (1967) recorded whether passersby donated to a Salvation Army kettle at Christmas time. In other cases, researchers record whenever one of several behaviors is observed. For example, many researchers have used the Interaction Process Analysis (Bales, 1970) to study group interaction. In this checklist system, observers record whenever any of 12 behaviors is observed: seems friendly, dramatizes, agrees, gives suggestion, gives opinion, gives information, asks for information, asks for opinion, asks for suggestion, disagrees, shows tension, and seems unfriendly.

Although checklists may seem an easy and straightforward way of recording behavior, researchers must struggle to develop clear, explicit operational definitions of the target behaviors. Whereas we may find it relatively easy to determine whether a passerby dropped money into a Salvation Army kettle, we may have more difficulty defining explicitly what we mean by "seems friendly" or "shows tension." As we discussed in Chapter 1, researchers use *operational definitions* to define unambiguously how a particular construct will be measured in a particular research setting.

Temporal measures: Latency and duration.   Sometimes researchers are interested not only in whether a behavior occurred but also in *when* it occurred and *how long* it lasted. Researchers are often interested in how much time elapsed between a particular event and a behavior or between two behaviors (**latency**). The most obvious and commonplace measure of latency is **reaction time**—the time that elapses between the presentation of a stimulus and the subject's response (such as pressing a key). Reaction time is used by cognitive psychologists as an index of how much processing of information is occurring in the nervous system; the longer the reaction time, the more internal processing must be occurring.

Another latency measure is **task completion time**—the length of time it takes subjects to solve a problem or complete a task. In a study of the effects of altitude on cognitive performance, Kramer, Coyne, and Strayer (1993) tested climbers before, during, and after climbing Mount Denali in Alaska. Using portable microcomputers, the researchers administered several perceptual, cognitive, and sensorimotor tasks, measuring both how well subjects performed and *how long* it took subjects to complete the task. Compared to a control group, the climbers showed deficits in their ability to learn and remember information, and they performed more slowly on most of the tasks.

Other measures of latency involve **interbehavior latency**—the time that expires between the performance of two behaviors. In a study of emotional expressions, Asendorpf (1990) observed the temporal relationship between smiling and gaze during embarrassed and nonembarrassed smiling. Observation of different smiles showed that nonembarrassed smiles tend to be followed by immediate gaze aversion (people look away briefly right as they stop smiling), but when people are embarrassed, they avert their gaze 1.0 to 1.5 seconds *before* they stop smiling.

In addition to latency measures, a researcher may be interested in how long a particular behavior lasted—in its **duration**. For example, researchers interested in social interaction often measure how long people talk during a conversation or how long people look at one another when they interact (eye contact). Researchers interested in infant behavior have studied the temporal patterns in infant crying, such as, for example, how long bursts of crying last (duration) and how much time elapses between bursts (interbehavior latency) (Zeskind, Parker-Price, & Barr, 1993).

Observational rating scales. For some purposes, researchers are interested in measuring the *quality* or *intensity* of a behavior. A developmental psychologist may want to know not only whether a child cried when teased but *how hard* he or she cried. Or a counseling psychologist may want to assess *how anxious* speech-anxious subjects appeared while giving a talk. In such cases, observers often go beyond recording the presence of a behavior to judge its intensity or quality. The observer may rate the child's crying on a 3-point scale (1 = slight, 2 = moderate, 3 = extreme) or how nervous a public speaker appeared on a 5-point scale (1 = not at all, 2 = slightly, 3 = moderately, 4 = very, 5 = extremely).

Because these kinds of ratings necessarily entail a certain degree of subjectivity, special care must be devoted to clearly defining the rating scale categories. Unambiguous criteria must be established so that observers know what distinguishes "slight crying" from "moderate crying" from "extreme crying."

Increasing the Reliability of Observational Methods

To be useful, observational coding strategies must demonstrate adequate **interrater reliability**. As we saw in the previous chapter, interrater reliability refers to the degree to which the observations of two or more independent raters or observers agree. Low interrater reliability indicates that the raters are not using the observation system similarly and that their ratings contain excessive measurement error.

The reliability of observational systems can be increased in two ways. First, as noted earlier, clear and precise operational definitions must be provided for the behaviors of interest. All observers must use precisely the same criteria in recording and rating subjects' behaviors.

Second, raters should practice using the coding system and discuss their practice ratings with one another before observing the behavior to be analyzed. In this way, they can resolve differences in how they are using the observation system. This also allows researchers to check the interrater reliability to be sure that the observational coding system is sufficiently reliable before observing the behavior of the actual subjects.

Self-Report Measures

Behavioral researchers generally prefer to observe behavior directly, rather than to rely on subjects' reports of how they behave. However, practical and ethical issues often make direct observation implausible or impossible. Furthermore, some information—such as about past experiences, feelings, and attitudes—is most directly assessed through self-report measures obtained either on questionnaires or in interviews. On **questionnaires**, subjects respond to written questions or statements; in **interviews**, an interviewer asks the questions and the subject responds orally.

Both questionnaires and interviews have advantages and disadvantages, and researchers must decide which strategy will best serve a particular research purpose. On one hand, because questionnaires require less extensive training of researchers and can usually be administered to groups of people simultaneously, they are often less expensive and time-consuming than interviews. Furthermore, if the topic is a sensitive one, subjects can be assured that their responses to a questionnaire will be anonymous, whereas anonymity is impossible in a face-to-face interview. Thus, subjects may be more honest on questionnaires than in interviews.

On the other hand, if respondents are drawn from the general population, questionnaires are inappropriate for those who are functionally illiterate—approximately 10% of the adult population of the United States. Similarly, interviews are necessary for young children who are incapable of completing questionnaires on their own. Unlike questionnaires, interviews can be administered to both literate and illiterate respondents. Also, interviews allow the researcher to be sure respondents understand each question before answering. We have no way of knowing whether respondents understand all of the questions on a questionnaire. Perhaps the greatest advantage of interviews is that detailed information can be obtained about complex topics. A skilled interviewer can probe respondents for elaboration of details in a way that is impossible on a questionnaire. Table 4.1 presents a comparison of the advantages of questionnaires and interviews.

Questionnaires

Questionnaires are perhaps the most ubiquitous of all psychological measures. Not only are they used at one time or another by most researchers who study human behavior, but questionnaires are used by clinical psychologists to obtain information about their clients, by companies to collect data on applicants and employees, by members of Congress to poll their constituents, by restaurants to assess the quality of their food and service, and by colleges to obtain students' evaluations of their teachers. You have undoubtedly completed many questionnaires, and you may even have designed a questionnaire for use in a class, club, church, or other activity.

Designing a good questionnaire involves much more than writing a few ques-

TABLE 4.1

Advantages of Questionnaires Versus Interviews

Questionnaires	Interviews
Less expensive	Necessary for illiterate respondents
Easier to administer	Necessary for young children and persons with low IQ
May be administered in groups	
Less training of researchers	Can ensure that respondents understand questions
Anonymity can be assured	Allows for follow-up questions
	Can explore complex issues more fully

tions. Researchers must keep several issues in mind as they design questionnaires for use in descriptive, correlational, experimental, or quasi-experimental research. Following are guidelines for designing a useful questionnaire.

Use precise terminology in phrasing the questions. Be certain that your respondents will interpret each question exactly as you intended. What reply would you give, for example, to the question, "What kinds of drugs do you take?" One person might list the recreational drugs he or she has tried, such as marijuana or cocaine. Other respondents, however, might interpret the question to be asking what kinds of prescription drugs they are taking and list things such as penicillin or insulin. Still others might try to recall the brand names of the various over-the-counter remedies in their medicine cabinets.

Write the questions as simply as possible, avoiding difficult words, unnecessary jargon, and cumbersome phrases. Many respondents would stumble over instructions such as, "Rate your self-relevant affect on the following scales." Why not just say, "Rate how you feel about yourself"? Keep the questions short and uncomplicated. Testing experts recommend limiting each question to no more than 20 words.

Avoid making unwarranted assumptions about the respondents. We often tend to assume that most other people are just like us, and so we write questions that make unjustified assumptions based on our own experiences. The question, "How do you feel about your mother?" for example, assumes that the subject knows his or her mother, which might not be the case. Similarly, consider whether respondents have the necessary knowledge to answer each question. A respondent who does not know the details of a new international treaty would not be able to give his or her attitude about it.

Conditional information should precede the key idea of the question. When a question contains conditional or hypothetical information, that information should precede the central part of the question. It would be better to ask, "If a good friend were depressed for a long time, would you suggest he or she see a therapist?" rather than "Would you suggest a good friend see a therapist if he or she were depressed for a long time?" When the central idea in a question is presented first, respondents may begin formulating an answer before considering the essential conditional element.

Do not use double-barreled questions. A double-barreled question asks more than one question but provides the respondent with the opportunity for only one response. Consider the question, "Do you eat healthily and exercise regularly?" How should I answer the question if I eat healthily but don't exercise, or vice versa? Rewrite double-barreled questions as two separate questions.

Choose an appropriate response format. The **response format** refers to the manner in which the subject indicates his or her answer to the question. There are three basic response formats, each of which works better for some research purposes than for others.

In a *free-response format* (or open-ended question), the subject fills in a blank or writes an unstructured response to the question. In simple cases, the question may ask for a single number, as when respondents are asked how many siblings they have or how many minutes they think have passed as they worked on an experimental task. In more complex cases, the subject may be asked to write an essay-type answer to a question. For example, respondents might be asked to describe themselves in a paragraph. Open-ended questions can provide a wealth of information but, if verbal (as opposed to numerical) responses are obtained, the answers must be coded or content-analyzed before they can be analyzed and interpreted. (Content analysis is discussed later in the chapter.)

When questions are asked about behaviors, thoughts, or feelings that can vary in frequency or intensity, a *rating scale response format* should be used. Often, a 5-point scale is used, as in the following example.

To what extent do you oppose or support capital punishment?

_____ Strongly oppose

_____ Moderately oppose

_____ Neither oppose nor support

_____ Moderately support

_____ Strongly support

However, other length scales are also used, as in this example of a 4-point rating scale:

How depressed did you feel after failing the test?

_____ Not at all

_____ Slightly

_____ Moderately

_____ Very

When people are asked to rate themselves, other people, or objects on descriptive adjectives, researchers have often used 7-point scales, asking respondents to write an X in one of seven spaces to indicate their answer.

Not Lonely :____:____:____:____:____:____:____: Lonely

Depressed :____:____:____:____:____:____:____: Not Depressed

This kind of measure is often called a *bipolar adjective scale* because each item consists of an adjective and its opposite.

Finally, sometimes respondents are asked to choose one response from a set of possible alternatives—the *multiple choice* or *fixed-alternative response format*.

What is your attitude toward abortion?

_____ Disapprove under all circumstances

_____ Approve only under special circumstances, such as when the woman's life is in danger

_____ Approve whenever a woman wants one

The *true–false response format* is a special case of a fixed-alternative format in which only two alternatives are available—"true" and "false." A true–false format is most useful for questions of fact (for example, "I attended church last week"), but is not recommended for measuring attitudes and feelings. In many cases, people's subjective reactions are not clear-cut enough to fall neatly into a true or false category. For example, if asked to respond true or false to the statement, "I feel nervous in social situations," most people would have difficulty answering either true or false and would probably say, "It depends."

Researchers should consider various options when deciding on a response format, then choose the one that provides the best information.

Pretest the questionnaire. Whenever possible, researchers pretest their questionnaires before using them in a study. Questionnaires are pretested by asking a few people to complete the questionnaire, tell the researcher what they think each question is asking, report on difficulties they have understanding the questions or using the response formats, and express other reactions to the items. Based on subjects' responses during pretesting, the questionnaire can be revised before it is actually used in research.

BEHAVIORAL RESEARCH CASE STUDY

SELF-REPORT DIARIES

One shortcoming with some self-report questionnaires is that respondents have difficulty remembering the details needed to answer the questions accurately. Suppose, for example, that you are interested in the relationship between loneliness and the number of social interactions people have with close friends versus acquaintances during the week. Specifically, you are interested in whether lonely people have fewer contacts with close friends than nonlonely people do.

The most accurate way to examine this question would be to administer a measure of loneliness, then follow subjects around for a week and directly observe who they interact with. Obviously, practical and ethical problems preclude such an approach, not to mention the fact that people would be unlikely to behave naturally with a researcher trailing them 24 hours a day.

Alternatively, you could measure subjects' degree of loneliness and, then ask subjects to report how many times (and for how long each time) they interacted with certain friends and acquaintances during the past week. If subjects' memories were infallible, this would be a reasonable way to address the research question, but people's memories are simply not that good. Can you really recall everyone you interacted with during the past seven days, and how long you interacted with each? Thus, neither observational methods nor retrospective self-reports are likely to yield viable data in a case such as this.

An approach that has seen increased use during the past 10 years involves **diary methodologies**. Several different kinds of diary methodologies have been developed, but all of them ask subjects to keep a *daily record* of information pertinent to the researcher's question. For example, Wheeler, Reis, and Nezlek (1983) used a diary approach to study the relationship between loneliness and social interaction. In this study, participants completed a standard measure of loneliness and kept a daily record of their social interactions for about two weeks. For every interaction they had that lasted 10 minutes or longer, the participants filled out a short form on which they recorded who they had interacted with, how long the interaction lasted, the gender of the other interactant(s), and other information such as who had initiated the interaction and how pleasant the encounter was. By having subjects record this information as soon as possible after each interaction, the researchers decreased the likelihood that the data would be contaminated by participants' faulty memories.

The results showed that, for both male and female participants, loneliness was negatively related to the amount of time they interacted with women; spending more time with women was associated with lower loneliness. Furthermore, although loneliness was not associated with the number of different people participants interacted with, lonely participants rated their interactions as less meaningful than less lonely participants did. In fact, the strongest predictor of loneliness was how meaningful participants found their daily interactions.

Diary methods have been used to study the relationship between everyday interaction and a variety of variables, including academic performance, gender, social support, alcohol use, self-presentation, physical attractiveness, and friendship (see Reis & Wheeler, 1991).

Effective Interviewing

For some research purposes, self-report responses are better obtained in face-
or telephone interviews rather than on questionnaires. Each of the guidelines
discussed for writing questionnaire items is equally relevant for designing an **interview schedule**—the series of questions that are used in an interview.

In addition, the researcher must consider how the interview process itself—the
interaction between the interviewer and respondent—will affect subjects' responses. Following are a few suggestions of ways for interviewers to improve the
quality of the responses they receive from interviewees.

- *Create a friendly atmosphere.* The interviewer's first goal should be to put the
  respondent at ease. Respondents who like and trust the interviewer will be
  more open and honest in their responses than those who are angered or
  intimidated by the interviewer's style.

- *Maintain an attitude of friendly interest.* The interviewer should appear truly
  interested in the respondent's answers, rather than mechanically recording
  the responses in a disinterested manner.

- *Order the sections of the interview to facilitate rapport building and to create a
  logical sequence.* The interviewer should start with the most basic and least
  threatening topics, then move slowly to more specific and sensitive
  questions as the respondent becomes more relaxed.

- *Conceal personal reactions to the respondent's answers.* The interviewer should
  never show surprise, approval, disapproval, or other reactions to the
  respondent's replies.

- *Ask questions exactly as they are worded.* In most instances, the interviewer
  should ask the question in precisely the same way to all respondents.
  Impromptu rewording of the questions introduces differences in how various
  respondents are interviewed, thereby increasing measurement error and
  lowering the reliability of subjects' responses.

- *Don't lead the respondent.* In probing the respondent's answer by asking for
  clarification or details, the interviewer must be careful not to put words in
  the respondent's mouth.

Biases in Observational and
Self-Report Measurement

Although measurement in all sciences is subject to biases of various sorts (scientists
of all kinds are prone to see what they expect to see), the measures used in
behavioral research are susceptible to certain biases that those in many other
sciences are not. Unlike the objects of study in the physical sciences, for example,
the responses of the subjects used in behavioral research are sometimes biased. A

piece of crystal will not change how it responds while being studied by a geologist, but a human subject may well act differently when being studied by a psychologist or other behavioral researcher. In this section, we briefly discuss three measurement biases.

The Social Desirability Bias

Research subjects are often concerned with how they will be perceived and evaluated by the researcher or by other subjects. As a result, they sometimes respond in a socially desirable manner rather than naturally and honestly. People are hesitant to admit certain problems or express certain attitudes, for example. This **social desirability response bias** can lower the validity of certain observational and self-report measures. When people bias their answers or behaviors in a socially desirable direction, the instrument no longer measures what it was supposed to measure; instead, it measures subjects' proclivity for responding in a socially desirable fashion.

Social desirability biases can never be eliminated entirely, but steps can be taken to reduce their effects on subjects' responses. First, questions should be worded as neutrally as possible so that concerns with social desirability do not arise. Second, when possible, subjects should be assured that their responses are anonymous, thereby lowering their concern with others' evaluations. (As we noted, this is easier to do when information is obtained on questionnaires rather than in interviews.) Third, in observational studies, observers should be as unobtrusive as possible to minimize subjects' concerns about being watched.

Acquiescence and Naysaying Response Styles

Some individuals show a tendency to agree with statements regardless of the content (**acquiescence**), whereas others have a tendency to express disagreement (**naysaying**). These response styles were first discovered during early research on authoritarianism. Two forms of a measure of authoritarian attitudes were constructed, with the items on one form written to express the reverse of the items on the other form. Given that the forms were reversals of one another, we would expect a strong negative relationship between scores on the two forms; people who scored high on one form should score low on the other, and vice versa. Instead, scores on the two forms were *positively* related. This surprising finding alerted the researchers to the possibility that some respondents were agreeing or disagreeing with the statements regardless of the content of the statements.

Fortunately, years of subsequent research suggest that the tendency for some research participants to agree or disagree with questionnaire items regardless of content has only a very minor effect on the validity of psychological measurement as long as one essential precaution is taken: a measure that asks respondents to indicate agreement or disagreement (or true or false) to various statements should have an approximately equal number of items on which people who score high on the construct would indicate "agree" versus "disagree" (or "true" versus "false") (Nunnally, 1978). For example, on a measure of the tendency to experience stage fright, we would need an equal number of items that express high stage fright ("I am often nervous before speaking in public") and items that express low stage fright ("I usually feel comfortable when speaking or performing before an audience").

Observer Biases

Not all measurement biases can be blamed on research subjects; some result from the researcher. In observational research, in particular, the biases of observers who observe and rate subjects' behavior can compromise the validity of a measure.

A **halo bias** occurs when observers' ratings of a subject's behavior are affected by their overall positive or negative evaluation of the subject (Cooper, 1981). For example, an observer who forms a positive impression of a subject may interpret the subject's behavior differently than an observer who forms a negative impression of the same subject. If the observers are counting how many times the subject interrupts another person during a conversation, an observer who views the subject negatively may "count" more interruptions than one who views the subject positively.

Other biases result from the frame of reference that an observer uses to rate subjects. The *contrast error*, for example, is the tendency for observers to rate subjects as opposite to them on a trait: the more extreme an observer sees him- or herself on a particular characteristic, the more extreme he or she will rate others in the opposite direction (Murray, 1938). Imagine that a researcher is rating how "outgoing" subjects are during a laboratory conversation with a confederate. An friendly, personable researcher is likely to rate subjects as less outgoing than an quiet, shy researcher will because each researcher implicitly uses him- or herself as a frame of reference when rating other people.

IN DEPTH

ASKING FOR MORE THAN SUBJECTS CAN REPORT

When using self-report measures of any kind, researchers should be alert to the possibility that they may sometimes ask questions that subjects cannot answer accurately. In some cases, subjects *know* they do not know the answer to a particular question, such as "How old were you, in months, when you were toilet-trained?" When they know they don't know the answer to a question, subjects may indicate that they do not know the answer or they may simply guess. Obviously, researchers who treat subjects' uninformed guesses as accurate responses are asking for trouble.

In other cases, subjects *think* they know the answer to a question—in fact, they may be quite confident of their response—yet it is entirely wrong. Research shows, for example, that people are often not aware that their memories of past events are distorted; nor do they always know why they behave or feel certain ways. Although we often assume that people know why they do what they do, people can be quite uninformed regarding the factors that affect their behavior (Nisbett & Wilson, 1977).

People's beliefs about their motives are important to study in their own right, whether or not those beliefs are correct. But behavioral researchers should not blithely assume that subjects are always able to report the reasons they act or feel certain ways accurately.

Content Analysis

In many studies that use observational or self-report measures, the behavior of interest involves the *content* of people's speech or writing. For example, behavioral researchers may be interested in what children say aloud as they solve difficult problems, what shy strangers talk about during a getting-acquainted conversation, or what married couples express during marital therapy. Similarly, researchers may want to analyze the content of essays that subjects write about themselves or subjects' answers to open-ended questions. In other cases, researchers want to study existing archival data such as newspaper articles, letters, or personal diaries.

Researchers interested in such topics are faced with the task of converting written or spoken material to meaningful data that can be analyzed. In such situations, researchers turn to **content analysis**, a set of procedures designed to convert textual information to more relevant, manageable data (Berelson, 1952; Rosengren, 1981; Weber, 1990). Content analysis has been used to study topics as diverse as historical changes in the lyrics of popular songs, differences in the topics men and women talk about in group discussions, suicide notes, racial and sexual stereotypes reflected in children's books, election campaign speeches, biases in newspaper coverage of various events, television advertisements, the content of the love letters of people in troubled versus untroubled relationships, and psychotherapy sessions.

The central goal of content analysis is to classify words, phrases, or other units of text into a limited number of meaningful categories, that is, categories that are relevant to the researcher's hypothesis. Any text can be content analyzed, whether it is written material (answers, essays, articles) or transcriptions of spoken material (conversations, public speeches, talking aloud)

The first step in content analysis is to decide what units of text will be analyzed—words, phrases, sentences, or whatever. Often, the most useful unit of text is the *utterance* (or theme), which roughly corresponds to a simple sentence having a noun, a verb, and supporting parts of speech (Stiles, 1978). For example, the statement, "I hate my mother" is a single utterance. In contrast, "I hate my mother and father" reflects *two* utterances: "I hate my mother," and "(I hate) my father." The researcher goes through the text or transcript, marking and numbering every discrete utterance.

The second step is to define how the units of text will be coded. At the most basic level, the researcher must decide whether to (1) *classify* each unit of text into one of several mutually exclusive categories or (2) *rate* each unit on some specified dimensions. For example, imagine that we were interested in people's responses to others' complaints. On one hand, we could classify reactions to complaints into one of four categories, such as disinterest (simply not responding to the complaint), refutation (denying that the person has a valid complaint), nonempathic responsivity (simply acknowledging the complaint), or validation (agreeing with the complaint). On the other hand, we could *rate* responses on the degree to which they are supportive. For example, we could rate subjects' responses to complaints on a 5-point scale where 1 = nonsupportive and 5 = extremely supportive.

Whichever system is used, clear rules must be developed for classifying or rating the text. These rules must be so explicit and clear that two raters using the system will rate the material in the same way. To maximize the degree to which their ratings agree, raters often discuss and practice the system before actually coding the textual material from the study. Also, researchers typically assess the interrater reliability of the system by determining the degree to which the raters' classifications or ratings are consistent (see Chapter 3). If the reliability is low, the coding system is clarified or redesigned. After the researcher is convinced that interrater reliability is sufficiently high, raters code the entire text. They must do so independently and without conferring with one another so that interrater reliability can again be assessed based on ratings of the material obtained in the study.

Although researchers must sometimes design a content analysis coding system for use in a particular study, they should always explore whether a system that will serve their purposes already exists. Coding schemes have been developed for analyzing everything from newspaper articles to evidence of inner psychological states (such as hostility and anxiety) to group discussions and conversations (Bales, 1970; Rosengren, 1981; Stiles, 1978; Viney, 1983).

BEHAVIORAL RESEARCH CASE STUDY

IMPRESSION MANAGEMENT AND PSYCHOLOGICAL DISORDERS

We began this chapter with the question of how we might go about testing the hypothesis that some schizophrenics purposely convey the impression of being either more or less disturbed, depending on which will have the greatest benefits for them. Researchers who have studied the impression-management behavior of mental patients have measured patients' behavior using both observational and self-report strategies.

For example, Braginsky and Braginsky (1967) videotaped patients' behavior under conditions in which the patients thought appearing disturbed would have either benefits or negative consequences (being transferred to a "back ward" for more disturbed patients) for them. The subjects' behavior on these videotapes was then analyzed for evidence of psychotic symptoms. In contrast, Fontana and Gessner (1969) had patients complete self-report measures on which they rated their psychological symptoms. In another study, Watson (1972) both interviewed patients and had them complete self-report questionnaires.

Although these studies used different measurement strategies (observation versus questionnaires versus interviews), each obtained some evidence that people use psychiatric symptoms strategically by emphasizing their problems when doing so has benefits for them but downplaying them when they will benefit from appearing less disturbed.

Summary

1. Researchers who use observational measures must decide whether the observation will occur in a natural or a contrived setting. Naturalistic observation involves the observation of behavior as it occurs naturally with no intrusion by the researcher. Contrived observation involves the observation of behavior in settings that the researcher has arranged specifically for observing and recording behavior.

2. Participant observation, in which the researcher engages in the same activities as the people he or she observes, is a special case of naturalistic observation.

3. When researchers are concerned that behaviors may be reactive, they sometimes use disguised observation, concealing from subjects the fact they are being observed. However, because this may raise ethical issues, researchers sometimes turn to undisguised observation or to partial concealment.

4. Behavioral recordings fall into four general categories: narrative records (relatively complete descriptions of a subject's behavior), checklists (tallies of whether or not certain behaviors were observed), temporal measures (including measures of latency and duration), and observational rating scales (on which researchers rate the intensity or quality of subjects' reactions).

5. Interrater reliability can be increased by developing precise operational definitions of the behaviors being observed and by giving observers the opportunity to practice using the observation coding system.

6. Subjects' self-reports can be obtained using either questionnaires or interviews, each of which has its advantages and disadvantages.

7. To design reliable and valid questionnaires and interviews, researchers must use precise terminology, write the questions as simply as possible, put conditional information before the key part of the question, avoid making unwarranted assumptions about the respondents, avoid doubled-barreled questions, and choose an appropriate response format.

8. Self-report measures may use one of three general response formats: free response, rating scale, and multiple choice.

9. When a diary methodology is used, respondents keep a daily record of certain target behaviors.

10. When interviewing, researchers must structure the interview setting in a way that enhances the comfort, honesty, and accuracy of the respondents.

11. Whenever self-report measures are used, researchers must guard against the social desirability response bias—the tendency for people to respond in ways that convey a socially desirable impression.

12. If spoken or written textual material is collected, it must undergo content analysis. The goal of content analysis is to classify units of text into meaningful categories for analysis.

Key Terms

observational method

naturalistic observation

participant observation

contrived observation

undisguised observation

reactive measure

disguised observation

narrative record

field notes

checklist

latency

reaction time

task completion time

interbehavior latency

duration

observational rating scale

interrater reliability

self-report measure

questionnaire

interview

response format

diary methodology

interview schedule

social desirability response bias

acquiescence

naysaying

halo effect

contrast error

content analysis

Review Questions

1. Discuss the pros and cons of using naturalistic versus contrived observation.

2. What special opportunities and problems does participant observation create for researchers?

3. What does it mean to say a behavior is reactive? How do researchers minimize the problem of reactivity?

4. Is it true that disguised observation always occurs in naturalistic settings, whereas undisguised observation always occurs in contrived settings? Explain.

5. What are the advantages and disadvantages of using narrative records in observational research?

6. Distinguish between a structured and an unstructured observation method.

7. What do measures of reaction time, task completion time, and interbehavior latency all have in common?

8. Give examples (other than those in the chapter) of three measures of duration.

9. When would you use an observational rating scale?

10. How could you increase the interrater reliability of an observational method?

11. Discuss the advantages and disadvantages of using questionnaires versus interviews to obtain self-report data.

12. What considerations must a researcher keep in mind when writing the questions to be used on a questionnaire or in an interview?

13. Describe the three types of response formats.

14. Tell what kind of response format would be most useful to obtain the following information:
    a. To ask whether the respondent's materal grandfather was still living
    b. To obtain subjects' impressions of another person with whom they had just interacted
    c. To find out whether the subject was single, married, divorced, or widowed
    d. To obtain a self-report measure of how anxious subjects felt

15. What are diary methodologies, and why are they used?

16. Discuss ways that interviewers can increase the reliability and validity of the information they obtain.

17. How can researchers minimize the effects of the social desirability response bias on subjects' self-reports?

18. When would you use content analysis?

Questions for Thought and Discussion

1. Design a questionnaire that assesses people's eating habits. Your questions could address topics such as what they eat, when they eat, how much they eat, who they eat with, where they eat, how health-conscious their eating habits are, and so on. In designing your questionnaire, be sure to consider the issues discussed throughout this chapter.

2. Pretest your questionnaire by giving it to three people. Ask for their reactions to each question, looking for potential problems in how the questions are worded and in the response formats.

3. Do you think that people's responses on your questionnaire might be affected by response biases? If so, what steps could you take to minimize them?

4. Obtain two textbooks—one in a social or behavioral science (such as psychology, sociology, communication, or anthropology) and the other in a natural science (such as biology, chemistry, or physics). Pick a page from each at random, but be sure to choose a page that is all text, with no figures or tables. Do a content analysis of the text on these pages that will address the question, "Are textbooks in behavioral and social science written in a more personal style than textbooks in natural science?" You will need to (1) decide what unit of text will be analyzed, (2) operationally define what it means for something to be written in a "personal style," (3) develop your coding system, (4) code the material on the two pages of text, and (5) describe the differences you discovered between the two texts. (Note: Because there will likely be a different number of units of text on the two pages, you will need to adjust the scores for the two pages by the number of units on that page.)

CHAPTER 5

Describing and Presenting Data

After a study is completed, one of the first tasks a researcher faces is to summarize the data that were collected. No matter the topic being investigated, the measures used, or the research strategy employed, researchers must find meaningful ways to summarize their data. Not only is summarizing the data essential for analyzing the results of a study, but researchers must describe and present the data so that they are easily comprehended by others.

In descriptive studies, the sole purpose of the research is to describe patterns of behavior. Survey research, for example, aims to describe the attitudes or behavior of a particular group of people. Similarly, studies of sexual response, such as those conducted by Masters and Johnson (1966), involved observing and describing the sexual response cycle in large numbers of people.

In correlational, experimental, and quasi-experimental studies, researchers are interested not in simply describing what their subjects do but rather in exploring variables that cause or are related to subjects' behavior. Even when description is not the primary goal, however, researchers must always find ways to summarize and describe their data in the most meaningful and useful fashion possible.

Criteria of a Good Description

To be useful, the description of data should meet three criteria: accuracy, conciseness, and understandability.

Accuracy

Obviously, data must be summarized and described accurately in order to be useful. Some ways of describing the findings of a study are more accurate than others. For example, as we'll see later, certain ways of graphing data may be misleading. Similarly, depending on the nature of the data (whether extreme scores exist, for example), certain descriptive statistics may summarize and describe the data more accurately than others. Researchers should always present their data in ways that represent the data most accurately.

Conciseness

Unfortunately, the most accurate descriptions of data are often the least useful because they overwhelm the reader with information. Strictly speaking, the most accurate description of a set of data would involve a table of the **raw data**—all subjects' scores on all measures. Only when dealing with raw data is there no possibility that the data will be distorted by condensing and summarizing. However, imagine trying to make sense out of a table that contained the raw data for a study that collected 20 measures on 160 subjects; the table would contain 3200 entries! To be interpretable, data must be summarized in a concise and meaningful form. At the same time, the summary should sacrifice as little information as possible.

Understandability

The description of one's data must be easily understood. Overly complicated tables, graphs, or statistics can obscure the findings of a study and lead to confusion. Researchers must be selective in the data they choose to present, offering only the data that most clearly describe the results. Having decided which aspects of the data best portray the findings of a study, researchers must then choose the clearest, most straightforward manner of describing the data.

The Raw Data

All descriptions of behavioral data begin with a **raw data matrix**. The raw data matrix is a table in which each subject is represented by a row and each variable is represented by a column. I recently asked 24 undergraduates to tell me at what age they thought they would die. Table 5.1 shows the raw data matrix for their answers.

This raw data matrix contains only one column of data (other than the subject numbers) because only one variable was measured. More commonly, a raw data matrix will have many columns, one for each variable.

Researchers often find it useful to construct a raw data matrix as they begin to analyze their data. In fact, when analyzing data on a computer, the data are usually entered into the computer in the form of a raw data matrix, with each row of data representing a single subject's data. However, because it is quite difficult to make much sense out of a raw data matrix (even a small one such as Table 5.1) by just eyeballing the data, the information in the raw data matrix must be summarized and presented in a more concise manner.

TABLE 5.1	

A Raw Data Matrix

Subject	Estimated age of death
1	70
2	75
3	82
4	72
5	72
6	81
7	78
8	75
9	87
10	72
11	70
12	68
13	75
14	75
15	85
16	72
17	80
18	74
19	75
20	88
21	82
22	78
23	76
24	80

Methods of summarizing and describing sets of numerical data can be classified as either **graphical methods** or **numerical methods**. Graphical methods involve the presentation of data in graphical or pictorial form such as graphs or pie charts; numerical methods summarize data in the form of numbers such as percentages or means. As we'll see, often such numbers are presented in a table.

Frequency Distributions

The basis of many data descriptions is the frequency distribution. A **frequency distribution** summarizes the information in a raw data matrix by showing the number of scores that fall within each of several categories.

Simple Frequency Distributions

One way to summarize a raw data matrix is to construct a **simple frequency distribution** of the data. A simple frequency distribution is a table that indicates the number of subjects who obtained each score. All possible scores are arranged from lowest to highest (or, less commonly, from highest to lowest). Then, in a second column, the number of scores, or **frequency** of each score, is shown. Table 5.2 shows the simple frequency distribution for the raw data matrix in Table 5.1.

Constructing a simple frequency distribution makes it easier to describe and comprehend the data. For example, in Table 5.2, it is easy to see the range of scores (88 − 68 = 20) and to see which scores occur most frequently (72 and 75).

Grouped Frequency Distributions

In many instances, a simple frequency distribution provides a meaningful, easily comprehended summary of the raw data; in other cases it is less useful. Imagine, for

TABLE 5.2

A Simple Frequency Distribution

Age	Frequency	Age	Frequency
68	1	79	0
69	0	80	2
70	2	81	1
71	0	82	2
72	4	83	0
73	0	84	0
74	1	85	1
75	5	86	0
76	1	87	1
77	0	88	1
78	2		

TABLE 5.3

A Grouped Frequency Distribution

Class interval	Frequency
68–70	3
71–73	4
74–76	7
77–79	2
80–82	5
83–85	1
86–88	2

example, that instead of having a range of 20 (as do the data in Table 5.2), the range of the data was much greater. If the scores in the table had been IQ scores rather than the ages at which subjects expected to die, for example, the range would be larger, perhaps spanning 100 points or more. If the range had been this large, our simple frequency distribution would contain 100 rows instead of 21. Such a table would be difficult both to summarize and to interpret.

In cases such as this, researchers use a **grouped frequency distribution**. Rather than presenting the frequency of each individual score, a grouped frequency distribution shows the frequency of *subsets of scores*. To make a grouped frequency distribution, you first break the range of scores into several subsets, or **class intervals**, of equal size. For example, for the data in Table 5.2, we could clump the scores together in class intervals of three scores. Subjects who indicated they would die at ages 68, 69, and 70 could be grouped together into a single class interval; those who expected to die at 71, 72, and 73 could be grouped together; and so on. We could then indicate the frequency of scores in each of the class intervals, as shown in Table 5.3.

If you compare the grouped frequency distribution (Table 5.3) to the simple frequency distribution (Table 5.2), you will see that the grouped frequency distribution provides a clearer picture of the data.

You should notice three things about the grouped frequency distribution. First, the class intervals are mutually exclusive; a person could not fall into more than one class interval. Second, the class intervals capture all possible responses; there are no data in the raw data matrix that cannot be included in one of the class intervals of the grouped frequency distribution. Third, all of the class intervals are the same size; in this example, each class interval spans three years. All grouped frequency distributions must have these three characteristics.

| TABLE 5.4 | | |

A Relative Frequency Distribution

Class interval	Frequency	Relative frequency
68–70	3	.13
71–73	4	.17
74–76	7	.29
77–79	2	.08
80–82	5	.21
83–85	1	.04
86–88	2	.08

Relative Frequency Distributions

In some instances, researchers include relative frequencies in their distribution tables. The **relative frequency** of each class is the *proportion* of the total number of scores that falls in each class interval. It is calculated by dividing the frequency for a class interval by the total number of scores. For example, the relative frequency for the class interval 68–70 in Table 5.3 is 3/24, or .13. A relative frequency distribution for our estimated-age-of-death data is shown in Table 5.4.

Frequency Histograms and Polygons

Simple and grouped frequency distributions provide useful summaries of data. In many cases, however, the information given in a frequency distribution is more easily grasped by others if it is presented graphically rather than in a table.

Frequency distributions are often portrayed graphically in the form of **histograms** and **bar graphs**. The horizontal x-axis of histograms and bar graphs presents the class intervals, and the vertical y-axis shows the number of scores in each class interval (the **frequency**). Bars are drawn to a height that indicates the frequency of cases in each response category. For example, if we graphed the data in Table 5.3, the histogram would look like the graph in Figure 5.1.

Although histograms and bar graphs look similar, they differ in an important way. A histogram is used when the variable on the x-axis is on an interval or ratio scale of measurement. When a variable is measured on an interval or ratio scale, the scores of the variable are continuous and equal differences in the scale values represent equal differences in the attribute being measured. As a result, the bars on a histogram touch one another (as in Figure 5.1). However, when the variable on

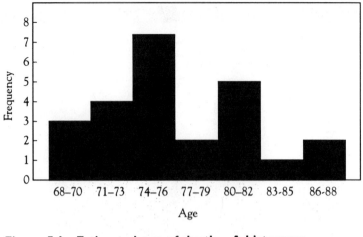

Figure 5.1   Estimated age of death—A histogram

the *x*-axis is on a nominal or ordinal scale (and, thus, equal differences in scale values do not reflect equal differences in the characteristic being measured), a bar graph is used in which the bars are separated to avoid any implication that the categories of the variable are on a continuous scale.

Researchers also present frequency data as a **frequency polygon**. The axes on the frequency polygon are labeled as they are for the histogram, but rather than using bars (as in the histogram), lines are drawn to connect the frequencies of the class intervals. Typically, this type of graph is used only for data that are on an

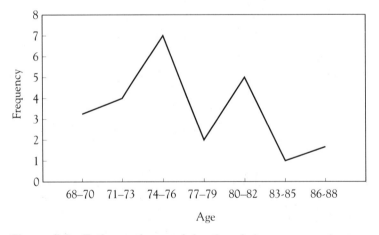

Figure 5.2   Estimated age of death—A frequency polygon

interval or ratio scale. The data from Table 5.3, which was shown in Figure 5.1 as a histogram, looks like Figure 5.2 when illustrated as a frequency polygon.

DEVELOPING YOUR RESEARCH SKILLS

HOW TO LIE WITH STATISTICS: PART I—BAR CHARTS AND LINE GRAPHS

In 1954, Darrell Huff published a humorous look at the misuse of statistics, entitled *How to Lie with Statistics*. Among the topics Huff discussed was what he called the "gee-whiz graph." A gee-whiz graph is a graph that, although technically accurate, is constructed in such a way as to give a misleading impression of the data—usually to catch the reader's attention or to make the data appear more striking than they really are.

Consider the graph in Figure 5.3, which shows the number of murders and other cases of nonnegligent manslaughter in the United States from 1985 to 1991. From just glancing at the graph, it is obvious that the murder rate has increased sharply over these years. Or has it?

Look at another graph of the same data. In the graph in Figure 5.4, we can see that the murder rate has indeed risen between 1985 and 1991. However, its rate of increase is nowhere as great as implied by the first graph.

If you'll look closely, you'll see that the two graphs present *exactly the same data*; technically speaking, they both portray the data accurately. The only difference in these graphs involves the units along the *y*-axis. The first graph used very small units

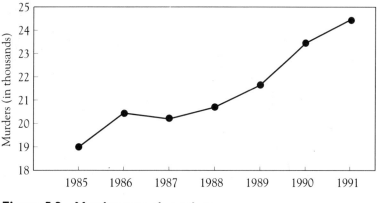

Figure 5.3   Murder rate skyrockets

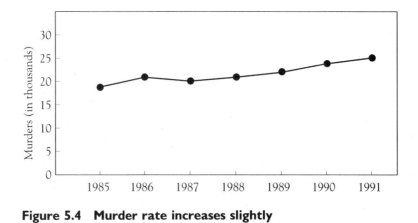

Figure 5.4   Murder rate increases slightly

and no zero point to give the impression of a large change in the murder rate. The second graph provided a more accurate perspective by using a zero point.

A similar tactic for misleading readers employs bar graphs. Again, the *y*-axis can be adjusted to give the impression of more or less difference between categories than actually exists. For example, the bar graph in Figure 5.5(a) shows the effects of two different antianxiety drugs on patients' ratings of anxiety. From this graph it appears that subjects who took drug B expressed much less anxiety than those who took drug A.

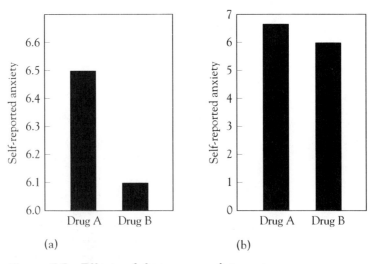

Figure 5.5   Effects of drugs on anxiety

Note, however, that the actual difference in anxiety ratings is quite small. This fact is seen more clearly in Figure 5.5(b), where the scale on the y-axis is extended.

Misleading readers with such graphs is common in advertising. However, the goal of research is to express the data as accurately and as honestly as possible. Rather than using gee-whiz graphs, researchers should present their data in ways that most clearly and accurately portray their findings.

Measures of Central Tendency

Frequency distributions, however they are portrayed, convey important information about subjects' responses. However, researchers typically are interested in summarizing the data for an entire group of subjects. To do this, they use descriptive statistics—numbers that summarize an entire distribution of data.

Much information can be obtained about a distribution of scores by knowing only the average or typical score in the distribution. For example, rather than presenting you with a detailed table showing the number of hospitalized mental patients per state last year, I might simply tell you that there were an average of 4282 patients per state. Or, rather than drawing a frequency polygon of the distribution of students' IQ scores in my city's school system, I might simply tell you that the average IQ is 104.6.

Measures of central tendency convey information about a distribution by describing the average, or most typical, score. In many instances, such descriptive statistics are all that are needed to describe the important characteristics of the data for a particular study.

Three measures of central tendency are most often used, each of which tells us something different about the data. These are the mean, the median, and the mode.

The Mean

By far the most commonly used measure of central tendency is the **mean**, or average. As we saw in Chapter 2, the mean is calculated by summing the scores for all cases, and then dividing by the number of cases. You may recall that the statistical formula for the mean is

$\Sigma y_i / n$

which tells us to add (Σ) the individual scores (y_i), and divide by the number of scores (n).

When researchers wish to present the means of several variables in an easily comprehended manner, they often do so using either tables or line graphs. For example, Orbach, Kedem, Gorchover, Apter, and Tyano (1993) examined how adolescents who had attempted suicide differed from adolescents who had not

TABLE 5.5

Means for the Five Fear-of-Death Measures

Measure	Suicidal group (n = 24)	Nonsuicidal group (n = 27)
Fear of loss of self-fulfillment (death will bring an end to my plans)	3.40	4.47
Fear of self-annihilation (I won't exist anymore)	3.10	3.13
Fear of loss of social identity (other people will forget me)	3.27	2.52
Fear of effects on my family (my family will experience pain if I die)	4.08	3.91
Fear of the unknown (not knowing what will happen to me)	3.56	4.53

attempted suicide in terms of their fears about death. Table 5.5 shows the mean ratings that the suicidal and nonsuicidal subjects gave to five common fears about death. (Scores could range from 1 to 5.)

This same set of means could also be presented in a **line graph**. A line graph is similar to a frequency polygon except that the data being graphed are means rather than frequencies. A line graph of the means in Table 5.5 is shown in Figure 5.6.

TABLE 5.6

Ages of Students in a Senior Seminar

21
20
21
22
54
21
20
24
25

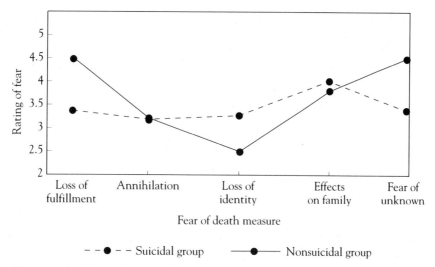

Figure 5.6   Mean fear of death ratings for suicidal and nonsuicidal adolescents

Explanation: This line graph presents the same means that were shown in Table 5.5. Each group's mean rating is plotted for each of the five measures. Then, the means for a particular group are joined by a line.

In general, the mean is the most common and useful measure of central tendency, but on occasion it can be misleading. Consider the raw data shown in Table 5.6.

The mean of the distribution of the data is 25.3. However, as you can see, the mean overshoots all of the ages except one (an older student who was returning to college later in life). In a case such as this, when the mean does not accurately represent the average or typical case, researchers also report the median and the mode of the distribution.

The Median

The **median** is the middle score of a distribution. If we rank-order the scores according to their magnitude, the median is the score that falls in the middle, or the score below which 50% of the measurements fall. For example, we can rank-order the nine ages of our students in Table 5.7.

The middle score, or median, of this distribution is 21, which more closely represents the typical score than the mean of 25.3 does. The advantage of the median over the mean is that it is less affected by extreme scores, or **outliers**. In the data involving students' ages, the 54-year-old student is an outlier.

TABLE 5.7

Rank-Ordered Ages

20

20

21

21

21 ← Median

22

24

25

54

The median is easy to identify when there is an odd number of scores because it is the middle score. When there are an even number of scores, however, there is no middle score. In this case, the median falls halfway between the two middle scores. For example, if the two middle scores in a distribution were 48 and 50, the median would be 49, even though no subject actually obtained that score.

The Mode

The **mode** is the most frequent score. The mode of the distribution of our students' ages is 21; more students were 21 years old than any other age. In this instance the mode is the same as the median, but this is not always the case. If all of the scores in the distribution are different, there is no mode. Occasionally, a distribution may have more than one mode. Such distributions are called bimodal (two modes) or trimodal (three modes).

DEVELOPING YOUR RESEARCH SKILLS

HOW TO LIE WITH STATISTICS: PART II—CENTRAL TENDENCY

In *How to Lie with Statistics*, Huff (1954) also discussed the misleading uses of measures of central tendency. He pointed out that, in everyday language, the word *average* has a loose meaning and can be used to indicate mean, median, or mode. If the reader does not know which use is meant, he or she may be misled.

Imagine that you own a business and that you have ten employees. Five of them earn $25,000 a year, four earn $35,000 a year, and one earns $50,000 a year. As owner, your salary is approximately $100,000. Your employees want to know the average salary in the company (*including yours*) for last year. What do you tell them?

On the one hand, you could report the *mean salary*, which would be $37,727.27. This might create some hostility among your employees, however, because all but one would perceive they are being paid less than average. Alternatively, you could report that the *modal salary* was $25,000. Although perfectly accurate, such a statement distorts the true distribution, ignoring the higher salaries. Finally, you could tell them that the *median salary* was $35,000. In this instance, the median seems to distort the true picture least. Even so, it hides the extreme range of salaries in the company.

Although behavioral researchers generally prefer the mean over the median and mode as a measure of central tendency, they are alert to instances in which the mean fails to describe the data accurately. In many cases, researchers report all three measures of central tendency to provide the fullest and clearest picture of their data.

Measures of Variability

In the preceding example, your employees would have learned more information about company salaries if given information about the *variability* in the salaries. In addition to knowing the average or typical score in a data distribution, it is helpful to know how much the scores in the distribution vary around the average score. As we saw in Chapter 2, because the entire research enterprise is oriented toward accounting for behavioral variability, researchers often use statistics that indicate the amount of variability in the data.

Among other things, knowing about the variability in a distribution tells us how typical the mean is of a set of scores. If the variability in a set of data is very small, the mean is highly representative of the scores as a whole and the mean tells us a great deal about the typical subject's score. In fact, if asked to guess what any particular subject's score was, we would not be too far off if we guessed the mean of a distribution that had very low variability. On the other hand, if the variability is large, the mean is not very representative of the scores as a set. Guessing the mean for a particular subject would probably miss his or her score by a wide margin if the scores show a great deal of variability.

Put another way, the variability tells us how homogeneous versus heterogeneous the subjects are on the attribute being measured. Large variability indicates that the subjects are heterogeneous, whereas low variability indicates that the subjects are more homogeneous. To examine the extent to which scores in a distribution vary from one another (and, thus, the degree to which the scores are homogeneous versus heterogeneous), researchers use **measures of variability**—

descriptive statistics that convey information about the spread or variability of a set of data.

We briefly mentioned two measures of variability (the range and the variance) in Chapter 2, but we will discuss them more fully here.

The Range

Earlier, we saw that the **range** was the difference between the largest and smallest scores in a distribution. The range is the least useful of the measures of variability because it is based entirely on the two extreme scores and does not take the variability of the remaining scores into account. Thus, although researchers often report the range of their data, they provide other measures of variability as well.

The Interquartile Range

Because the range is determined only in reference to the two extreme scores in a set of data, it tells us little about the overall variability in our data if the lowest and/or highest scores are extremely discrepant from most of the other scores (that is, if they are outliers). The interquartile range solves this problem by focusing on the variability of only the middle 50% of the scores and ignoring those at the extremes of the distribution.

To calculate the interquartile range, we first rank-order our data, then divide it into four parts of equal size. In Figure 5.7, we see a graph of a distribution of scores that has been divided into four parts, each of which contains one quarter of the subjects. The point at the upper limit of each quarter of the scores is called a **quartile**, shown in Figure 5.7 as Q1, Q2, and Q3; Q1 is the score below which 25% of the scores fall, Q2 is the score below which 50% of the scores fall, and Q3 is the score below which 75% of the scores fall. (What measure of central tendency is

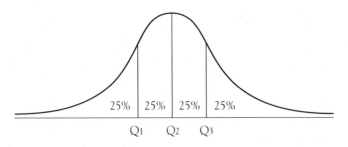

Figure 5.7   The interquartile range

Explanation: The interquartile range is expressed as the difference between the value of the third and first quartiles (that is, Q3 - Q1).

equivalent to the second quartile, Q2?) The **interquartile range** is the interval, or range, from the first to the third quartile, from Q1 to Q3. To calculate the interquartile range, simply subtract Q1 from Q3.

One way to think about the interquartile range is that it tells us the degree to which scores in a set of data vary around the median score, that is, around Q2. If the interquartile range is small, the middle 50% of the scores cluster tightly around the median, telling us that the variability in the data is low. On the other hand, if the interquartile range is large, we know that the middle 50% of the scores are widely dispersed around Q2 and that the variability of the data is large.

Variance

Although the range and the interquartile range provide useful information, re-searchers more typically use the **variance** and its square root (the *standard deviation*) when they describe and analyze the variability in their data. The advantage of the variance is that, unlike the range and interquartile range, the variance takes into account *all* the scores when calculating the variability in a set of data.

In Chapter 2, we learned that the variance is based on the sum of the squared differences between each score and the mean. You may recall that we can calculate the variance by subtracting the mean of our data from each subject's score, squaring these differences (or deviation scores), summing the squared deviation scores, and dividing by the number of scores minus 1. The variance is an index of the average amount of variability in a set of data—the average amount that each subject's score differs from the mean of the data—expressed in squared units.

Standard Deviation

Variance is the most commonly used measure of variability for purposes of statisti-cal analysis. However, when researchers simply want to *describe* how much variabil-ity exists in their data, variance has a shortcoming. As you'll recall, we squared the deviation scores as we calculated s^2. As a result, the variance is expressed in terms of squared units and thus is difficult to interpret conceptually. For example, if we are measuring systolic blood pressure in a study of stress, the variance is expressed not in terms of the original blood pressure readings but in terms of *blood pressure squared*! When researchers want to express behavioral variability in the original units of their data, they use the standard deviation. The **standard deviation** (for which we'll use the symbol s) is the square root of the variance.

The standard deviation is very useful for describing how much the scores in a set of data vary. As we'll see in a moment, a great deal can be learned from knowing only the mean and standard deviation of the data—much more than is apparent at first glance. For this reason, researchers often report the mean and standard devia-tion of their data as a matter of course.

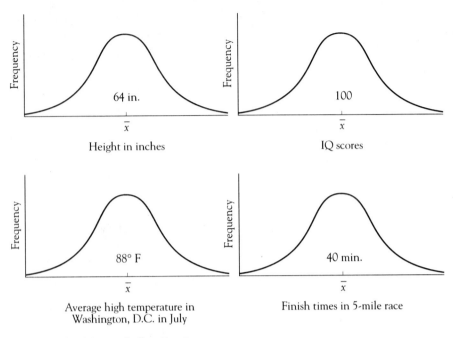

Figure 5.8   Normal distributions

Explanation: Figure 5.8 shows four idealized normal distributions. In normal distributions such as these, most scores fall toward the middle of the range, with the greatest number of scores falling at the mean of the distribution. As we move in both directions away from the mean, the number of scores tapers off symmetrically, indicating an equal number of low and high scores.

Standard Deviation and the Normal Curve

In the 19th century, the Belgian statistician and astronomer Quetelet demonstrated that many bodily measurements, such as height and chest circumference, showed identical distributions when plotted on a graph. When plotted, such data form a curve, with most of the points on the graph falling near the center, and fewer and fewer points lying toward the extremes. Four such curves are shown in Figure 5.8.

Sir Francis Galton, an eminent British scientist and statistician, extended Quetelet's discovery to the study of psychological characteristics. He found that no matter what attribute he measured, graphs of the data nearly always followed the same bell-shaped distribution. For example, Galton showed that scores on university examinations fell into this pattern.

In fact, many, if not most, of the variables studied by behavioral scientists fall at least roughly into a **normal distribution**. A normal distribution rises to a rounded peak at its center and then tapers off at both tails, indicating that most of the scores

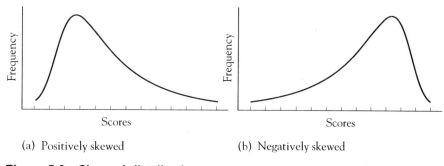

Figure 5.9 Skewed distributions

Explanation: In skewed distributions, most scores fall toward one end of the range. In a positively skewed distribution (a), there are more low scores than high scores. In a negatively skewed distribution (b), there are more high scores than low scores.

fall toward the middle of the range of scores (that is, around the mean), with fewer scores toward the extremes. That many data distributions, regardless of what attribute is being measured, approximate a normal curve is really not surprising, because most people are about average and extreme scores are relatively few.

Occasionally, however, our data distributions are skewed. In a **positively skewed distribution**, such as Figure 5.9(a), there are more low scores than high scores in the set of data; if data are positively skewed, one observes a clustering of scores toward the lower, left-hand end of the scale, with the tail of the distribution extending to the right. In a **negatively skewed distribution**, such as Figure 5.9(b), there are more high scores than low scores; the hump is to the right of the graph, and the tail of the distribution extends to the left.

Assuming we have a roughly normal distribution, we can estimate the percentage of subjects who obtained certain scores just by knowing the mean and standard deviation of the data. For example, in any normally distributed set of data, approximately 68% of the scores (68.26%, to be exact) will fall in the range defined by ± 1 standard deviation from the mean. In other words, roughly 68% of the subjects will have scores that fall between 1 standard deviation below the mean and 1 standard deviation above the mean.

Let's consider IQ scores, for example. One commonly used IQ test has a mean of 100 and a standard deviation of 15. The score falling one standard deviation below the mean is 85 (that is $100 - 15$), and the score falling 1 standard deviation above the mean is 115 (that is, $100 + 15$). Thus, approximately 68% of all people have IQ scores between 85 and 115.

Figure 5.10 shows this principle graphically. As you can see, 68.26% of the scores fall within 1 standard deviation ($\pm 1\ s$) from the mean. Approximately 95% of the scores in a normal distribution fall ± 2 standard deviations from the mean.

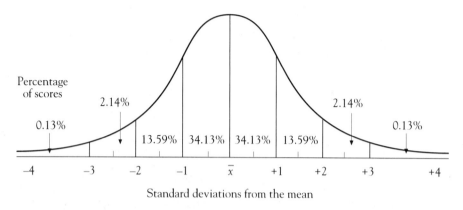

Standard deviations from the mean

Figure 5.10   Percentage of scores under ranges of the normal distribution

Explanation: This figure shows the percentage of subjects who fall in various portions of the normal distribution. For example, 34.13% of the scores in a normal distribution will fall between the mean and 1 standard deviation above the mean. Similarly, 13.59% of subjects's scores will fall between −1 and −2 standard deviations below the mean.

On an IQ test with a mean of 100 and standard deviation of 15, 95% of people score between 70 and 130. Less than 1% of the scores fall further than 3 standard deviations below or above the mean. If you have an IQ score below 55 or above 145, you are quite unusual in that regard.

It is easy to see why the standard deviation is so useful. By knowing the mean and standard deviation of a set of data, we can tell not only how much the data vary, but how they are distributed across various ranges of scores. With real data, which are seldom perfectly normally distributed, these ranges are only approximate. Even so, researchers find the standard deviation very useful when trying to describe and understand the data they collect.

DEVELOPING YOUR RESEARCH SKILLS

CALCULATING THE VARIANCE AND STANDARD DEVIATION

In Chapter 2, we introduced the following formula for the variance:

$$\Sigma \, (y_i - \bar{y})^2 / n - 1$$

Although this formula shows clearly what the variance is (the sum of the squared deviations of each score from the mean, divided by $n - 1$), it is rarely used to actually calculate the variance. Not only is this particular formula time-consuming with large samples, but rounding errors accumulate as we add all of the deviation scores. As a result, researchers use the following formula when they actually calculate the variance:

$$s^2 = \frac{\Sigma y_i^2 - [(\Sigma y_i)^2/n]}{n - 1}$$

Remember that Σ is summation, y_i refers to each subject's score, and n reflects the number of subjects. Although it may look different, this computational formula is mathematically equivalent to the demonstrational formula you learned in Chapter 2.

To use this formula, first square each score (y_i^2) and add these squared scores together (Σy_i^2). Then, add up all of the orginal scores (Σy_i) and square the sum $[(\Sigma y_i)^2]$. Finally, plug these numbers into the formula, along with the sample size (n), to get the variance.

We can simplify the calculations by setting up a table with two columns—one for the raw scores and one for the square of the raw scores. Here is the calculation for the data we analyzed in Chapter 2 dealing with attitudes about capital punishment.

Subject	y_i	y_i^2
1	4	16
2	1	1
3	2	4
4	2	4
5	4	16
6	3	9

$$\Sigma y_i = 16 \qquad \Sigma y_i^2 = 50$$
$$(\Sigma y_i)^2 = 256$$

Then,

$$s^2 = \frac{50 - 256/6}{6 - 1} = \frac{50 - 42.67}{5} = 1.47$$

Thus, the variance (s^2) of these data is 1.47. To obtain the standard deviation (s), we simply take the square root of the variance. The standard deviation of these data is the square root of 1.47, or 1.21.

The z-Score

Sometimes researchers need to describe where a particular subject falls in the data distribution. Just knowing that a certain subject's score was 47 does not tell us very much. Knowing the mean of the data tells us whether the subject's score was above or below average, but without knowing something about the variability of the data, we still cannot tell how far above or below the mean the subject's score is, relative to other subjects.

The **z-score**, or *standard score*, is used to describe a particular subject's score relative to the rest of the data. A subject's z-score indicates how far the subject's score varies from the mean in terms of standard deviations. Positive z-scores indicate scores above the mean, whereas negative z-scores indicate scores below the mean.

For example, if we find that a subject has a z-score of -1.00, we know that his or her score is 1 standard deviation below the mean. Referring to Figure 5.10, we can see that only about 16% of the other subjects scored lower than our subject. Similarly, a z-score of $+2.9$ indicates a score nearly 3 standard deviations above the mean—in the uppermost ranges of the distribution.

If we know the mean and standard deviation of a sample, a subject's z-score is easy to calculate:

$$z = (y_i - \bar{y})/s$$

where y_i is the subject's score, $\bar{y}$ is the mean of the sample, and s is the standard deviation of the sample.

Sometimes researchers standardize an entire set of data by converting all the subjects' raw scores to z-scores. This is a useful way to identify extreme scores or outliers. An outlier can be identified by a very low or very high z-score—one that falls below -3.00 or above $+3.00$, for example. Also, certain statistical analyses require standardization prior to the analysis. When a set of scores is standardized, the new set of z-scores always has a mean equal to 0 and a standard deviation equal to 1, regardless of the mean and standard deviation of the original data.

DEVELOPING YOUR RESEARCH SKILLS

CALCULATING Z-SCORES

In the previous box, "Calculating the Variance and Standard Deviation," we found that the standard deviation of the data was 1.21. Using the formula for z,

$$z = (y_i - \bar{y})/s$$

calculate the z-scores for Subject 1 (who had a score of 4) and Subject 2 (who had a score of 1).

First, you'll need to calculate the mean of the six scores (4, 1, 2, 2, 4, 3). Then, subtract the mean from Subject 1's score. Finally, divide this difference by the standard deviation to get z. Do the same for Subject 2. What do each of these z-scores tell you?

Summary

1. Researchers attempt to describe their data in ways that are accurate, concise, and easily understood.

2. Some methods of describing data are graphical, such as histograms and line graphs, whereas other methods, such as the mean and variance, are numerical.

3. A simple frequency distribution is a table that indicates the number (frequency) of subjects who obtained each score.

4. A grouped frequency distribution indicates the frequency of scores that fall in each of several mutually exclusive class intervals. Often, the proportion of scores falling in each class interval is also presented—a relative frequency distribution.

5. Histograms, bar graphs, and frequency polygons (line graphs) are common graphical methods of describing data.

6. A full statistical description of a set of data usually involves both measures of central tendency (mean, median, mode) as well as measures of variability (range, interquartile range, variance, standard deviation).

7. The mean is the numerical average of a set of scores, the median is the middle score when a set of scores is rank ordered, and the mode is the most common score. The mean is the most commonly used measure of central tendency, but it can be misleading if the data are very skewed.

8. The range is the difference between the largest and smallest scores. The interquartile range is the range between the first and third quartiles. The variance and its square root (the standard deviation) indicate the total variability in a set of data. Among other things, the variability in a set of data indicates how representative the mean is of the scores as a whole.

9. In a normally distributed set of data, approximately 68% of the scores fall between + and − 1 standard deviation from the mean. Approximately 95% of the scores·fall ±2 s, and 99% fall in the range bounded by −3 and +3 s.

10. A z-score expresses a particular subject's score in terms of its distance from the mean in standard deviations.

Key Terms

raw data	frequency distribution
raw data matrix	simple frequency distribution
graphical method	frequency
numerical method	grouped frequency distribution

class interval

relative frequency

histogram

bar graph

frequency polygon

measures of central tendency

mean

line graph

median

outlier

mode

measures of variability

range

quartile

interquartile range

variance

standard deviation

normal distribution

positively skewed distribution

negatively skewed distribution

z-score

standard score

Review Questions

1. What three criteria characterize good descriptions of data?

2. Why might it be said that the raw data matrix is the most accurate, but least useful, way of describing data?

3. Distinguish between graphical and numerical methods of describing data.

4. Under what conditions is a grouped frequency distribution more useful as a means of describing a set of scores than a simple frequency distribution? Why do researchers often add relative frequencies to their tables?

5. What three rules govern the construction of a grouped frequency distribution?

6. What are the most commonly used measures of central tendency? What are the most commonly used measures of variability?

7. Discuss the conditions under which the median is a more meaningful measure of central tendency than the mean.

8. Why do researchers prefer the standard deviation over the range as a measure of variability?

9. In a normal distribution, what percentage of scores fall above one standard deviation below the mean? above one standard deviation above the mean? between two standard deviations below and two standard deviations above the mean?

10. What does it indicate if a subject's z-score is .00?

Exercises

Table of Scores

110	124	100	125	104	119
98	130	76	95	143	90
132	102	125	96	99	78
100	80	112	112	103	88
94	108	88	132	87	119
109	104	104	100	119	99
135	128	92	110	90	92
120	95	110	78		

1. Construct a simple frequency distribution of the scores given above.

2. Construct a grouped frequency distribution of these scores that includes both frequencies and relative frequencies.

3. Construct a frequency polygon, using the grouped frequency data.

4. Find the mean, median, and mode of the data. Does one of these measures of central tendency represent the data better than the others?

CHAPTER 6

Sampling in Behavioral Research

In 1936, *Literary Digest* magazine polled a sample of more than two million voters regarding their preference for Alfred Landon versus Franklin Roosevelt in the upcoming presidential election. Based on the responses they received, the *Digest* predicted that Landon would defeat Roosevelt by approximately 15 percentage points. When the election was held, however, not only was Roosevelt elected president, but the margin of victory was overwhelming. Roosevelt received 62% of the popular vote, compared to 38% for Landon. What happened?

The problem in the *Literary Digest* poll was purely one of sampling. The names of the respondents contacted for the poll were taken from telephone directories and automobile registration lists. This sampling procedure had yielded accurate predictions in the presidential elections of 1920, 1924, 1928, and 1932. However, unlike those previously polled, the people who had telephones and automobiles in 1936 were not representative of voters in the country at large. In the aftermath of the Great Depression, many voters had neither cars nor phones, and those voters overwhelmingly supported Roosevelt. Because the sample was not representative, the results of the survey were biased.

Among the decisions behavioral scientists face when they design research is how to select subjects to participate in the study. Researchers rarely can examine every individual in the population that is relevant to their interests—all newborns, all paranoid schizophrenics, all color-blind adults, all registered voters in California, all female porpoises, or whatever.

Fortunately there is absolutely no need to study *every* individual in the population of interest. Instead, researchers collect data from a subset, or **sample**, of subjects in the population. Researchers do this under the assumption that what they learn from studying the sample more or less generalizes to other individuals in the population at large. (As we'll see, this assumption may or may not be warranted depending on how the sample was selected.) Just as a physician can learn certain things about a patient from analyzing a small sample of the patient's blood (and need not drain every drop of blood for analysis), researchers can learn about a population from analyzing a relatively small sample.

Sampling is the process by which a researcher selects a sample of subjects for a study from the population of interest. Researchers must consider the manner in which they select their samples because the sampling procedure they use has implications for the external validity of a study's findings. **External validity** refers to the degree to which the findings of a particular study can be generalized, such as to other research settings, procedures, and samples, and of greatest relevance to this chapter, to the population from which the sample was drawn.

In some (but not all) research contexts, researchers wish to use the findings they obtained from a particular sample to draw conclusions about a larger population; that is, they want to *generalize* the findings from the sample to the population. When this is the case, external validity is of paramount importance. As we will see, the external validity of a study depends, in part, on how the subjects were selected.

Probability Samples

The purpose of some research is to describe accurately the thoughts, feelings, or behavior of a large population on the basis of data collected from a smaller sample. In survey research, for example, the goal is to estimate the attitudes or behavior of a large group from the answers of a small number of respondents. When accurate description is the goal, researchers *must* ensure that the sample they select is representative of the population at large. A **representative sample** is one from which we can draw accurate, unbiased estimates of the characteristics of the larger population. Only if we have a representative sample can we draw accurate inferences about the population from data obtained on the sample.

The Error of Estimation

Unfortunately, samples rarely mirror their parent populations in every respect. The characteristics of the individuals selected for the sample almost always differ somewhat from the characteristics of the general population. This difference, called **sampling error**, causes results obtained from the sample to differ from what would have been obtained had the entire population been studied. As a result of sampling error, the data collected from a sample rarely perfectly reflects the population. If you calculate the average grade point average of a representative sample of 200 students at your college or university, the mean for this sample will not perfectly match the mean you would obtain based on *all* students in your school. If the sample is truly representative however, the value obtained on the sample should be close to what would be obtained from the entire population.

Fortunately, when certain sampling procedures known as probability sampling techniques are used, researchers can estimate how much sampling error is in their sample data. The **error of estimation** (also called the **margin of error**) specifies the degree to which the data obtained from the sample would be expected to differ from the population as a whole. For example, you may have heard television newscasters report the results of a political opinion poll and then add that the results "are accurate within 3 percentage points." What this means is that if 45% of the respondents in the sample endorsed Smith for president, we know that there is a very high probability (usually over 95%) that the true percentage of people in the population who support Smith is between 42% and 48% (that is, 45% ±3%). By allowing researchers to estimate the sampling error in their data, probability samples permit them to specify how confident they are that the sample results accurately reflect the behavior of the population. Their confidence is expressed in terms of the error of estimation.

The smaller the error of estimation, the more closely the results from the sample estimate the behavior of the larger population. For example, if the limits on the error of estimation are only ±1%, the sample data are a better indicator of the population than if the limits on the error of estimation are ±10%. Obviously, researchers prefer the error of estimation to be as small as possible. The error of estimation is a function of three things: the sample size, population size, and variance of the data.

Most important is the size of the sample. The larger a probability sample, the more similar to the population the sample tends to be (that is, the smaller the sampling error) and the more accurately the sample data estimate the population. In light of this, you might expect that researchers always obtain as large a sample as possible. This is not the case, however. Rather, researchers opt for an **economic sample**—one that provides a reasonably accurate estimate of the population (within a few percentage points, for example) at reasonable effort and cost. After a sample of a certain size is obtained, collecting additional data does little to add to the accuracy of the results. (Formulas have been developed for determining the most economical sample size.)

For example, if we are trying to estimate the percentage of voters in a population of 10,000 who will vote for a particular candidate in a very close election, interviewing a sample of 500 will allow us to estimate the percentage of voters in the population who will support each candidate within 9 percentage points. Increasing the sample size to 1000 (an increase of 500 respondents) lowers the error of estimation to only 3%. However, adding an additional 500 subjects to the sample beyond that helps relatively little; with 1500 respondents in the sample, the error of estimation drops only to 2.3%. From a practical standpoint, it may make little sense to increase the sample size beyond 1000 in this instance.

The error of estimation also is affected by the size of the population from which the sample was drawn. Imagine we have two samples of 200 respondents. The first was drawn from a population of 400, the second from a population of 10 million. In which sample would we expect the results to mirror more closely the behavior of the population? I think you can guess that the error of estimation will be lower when the population contains 400 cases than when it contains 10 million cases.

The third factor that affects the error of estimation is the variance of the data. The greater the variability in the data, the more difficult it is to estimate the population accurately. We saw in earlier chapters that the larger the variance, the less representative the mean is of the scores as a whole. As a result, the larger the variance in the data, the larger the sample must be to draw accurate inferences about the population.

Researchers can calculate the error of estimation only if they know the probability that a particular individual in the population was included in the sample. Probability samples are used for this purpose. When a **probability sample** is used, the researcher can specify the probability that any individual in the population will be included in the sample. Typically, for example, researchers use an **epsem design**, which specifies that all cases in the population have an equal probability of being chosen for the sample (Schuman & Kalton, 1985). (Epsem stands for *equal probability selection method*.) Knowing the probability that a particular case will be included tells the researcher how representative the sample is of the population and allows him or her to estimate the sampling error.

Probability samples may be obtained in several ways, but the three basic methods involve simple random sampling, stratified random sampling, and cluster sampling.

Simple Random Sampling

When a sample is chosen in such a way that every possible sample of the desired size has the same chance of being selected from the population, the sample is a **simple random sample**. For example, suppose we want to select a sample of 200 subjects from a school district that has 5000 students. If we wanted a simple random sample, we select our sample in such a way that every possible combination of 200 students has an equal probability of being chosen. To obtain a simple random sample, the researcher must have a **sampling frame**—a listing of the population from which the sample will be drawn. Then subjects are chosen randomly from this list.

You might think that you could simply take every 25th name from the list to get your sample of 200. Although this procedure, called **systematic sampling**, is sometimes used, it is not a truly random procedure; after all, the names may be listed in some particular order. If the names were in alphabetical order, for example, most children from the same family (that is, those with the same last name) would be listed together. Taking every 25th name would preclude the possibility of obtaining any siblings in the sample, thereby introducing a systematic bias into the sample. In a truly random sample, it would be possible to obtain a sample that included siblings.

Generally, researchers who need a representative sample prefer to use a truly random procedure. If the population is small, one approach is to write the name of each case in the population on a slip of paper, shuffle the slips of paper, then pull slips out until a sample of the desired size is obtained. For example, we could type each of the 5000 students' names on cards, shuffle the cards, then randomly pick 200. However, with larger populations, pulling names "out of a hat" becomes unwieldy. One common procedure is to use a **table of random numbers**. A portion of such a table is shown below, along with an explanation of how to use it.

DEVELOPING YOUR RESEARCH SKILLS

USING A TABLE OF RANDOM NUMBERS

When researchers want to obtain a random sample from a larger population, they often use a table of random numbers. The numbers on such a table are generated randomly, usually by a computer, such that there is absolutely no order to the sequence of numbers in the table. A small portion of a table of random numbers is shown below for demonstration. A complete table of random numbers appears in Appendix A-1.

Random Numbers

54 83 80 53 90 50 90 46 47 12 62 68 30 91 21 01 37 36 20
36 85 49 83 47 89 46 28 54 02 87 98 10 47 22 67 27 33 13
60 98 76 53 02 01 82 77 45 12 68 13 09 20 73 07 92 53 45
62 79 39 83 88 02 60 92 82 00 76 30 77 98 45 00 97 78 16
31 21 10 50 42 16 85 20 74 29 64 72 59 58 09 30 73 43 32

You will note that the table consists of two-digit numbers (54, 83, 80 . . .). These are arranged in columns to make them easier to read and use. In practice, you should disregard the two-digit numbers and columns and think of the table as a very long list of single-digit numbers (5, 4, 8, 3, 8, 0, 5, 3, 9, 0 . . .).

To use the table to select a random sample, first number the cases in your population. For example, if the school system from which you are sampling has 5000 students, number the students from 0001 to 5000. Then, beginning anywhere in the table, take 200 sets of four-digit numbers. For example, let's say you randomly entered the table at the fifth digit in the second row:

36 85 **4**9 83 47 89 46 28 54 02 87 98 10 47 22 67 27 33 13

    ↑
Imagine you selected this
digit as your starting
point.

Starting with this number, take the next four digits, which are 4983. Thus, the first subject you select for your sample is the student who was number 4983 in your original list of 5000. The next four digits are 4789, so take student number 4789 for your sample; the third subject is number 4628.

The next four digits are 5402. However, there were only 5000 students in the population, so 5402 and the next number 8798, are out of the range of your population size. Ignore numbers on the table that exceed the size of the population, such as 5402 and 8798. However, the next four digits, do represent a student in the population—number 1047—so this student would be included in the sample.

Continue this process until you reach your desired sample size. In our example, in which we wanted a sample of 200, we would continue until we obtained 200 four-digit random numbers between 0001 and 5000, inclusive. (Obviously, to draw a sample of 200, you would need to use the full table in Appendix A-1 rather than the small portion of the table shown here.) The cases in the population that correspond to these numbers would then be used in the sample.

Tables of random numbers are used for purposes other than selecting a sample. For example, when using an experimental design, researchers must assign subjects to the various experimental conditions in a random fashion. A random numbers table can be used to ensure that the manner in which subjects are assigned to conditions is truly random. We'll return to this use of random numbers in a later chapter.

Stratified Random Sampling

Stratified random sampling is a variation of simple random sampling. Rather than selecting cases directly from the population, we first divide the population into two or more strata. A **stratum** is a subset of the population that shares a particular characteristic. For example, we might divide the population into men and women, or into six age ranges (20–29, 30–39, 40–49, 50–59, 60–69, over 69). Then, cases are randomly sampled from each of the strata.

By first dividing the population into strata, we sometimes increase the probability that the subjects we select will be representative of those in the population. In addition, stratification ensures that the researcher has an adequate number of subjects from each strata, so he or she can analyze differences in responses among the various strata. For example, the researcher might want to compare younger respondents (20–29 years old) with older respondents (60–69 years old). By first stratifying the sample, the researcher ensures that there will be an ample number of both young and old respondents in the sample.

Cluster Sampling

Although they provide us with the most accurate pictures of the population, simple and stratified random sampling have a major drawback. To use random sampling, we must have a sampling frame of all of the cases in the population; only then can we specify the probability that any particular case will be included in the sample and be assured that our sample was selected truly at random. Obtaining the listing for small, easily identified populations is no problem. You would find it relatively easy to obtain a list of all students in your college or all members of the American Psychological Society, for example.

Unfortunately, not all populations are easily identified. Could we, for example, obtain a list of every person in the United States or, for that matter, in New York City? Could we get a sampling frame of all Hispanic 3-year-olds, all retired persons in California, all deaf people who know sign language, or all single-parent families in Canada headed by the father? In cases such as these, random sampling is not possible, because without a listing we cannot locate potential subjects or specify the probability that a particular case will be included in the sample.

In such instances, **cluster sampling** is typically used. To obtain a cluster sample, the researcher first samples not subjects but groupings or **clusters** of subjects. These clusters are often based on naturally occurring groupings, such as geographical areas or particular institutions. For example, if we wanted a sample of elementary school children in West Virginia, we might first randomly sample from the 55 county school systems in West Virginia. Perhaps we would pick 15 counties at random. Then, after selecting this small random sample of counties, we could get lists of students for those counties and obtain random samples of students from the selected counties.

Often, cluster sampling involves a **multistage sampling** process in which we begin by sampling large clusters, then we sample smaller clusters from within the large clusters, then we sample even smaller clusters, and finally we obtain our sample of subjects. For example, we could randomly pick counties, then randomly choose several particular schools from the selected counties. We could then randomly select particular classrooms from the schools we selected, and finally randomly sample students from each classroom.

Cluster sampling has two distinct advantages. First, a sampling frame of the population is not needed to begin, only a listing of the clusters. In this example, all we would need to start is a list of counties in West Virginia, which is far easier to obtain than a census of all children enrolled in West Virginia schools. Then, after sampling the clusters, we could get lists of students within each cluster (that is, county) that was selected, which is much easier than getting a census for the entire population of students in West Virginia.

The second advantage is that, if each cluster represents a grouping of subjects that are close together geographically (such as students in a certain county or school), less time and effort are required to contact the subjects. Focusing on only 15 West Virginia counties would require considerably less time, effort, and expense than sampling students from all 55 counties in that state.

DEVELOPING YOUR RESEARCH SKILLS

CALCULATING THE ERROR OF ESTIMATION

As we've seen, probability samples permit us to calculate the error of estimation. Formulas have been developed for calculating the error of estimation for various kinds of probability samples. The details of these formulas go beyond the scope of this book, but one example will show how they work.

For our example, let's return to data we discussed in Chapter 2. As you may recall, we had data from six respondents regarding their attitudes toward capital punishment. Responses were measured on a 5-point scale, where 1 indicated opposition and 5 indicated support for capital punishment. The scores for the six respondents are 4, 1, 2, 2, 4, and 3; the mean of the responses for the sample is 2.67.

Let's assume that the six respondents are a random sample chosen from a class of 40 students, and that we want to estimate the average attitude toward capital punishment in the class (the population) from the responses of the sample. To calculate the error of estimation in this case, we use the following formula:

$$\text{Error of estimation } (E) = 2\sqrt{\left(\frac{s^2}{n}\right)\left(\frac{N-n}{N}\right)}$$

where s^2 is the variance of the data (1.47), n is the sample size (6), and N is the size of the population (40).

Entering the appropriate numbers in our formula, we get

$$
\begin{aligned}
E &= 2\sqrt{\left(\frac{1.47}{6}\right)\left(\frac{40-6}{40}\right)} \\
&= 2\sqrt{(.025)(.085)} \\
&= 2\sqrt{(.021)} \\
&= 2(.046) \\
&= 0.92
\end{aligned}
$$

The error of estimation is 0.92. This means that there is a 95% probability that the true average attitude toward capital punishment in the population is 2.67 (the mean) ± 0.92, or between 1.75 and 3.59.

The Problem of Nonresponse

Strictly speaking, researchers are rarely able to obtain perfectly representative samples, even in those situations in which representativeness is essential for their research purposes. Imagine, for example, that we wish to obtain a representative sample of family physicians for a study of professional burnout. We design a questionnaire to assess burnout and mail this questionnaire to a random sample of family physicians in our state (using a professional directory to obtain the names).

To obtain a truly representative sample, *every* physician we choose must complete and return the questionnaire. If our return rate is less than 100%, the data we obtain may be biased in ways that are impossible to determine. For example, physicians who are exceptionally busy (and, thus, particularly likely to be "burned out") may be unlikely to take the time to complete and return our questionnaire. On the other hand, those who do return it may be highly conscientious or have especially positive attitudes toward behavioral research. In any case, the representativeness of our sample is compromised.

A similar problem arises when telephone surveys are used. Aside from the fact that a telephone sample is not representative of the country at large (only 90% of American households have telephones; Schuman & Kalton, 1985), the nonresponse rate for telephone research is often high. We will find it difficult, if not impossible, to contact some of the people who were randomly selected for our sample. People who travel frequently, work at odd hours, live somewhere other than where their phone is, or screen their calls on answering machines may be inaccessible. Furthermore, we are likely to encounter many people who are simply unwilling to answer our questions. Given these limitations, the final set of respondents we contact may not be representative of the population.

Researchers can do at least two things to tackle the nonresponse problem. First, they can take extra steps to increase the response rate. When mail surveys are used, researchers often follow the initial mailing of the questionnaire with telephone calls or postcards to urge the respondents to complete and return them. Although we rarely get 100% of the sample to respond, we can be much more confident of our findings if we get at least an 80% response rate.

Second, to the extent possible, researchers try to determine whether respondents and nonrespondents differ in any systematic ways. Based on what they know about the sample they selected, researchers can see whether those who did and did not respond differed. For example, the professional directory we used to obtain a sample of physicians may provide their birthdates, the year they obtained their medical degree, their workplace (hospital versus private practice), specialty area, and other information. Using this information, we may be able to show that those who returned the survey did not differ from those who did not. (Of course, they may differ on dimensions about which we have no information.)

BEHAVIORAL RESEARCH CASE STUDY

SAMPLING AND SEX SURVEYS

People are understandably interested in how they compare with others. One dimension that people are often interested in is sexual behavior. Am I more or less sexually active than other people my age? How do my sexual attitudes and experiences compare to most other people's?

The first major surveys of sexual behavior were published by Kinsey, Pomeroy, and Martin in 1948 (*Sexual Behavior in the Human Male*) and by Kinsey, Pomeroy, Martin, and Gebhard in 1953 (*Sexual Behavior in the Human Female*). Kinsey's researchers interviewed over 10,000 American men and women, asking about their sexual histories and current sexual practices. You might think that with such a large sample, Kinsey would have obtained valid data regarding sexual behavior in the United States. Unfortunately, although Kinsey's data are often cited as if they reflect the typical sexual experiences of Americans, his sampling techniques do not permit us to draw confident conclusions about sexual behavior in this country.

Rather than using a probability sample that would have allowed him to calculate the error of estimation in his data, Kinsey relied upon what he called "100 percent sampling." His researchers would contact a particular group, such as a professional organization or sorority, and then obtain responses from 100% of its members. Although 100% samples were obtained, the groups were *not* selected at random. As a result, there were a disproportionate number of respondents from Indiana in the sample, as well as an overabundance of college students, Protestants, and well-educated people (Kirby, 1977). In an analysis of Kinsey's sampling technique, Cochran, Mosteller, and Tukey (1953) concluded that, because he had not used a probability sample, Kinsey's results "must be regarded as subject to systematic errors of unknown magnitude due to selective sampling" (p. 711).

Other surveys of sexual behavior have encountered similar difficulties. In the Hunt (1974) survey, names were chosen at random from the phone books of 24 selected American cities. This technique produced three sampling biases. First, the cities were not selected randomly. Second, by selecting names from the phone book, the survey overlooked people without phones and those with unlisted numbers (approximately one-fourth of the population). Third, only 20% of the people who were contacted agreed to participate in the study; how these respondents differed from those who declined is impossible to judge.

Several popular magazines, such as *McCall's*, *Psychology Today*, and *Redbook*, have also conducted large surveys of sexual behavior. Again, because probability samples were not obtained, the accuracy of their data is questionable. The most obvious sampling bias in these surveys is that only people who can read responded to the questionnaires in the magazines, thereby eliminating the estimated 10% of the adult population that is illiterate. Also, readers of particular magazines are unlikely to be representative of the population at large.

Most recently, Hite (1987) published a 922-page book, *Women and Love*, that described the findings of a nationwide study of how women view themselves and their relationships with men. Some of Hite's findings were surprising and created quite a stir when they were released. For example, 95% of the women in her sample reported feeling "emotionally harrassed by the men they love." However, before jumping to conclusions about the state of male–female relationships in this country, let us consider Hite's sampling procedure.

To ensure anonymity, questionnaires were sent to organizations rather than to individuals, with the idea that the organizations would distribute the questionnaires to their members, who would return them anonymously. Thus, the sample includes primarily women who belong to some kind of organization. Furthermore, out of the 100,000 questionnaires that were sent out, only 4500 completed surveys were returned—a return rate of only 4.5%. How respondents differed from nonrespondents is impossible to determine, but the nonrepresentativeness of the sample should make us hesitant to generalize the findings to the population at large.

In fairness to all of these studies, obtaining accurate information about sexual behavior is a difficult and delicate task. Aside from the problems associated with obtaining any probability sample, the fact that a high percentage of people will refuse to answer questions about sexuality also biases the findings. The bottom line is that, although the results of such surveys are interesting, we should not regard them as true indicators of sexual behavior in the general population.

Nonprobability Samples

Although probability samples provide the most externally valid picture of the population of interest, relatively little behavioral research is conducted on probability samples. In most research contexts, it is impossible, impractical, or unnecessary for a researcher to obtain a probability sample; in such cases, nonprobability samples are used. With a **nonprobability sample**, the researcher has no way of knowing the probability that a particular case will be chosen for the sample. As a result, there is no way either to determine precisely how representative the sample is of the population at large or to calculate the error of estimation. However, in many research contexts, this does not necessarily create a problem for the interpretation of our results.

When a researcher is interested in accurately describing the typical attitudes, feelings, or behavior of a particular population, probability sampling is a necessity. Without probability sampling, we cannot be sure of the degree to which the data provided by the sample approximate the behavior of the larger population. Thus, in survey research, such as opinion polls, probability sampling is essential.

The difficulty with probability sampling, however, is that it is often time-consuming, expensive, and difficult, if not impossible. A developmental psychologist who was interested in studying language development would find it difficult to obtain a probability sample of all preschool children in the United States. Similarly, a psychophysiologist who was interested in hearing loss would not be able to obtain a probability sample of all deaf people.

As a result, probability samples are virtually never used in experimental research. Much psychological research is conducted on samples (such as college students) that are clearly not representative of all people. Similarly, the animals used in behavioral research are never sampled randomly from all animals of that species, but instead consist of particular species that were raised for laboratory use. You might wonder, then, about the validity of research that does not use probability samples.

Contrary to what you might expect, nonprobability samples are perfectly acceptable for many kinds of behavioral research. The goal of most behavioral research is *not* to describe how a particular population behaves, but rather to test hypotheses regarding the effects of particular variables on behavior. Hypotheses are derived from theories, and then research is conducted to see whether the predicted effects of the independent variables are obtained. If the data are consistent with the researcher's hypotheses, they provide evidence in support of the theory regardless of the nature of the sample.

In the case of experimental studies that use nonprobability samples, the external validity of the findings can be assessed through replication. The same experiment can be conducted using other samples of subjects who differ in age, education level, socioeconomic status, region of the country, and so on. If similar findings are obtained using several different samples, we have increased faith in the validity of the results.

To the extent that many of the processes studied in research are basic and universal, there is often little reason to expect different samples to respond differently. If this is true, then it matters little what kind of sample one uses; the processes involved will be similar. Of course, we cannot blithely assume that certain psychological processes are, in fact, universal; only replication can show whether findings generalize across samples. But it is erroneous to assume that research conducted on nonprobability samples tells us nothing about people in general.

Although the nature of one's sample is important, other considerations sometimes outweigh sampling as researchers design their studies. For example, experimental psychologists are willing to risk sampling bias to increase their control over experimental variables. Furthermore, the time and expense involved in obtaining a representative sample would prohibit much important research from being done at all. Researchers must weigh the advantages of probability samples against other considerations.

Three primary types of nonprobability samples include convenience, quota, and purposive samples.

Convenience Sampling

In **convenience sampling**, the researcher simply uses whatever subjects are readily available. Subjects are chosen until a sample of the desired size is obtained without regard to its representativeness. For example, we could stop the first 150 shoppers we encounter on a downtown street; or we could sample people waiting in an airport or bus station, or patients at a local hospital. Behavioral researchers often use convenience samples of psychology students as subjects for their experiments. No one argues that students are representative of people in general or even of 18- to 22-year-olds. Even so, such samples are often used because they are convenient.

Although using students as subjects does not necessarily invalidate the results of a study, researchers should be aware of the potential biases involved in student samples. For example, college students tend to be more intelligent than the general population. They also tend to come from middle- and upper-class backgrounds and to hold slightly more liberal attitudes than the population at large. Additional sampling biases are introduced when students are asked to *volunteer* to participate in research. Volunteers tend to differ in systematic ways from students who choose not to volunteer; volunteers tend to be more unconventional, more self-confident, more extroverted, and higher in need for achievement (Bell, 1962).

Quota Sampling

A **quota sample** is a convenience sample in which the researcher takes steps to ensure that certain kinds of subjects are obtained in particular proportions. The researcher specifies in advance that the sample will contain certain percentages of particular kinds of subjects. For example, if a researcher wanted to obtain an equal proportion of male and female subjects, he or she might decide to obtain a sample of 75 women and 75 men on a downtown street or from a psychology class.

Purposive Sampling

In **purposive sampling**, the researcher uses his or her judgment to decide which respondents to include in the sample. The researcher tries to choose respondents that are typical of the population in which he or she is interested. Unfortunately, researchers' judgments are not a trustworthy way of selecting a sample.

One area in which purposive sampling has been used successfully involves forecasting the results of national elections. On the basis of previous election results, it is possible to identify particular areas of the country where voting patterns tend to mirror the country's as a whole. Voters from these areas are then interviewed and their political preferences used to predict the outcome of an upcoming election.

IN DEPTH

SAMPLING AND GENDER DIFFERENCES

The nature of one's sample has a direct impact on the results that are obtained in a study. If the sample is biased or nonrepresentative, erroneous conclusions may be drawn from the data.

A case in point involves the use of samples that consist entirely of one sex (Grady, 1981). In the early days of psychology, when a disproportionate number of college students were men, researchers commonly used only male subjects in research. For example, early work on achievement motivation (McClelland, Atkinson, Clark, & Lowell, 1953) used only male subjects. Even as late as 1968, an analysis of articles in the *Journal of Personality and Social Psychology*—one of the leading journals in behavioral science—showed that all-male samples were used twice as frequently as all-female samples (31% versus 15%; Carlson, 1971).

Currently, about one-fourth of behavioral research uses only one sex. In many instances, single-sex samples are justified by the researcher's interest; a study of postpartum depression necessarily involves a female sample, for example. The problem is that the vast majority of the studies that use only one sex generalize their findings to the population as a whole (Reardon & Prescott, 1977).

Are findings obtained with members of one sex generalizable to the other? Often they are. Studies that look for potential sex differences often find none; men and women respond similarly in many respects. However, because many findings are specific to one sex or the other, a researcher is never justified in generalizing from the behavior of one sex to the behavior of people in general. Only by using samples composed of both men and women can conclusions be drawn about ways in which the sexes do or do not differ from each other.

Summary

1. Sampling is the process by which a researcher selects a group of subjects for research (the sample) from a larger population.

2. When a probability sample is used, the researcher can specify the probability that any individual in the population will be included in the sample. In a probability sample, the degree to which the data obtained from the sample accurately reflect the population—the error of estimation—can be calculated.

3. Most probability samples are selected by epsem—an equal-probability selection method. Simple random samples, for example, are selected in such a way that every possible sample of the desired size has an equal probability of being chosen.

4. Researchers often use a table of random numbers to select random samples.

5. A stratified random sample is chosen by first dividing the population into subsets or strata that share a particular characteristic. Then subjects are sampled randomly from each stratum.

6. In cluster sampling, the researcher first samples groupings, or clusters, of subjects, then samples subjects from the selected clusters. In multistage sampling, the researcher sequentially samples clusters from within clusters before choosing the final sample of subjects.

7. Error of estimation is a function of the size of the sample, the size of the population, and the variance of the data. Researchers usually opt for an economical sample that provides an acceptably low error of estimation at reasonable cost and effort.

8. When the response rate for a probability sample is less than 100%, the findings of the study may be biased in unknown ways.

9. When nonprobability samples—such as convenience, quota, and purposive samples—are used, the researcher has no way of determining the degree to which they are representative of the population, nor of calculating the error of estimation. Even so, nonprobability samples are used far more often in behavioral research than probability samples.

Key Terms

sample	systematic sampling
sampling	table of random numbers
external validity	stratified random sample
representative sample	stratum
sampling error	cluster sampling
error of estimation	cluster
margin of error	multistage sampling
economic sample	nonprobability sample
probability sample	convenience sample
epsem design	quota sample
simple random sample	purposive sample
sampling frame	

Review Questions

1. Why are probability samples generally preferred over nonprobability samples?

2. What is the central difficulty involved in obtaining simple random samples from large populations?

3. How does cluster sampling solve the practical problems involved in simple random sampling?

4. What is the difference between a stratum and a cluster?

5. What is the drawback of obtaining random samples by telephone?

6. What does the error of estimation tell us about the results of a study conducted using probability sampling?

7. What happens to the error of estimation as one's sample size increases?

8. What factors affect the error of estimation?

9. What type of sample is used most frequently in behavioral research?

10. What are the advantages and disadvantages of using convenience samples?

11. Why do behavioral researchers tend to use nonprobability samples more frequently than probability samples?

Questions for Thought and Discussion

1. Suppose that you wanted to obtain a simple random sample of lawyers in your state. How would you do it?

2. Suppose that you wanted to study children who have Down's syndrome. How might you use cluster sampling to obtain a probability sample of children with Down's syndrome in your state?

3. Using the table of random numbers in Appendix A-1, draw a stratified random sample of 10 boys and 10 girls from the population below:

Tom	Carlos	Jenny
Jerry	Dale	Rupert
Kevin	Erin	Brandon
Chris	Li	Stacey
Collin	Tom	Ryan
Milou	Clem	Andrew
Shannon	Gary	Patrick
Daniel	Wes	Mario
Susan	José	Kelly
Robin	Taylor	Usha
Mark	Greg	Teresa
Pam	Wendy	Marilyn
Raji	Jack	Richard
Vincent	Sergei	Barry
Anne	Kathy	Paul
Brenda	Philip	Elvis
Rowland	Debbie	Elisha
Gail	Patsy	Mike
Tan	Julie	Betsy

4. In defending the sampling methods used for *Women and Love*, Hite (1987) wrote: "Does research that is not based on a probability or random sample give one the right to generalize from the results of the study to the population at large? If a study is large enough and the sample is broad enough, and if one generalizes carefully, yes" (p. 778). Do you agree with Hite? Why or why not?

5. Imagine that you are a researcher employed by a local board of education. The board wants to know the average IQ of the 2500 seventh-grade students in your school district. You administer an IQ test to a simple random sample of 350 students and find that the mean IQ score for the sample is 103.7 and the variance of the scores is 196. Calculate the error of estimation and tell how you would explain your findings to members of the school board (who we will assume know nothing about research or sampling). The answer appears below.

Answer to Question 5:
The error of estimation is 1.39. This means that there is a 95% probability that the average IQ score of the 2,500 seventh-graders in the school district is between 102.3 and 105.1 (that is, 103.7 plus or minus 1.39).

CHAPTER 7

Correlational Research

My grandfather, a farmer for more than 50 years, has told me on several occasions that the color and thickness of a caterpillar's coat is related to the severity of the coming winter. When "woolly worms" have dark, thick furry coats, he says, we can expect an unusually harsh winter.

Whether this common bit of folk wisdom is true, I don't know. But, like my grandfather, we all hold many beliefs about associations between events in the world. Some of our beliefs are true; others are undoubtedly false. Many people believe, for instance, that hair color is related to personality and intelligence—that people with red hair have fiery tempers and that blondes are often "dumb." Others think that geniuses are particularly likely to suffer from mental disorders or that people who live in large cities are apathetic and uncaring. Those who believe in astrology claim the date on which a person is born is associated with the person's personality later in life. Sailors capitalize on the relationship between the appearance of the sky and approaching storms, as indicated by the old saying: Red sky at night, sailor's delight; red sky at morning, sailors take warning. You probably hold many such beliefs about things that tend to go together.

Like all of us, behavioral researchers are also interested in whether certain variables are related to each other. Is outside temperature related to the incidence of urban violence? To what extent are children's IQ scores related to the IQs of their parents? Is shyness associated with low self-esteem? What is the relationship between the degree of students' test anxiety and their performance on exams? Are SAT scores related to college grades? Each of these questions asks whether two variables (such as SAT scores and grades) are related and, if so, how strongly they are related.

We determine whether one variable is related to another by seeing whether scores on the two variables *covary*—whether they *vary together*. If self-esteem is related to shyness, for example, we should find that scores on measures of self-esteem and shyness vary together. Higher self-esteem scores should be associated with lower shyness scores, and lower self-esteem scores should be associated with greater shyness. Such a pattern would indicate that scores on the two measures covary, or vary together. On the other hand, if self-esteem and shyness bear no consistent relationship to each other—if we found that high self-esteem scores were as likely to be associated with high shyness scores as with low shyness scores—the scores would not vary together, and we would conclude that no relationship existed between self-esteem and shyness.

When researchers are interested in such questions, they often conduct **correlational research**. Correlational research is used to describe the relationship between naturally occurring variables by assessing the degree to which the variables covary. Before delving into details regarding correlational research, let's look at an example of a correlational study that we'll return to throughout the chapter.

Personality Resemblance Between Children and Parents

Since the earliest days of psychology, researchers have debated the relative importance of genetic versus environmental influences on behavior, often dubbed the *nature-nurture controversy*. Scientists have disagreed regarding whether people's behaviors are affected more by their inborn biological makeup or by their experiences in life. Most psychologists now agree that the debate is a complex one; behavior and mental ability are a product of *both* inborn *and* environmental factors. So, rather than discuss whether a particular behavior should be classified as *innate* or *acquired*, researchers have turned their attention to studying the interactive effects of nature and nurture on behavior and to identifying aspects of behavior that are more affected by nature than nurture, and vice versa.

Part of this work has focused on the relationship between the personalities of children and their parents. Common observation tells us that children display many of the psychological characteristics of their parents. But is this similarity due to genetic factors or to the fact that the parents raised their children in a particular way? Is this resemblance due to nature or to nurture?

If we only study children who were raised by their natural parents, we cannot answer this question; both genetic and environmental influences can explain similarities with their parents found in children who were raised by their biological parents. For this reason, many researchers have turned their attention to children who were adopted in infancy. Because any resemblance between children and their adoptive parents is unlikely to be due to genetic factors, it must be due to environmental variables.

In one such study, Sandra Scarr and her colleagues administered several personality measures to 120 adolescents and their natural parents and to 115 adolescents and their adoptive parents (Scarr, Webber, Weinberg, & Wittig, 1981). These scales measured a number of personality traits, including introversion–extraversion (the tendency to be inhibited versus outgoing) and neuroticism (the ten-

TABLE 7.1

Correlations Between Children's and Parents' Personalities

Personality measure	Biological parents	Adoptive parents
Introversion–extraversion	.19	.00
Neuroticism	.25	.05

dency to be anxious and insecure). The researchers wanted to know whether children's personalities were related more closely to their natural parents' personalities or to their adoptive parents' personalities.

This study produced a wealth of data, a small portion of which is shown in Table 7.1. This table shows *correlation coefficients* that express the nature of the relationships between the children's and parents' personalities. These correlation coefficients indicate both the strength and the direction of the relationship between parents' and children's scores on the two personality measures. One column lists the correlations between children and their biological parents, and the other column shows correlations between children and their adoptive parents. This table can tell us a great deal about the relationship between children's and parents' personalities, but first we must learn how to interpret correlation coefficients.

The Correlation Coefficient

A **correlation coefficient** is a statistic that indicates the degree to which two variables are related to one another. In the study just described, the researchers were interested in the relationship between children's personalities and those of their parents. Any two variables can be correlated: self-esteem and shyness, enjoyment of rock music and hearing acuity, marijuana use and scores on a test of memory, and so on. We could even do a study that looked at the correlation between the thickness of caterpillars' coats and winter temperatures. The only requirement for a correlational study is that we obtain scores on two variables for each subject in our sample.

The **Pearson correlation coefficient**, designated by the letter r, is the most commonly used measure of correlation. There are other kinds of correlations, but they are alternative approximations of the Pearson correlation coefficient.

The numerical value of a correlation coefficient always ranges between -1.00 and $+1.00$. When interpreting a correlation coefficient, a researcher considers two things: its sign and its magnitude.

The *sign* of a correlation coefficient (+ or −) indicates the *direction* of the relationship between the two variables. Variables may be either positively or negatively correlated. A **positive correlation** indicates a direct, positive relationship between the two variables. If the correlation is positive, scores on one variable tend to increase as scores on the other variable increase. For example, the correlation between SAT scores and college grades is a positive one; people with higher SAT scores tend to have higher grades, whereas people with lower SAT scores tend to have lower grades. Similarly, the correlation between educational attainment and income is positive; better educated people tend to make more money. In Chapter 2, we saw that optimism and health are positively correlated; more optimistic people tend to be healthier.

A **negative correlation** indicates an inverse, negative relationship between two variables. As values of one variable increase, values of the other variable decrease. For example, the correlation between self-esteem and shyness is negative. People with higher self-esteem tend to be less shy, whereas people with lower self-esteem tend to be more shy. The correlation between alcohol consumpton and college grades is also negative. On the average, the more alcohol a student consumes in a week, the lower his or her grades are likely to be. Likewise, the degree to which people have a sense of control over their lives is negatively correlated with depression; lower perceived control is associated with greater depression, whereas greater perceived control is associated with lower depression.

The *magnitude of the correlation*—its numerical value, ignoring the sign— expresses the strength of the *linear relationship* between the variables. If subjects' scores on the two variables are plotted on a graph as in Figure 7.1, do the scores relate to one another in a straight line? When r is zero ($r = .00$), we know that the variables are not linearly related. As the numerical value of a correlation coefficient increases, so does the strength of the linear relationship. Thus, a correlation of +.78 indicates the variables are more strongly related than does a correlation of +.30. Keep in mind that the sign of a correlation coefficient indicates only the direction of the relationship and tells us nothing about its strength. Thus, a correlation of −.78 indicates a larger correlation (and a stronger relationship) than a correlation of +.40, but the first relationship is negative whereas the second one is positive.

A Graphic Representation of Correlations

The relationship between any two variables can be portrayed graphically on an *x*- and *y*-axis. For each subject, we can plot a point that represents his or her combination of scores on the two variables (which we can designate *x* and *y*). When scores for an entire sample are plotted, the resulting graphical representation of the data is called a **scatter plot**.

Figure 7.2 shows several scatterplots of relationships between two variables. Positive correlations can be recognized by their upward slope to the right, which

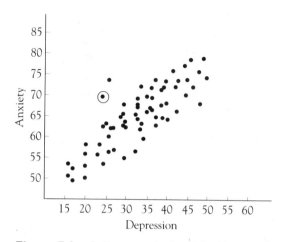

Figure 7.1   A linear relationship: Depression and anxiety

Explanation: This graph shows subjects' scores on two measures (depression and anxiety) plotted on an axis, where each dot represents a single subject's score. For example, the circled subject scored 25 on depression and 70 on anxiety. As you can see from this scatterplot, depression and anxiety are linearly related; that is, the pattern of the data tends to follow a straight line.

indicates that subjects with high values on one variable (*x*) also tend to have high values on the other variable (*y*), whereas low values on one variable are associated with low values on the other. Negative correlations slope downward to the right, indicating that subjects who score high on one variable tend to score low on the other variable, and vice versa.

The stronger the correlation, the more tightly the data are clustered around an imaginary line running through them. When we have a **perfect correlation** (-1.00 or $+1.00$), all the data fall in a straight line, as in Figure 7.2(e). At the other extreme, a zero correlation appears as a random array of dots because the two variables bear no relationship to one another [see Figure 7.2(f)].

As noted, a correlation of zero indicates the variables are not linearly related. However, it is possible they are related in a *curvilinear* fashion. Look, for example, at Figure 7.3. This graph shows the relationship between physiological arousal and performance; people perform better when they are moderately aroused than when arousal is either very low or very high. If we calculate a correlation coefficient for these data, *r* will be nearly zero. Can we conclude that arousal and performance are unrelated? No, for as Figure 7.3 shows, they are closely related. But the relationship is curvilinear, and correlation tells us only about linear relationships. Many researchers regularly examine a graph of their data to be sure the variables are not

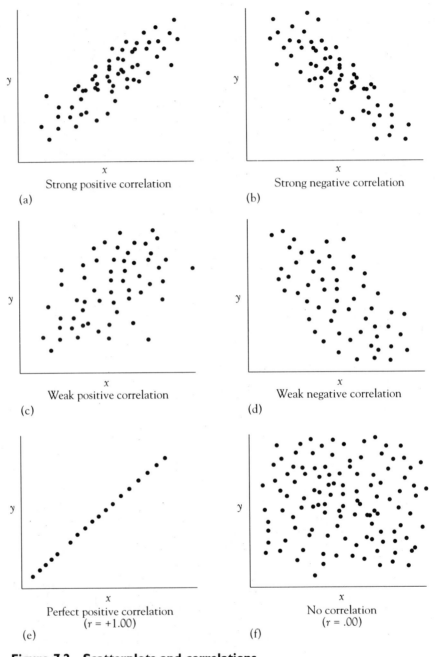

Figure 7.2 Scatterplots and correlations

curvilinearly related. There are statistics for measuring the degree of curvilinear relationship between two variables, but those statistics don't concern us here. Simply remember that correlation coefficients tell us only about linear relationships between variables.

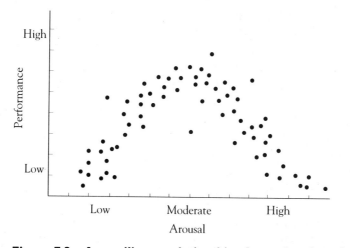

Figure 7.3   A curvilinear relationship: Arousal and performance

Explanation: This is a scatterplot of 70 subjects' scores on a measure of arousal (*x*-axis) and a measure of performance (*y*-axis). The relationship between arousal and performance is curvilinear; subjects with moderate arousal performed better than those with low or high arousal. Because *r* is a measure of linear relationships, calculating a correlation coefficient for these data would yield a value of *r* that was approximately zero. Obviously, this cannot be taken to indicate that arousal and performance are unrelated.

Interpreting the Example

You should now be able to make sense out of the correlation coefficients in Table 7.1. First, we see that the correlation between the introversion–extraversion scores of children and their natural parents is +.19. This is a positive correlation, which means children who scored high in introversion–extraversion tended to be those whose natural parents also had high introversion–extraversion scores. Conversely, children with lower scores tended to be those whose natural parents also scored low. The correlation is only .19, however, which indicates a relatively weak relationship between the scores of children and their natural parents.

The correlation between the introversion–extraversion scores of children and their adoptive parents, however, was .00; there was no relationship. Taking these two correlations together suggests that a child's level of introversion–extraversion is more closely related to that of his or her natural parents than to that of his or her adoptive parents. The same appears to be true of neuroticism. The correlation for children and their natural parents was +.25, whereas the correlation for children and adoptive parents was only +.05. Again, these positive correlations are small, but they are stronger for natural than for adoptive parents.

The Coefficient of Determination

We've seen that the correlation coefficient, r, expresses the direction and strength of the relationship between two variables. But what, precisely, does the value of r indicate? If children's neuroticism scores correlate $+.25$ with the scores of their parents, we know there is a positive relationship, but what does the number itself tell us?

To interpret a correlation coefficient fully, we must first square it, because the statistic r is not on a ratio scale. As a result, we can't add, subtract, multiply, or divide correlation coefficients, nor can we compare them directly. Contrary to how it appears, a correlation of .8 is *not* twice as large as a correlation of .4! To make r more easily interpretable, we square it to obtain the **coefficient of determination**, which is on a ratio scale of measurement and is easily interpretable. What does it show? To answer this question, let us return momentarily to the concept of variance.

We learned in Chapter 2 that variance indicates the amount of variability in a set of data. We learned also that the total variance in a set of data can be partitioned into systematic variance and error variance. Systematic variance is that part of the total variability in subjects' responses that is related to variables the researcher is investigating. Error variance is that portion of the total variance that is unrelated to the variables under investigation in the study.

We also learned in Chapter 2 that researchers can assess the strength of the relationships they study by determining the proportion of the total variance in subjects' responses that is systematic variance related to other variables under study. (This proportion equals the quantity, systematic variance/total variance.) The higher the proportion of the total variance in one variable that is systematic variance related to another variable, the stronger is the relationship between them.

The squared correlation coefficient (or coefficient of determination) tells us *the proportion of variance in one of our variables that is accounted for by the other variable.* Viewed another way, the coefficient of determination is the proportion of the total variance in one variable that is systematic variance shared with the other variable. For example, if we square the correlation between children's neuroticism scores and those of their biological parents ($.25 \times .25$), we obtain a coefficient of determination of .0625. This tells us that 6.25% of the variance in children's neuroticism scores can be accounted for by their parents' scores, or, 6.25% of the total variance in children's scores is systematic variance related to the parents' scores.

When two variables are uncorrelated—when r is .00—they are totally independent and we cannot account for any of the variance in one of our variables by the other variable. However, to the extent that two variables are correlated with one another, scores on one variable *are* related to scores on the other variable, and systematic variance is present. The existence of a correlation (and systematic variance) means that we can account for some of the variance in one variable by the other variable.

If we were omniscient and knew everything there is to know about neuroticism, we would know *all* the factors that account for the variance in children's neuroticism scores. Some possible contributors to neuroticism include genetic factors, the absence of a secure home life as a child, neurotic parents who provide models of neurotic behavior, low self-esteem, exploitation by other people, and so on. If we knew everything about neuroticism, we could account for 100% of the variance in children's neuroticism scores.

But we are not all-knowing. The best we can do is conduct research that looks at the relationship between neuroticism and a handful of other variables. In the case of the research conducted by Scarr and her colleagues (1981) discussed earlier, we can account for only a relatively small portion of the variance in children's neuroticism scores—that portion associated with the neuroticism of their natural parents. Given the myriad factors that influence neuroticism, it is really not surprising that one particular factor, such as parental neuroticism, is related only weakly to children's neuroticism.

In summary, the square of a correlation coefficient—its coefficient of determination—indicates the proportion of variance in one variable that can be accounted for by another. If r is zero, we account for none of the variance. If r equals -1.00 or $+1.00$, we can perfectly account for 100% of the variance. And if r is in between, the more variance we account for, the stronger the relationship.

DEVELOPING YOUR RESEARCH SKILLS

CALCULATING THE PEARSON CORRELATION COEFFICIENT

Now that we understand what a correlation coefficient tells us about the relationship between two variables, let's look at how it is calculated. To calculate the Pearson correlation coefficient (r), we must sample several individuals and obtain two measures on each.

The Formula

The equation for calculating r is

$$r = \frac{\Sigma xy - \frac{(\Sigma x)(\Sigma y)}{n}}{\sqrt{\left(\Sigma x^2 - \frac{(\Sigma x)^2}{n}\right)\left(\Sigma y^2 - \frac{(\Sigma y)^2}{n}\right)}}$$

In this equation, x and y represent subjects' scores on the two variables of interest, for example shyness and self-esteem, or neuroticism scores for oneself and one's parents. The term Σxy indicates that we multiply each subject's x- and y-scores together, then sum these products across all subjects. Likewise, the term $(\Sigma x)(\Sigma y)$

indicates that we sum all subjects' x-scores, sum all subjects' y-scores, then multiply these two sums. The rest of the equation should be self-explanatory. Although calculating r may be time-consuming with a large number of subjects, the math involved is only simple arithmetic.

An Example

Many businesses use ability and personality tests to help them hire the best employees. Before they may legally use such tests, however, employers must demonstrate that scores on the tests are, in fact, related to job performance. Psychologists are often called upon to examine the predictive validity of employment tests by showing that test scores correlate with performance on the job.

Suppose we are interested in whether scores on a particular test relate to job performance. First, we obtain employment test scores for 10 employees. Then, 6 months later, we ask these employees' supervisors to rate their employees' job performance on a scale of 1 to 10, where a rating of 1 represents extremely poor job performance and a rating of 10 represents superior performance.

Table 7.2 shows the test scores and ratings for the 10 employees, along with some of the products and sums we need to calculate r. In this example, two scores have been obtained for each employee: an employment test score (x) and a job performance rating (y).

TABLE 7.2

Calculating the Pearson Correlation Coefficient

Employee	Test score (x)	Job performance rating (y)	x^2	y^2	xy
1	85	9	7225	81	765
2	60	5	3600	25	300
3	45	3	2025	9	135
4	82	9	6724	81	738
5	70	7	4900	49	490
6	80	8	6400	64	640
7	57	5	3249	25	285
8	72	4	5184	16	288
9	60	7	3600	49	420
10	65	6	4225	36	390
	$\Sigma x = 676$	$\Sigma y = 63$	$\Sigma x^2 = 47{,}132$	$\Sigma y^2 = 435$	$\Sigma xy = 4451$
	$(\Sigma x)^2 = 456{,}976$	$(\Sigma y^2) = 3969$			

As you can see, we've obtained x^2, y^2, and the product of x and y (xy) for each subject, along with the sums of x, y, x^2, y^2, and xy. Once we have these numbers, we simply substitute them for the appropriate terms in the formula for r:

$$r = \frac{\Sigma xy - \frac{(\Sigma x)(\Sigma y)}{n}}{\sqrt{\left(\Sigma x^2 - \frac{(\Sigma x)^2}{n}\right)\left(\Sigma y^2 - \frac{(\Sigma y)^2}{n}\right)}}$$

Entering the appropriate numbers into the formula yields:

$$r = \frac{4451 - (676)(63)/10}{\sqrt{(47{,}132 - 456{,}976/10)(435 - 3969/10)}}$$

$$= \frac{4451 - 4258.8}{\sqrt{(47{,}132 - 45{,}697.6)(435 - 396.9)}}$$

$$= \frac{192.2}{\sqrt{(1434.4)(38.1)}} = \frac{192.2}{\sqrt{54{,}650.64}} = \frac{192.2}{233.77} = .82$$

The obtained correlation for the example in Table 7.2 is $+.82$.

Can you interpret this number? First, the sign of r is positive, indicating that test scores and job performance are directly related; employees who score higher on the test tend to be evaluated more positively by their supervisors, whereas employees with lower scores tend to be rated less positively. The value of r is .82, which is a strong correlation. To see precisely how strong the relationship is, we square .82 to get the coefficient of determination, .67. This indicates that 67% of the variance in employees' job performance ratings can be accounted for by knowing their test scores. The test seems to be a valid indicator of job performance.

CONTRIBUTORS TO BEHAVIORAL RESEARCH

THE INVENTION OF CORRELATION

The development of correlation as a statistical procedure began with the work of Sir Francis Galton. Intrigued by the ideas of his cousin, Charles Darwin, regarding evolution, Galton began investigating human heredity. One aspect of his work on inheritance involved measuring various parts of the body of hundreds of people and their parents. In 1888, Galton introduced the "index of co-relation" as a method of describing the degree to which two such measurements were related. Rather than being a strictly mathematical formula, Galton's original procedure for estimating co-relation (which he denoted by the letter r for *reversion*) involved inspecting data that had been graphed on x- and y-axes (Cowles, 1989; Stigler, 1986).

Galton's seminal work provoked intense excitement among three British scientists who further developed the theory and mathematics of correlation. Walter Weldon, a Cambridge zoologist, began using Galton's ideas regarding correlation in his research on shrimps and crabs. In the context of his work examining correlations among various crustacean body parts, Weldon first introduced the concept of *negative correlation*. (Weldon tried to name *r* after Galton, but the term *Galton's function* never caught on; Cowles, 1989).

In 1892, Francis Edgeworth published the first mathematical formula for calculating the coefficient of correlation directly. Unfortunately, Edgeworth did not initially recognize the importance of his work, which was buried in a more general, "impossibly difficult to follow paper" on statistics (Cowles, 1989, p. 139).

Thus, when Galton's student Karl Pearson derived a formula for calculating *r* in 1895, he didn't know that Edgeworth had obtained an essentially equivalent formula a few years earlier. Edgeworth himself notified Pearson of this fact in 1896, and Pearson later acknowledged that he had not carefully examined others' previous work. Even so, Pearson recognized the importance of the discovery and went ahead to make the most of it, applying his formula to research problems in both biology and psychology (Pearson & Kendall, 1970; Stigler, 1986). Because Pearson was the one to popularize the formula for calculating *r*, the coefficient became known as the *Pearson correlation coefficient*, or Pearson *r*.

Statistical Significance of r

When calculating a correlation between two variables, researchers are interested not only in the value of the correlation coefficient but also in whether the value of *r* is statistically significant. A correlation coefficient calculated on a sample is **statistically significant** if it has a very low probability of being zero in the population.

To understand what this means, let's imagine for a moment that we are all-knowing beings, and that, as all-knowing beings, we *know* that if we tested every human being on the face of the earth we would find that the correlation between two particular variables, *x* and *y*, was absolutely zero (that is, $r = .00$). Now, imagine that a mortal behavioral researcher wishes to calculate the correlation between these two variables. Of course, as a mortal, this researcher cannot collect data on millions of people around the world, so she obtains a sample of 200 respondents, measures *x* and *y* for each respondent, and calculates *r*. Will the value of *r* she obtains be .00? I suspect that you can guess that the answer is no. Because of sampling error, measurement error, and other sources of error variance, she will likely obtain a nonzero correlation coefficient *even though the true correlation in the population is zero*.

Of course, this discrepancy creates a problem. When we calculate a correlation coefficient, how do we know whether we can trust the value we obtain or whether the true value of *r* in the population may, in fact, be zero? We can't know for certain, but we can estimate the probability that the value of *r* we obtain in our research would really be zero if we had tested the entire population from which our sample was drawn. And, if the probability that our correlation is truly zero in the population is sufficiently low (usually less than .05), we refer to it as statistically significant.

The statistical significance of a correlation correlation is affected by three things: first is our sample size. Assume that, unbeknown to each other, you and I independently calculated the correlation between shyness and self-esteem and that we both obtained a correlation of −.50. However, your calculation was based on data from 300 subjects, whereas my calculation was based on data from 30 subjects. Which of us should feel more confident that the true correlation between shyness and self-esteem in the population is not .00? You can probably guess that your sample of 300 should give you more confidence in the value of r you obtained than my sample of 30.

Second, the statistical significance of a correlation coefficient depends on the magnitude of the correlation. For a given sample size, the larger the value of r we obtain, the less likely it is to be .00 in the population. Imagine you and I both calculated a correlation coefficient based on data from 300 subjects; your calculated value of r was .75, whereas my value of r was .20. You would be more confident that your correlation was not truly .00 in the population than I would be.

Third, statistical significance depends on how careful we want to be not to draw an incorrect conclusion about whether the correlation we obtain could be zero in the population. The more careful we want to be, the larger the correlation must be to be declared "significant." Typically, researchers decide they will consider a correlation to be significantly different from zero if there is less than a 5% chance (that is, less than 5 chances out of 100) that a correlation as large as the one they obtained *could* have come from a population with a true correlation of zero.

Formulas and tables for testing the statistical significance of correlation coefficients can be found in many statistics books (see, for example, Minium, 1978). Table 7.3 shows part of one such table. This table shows the minimum value of r that would be considered statistically significant if we set the chances of making an incorrect decision at 5%. For example, imagine that you obtained a value of r of .32 based on a sample of 100 subjects. Looking down the left-hand column, find the number of subjects (100). Looking at the other column, we see that the minimum value of r that is significant with 100 subjects is .16. Because our correlation coefficient (.32) exceeds .16, we conclude that the population correlation is *very unlikely* to be zero (in fact, there is less than a 5% chance that the population correlation is zero).

If the correlation coefficient we calculated had been less than .16, however, we would have concluded that it easily could have come from a population in which the correlation between our variables was zero. Thus, it is regarded as statistically nonsignificant, and we must treat it as if it were zero.

Keep in mind that, with large samples, even very small correlations are statistically significant. Thus, finding that a particular r is significant tells us only that it is

TABLE 7.3

Critical Values of r

Number of subjects	Minimum value of r that is significant
10	.52
20	.37
30	.30
40	.26
50	.23
60	.21
70	.20
80	.18
90	.17
100	.16
200	.12
300	.10
400	.08
500	.07
1000	.05

Explanation: These are the minimum values of r that are considered statistically significant, with less than a 5% chance that the correlation in the population is zero.

very unlikely to be .00 in the population; it does *not* tell us whether the relationship between the two variables is a strong or an important one. The strength of a correlation is assessed only by examining its magnitude, not whether or not it is statistically significant. Although only a rule of thumb, behavioral researchers tend to regard correlations at or below about 0.10 as *weak* in magnitude (they account for only 1% of the variance), correlations around 0.30 as *moderate* in magnitude, and correlations over 0.50 as *strong* in magnitude (Cohen, 1977).

BEHAVIORAL RESEARCH CASE STUDY

CORRELATES OF SATISFYING RELATIONSHIPS

Although relationships are an important part of most people's lives, behavioral researchers did not begin seriously to study processes involved in liking and loving until the 1970s. Since that time, we have learned a great deal about factors that affect

---

TABLE 7.4

Correlates of Relationship Satisfaction Among Adolescents

	Correlation with satisfaction	
Receiving from relationships	Males	Females
Togetherness	.48*	.30*
Personal growth	.44*	.22*
Appreciation	.33*	.21*
Exhilaration/happiness	.46*	.39*
Painfulness/emotional turmoil	−.09	−.09
Passion/romance	.19	.21*
Emotional support	.34*	.23*
Good communication	.13	.17

---

liking and love, determinants of people's satisfaction with their relationships, and the reasons people decide to end their romantic relationships. However, researchers have focused primarily on the relationships of adults and have largely ignored adolescent love experiences.

To remedy this shortcoming in the research, Levesque (1993) conducted a correlational study of the factors associated with a satisfying love relationship in adolescence. Using a sample of more than 300 adolescents between the ages of 14 and 18 who were involved in a dating relationship, Levesque administered measures of relationship satisfaction and obtained other information about the respondents' perceptions of their relationships.

A small portion of the results of the study is given in Table 7.4, which shows the correlations between respondents' ratings of the degree to which they were receiving certain things from their relationships and their satisfaction with the relationship. Correlations with an asterisk (*) were found to be statistically significantly different from zero.

As you can see from the table, many different aspects of relationships correlated with relationship satisfaction, and. in most instances, the correlations were similar for male and female respondents.

Considerations in Interpreting r

Assuming they have obtained a significant correlation, researchers must keep several matters in mind when they interpret correlation coefficients.

Artificially Large and Small Correlations Are Possible

Correlation coefficients are not always what they appear to be. Many factors can cause coefficients to either underestimate or overestimate the true degree of relationship between two variables. Therefore, when interpreting correlation coefficients, one must be on the lookout for three factors that may artificially inflate or deflate the magnitude of correlations.

Restricted range.   Look for a moment at Figure 7.4(a). From this scatterplot, do you think SAT scores and grade point averages are related? There is an obvious positive linear trend to the data, which reflects a moderate positive correlation. Now look at Figure 7.4(b). In this set of data, are SAT scores and grade point average correlated? In this case, the pattern, if indeed there is one, is much less pronounced. It is difficult to tell whether there is a relationship or not.

If you look at Figure 7.4(c), you'll see that Figure 7.4(b) is actually taken from a small section of Figure 7.4(a). However, rather than representing the full range of possible SAT scores and grade point averages, the range of the data shown in Figure 7.3(b) is quite narrow, or **restricted**. Instead of ranging from 200 to 1600, the entrance exam scores fall only in the range from 1000 to 1150.

These figures show graphically what happens to correlations when the range of data is restricted. Correlations obtained on a relatively homogeneous group of subjects whose scores fall in a narrow range are smaller than those obtained from a heterogenous sample with a wider range of scores. If the range of scores is restricted, a researcher may be misled into concluding that the two variables are only weakly correlated, if at all. However, had a broader range of scores been sampled, a strong relationship would have emerged. The lesson here is to examine one's raw data to be sure the range of scores is not artificially restricted.

The problem may be even more serious if the two variables are curvilinearly related *and* the range of scores is restricted. Look, for example, at Figure 7.5. This graph shows the relationship between anxiety and performance on a task, and the relationship is obviously curvilinear. Now imagine you selected a sample of 200 respondents from a phobia treatment center and examined the relationship between anxiety and performance for these 200 subjects. Because your sample had a restricted range of scores (being phobic, these subjects were higher than average in anxiety), you would likely detect a negative *linear* relationship between anxiety and performance, not a curvilinear relationship. You can see this graphically in Figure 7.5 if you look only at the data for subjects who scored above average in anxiety. For these subjects, there is a strong negative relationship between their anxiety scores and their scores on the measure of performance.

Outliers.   Outliers are scores that are so obviously deviant from the remainder of the data that one can question whether they belong in the data set at all. Many researchers consider a score to be an outlier if it is further than three standard deviations from the mean of the data. You may remember from Chapter 5 that,

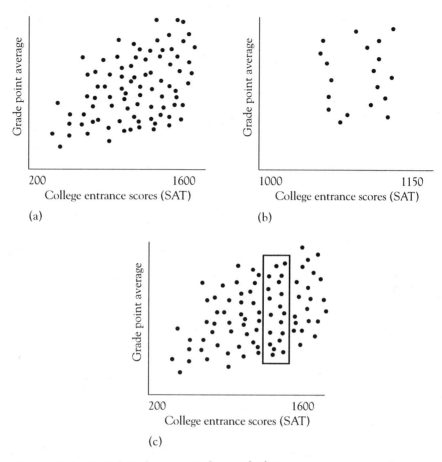

Figure 7.4   Restricted range and correlation

Explanation: Scatterplot (a) shows a distinct positive correlation between SAT scores and grade point averages when the full range of SAT scores (from 200 to 1600) is included. However, when a more restricted range of scores is examined (those from 1000 to 1150), the correlation is less apparent (b). Scatterplot (c) graphically displays the effects of restricted range on correlation.

assuming we have a roughly normal distribution, scores that fall more than three standard deviations below the mean are smaller than more than 99% of the scores; a score that falls more than three standard deviations above the mean is larger than more than 99% of the scores. Clearly, scores that deviate from the mean by more than ±3 standard deviations are very unusual.

Figure 7.6 shows two kinds of outliers. Figure 7.6(a) shows two *on-line outliers*. Two subjects' scores, although falling in the same pattern as the rest of the data, are extreme on both variables. On-line outliers tend to artificially inflate correlation coefficients, making them larger than is warranted by the rest of the data. Figure

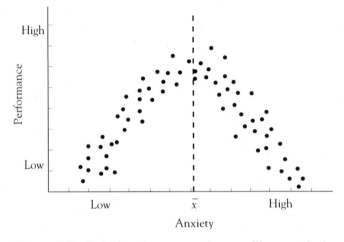

Figure 7.5   Restricted range and a curvilinear relationship

Explanation: As shown here, the relationship between anxiety and performance is curvilinear, and, as we have seen, the calculated value of *r* will be near .00. Imagine what would happen, however, if data were collected on only highly anxious subjects. If we calculate *r* only for subjects scoring above the mean of the anxiety scores, the obtained correlation will be strong and negative.

7.6(b) shows two *off-line outliers*. Off-line outliers tend to artificially deflate the value of *r*. The presence of even a few off-line outliers will cause *r* to be smaller than indicated by most of the data.

Because outliers can lead you to make erroneous conclusions about the strength of the correlation between variables, you should examine scatterplots to look for outliers. Some researchers exclude outliers from their analyses, arguing that such extreme scores are flukes that don't really belong in the data. Other researchers change outliers' scores to the value of the variable that is 3 standard deviations from the mean. By making the outlier less extreme, the researcher can include the subject's data in the analysis while minimizing the degree to which it distorts the correlation coefficient. You need to realize that changing data in these ways is highly controversial and strongly discouraged by many researchers. On the other hand, only one or two extreme outliers can badly distort correlation coefficients and lead to incorrect conclusions.

Reliability of measures.   Unreliable measures attenuate the magnitude of correlation coefficients. All things being equal, the less reliable our measures, the lower the correlation coefficients we will obtain. (You may wish to review the section on reliability in Chapter 3.)

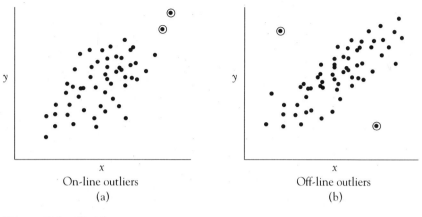

Figure 7.6   Outliers

Explanation: Two on-line outliers are circled in (a). On-line outliers lead to inflated correlation coefficients. Off-line outliers, such as those circled in (b), tend to artificially deflate the magnitude of *r*.

To understand why this is so, let us again imagine we are omniscient. In our infinite wisdom, we know that the real correlation between a child's neuroticism and the neuroticism of his or her parents is, say, +.45. However, let's also assume that a poorly trained, fallible researcher uses a measure of neuroticism that is *totally unreliable*. That is, it has absolutely no test–retest or interitem reliability. If the researcher's measure is completely unreliable, what value of *r* will he or she obtain between parents' and children's scores? Not +.45 (the true correlation), but rather .00. Of course, researchers seldom use measures that are totally unreliable. Even so, the less reliable the measure, the lower the correlation will be.

Correlation Does Not Imply Causality

We've saved perhaps the most important consideration regarding correlational research until last. People will often conclude that two things that go together must be causally related in some way. This is not necessarily so; one variable can be strongly related to another, yet not cause it. Even if the thickness of a caterpillar's coat correlates closely with the severity of winter weather, we wouldn't conclude that caterpillars *cause* blizzards, ice storms, and freezing temperatures. This principle is important when doing correlational research. A correlation can never be used to conclude that one of the variables causes or influences the other, no matter how large the correlation may be. Put simply, *correlation does not imply causality*.

For us to conclude that one variable *causes* another variable, three criteria must be met: covariation, directionality, and elimination of extraneous variables. However, most correlational research satisfies unequivocally only the first of these criteria.

Covariation.   To conclude that two variables are causally related, they first must be found to covary, or correlate. If one variable causes the other, then changes in the values of one variable should be associated with changes in values of the other variable. Of course, this is what correlation is by definition, so if two variables are found to be correlated, this first criterion for inferring causality is met.

Directionality.   Second, to infer that two variables are causally related, we must show that the presumed cause precedes the presumed effect in time. However, in most correlational research, both variables are measured at the same time. For example, if a researcher correlates subjects' scores on two personality measures that were collected at the same time, there is no way for him or her to determine the direction of causality. Does variable x cause variable y, or does variable y cause variable x (or, perhaps, neither)?

Elimination of extraneous variables.   The third criterion for inferring causality is that all extraneous factors that might influence the relationship between the two variables are controlled or eliminated. Correlational research never satisfies this requirement completely. Two variables may be correlated not because they are causally related to one another but because they are both related to a third variable.

For example, Levin and Stokes (1986) were interested in correlates of loneliness. Among other things, they found that loneliness correlated +.60 with depression. Does this mean that being lonely makes people depressed or that being depressed makes people feel lonely? Perhaps neither. Another option is that both loneliness and depression are caused by a third variable, such as the quality of a person's social network. Having a large number of friends and acquaintances, for example, may reduce both loneliness and depression.

IN DEPTH

CORRELATION, CIGARETTES, AND CANCER

The inability to draw conclusions about causality from correlational data is the basis of the tobacco industry's insistence that no research has produced evidence of a causal link between smoking and cancer in humans. Plenty of research shows that smoking and the incidence of cancer are *correlated* in humans; more smoking is associated with a greater likelihood of getting lung cancer. But because the data are correlational, we cannot, strictly speaking, infer a causal link between smoking and health.

Research *has* established that smoking causes cancer in laboratory animals, however. Animal research involves experimental studies that allow us to infer cause-and-effect relationships. Such research on humans would require that a randomly assigned group of subjects smoke heavily, which would be unethical. (Would you volunteer to participate in a study that might give you cancer?) Thus, we are unable to conduct the kind of study that could conclusively demonstrate that smoking causes cancer in human beings.

Although research that unequivocally documents that smoking causes cancer in humans has not been conducted, the animal experimental data, in combination with the human correlational data, have resulted in the Surgeon General's warning that smoking may be hazardous to your health.

A caveat. Although correlation does not imply causality, researchers have at their disposal research strategies that allow them to make informed guesses about whether one variable might be causally related to another. These strategies cannot provide definitive causal conclusions, but they can provide evidence that either does or does not lend support to a particular causal explanation of the relationship between two variables that are correlated. We'll examine some of these strategies in the next chapter.

Summary

1. Correlational research is used to describe the relationship between two variables. A correlation coefficient (r) expresses both the direction and magnitude of the relationship.

2. If the scores on the two variables tend to increase and decrease together, the variables are positively correlated. If the scores are inversely related, the variables are negatively correlated.

3. The magnitude of a correlation coefficient ranges from .00 to ±1.00 and indicates the strength of the relationship between the variables.

4. The square of the correlation coefficient, the coefficient of determination (r^2), reflects the proportion of the variance in one variable that can be accounted for by the other variable.

5. Researchers test the statistical significance of a correlation to gauge the likelihood that the correlation coefficient obtained in their research might have come from a population in which the true correlation was zero. A correlation is usually considered statistically significant if there is less than a 5% chance that the true population correlation is zero.

6. When interpreting correlations, researchers consider the possibility that the variables are curvilinearly related. They are also on the lookout for factors that may artificially inflate and deflate the magnitude of the correlation—restricted range, outliers, and reliability.

7. Correlational research seldom if ever meets all three criteria for inferring causality—covariation, directionality, and elimination of extraneous variables. Thus, correlation does not imply causality.

Key Terms

covary	scatterplot
correlational research	perfect correlation
correlation coefficient	coefficient of determination
Pearson correlation coefficient	statistical significance
positive correlation	restricted range
negative correlation	outlier
linear relationship	

Review Questions

1. The correlation between self-esteem and shyness is −.50. Interpret this correlation.

2. Which is larger, a correlation of +.45 or a correlation of −.60? Explain.

3. Tell whether each of the following relationships reflects a positive or a negative correlation.
   a. The amount of stress in people's lives and the number of colds they get during the winter
   b. The amount of time a person spends trying to get a suntan and an index of skin damage
   c. Age and computer literacy
   d. Happiness and suicidal thoughts

4. Why do researchers often examine scatterplots of their data when doing correlational research?

5. The correlation between self-esteem and shyness is −.50, and the correlation between self-consciousness and shyness is +.25. How much stronger is the first relationship than the second? (Be careful on this one.)

6. Why do researchers calculate the coefficient of determination?

7. Why can it be argued that the formula for calculating r should be named the Edgeworth, rather than the Pearson, correlation coefficient?

8. What does it mean if a correlation coefficient is statistically significant?

9. Discuss the effects of restricted range and outliers on correlation coefficients. How would you detect and correct these two problems in your data?

10. Why can't we infer causality from correlation?

Exercises

Imagine you are a college professor. You notice that fewer students appear to attend class on Friday afternoons when the weather is warm than when it is cold outside. To test your hunch, you collect data regarding outside temperature and attendance for several randomly selected weeks during the academic year. Your data are as follows:

Temperature (degrees F)	Attendance (number of students)
58	85
62	83
78	64
77	62
67	66
50	86
80	60
85	82
70	65
75	62

1. Draw a scatterplot of the data.
   a. Do the data appear to be roughly linear?
   b. Do you see any evidence of outliers?
   c. Does there *appear* to be a correlation between temperature and attendance? If so, is it positive or negative?

2. Calculate and interpret r for these data. The answer appears below.

Answer to Exercise 2:
The correlation for this set of data is $-.61$.

CHAPTER 8

Advanced Correlational Strategies

K nowing whether variables are related to one another provides the corner-stone for much scientific investigation. The first step in understanding any behavioral phenomenon typically is to document that certain variables are somehow related, and correlational research methods are indispensible for this purpose. However, as we saw in Chapter 7, correlational research can provide only tentative conclusions about cause-and-effect relationships, and simply demonstrating that variables are correlated is of only limited usefulness. Once they know that variables are correlated, researchers usually want to understand *how* and *why* they are related.

In this chapter, we look at four advanced correlational strategies that are used to explore how and why variables are related to one another. These methods allow researchers to go beyond simple correlations to a fuller and more precise understanding of what correlations tell us about the variables under study. Specifically, these methods allow researchers to (1) investigate other variables that may be responsible for correlations they obtain (partial correlation), (2) develop equations that describe how variables are related and that allow prediction of one variable from another (regression analysis), (3) explore the likely direction of causality between two or more variables that are correlated (path analysis), and (4) identify basic dimensions that underlie sets of correlations (factor analysis).

Our emphasis in this chapter is on understanding what each of these methods can tell us about the relationships among correlated variables and *not* on how to actually use them. Each of these strategies utilizes relatively sophisticated statistical analyses that would take us beyond the scope of this book.

Testing Causal Alternatives: Partial Correlation

We saw in Chapter 7 that three criteria must be met for us to infer that one variable causes another: (1) the two variables must covary or correlate, (2) the presumed causal variable must precede the presumed effect in time, and (3) extraneous factors that might influence the relationship between the two variables must be controlled or eliminated. Obtaining a correlation between two variables satisfies the first criteria, but rarely the second and never the third. As a result, researchers are careful never to infer causality from the presence of a correlation.

Even so, researchers are sometimes able to test the plausibility of certain causal explanations of the correlations they obtain. Although they can never conclude in an absolute sense that one correlated variable causes another, they may be able to conclude that a particular explanation of the relationship between the variables is more likely to be correct than are other explanations.

If we find that two variables, x and y, are correlated, there are three general explanations of their relationship: x may cause y, y may cause x, or some other variable or variables (z) may cause *both* x and y. Imagine we find a negative correlation between alcohol consumption and college grades: the more alcohol a student drinks per week, the lower his or her grades are likely to be. Such a correlation could be explained in three ways. On one hand, excessive alcohol use may cause students' grades to go down—perhaps because they are drinking instead of studying, or they miss class because of hangovers. Alternatively, obtaining poor grades may cause students to drink—to relieve the stress of failing, for example.

A third possibility is that the correlation between alcohol consumption and grades is due to some third variable. Perhaps depression is the culprit: students who are highly depressed do not do well in class, and they may try to relieve their depression by drinking. Thus, alcohol use and grades may be correlated only indirectly, by virtue of their relationship with depression. Alternatively, the relationship between alcohol and grades may be caused by the value students place on social relationships versus academic achievement. Students who place a great deal of importance on their social lives may study less and party more. As a result, they coincidentally receive lower grades *and* drink more alcohol, but the grades and drinking are not directly related. (Can you think of third variables other than depression and sociability that might mediate the relationship between alcohol consumption and grades?)

Researchers can test the plausibility of hypotheses about the possible effects of third variables on correlations by using partial correlation. Partial correlation allows researchers to examine a third variable's possible influence on a correlation between two other variables. Specifically, a **partial correlation** is the correlation between two variables with the influence of one or more other variables statistically removed.

Imagine we obtain a correlation between x and y and we want to know whether the relationship is due to the fact that x and y are both caused by some third variable, z. We can use partial correlation techniques to statistically remove the variability in x and y associated with z and see whether x and y are still correlated. If x and y still correlate after we partial out the influence of z, we can conclude the relationship between x and y is unlikely to be due to z. Stated differently, if x and y are correlated even when systematic variance due to z is removed, z is unlikely to be causing the relationship between x and y.

However, if x and y are no longer correlated after the influence of z is statistically removed, we have evidence that the correlation between x and y is due to z or to some other variable that correlates with z. That is, systematic variance associated with z must be responsible for the relationship between x and y.

Let's return to our example involving alcohol consumption and college grades. If we want to know whether a third variable, such as depression, is responsible for the correlation between alcohol and grades, we could calculate the partial correlation between alcohol use and grade point average while statistically removing (partialing out) the variability related to depression scores. If the correlation between alcohol use and grades remains unchanged when depression is partialed out, we would have good reason to conclude that the relationship between alcohol use and grades is *not* related to depression. However, if the partial correlation between alcohol and grades with depression removed is substantially lower than their true correlation, we would conclude that depression—or something else associated with depression—mediates the relationship.

Keep in mind a caution raised in Chapter 7: *correlation does not imply causality*. This admonition is particularly important to remember when interpreting partial correlations. When we find that the relationship between two variables (such as alcohol use and grades) disappears when the variability due to a third variable (such as depression) is removed, we may be tempted to conclude that the third variable *caused* the relationship between the other two—that depression causes students to do poorly in class and causes them to consume more alcohol, for example.

But such reasoning is fallacious. For one thing, we do not know whether the particular third variable we examined (such as depression) is responsible for the relationship between the two other variables or whether the relationship is due to yet another variable correlated with the third variable (such as self-esteem, lack of a social support network, drug dependency, or hundreds of other variables).

Furthermore, if the relationship between two variables does *not* disappear when variability due to the third variable is partialed out, we cannot conclude that the two variables are directly related. No matter how many plausible variables we partial out of the relationship, we may have missed the one variable that accounts for the relationship between them. In fact, it is possible that *none* of the variables we could potentially measure is causally related to another. Perhaps there is a single cause (an unhappy childhood, for example) that leads to poor grades, alcohol use, depression, low self-esteem, social difficulties, drug use, and so on.

These considerations should not lead you to conclude that partial correlation techniques are worthless. On the contrary, partial correlation is an important tool that helps researchers test the *plausibility* of various hypotheses about the relationship between the variables. However, we must be careful not to take the big (and unwarranted) step from examining plausible connections to inferring causality.

BEHAVIORAL RESEARCH CASE STUDY

PARTIAL CORRELATION: DEPRESSION, LONELINESS, AND SOCIAL SUPPORT

In Chapter 7, we discussed a study by Levin and Stokes (1986) that found a correlation of .60 between loneliness and depression. These researchers hypothesized that one reason lonely people tend to be more depressed is that they have smaller social support networks; people who have fewer friends are more likely to feel lonely *and* are more likely to be depressed (because they lack needed social and emotional support). Thus, the relationship between loneliness and depression may be due to a third variable, social support.

To test this possibility, Levin and Stokes calculated the partial correlation between loneliness and depression, removing the influence of subjects' social networks. When they removed the variability due to social networks, the correlation dropped from .60 to .39. This suggests that some of the relationship between loneliness and depression is mediated by social network variables. However, even with the social network factor removed, loneliness and depression were still correlated, which suggests that factors other than social network also contribute to the relationship between them.

Predicting Behavior: Regression Strategies

Image you are an industrial–organizational psychologist who works for a large company. One of your responsibilities is to develop better ways of selecting employees from the large number of people who apply for jobs with this company. You have developed a job aptitude test that is administered to everyone who applies for a job. When you looked at the relationship between scores on this test and how employees were rated by their supervisors after working for the company for six months, you found that scores on the aptitude test correlated positively with ratings of job performance.

Armed with this information, you should be able to *predict* applicants' future job performance, allowing you to make better decisions about whom to hire. One consequence of two variables being correlated is that if we know a person's score on one variable, we can predict his or her score on the other variable. Our prediction is seldom perfectly accurate, but if the two variables are correlated, we can predict scores (within limits) at better than chance levels.

Linear Regression

This ability to predict scores is accomplished through **linear regression analysis**. The goal of regression analysis is to develop a **regression equation** from which we can predict one score on the basis of one or more other variables. This procedure is quite useful in situations in which psychologists must make predictions. For example, regression equations are used to predict students' college performance from entrance exams and high school grades. They are also used in business and industrial settings to predict a job applicant's potential job performance on the basis of test scores and other factors. Regression analysis is also widely used in basic research settings to describe mathematically the relationships between sets of variables. The precise manner in which a regression equation is calculated does not concern us here. What is important is that you know what a regression analysis is and the rationale behind it, should you encounter one in the research literature.

Remember that correlation indicates a *linear* relationship between two variables. If the relationship between two variables is linear, a straight line can be drawn through the data to represent the relationship between the variables. For example, Figure 8.1 shows the scatterplot for the relationship between the employees' test scores and job performance ratings we analyzed in Chapter 7. (Remember, we found that the correlation between the test scores and job performance was +.82; see page 145.) The line drawn through the scatterplot portrays the nature of the relationship between test scores and performance ratings. In following the trend in the data, this line reflects how test scores and job performance tend to be related.

The goal of regression analysis is to find the equation for the line that best fits the pattern of the data. If we can find the equation for the line that best portrays the relationship between the two variables, this equation will provide us with a useful mathematical description of how the variables are related.

You may remember from high school geometry class that a line can be represented by the equation $y = mx + b$, where m is the slope of the line and b is the y-intercept. In linear regression, the symbols are different and the order of the terms is reversed, but the equation is the same:

$$y = B_0 + B_1 x$$

In a regression equation, y is the variable we would like to predict. This is usually called the **dependent variable** or **criterion variable.** x is the variable we are using to predict y; x is called the **predictor variable.** B_0 is called the **regression constant** (or beta-zero) and is the y-intercept of the line that best fits the data in the scatterplot; it is equivalent to b in the formula you learned in geometry class. The **regression coefficient,** B_1, is the slope of the line that best represents the relationship between the predictor variable (x) and the criterion variable (y). It is equivalent to m in the formula for a straight line. The regression equation for the

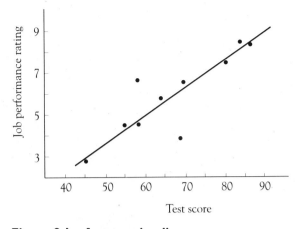

Figure 8.1   A regression line

Explanation: This is a scatterplot of the data in Table 7.2. The x-axis shows scores on an employment test, and the y-axis shows employees' job performance ratings six months later. The line running through the scatterplot is the regression line for the data—the line that best represents, or fits, the data. A regression line such as this can be described mathematically by the equation for a straight line. The equation for this particular regression line is $y = -2.76 + .13x$.

line for the data in Figure 8.1 is

$$y = -2.76 + .13x$$

or

$$\text{Job performance rating} = -2.76 + .13(\text{test score})$$

If x and y represent any two variables that are correlated, we can predict a person's y-score by plugging his or her x-score into the equation. For example, suppose a job applicant obtained a test score of 75. Using the regression equation for the scatter-plot in Figure 8.1, we can solve for y (job performance rating):

$$y = -2.76 + .13\ (75) = 6.99$$

On the basis of knowing how well he or she performed on the test, we would predict this applicant's job performance rating after six months to be 6.99. Thus, if job ability scores and job performance are correlated, we can, within limits, predict an applicant's job performance from the score he or she obtains on the employment test.

We can extend the idea of linear regression to include more than one predictor variable. For example, you might decide to predict job performance on the basis of three variables: aptitude test scores, a measure of work motivation, and an index of physical strength. Using **multiple regression,** you could develop a regression equation that includes three predictors. Once the equation is determined, you can predict job performance from an applicant's scores on the three predictor variables.

Multiple Correlation

When researchers use multiple regression analysis, they want not only to develop an equation for predicting subjects' scores but also to know *how well* the predictor, or *x*, variables predict *y*. After all, if the predictors do a poor job of predicting the outcome variable, we wouldn't want to use the equation to make decisions about job applicants. To express the usefulness of a regression equation for predicting, researchers calculate the **multiple correlation coefficient,** symbolized by the letter *R*. *R* describes the degree of relationship between the criterion variable (*y*) and the *set* of predictor, or *x*, variables. Unlike the Pearson *r*, multiple correlation coefficients range only from .00 to 1.00. The larger *R* is, the better job the equation does of predicting the outcome variable from the predictor variables.

Just as a Pearson correlation coefficient can be squared to indicate the percentage of variance in one variable that is accounted for by the other, a multiple correlation can be squared to show the percentage of variance in the criterion variable (*y*) that can be accounted for by the *set* of predictor variables.

BEHAVIORAL RESEARCH CASE STUDY

MULTIPLE REGRESSION AND CORRELATION: PREDICTORS OF BLUSHING

In the preceding example, regression analysis was used for a decidedly applied purpose—to improve the hiring of employees within a particular company. However, regression analysis is also widely used in basic research settings to identify variables that predict some behavior of interest.

We once conducted a study in which we were interested in identifying factors that predict the degree to which people blush (Leary & Meadows, 1991). We administered a Blushing Propensity Scale to 220 subjects, along with measures of 13 other psychological variables. We then conducted a multiple regression analysis from which we obtained a regression equation showing how the 13 predictor variables were related to the propensity to blush (our dependent, or criterion, variable).

The results of the regression analysis showed that blushing propensity was best predicted by a set of only 4 of the original 13 predictor variables: (1) embarrassability (the ease with which a person becomes embarrassed), (2) social anxiety (the tendency to feel nervous in social situations), (3) self-esteem (the positivity of one's self-evaluations), and (4) refinement (the degree to which a person is repulsed or offended by crass and vulgar behavior).

The multiple correlation, *R*, between this set of four predictors and blushing propensity was .63. Squaring *R* (.63 × .63) gives us .40, indicating that 40% of the variance in subjects' blushing propensity scores was accounted for by the set of four predictors.

Assessing Directionality: Path Analysis

We've stressed several times that researchers cannot infer causality from correlation. Earlier in this chapter, we saw how partial correlation can be used to tentatively test whether certain third variables are responsible for the correlation between two variables. But even if we conclude that the correlation between *x* and *y* is unlikely to be due to certain other variables, we still cannot determine from a simple correlation whether *x* causes *y* or *y* causes *x*. Fortunately, researchers have developed procedures for testing the viability of certain causal hypotheses. Although they cannot tell us *for certain* whether *x* causes *y* or *y* causes *x*, they can give us more or less confidence in one causal direction compared to the other.

A simple case involves the **cross-lagged panel correlation design** (Cook & Campbell, 1979). In this design, the correlation between two variables, *x* and *y*, is calculated at two different points in time. Then, correlations are calculated between measurements of the two variables across time. For example, we would correlate the scores on *x* taken at time 1 with the scores on *y* taken at time 2. Likewise, we would calculate the scores on *y* at time 1 with those on *x* at time 2. If *x* causes *y*, we should find that the correlation between *x* at time 1 and *y* at time 2 is larger than the correlation between *y* at time 1 and *x* at time 2; the relationship between a cause (variable *x*) and its effect (variable *y*) should be stronger if the causal variable is measured before rather than after its effect.

A cross-lagged panel design was used to study the link between violence on television and aggressive behavior. Nearly 30 years of research has demonstrated that watching violent television programs is associated with aggression. For example, the amount of violence a person watches on TV correlates positively with the person's level of aggressiveness. However, we should not infer from this correlation that television violence *causes* aggression. It is just as plausible to conclude that people who are naturally aggressive simply like to watch violent programs.

Eron, Huesmann, Lefkowitz, and Walder (1972) used a cross-lagged panel correlation design to disentangle the direction of the relationship between television violence and aggressive behavior. These researchers studied a sample of 427 subjects twice: once when the subjects were in the third grade and again 10 years later. On both occasions, subjects provided a list of their favorite TV shows, which were later rated for their violent content. In addition, each subject's aggressiveness was rated by his or her peers.

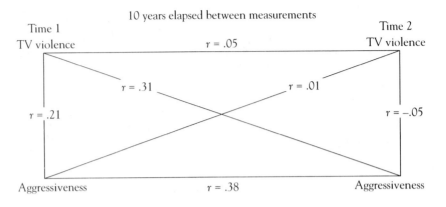

Figure 8.2   A cross-lagged panel design

Explanation: The important correlations in this cross-lagged panel design are on the diagonals. The correlation between the amount of TV violence watched by the children at Time 1 and aggressiveness 10 years later ($r = .31$) was larger than the correlation between aggressiveness at Time 1 and TV watching 10 years later ($r = .01$). This pattern is more consistent with the notion that watching TV violence causes aggressive behavior than with the idea that being aggressive disposes children to watch TV violence. Strictly speaking, however, we can never infer causality from correlational data such as these.

Correlations were calculated between TV violence and subjects' aggressiveness across the two time periods. The results for the male subjects are shown in Figure 8.2. The important correlations are on the diagonals of Figure 8.2—the correlations between TV violence at time 1 and aggressiveness at time 2, and between aggressiveness at time 1 and TV violence at time 2. As you can see, the correlation between earlier TV violence and later aggression ($r = .31$) is larger than that between earlier aggressiveness and later TV violence ($r = .01$). This pattern is consistent with the idea that watching television violence caused subjects to become more aggressive, rather than the other way around.

In recent years, this general idea has been extended through **path analysis.** Path analysis examines the possible causal directions among a *set* of correlated variables. Given the pattern of correlations among a set of variables, certain causal explanations (causal pathways) are more logical, or likely, than others. Some causal connections among the variables may be virtually impossible given the pattern of correlations among them, whereas other explanations are more consistent with the pattern of correlations among the variables. (For example, variables that are uncorrelated cannot be causally linked.) Sophisticated statistical analyses (sometimes called structural equations models) can be used to test the viability of alternative explanations.

BEHAVIORAL RESEARCH CASE STUDY

PATH ANALYSIS: TRACKING SUBSTANCE ABUSE FROM PARENTS TO CHILDREN

Children of alcoholics are at an increased risk for becoming alcoholics themselves as adults. However, researchers have had difficulty determining precisely why this is the case. One possibility is that parents who are alcoholics serve as models for their children and are less inclined to monitor their children's use of alcohol and other drugs. Another possibility is that children of alcoholics may turn to alcohol and other drugs as a way of coping with the stressfulness of their parents' alcoholism. A third explanation is that, if certain personality traits predispose people to abuse alcohol and drugs (such as impulsivity, sensation-seeking, and extraversion), children who have inherited or developed personalities like their parents' are likely to share some of the same behavioral tendencies including, perhaps, substance abuse.

To test these possible routes from parental alcoholism to substance abuse in adolescents, researchers (Chassin, Pillow, Curran, Molina, & Barrera, 1993) studied 416 adolescents and their parents. Of these adolescents, 246 had at least one biological parent who was an alcoholic. The researchers administered a large battery of measures, including measures of alcohol and drug use, psychopathology, life stress, parent–child relationships, and personality. The results of path analysis procedures provided support for all three of the models described above. Parents who were alcoholics did monitor their children less carefully, which appeared to lead to increased substance abuse in the child. In addition, having an alcoholic parent did appear to increase the child's stress which, in turn, both increased substance abuse directly and increased the probability of associating with peers who abused alcohol and drugs. Finally, some evidence was obtained for the possibility that alcohol abuse was mediated by personality traits parents and children shared. Interestingly, most of these effects were obtained only for mothers' alcoholism, not for fathers'. Overall, the variables studied by Chassin and her colleagues accounted for 59% of the variance in the children's substance abuse.

Uncovering Underlying Dimensions: Factor Analysis

Factor analysis refers to a class of statistical techniques used to analyze the interrelationships among a large number of variables. Its purpose is to identify the underlying dimensions or factors that account for the relationships observed among the variables.

If we look at the correlations among a large set of variables, we often see that certain variables correlate highly among themselves but weakly with other variables. Presumably, these patterns of correlations occur because the highly correlated variables measure the same general construct, but the uncorrelated variables measure different constructs. That is, the presence of correlations among several variables suggests the variables are each related to aspects of a more basic underlying factor. Factor analysis is used to identify the underlying factors that account for the observed patterns of relationships among a set of variables.

An Intuitive Approach

Suppose you obtained subjects' scores on five variables that we'll call A, B, C, D, and E. When you calculated the correlations among these five variables, you obtained the following correlation matrix:

	A	B	C	D	E
A	1.00	.78	.85	.01	−.07
B	—	1.00	.70	.09	.00
C	—	—	1.00	−.02	.04
D	—	—	—	1.00	.86
E	—	—	—	—	1.00

Look closely at the pattern of correlations. Based on the pattern, what conclusions would you draw about the relationships among variables A, B, C, D, and E? Which variables seem to be related to each other?

As you can see, variables A, B, and C correlate highly with each other, but each correlates weakly with variables D and E. Variables D and E, on the other hand, are highly correlated. This pattern suggests these five variables may be measuring only *two* different constructs; A, B, and C seem to measure aspects of one construct, whereas D and E measure something else. In the language of factor analysis, two **factors** underlie these data and account for the observed pattern of correlations among the variables.

Basics of Factor Analysis

Although identifying the factor structure may be relatively easy with a few variables, imagine trying to identify the factors in a data set that contained 20 or 30 or even 100 variables! Factor analysis identifies and expresses the factor structure using mathematical procedures, rather than by eyeballing the data as we have just done.

The mathematical details of factor analysis are complex and don't concern us here, but let us look briefly at how factor analyses are conducted. The grist for the factor analytic mill consists of correlations among a set of variables. Factor analysis attempts to identify the minimum number of factors, or dimensions, that will do a reasonably good job of accounting for the observed relationships among the variables. At one extreme, if all of the variables are highly correlated with one another, the analysis will identify a single factor; in essence, all the observed variables are measuring aspects of the same thing. At the other extreme, if the variables are totally uncorrelated, the analysis will identify as many factors as there are variables. This makes sense; if the variables are not at all related, there are no underlying factors that account for their interrelationships. Each variable is measuring something different, and there are as many factors as there are variables.

The solution to a factor analysis is presented in a **factor matrix**. Table 8.1 shows the factor matrix for the variables we examined in the preceding correlation matrix. Down the left column of the factor matrix are the original variables: A, B, C, D, and E. Across the top are the factors that have been identified from the analysis. The numerical entries in the table are **factor loadings,** which are the correlations of the variables with the factors. A variable that correlates with a factor is said to *load* on that factor. (Do not confuse these factor loadings with the correlations among the original set of variables.)

Researchers use these factor loadings to interpret and label the factors. By seeing which variables load on a factor, the researcher can usually identify the nature of a factor. In interpreting the factor structure, researchers typically consider the variables that load at least ±.30 with each factor. That is, they look at the variables that correlate at least ±.30 with a factor and try to discern what those variables have in common. By examining the variables that load on a factor, they can usually determine the nature of the underlying construct.

For example, as you can see in Table 8.1, variables A, B, and C each load greater than .30 on factor 1, whereas the factor loadings of variables D and E with

TABLE 8.1

A Factor Matrix

Variable	Factor	
	1	2
A	.97	−.04
B	.80	.04
C	.87	.00
D	.03	.93
E	−.01	.92

Explanation: This is the factor matrix for a factor analysis of the correlation matrix above. Two factors were obtained, suggesting these five variables measure two underlying factors. A researcher would interpret the factor matrix by looking at the variables that loaded highest on each factor. Factor 1 is defined by variables A, B, and C. Factor 2 is defined by variables D and E.

factor 1 are quite small. Factor 2, on the other hand, is defined primarily by variables D and E. This pattern indicates that variables A, B, and C reflect aspects of a single factor, whereas D and E reflect aspects of a different factor. In a real factor analysis, we would know what the original variables were measuring, and we would use that knowledge to identify and label the factors we obtained. For example, we might know that variables A, B, and C were all related to language and verbal ability, whereas variables D and E were measures of conceptual ability and reasoning. Thus, factor 1 would be a verbal ability factor and factor 2 would be a conceptual ability factor.

Uses of Factor Analysis

Factor analysis has two basic uses. First, it is used to study the underlying structure of psychological constructs. Many questions in behavioral science involve the structure of behavior and experience. How many distinct mental abilities are there? What are the basic traits that underlie human personality? What are the primary emotional expressions? What factors underlie job satisfaction? Factor analysis is used to answer such questions, thereby providing a framework for understanding behavioral phenomena. This use of factor analysis is portrayed in the accompanying case study, "Factor Analysis: The Five-Factor Model of Personality."

Researchers also use factor analysis to reduce a large number of variables to a smaller, more manageable set of data. Often, a researcher measures a large number of variables knowing these variables measure only a few basic constructs. For example, subjects may be asked to rate their current mood on 40 mood-relevant adjectives (such as happy, hostile, pleased, nervous). Of course, these do not reflect 40 distinct moods; instead, several items are used to measure each mood. So, a factor analysis may be performed to reduce these 40 scores to a small number of factors that reflect basic emotions. Once the factors are identified, common statistical procedures may be performed on the factors themselves rather than on the original items. Not only does this approach eliminate the redundancy involved in analyzing many measures of the same thing, but analyses of factors are usually more powerful and reliable than measures of individual items.

BEHAVIORAL RESEARCH CASE STUDY

FACTOR ANALYSIS: THE FIVE-FACTOR MODEL OF PERSONALITY

How many basic personality traits are there? Obviously, people differ on dozens, if not hundreds, of attributes, but presumably many of these variables are aspects of broader and more general traits. Factor analysis has been an indispensable tool in the search for the basic dimensions of personality. By factor analyzing people's ratings of themselves, researchers have been able to identify the basic dimensions of personality and see which specific traits load on these basic dimensions. In several studies of this nature, factor analyses have obtained five fundamental personality factors: extraversion, agreeableness, conscientiousness, emotional stability, and openness.

In a variation on this work, McCrae and Costa (1987) asked whether the same five factors would be obtained if we analyzed others' ratings of an individual rather than the individual's self-reports. Some 274 subjects were rated on 80 adjectives by a person who knew them well, such as a friend or co-worker. When these ratings were factor analyzed, five factors were obtained that closely mirrored the factors obtained when people's self-reports were analyzed.

A portion of the factor matrix is shown below. (Although the original matrix contained factor loadings for all 80 dependent variables, the portion of the matrix shown involves only 15 variables.) Recall that the factor loadings in the matrix are correlations between each item and the factors.

Based on the factor loadings, how would you interpret each of the five factors? Remember, factors are interpreted by looking for items that load at least ±.30 with a factor; in the table, factor loadings that meet this criterion are boldfaced.

	Factor				
Adjectives	I	II	III	IV	V
Calm–worrying	**.79**	.05	−.01	−.20	.05
At ease–nervous	**.77**	−.08	−.06	−.21	−.05
Relaxed–high-strung	**.66**	.04	.01	**−.34**	−.02
Retiring–sociable	−.14	**.71**	.08	.08	.08
Sober–fun-loving	−.08	**.59**	.12	.14	−.15
Aloof–friendly	−.16	**.58**	.02	**.45**	.06
Conventional–original	−.06	.12	**.67**	.08	−.04
Uncreative–creative	−.08	.03	**.56**	.11	.25
Simple–complex	.16	−.13	**.49**	−.20	.08
Irritable–good-natured	−.17	**.34**	.09	**.61**	.16
Ruthless–soft-hearted	.12	.27	.01	**.70**	.11
Selfish–selfless	−.07	−.02	.04	**.65**	.22
Negligent–conscientious	−.01	.02	.08	.18	**.68**
Careless–careful	−.08	−.07	−.01	.11	**.72**
Undependable–reliable	−.07	.04	.05	.23	**.68**

On the basis of their examination of the entire factor matrix, McCrae and Costa labeled five factors:

I　Neuroticism (worrying, nervous, high strung)

II　Extraversion (sociable, fun-loving, friendly, good-natured)

III　Openness (original, creative, complex)

IV   Agreeableness (friendly, good-natured, soft-hearted)

V   Conscientiousness (conscientious, careful, reliable)

These five factors, obtained from peers' ratings of subjects, closely mirror the five factors obtained from factor analyses of subjects' self-reports and lend further support to the five-factor model of personality.

Summary

1. Partial correlation is a procedure for statistically removing the influence of one or more variables (z) on the correlation between two other variables (x and y). If x and y are correlated even after the influence of z is removed, we have evidence for assuming the relationship between x and y is not caused by z. However, if removing the influence of z eliminates the correlation between x and y, we have reason to suspect their relationship is due to z (or to some variable that is associated with z).

2. Linear regression analysis is used to develop a regression equation for describing the relationships among variables that are correlated and for predicting subjects' scores on one variable based on their scores on other variables.

3. Multiple correlation expresses the strength of the relationship between one variable and a set of other variables.

4. Path analysis is a procedure for testing the plausibility of possible causal relationships among a set of correlated variables. The cross-lagged panel correlation design is a very simple variety of path analysis.

5. Factor analysis refers to a set of procedures for identifying the dimensions or factors that account for the observed relationships among a set of variables. A factor matrix shows the factor loadings for each underlying factor, which are the correlations between each variable and the factor. From this matrix, researchers can identify the basic factors in the data.

Key Terms

partial correlation

linear regression analysis

regression equation

dependent variable

criterion variable

predictor variable

regression constant

regression coefficient

multiple regression

multiple correlation coefficient

cross-lagged panel correlation design

path analysis

factor analysis

factor

factor matrix

factor loadings

Review Questions

1. Why do researchers use partial correlation?

2. Linear regression analysis is used for both descriptive and predictive purposes. Give an example of each.

3. What is the general form of a regression equation?

4. A regression equation is actually the equation for a straight line. When researchers calculate a regression equation, what line are they attempting to describe?

5. Interpret this regression equation: $y = 1.12 - .47x$

6. What is multiple regression?

7. When would you calculate a multiple correlation coefficient? What would you learn if you squared a multiple correlation?

8. Explain the basic rationale behind path analysis.

9. How does a cross-lagged panel correlation design provide evidence to support a casual link between two variables?

10. Why do researchers use factor analysis?

11. Imagine you conducted a factor analysis on a set of variables that were uncorrelated with one another. How many factors would you expect to find?

Questions for Thought and Discussion

1. Imagine you find that the correlation between variables x and y is $-.56$. You believe the relationship between x and y may be that they are both caused by variable z. You calculate the partial correlation between x and y, removing z, and obtain a partial correlation of $-.54$. What would you conclude?

2. What would you have concluded if the partial correlation were $-.02$? $-.35$?

3. In an exercise at the end of Chapter 7, you were asked to calculate the correlation between outside temperature and class attendance. The regression equation for the data in that exercise is

$$\text{Attendance} = 114.35 - .61 \text{ (temperature)}$$

Imagine the weather forecaster predicts that next Friday's temperature will be 82°F. How many students would you expect to attend class on that day?

4. Interpret the following factor matrix, which emerged from a factor analysis of mood ratings. Specifically, what do the three factors appear to be?

Mood rating	Factor 1	Factor 2	Factor 3
Happy	.07	.67	.03
Angry	.82	−.20	.11
Depressed	.12	−.55	.20
Nervous	.00	−.12	.67
Relaxed	.07	−.09	−.72

5. Researchers use partial correlation and path analysis to partially resolve the problems associated with inferring causality from correlation. Specifically, partial correlation addresses the possibility that the correlation is due to a third variable, and path analysis attempts to untangle the direction of the relationships among correlated variables. Even with partial correlation and path analysis, the causal inferences researchers draw must be considered only tentative and speculative. Explain why.

CHAPTER 9

Basic Issues in Experimental Research

Students in one of my courses once asked whether I would postpone for one week an exam that was scheduled for the next Monday. From my perspective as instructor, postponing the exam would have disrupted the course schedule, and I felt that delaying the test a week was too much to ask. So, I told them, "No, I think it would be better to have the test as scheduled." After a moment of silence, a student asked, "Well, if you won't postpone the test a week, will you postpone it at least until next Friday?" I was still reluctant, but finally agreed.

In retrospect, I think I was a victim of the "door-in-the-face" phenomenon. The door-in-the-face effect works like this: by first making an unreasonably large request, a person increases the probability that a second, smaller request will be granted. Refusing the students' request to postpone the test until Monday increased the chance that I would agree to postpone it until the preceding Friday.

This interesting phenomenon was studied by Robert Cialdini and his colleagues in a series of experiments (Cialdini, Vincent, Lewis, Catalan, Wheeler, & Darby, 1975). In one experiment, researchers approached people walking on the campus of Arizona State University and made one of three requests. Subjects in one group were first asked whether they would be willing to work as a nonpaid counselor for the County Juvenile Detention Center for two hours per week for two years. Not surprisingly, no one agreed to such an extreme request. However, after the subject has turned down this request, the researcher asked whether the subject would be willing to chaperone a group of children from the Juvenile Detention Center for a 2-hour trip to the zoo. Subjects in a second group were asked only the smaller request—to chaperone the trip to the zoo—without first being asked the more extreme request. For a third group of subjects, researchers described both the extreme and the small request, then asked subjects whether they would be willing to perform either one.

Which subjects should have been most likely to volunteer to chaperone the trip to the zoo? If the door-in-the-face effect occurred, they should have been the ones who first heard and rejected the extreme request. The results of the experiment are shown in Table 9.1. As you can see, compliance to the small request (going to the zoo) was greatest among subjects who had already turned down the extreme request. Fifty percent of the subjects in that condition agreed to go to the zoo—twice the number who complied after hearing both requests before responding (25%). In contrast, only 16.7% of those who were asked only the small request agreed to be a chaperone. In short, making an extreme request that was certain to be rejected increased the probability that the person would agree to the subsequent smaller request.

So far, we have discussed two general kinds of research in this book: descriptive and correlational. Descriptive and correlational studies are important, but they have a shortcoming when it comes to understanding behavior: they do not allow us to test directly hypotheses about the *causes* of behavior. Descriptive research allows us to describe how our subjects think, feel, and behave; and correlational research allows us to see whether certain variables are related to one another. Although both descriptive and correlational research provide hints about possible causes of behavior, we can never be sure from such studies that a particular variable does, in fact, cause changes in behavior. Experimental designs, on the other hand, allow researchers to draw conclusions about cause-and-effect relationships. Thus, when Cialdini and his colleagues wanted to know whether refusing an extreme request *causes* people to comply more frequently with a smaller request, they conducted an **experiment**.

Does the presence of other people at an emergency deter people from helping the victim? Does eating sugar increase children's hyperactivity and hamper their

TABLE 9.1

Results of the Door-in-the-Face Experiment

Experimental condition	Percentage of subjects who agreed to the small request
Large request, followed by small request	50.0
Small request only	16.7
Simultaneous requests	25.0

Source: From Reciprocal Concessions Procedure for Inducing Compliance: The Door-in-the-Face Technique by Cialdini, R. B., et al., 1975, *Journal of Personality and Social Psychology, 31*, pp. 206–215. Adapted with permission of Robert Cialdini.

school performance? Do stimulants affect the speed at which rats learn? Does observing cartoon violence cause children to behave more aggressively? Does making an extreme request cause people to comply with smaller requests? These kinds of questions about causality are ripe topics for experimental investigations. This chapter deals with the basic ingredients of a well-designed experiment. In Chapter 10, we will examine specific kinds of experimental designs, and in Chapters 11 and 12, we will discuss how the data from experimental designs are analyzed.

A well-designed experiment has three essential properties: (1) the researcher must *vary at least one independent variable* to assess its effects on subjects' behavior, (2) the researcher must have the power to *assign subjects to the various experimental conditions in a way that assures their initial equivalence,* and (3) the researcher must *control extraneous variables* that may influence subjects' behavior.

Manipulating the Independent Variable

The logic of experimentation stipulates that the researcher vary conditions under his or her control to assess the effects of those different conditions on subjects' behavior. By seeing how subjects' behavior varies with changes in the conditions controlled by the experimenter, we can then determine whether those variables affect subjects' behavior.

Independent Variables

In every experiment, the researcher varies or manipulates one or more **independent variables** to assess their effects on subjects' behavior. For example, a researcher interested in the effects of caffeine on memory would vary how much caffeine subjects receive in the study; some subjects might get capsules containing 100 milligrams (mg) of caffeine, some might get 300 mg, some 600 mg, and others might get capsules that contain no caffeine. After allowing time for the caffeine to enter the bloodstream, the subjects' memory for a list of words could be assessed. In this experiment the independent variable is the amount of caffeine subjects received.

An independent variable must have two or more **levels.** The levels refer to the different values of the independent variable. For example, the independent variable in the experiment just described had four levels: doses of 0, 100, 300, or 600 mg of caffeine. Often, researchers refer to the different levels of the independent variable as the experimental **conditions.** There were four conditions in this experiment; Cialdini's door-in-the-face experiment, on the other hand, had three experimental conditions (see Table 9.1).

Sometimes the levels of the independent variable involve *quantitative differences* in the independent variable. In the experiment on caffeine and memory, for example, the four levels of the independent variable reflect differences in the *quantity* of caffeine subjects received. In other experiments, the levels involve *qualitative differences* in the independent variable. In the experiment involving the door-in-the-face effect, subjects were treated qualitatively differently by being given different sequences of requests.

Types of independent variables.   Independent variables in behavioral research can be classified roughly into three types: environmental, instructional, and invasive. **Environmental manipulations** involve experimental modifications of the subject's physical or social environment. For example, a researcher interested in visual perception might vary the intensity of illumination; a researcher studying learning might manipulate the amount of reinforcement a pigeon receives; and an experimenter investigating attitude change might vary the characteristics of a persuasive message. In social and developmental psychology, **confederates**—researchers' accomplices who pose as other subjects or as uninvolved bystanders—are sometimes used to manipulate the subject's social environment.

Instructional manipulations vary the independent variable through the verbal instructions subjects receive. For example, subjects in a study of creativity may be given one of several different instructions for solving a particular task. In a study of how people's expectancies affect their performance, subjects may be led to expect that the task will be either easy or difficult.

Invasive manipulations involve creating physical changes in the subject's body through surgery or the administration of drugs. In studies that test the effects of chemicals on emotion and behavior, for example, the independent variable is often the amount of drug given to the subject. In physiological psychology, surgical procedures may be used to modify subjects' nervous systems to assess the effects of such changes on behavior.

BEHAVIORAL RESEARCH CASE STUDY

EMOTIONAL CONTAGION

Few experiments use all three types of independent variables we've described. One well-known piece of research that used environmental, instructional, and invasive independent variables in a single study was Schachter and Singer's (1962) classic experiment on emotion. This study was designed to test the hypothesis that emotions are affected by how people interpret their feelings of physiological arousal. According to this hypothesis, when people feel aroused, the precise emotion they experience will depend on what they think caused them to become emotionally aroused.

In this study, subjects received an injection of either epinephrine (which causes a state of physiological arousal) or an inactive placebo (which had no physiological effect). Subjects who received the epinephrine injection then received one of three explanations about the effect of the injection. Some subjects were accurately informed that the injection would cause short-lived changes in arousal such as shaking hands and increased heart rate. Other subjects were misinformed about the effects of the injection, being told either that the injection would cause (among other things) numbness and itching or that it would have no effect at all.

Subjects then waited for the injection to have an effect in a room with a confederate who posed as another subject. This confederate was trained to behave in either a playful, euphoric manner or an upset, angry manner. Subjects were observed during this time, and they completed self-report measures of their mood as well.

Results of the study showed that subjects who were misinformed about the effects of the epinephrine injection (believing it would either cause numbness or have no effects at all) tended to adopt the mood of the happy or angry confederate. In contrast, those who received the placebo or who were accurately informed about the effects of the epinephrine injection showed no emotional contagion.

The researchers interpreted this pattern of results in terms of differences in how subjects interpreted their feelings. Subjects who received an injection of epinephrine but did not know that the injection caused their arousal seemed to infer that their feelings were affected by the confederate's behavior. As a result, when the confederate was happy, they inferred that he was causing them to feel happy, whereas when he was angry, they labeled their feelings as anger. Subjects who knew the injection caused physiological changes, on the other hand, attributed their feelings to the injection rather than to the confederate and, thus, showed no mood change. Those who received the placebo did not feel aroused at all.

As you can see, this experiment involved an invasive independent variable (injection of epinephrine versus placebo), an instructional independent variable (information that the injection would cause arousal, numbness, or no effect), and an environmental independent variable (the confederate's behavior).

Experimental and control groups. In some experiments, one level of the independent variable involves the absence of the variable of interest. In the caffeine-and-memory study, some subjects received doses of caffeine, whereas other subjects received no caffeine at all. Subjects who receive a nonzero level of the independent variable compose the **experimental group,** and those who receive a zero level of the independent variable make up the **control group.** In this study, there were three experimental groups (subjects who received 100, 300, or 600 mg of caffeine) and one control group (subjects who received no caffeine).

Although control groups are useful in many experimental investigations, they are not always necessary. For example, if a researcher is interested in the effects of audience size on performers' stage fright, she may have subjects perform in front of audiences of 1, 3, or 9 people. In this example, there is no control group in which subjects perform without an audience. The door-in-the-face study also had no control group—one in which some subjects did not receive any sort of request.

Researchers must decide whether a control group will help them interpret the results of a particular study. Control groups are particularly important when the researcher wants to know the *baseline* level of a behavior. For example, if we are interested in the effects of caffeine on memory, we would probably want a control group to determine how well subjects remember words when they do not have any caffeine in their systems.

Assessing the impact of independent variables.

Many experiments fail not because the hypotheses being tested are incorrect but because the independent variable was not manipulated successfully. If the independent variable is not *strong enough* to produce the predicted effects, the study is doomed from the outset.

Imagine, for example, you are studying whether the brightness of lighting affects people's work performance. You conduct an experiment in which some subjects work at a desk illuminated by a 75-watt light bulb and others work at a desk illuminated by a 100-watt bulb. Although you have experimentally manipulated the brightness of the lighting, we might guess that the difference in brightness between the two conditions is not great enough to produce any detectable effects on behavior. In fact, subjects in the two conditions may not even perceive the amount of lighting as noticeably different.

Researchers often **pilot test** the levels of the independent variable they plan to use, trying them out on a handful of subjects before actually starting the experiment. The purpose of pilot testing is not to see whether the independent variable produces hypothesized effects on behavior (that's for the experiment itself to determine) but to ensure that the levels of the independent variable are different enough to be detected by subjects. If we are studying the effects of lighting on work performance, we could try out different levels of brightness to find out what levels of lighting pilot subjects perceive as dim versus adequate versus blinding.

In addition, during the experiment itself, researchers often use manipulation checks. A **manipulation check** is a question (or set of questions) designed to determine whether the independent variable was manipulated successfully. For example, we might ask subjects to rate the brightness of the lighting in the experiment. If subjects in the various experimental conditions rate the brightness of the lights differently, we would know that the difference in brightness was perceptible. However, if subjects in different conditions did not rate the brightness of the lighting differently, we would question whether the independent variable was successfully manipulated. If we obtained the latter result, our findings regarding the effects of brightness on work performance would be suspect.

Dependent Variables

In an experiment, the researcher is interested in the effect of the independent variable on one or more **dependent variables.** A dependent variable is the response being measured in the study. In behavioral research, this is typically a measure of subjects' thoughts, feelings, overt behavior, or physiological reactions. In the experiment involving caffeine, the dependent variable might involve how many words subjects remember. In Cialdini's study of the door-in-the-face phenomenon, the dependent variable was whether the subject agreed to chaperone the trip to the zoo. Most experiments have several dependent variables because few researchers are willing to expend the effort needed to conduct an experiment and collect data regarding only one behavior.

IDENTIFYING INDEPENDENT AND DEPENDENT VARIABLES

Are you a good or a poor speller? Research suggests that previous experience with misspelled words can undermine a person's ability to spell a word correctly. For example, teachers report they sometimes become confused about the correct spelling of certain words after grading the spelling tests of poor spellers.

To study this effect, Brown (1988) conducted an experiment using 44 university students. In the first phase of the study, the subjects took a spelling test of 26 commonly misspelled words (such as *adolescence, convenience,* and *vacuum*). Then, half the subjects were told to purposely generate two incorrect spellings for 13 of these words. (For example, a subject might write *vacume* and *vaccum* for *vacuum*.) The other half of the subjects were not asked to generate misspellings; rather, they performed an unrelated task. Finally, all subjects took another test of the same 26 words but presented in a different order.

As Brown had predicted, subjects who generated the incorrect spellings subsequently switched from correct to incorrect spellings on the final test at a significantly higher frequency than subjects who performed the unrelated task.

1. What was the independent variable in this experiment?
2. How many levels did it have?
3. How many conditions were there, and what were they?
4. What did subjects in the experimental group(s) do?
5. Was there a control group?
6. What was the dependent variable?

(Answers to these questions appear at the end of the chapter.)

Assigning Subjects to Conditions

We've seen that, in an experiment, subjects in different conditions receive different levels of the independent variable. At the end of the experiment, the responses of subjects in the various experimental and control groups are compared to see whether there is any evidence that their behavior was affected by the manipulation of the independent variable.

Such a strategy for testing the effects of independent variables on behavior makes sense only if we can assume our groups of subjects were roughly equivalent at the beginning of the study. If we see differences in the behavior of subjects in various experimental conditions at the end of the experiment, we want to have confidence that these differences were produced by the independent variable. The possibility exists, however, that the differences we observe at the end of the study are due to the fact that the groups of subjects differed at the *start* of the experiment, before they received one level or another of the independent variable.

For example, in our study of caffeine and memory, perhaps the subjects in the group receiving no caffeine were, on the average, simply more intelligent than subjects in the other groups, and thus they remembered more words. For the results of the experiment to be interpretable, we must be able to assume that subjects in our various experimental groups did not differ from one another before the experiment began. We would want to be sure, for example, that subjects in the four experimental conditions did not differ markedly in average intelligence as a group. Thus, an essential ingredient for every experiment is that the researcher take steps to ensure the initial equivalence of the groups prior to the introduction of the independent variable.

Simple Random Assignment

The easiest way to be sure experimental groups are roughly equivalent before manipulating the independent variable is to use a procedure known as **simple random assignment.** Simple random assignment involves placing subjects in conditions in such a way that every subject has an equal probability of being placed in any experimental condition. For example, if we had an experiment with only two conditions—the simplest possible experiment—we could flip a coin to assign each subject to one of the two groups. If the coin came up heads, the subject would be assigned to one experimental group; if it came up tails, the subject would be placed in the other experimental group. If we had an experiment with more than two groups, we could write the names of the experimental conditions on slips of paper, then randomly choose one slip to determine the condition in which each subject should be placed.

Random assignment ensures that, on the average, subjects in the groups do not differ. No matter what personal attribute we might consider, subjects with that attribute have an equal probability of being assigned to both groups. So, on average, the groups should be equivalent in intelligence, personality, age, attitudes, appearance, self-confidence, anxiety, and so on.

Matched Random Assignment

Research shows that simple random assignment is very effective in equating experimental groups at the start of an experiment, particularly if the number of subjects assigned to each experimental condition is sufficiently large. However, researchers sometimes try to increase the similarity among the experimental groups even further by using **matched random assignment.** When matched random assignment is used, the researcher obtains subjects' scores on a measure known to be relevant to the outcome of the experiment. Typically, this matching variable is a pretest measure of the dependent variable: for example, if we were doing an experiment on the effects of a counseling technique on math anxiety, we could pretest our subjects using a math anxiety scale. Subjects are then ranked on this measure from highest to lowest, and the researcher matches subjects by putting them in clusters, or blocks, of size k, where k is the number of conditions in the experiment. The first k subjects with the highest scores are matched together into a cluster, the next k subjects are matched together, and so on. Then, the researcher randomly assigns the k subjects in each cluster to each of the experimental conditions. For obvious reasons, an experiment that involves matched random assignment is called a **matched-subjects design.**

For example, assume we wanted to use matched random assignment in our study of caffeine and memory. We might obtain pretest scores on a memory test for 40 individuals, then rank these 40 subjects from highest to lowest. Because our study has four conditions, $k = 4$. We would take the four subjects with the highest memory scores and randomly assign each subject to one of the four conditions (0, 100, 300, or 600 mg of caffeine). We would then take the four subjects with the next highest scores and randomly assign each to one of the conditions, followed by the next block of four subjects, and so on until all 40 subjects were assigned to an experimental condition. This procedure ensures that each experimental condition contains subjects who possess comparable levels of memory ability.

Repeated Measures Designs

When different subjects are assigned to each of the conditions in an experiment, as in simple and matched random assignment, the design is called a **randomized groups design.** This kind of study is also sometimes called a **between-subjects,** or **between-groups, design** because we are interested in differences in behavior *between* different groups of subjects.

In some studies, however, a single group of subjects serves in all conditions of the experiment. For example, rather than randomly assigning subjects into four groups, each of which receives one of four dosages of caffeine, a researcher may test a single group of subjects under each of the four dosage levels. Such an experiment uses a **within-subjects design,** in which we are interested in differences in behavior across conditions within a single group of subjects. This is also commonly called a **repeated measures design** because each subject is measured more than once.

Using a within-subjects, or repeated measures, design eliminates the need for random assignment because every subject is tested under every level of the independent variable. What better way is there to be sure the groups do not differ than to use the same subjects in every experimental condition? In essence, each subject in a repeated measures design serves as his or her own control.

Advantages of within-subjects designs.   The primary advantage of a within-subjects design is that it is more *powerful* than a between-subjects design. In statistical terminology, the **power** of a research design refers to its ability to detect effects of the independent variable. Powerful designs are able to detect effects of the independent variable more easily than less powerful designs.

Within-subjects designs are more powerful because the subjects in all experimental conditions are identical in every way (after all, they are the same subjects). When this is the case, none of the observed differences in responses to the various conditions can be due to preexisting differences between subjects in the groups. Because we have repeated measures on every subject, we can more easily detect the effects of the independent variable on subjects' behavior. A second advantage of within-subjects designs in that they require fewer subjects. Because each subject is used in every condition, fewer are needed.

Disadvantages of within-subjects designs.   Despite their advantages, within-subjects designs create some special problems. The first involves **order effects.** Because each subject receives all levels of the independent variable, the possibility arises that the order in which the levels are received affects subjects' behavior.

For example, imagine that all subjects in our memory study are first tested with no caffeine, then with 100, 300, and 600 mg (in that order). Because of the opportunity to practice memorizing lists of words, subjects' performance may improve as the experiment progresses. Because all subjects receive increasingly higher doses of caffeine during the study, it may appear that their memory is best when they receive 600 mg of caffeine when, in fact, their memory may have improved as the result of practice alone.

To guard against the possibility of order effects, researchers use **counterbalancing,** which involves presenting the levels of the independent variable in different orders to different subjects. When feasible, all possible orders are used. In the caffeine-and-memory study, for example, there were 24 possible orders in which the levels of the independent variable could be presented:

	Order			
	1st	*2nd*	*3rd*	*4th*
1	0 mg	100 mg	300 mg	600 mg
2	0 mg	100 mg	600 mg	300 mg

| | **Order** | | | |
	1st	**2nd**	**3rd**	**4th**
3	0 mg	300 mg	100 mg	600 mg
4	0 mg	300 mg	600 mg	100 mg
5	0 mg	600 mg	100 mg	300 mg
6	0 mg	600 mg	300 mg	100 mg
7	100 mg	0 mg	300 mg	600 mg
8	100 mg	0 mg	600 mg	300 mg
9	100 mg	300 mg	0 mg	600 mg
10	100 mg	300 mg	600 mg	0 mg
11	100 mg	600 mg	0 mg	300 mg
12	100 mg	600 mg	300 mg	0 mg
13	300 mg	0 mg	100 mg	600 mg
14	300 mg	0 mg	600 mg	100 mg
15	300 mg	100 mg	0 mg	600 mg
16	300 mg	100 mg	600 mg	0 mg
17	300 mg	600 mg	0 mg	100 mg
18	300 mg	600 mg	100 mg	0 mg
19	600 mg	0 mg	100 mg	300 mg
20	600 mg	0 mg	300 mg	100 mg
21	600 mg	100 mg	0 mg	300 mg
22	600 mg	100 mg	300 mg	0 mg
23	600 mg	300 mg	0 mg	100 mg
24	600 mg	300 mg	100 mg	0 mg

If you look closely, you'll see that all possible orders of the four conditions are listed. Furthermore, every level of the independent variable appears in each order position an equal number of times.

Complete counterbalancing becomes unwieldy, however, when the number of conditions is large because of the sheer number of possible orders. Instead, researchers often randomly choose a smaller subset of these possible orderings. For example, a researcher might randomly choose orders 2, 7, 9, 14, 19, and 21 from the whole set of 24, then assign each subject randomly to one of these 6 orders.

Even when counterbalancing is used, the results of a repeated measures experiment can be affected by **carryover effects.** Carryover effects occur when the effects of one level of the independent variable are still present when another level of the independent variable is introduced. In the experiment involving caffeine, for example, a researcher would have to be sure that the caffeine from one dosage has worn off before giving subjects a different dosage.

BEHAVIORAL RESEARCH CASE STUDY

A WITHIN-SUBJECTS DESIGN: SUGAR AND BEHAVIOR

Parents and teachers have become increasingly concerned in recent years about the effects of sugar on children's behavior. The popular view is that excessive sugar consumption results in behavioral problems ranging from mild irritability to hyperactivity and attention disturbances. Interestingly, few studies have tested the effects of sugar on behavior, and those that have studied its effects have obtained inconsistent findings.

Against this backdrop of confusion, Rosen, Booth, Bender, McGrath, Sorrell, and Drabman (1988) used a within-subjects design to examine the effects of sugar on 45 preschool and elementary school children. All 45 subjects served in each of 3 experimental conditions. In the high-sugar condition, the children drank an orange-flavored breakfast drink that contained 50 grams (g) of sucrose (approximately equal to the sucrose in two candy bars). In the low-sugar condition, the drink contained only 6.25 g of sucrose. And in the control group, the drink contained aspartame (Nutrasweet), an artificial sweetener. Each child was tested five times in each of the three conditions. Each morning for 15 days each child drank a beverage containing 0, 6.25, or 50 g of sucrose. To minimize order effects, the order in which subjects participated in each condition was randomized across those 15 days.

Several dependent variables were measured. Subjects were tested on several measures of cognitive and intellectual functioning. In addition, their teachers (who did not know what each child drank) rated each student's behavior every morning. Observational measures were also taken of behaviors that may be affected by sugar, such as activity level, aggression, and fidgeting.

The results showed that high amounts of sugar caused a slight increase in activity, as well as a slight decrease in cognitive performance for girls. Contrary to the popular view, however, the effects of even excessive consumption of sugar were quite small in magnitude. The authors concluded that "the results did not support the view that sugar causes major changes in children's behavior" (Rosen et al., 1988, p. 583). Interestingly, parents' expectations about the effects of sugar on their child were uncorrelated with the actual effects. Apparently, parents often attribute their children's misbehavior to excessive sugar when sugar is not really the culprit.

Experimental Control

The third critical ingredient of a good experiment is **experimental control.** Experimental control refers to eliminating or holding constant extraneous factors that might affect the outcome of the study. If the effects of such factors are not eliminated, it will be difficult, if not impossible, to determine whether the independent variable had an effect on subjects' responses.

Systematic Variance

To understand why experimental control is important, let's return to the concept of variance. You will recall from Chapter 2 that variance is an index of how much subjects' scores differ or vary from one another. Furthermore, you may recall that the total variance in a set of data can be broken into two components: systematic variance and error variance.

In the context of an experiment, **systematic variance** (often called **between-groups variance**) is that part of the total variance that reflects differences among the experimental groups. The question to be addressed in any experiment is whether any of the total variability we observe in subjects' scores is systematic variance due to the independent variable. If the independent variable affected subjects' responses, then we should find that some of the variability in subjects' scores is associated with the manipulation of the independent variable.

Put differently, if the independent variable had an effect on behavior, we should observe *systematic differences* between the scores in the various experimental conditions. If scores differ systematically between conditions—if subjects remember more words in some experimental groups than in others, for example—systematic variance exists in the scores. This systematic, or between-groups, variability in the scores may come from two sources: the independent variable (in which case it is called treatment variance) and extraneous variables (in which case it is called confound variance).

Treatment variance. The portion of the variance in subjects' scores that is due to the independent variable is called **treatment variance** (or sometimes **primary variance**). If nothing other than the independent variable affected subjects' responses in an experiment, then all the variance in the data would be treatment variance. This is rarely the case, however. As we will see, subjects' scores typically vary for other reasons as well. Specifically, we can identify two other sources of variability in subjects' scores: confound variance (which we must eliminate from the study) and error variance (which we must minimize).

Confound variance. Ideally, all subjects in the various experimental conditions should be treated in precisely the same way, other than the fact that subjects in different conditions receive different levels of the independent variable. The only thing that may differ between the conditions is the independent variable. Only if this is so can we conclude that changes in the dependent variable were caused by manipulation of the independent variable.

Unfortunately, researchers sometimes design faulty experiments in which something other than the independent variable differs among the conditions. For example, if, in a study of the effects of caffeine on memory, all subjects who received 600 mg of caffeine were tested at 9:00 A.M. and all subjects who received no caffeine were tested at 3:00 P.M., the groups would differ not only in how much caffeine they received but also in the time at which they participated in the study. In this experiment, we would be unable to tell whether differences in memory between the groups were due to the ingestion of caffeine or the time of day.

When a variable other than the independent variable differs between the groups, **confound variance** is produced. Confound variance, which is sometimes called **secondary variance,** is that portion of the variance in subjects' scores that is due to extraneous variables that differ systematically between the experimental groups.

Confound variance must be eliminated at all costs, and the reason is clear: it is impossible for researchers to distinguish treatment variance from confound variance. Although we can easily determine how much systematic variance is present in our data, we cannot tell how much of the systematic variance is treatment variance and how much, if any, is confound variance. As a result, the researcher will find it impossible to tell whether differences in the dependent variable between conditions were due to the independent variable or to this unwanted, confounding variable. As we'll discuss in detail later in the chapter, confound variance is eliminated through careful experimental control in which all factors other than the independent variable are held constant or allowed to vary nonsystematically between the experimental conditions.

Error Variance

Recall that **error variance** (also called **within-groups variance**) is the result of *unsystematic* differences among subjects. Not only do subjects differ at the time they enter the experiment in terms of ability, personality, mood, past history, and so on, but also chances are the experimenter will treat individual subjects in slightly different ways. In addition, measurement error contributes to error variance by introducing random variability into the data (see Chapter 2).

In our study of caffeine and memory, we would expect to see differences in the number of words recalled by subjects who were in the same experimental condition; not all the subjects in a particular experimental condition will remember precisely the same number of words. This variability in scores within an experimental condition is not due to the independent variable, because all subjects in a particular condition receive the same level of the independent variable. Nor is this within-groups variance due to confounding variables, because all subjects within a group would experience the same confound. Rather, this variability—the error variance—is due to (1) individual differences among subjects within the group, (2) random variations in the experimental setting and procedure (time of testing, weather, researcher's mood, and so forth), and (3) other unsystematic influences. Similarly, in the study of the door-in-the-face phenomenon, various extraneous factors that had nothing to do with the independent variable likely affected subjects' willingness to chaperone the trip to the zoo. For example, the subjects undoubtedly differed in how busy they were as well as in their general willingness to be helpful, and the researcher would have found it impossible to approach each subject in precisely the same way.

Unlike confound variance, error variance does not invalidate an experiment, because there are statistical ways to distinguish between treatment variance (due to the independent variable) and error variance (due to unsystematic extraneous variables). Even so, the more error variance, the more difficult it is to detect effects of the independent variable. For this reason, researchers take steps to control the sources of error variance in an experiment, although they recognize that error variance will seldom be eliminated. We'll return to the problem of error variance later.

An Analogy

To summarize, the total variance in subjects' scores at the end of an experiment may comprise three components:

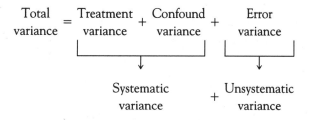

Together, the treatment and confound variance constitute systematic variance (creating systematic differences among experimental conditions), and the error variance is unsystematic variability within the various conditions.

In an ideal experiment, researchers maximize the treatment variance, eliminate confound variance, and minimize error variance. We can illustrate with the analogy of watching television. When you watch television, the image on the screen constantly varies or changes. In the terminology we have been using, there is *variance* in the picture. Three sets of factors can affect the image on the screen. The first is the signal being sent from the transmitting tower of the television station. This, of course, is the only source of image variance you're really interested in when you watch TV. Ideally, you would like the image on the screen to change only as a function of the signal being received from the station. Systematic changes in the picture due to changes in the signal from the TV station are analogous to treatment variance due to the independent variable.

Unfortunately, the picture on the tube may be altered in one of two ways. First, the picture may be systematically altered by images other than those of the program you want to watch. Perhaps "ghost figures" from another channel interfere with the image on the screen. This interference is much like confound variance because it distorts the primary image in a *systematic* fashion. In fact, depending on what you were watching, you might have difficulty distinguishing which images were from the program you wanted to watch and which were from the interfering signal. That is, you might not be able to distinguish the true signal (treatment variance) from the interference (confound variance).

The primary signal can also be weakened by static, fuzz, or "snow." Static produces *unsystematic* changes in the TV picture; it dilutes the image without actually distorting it. If the static is extreme enough, you may not be able to recognize the real picture at all. Similarly, error variance in an experiment clouds the signal produced by the independent variable.

To fully enjoy TV, you want to have the primary signal as strong as possible, to eliminate systematic distortions entirely, and to have as little static as possible. Only then will the true program come through loud and clear. In an analogous fashion, researchers want to maximize treatment variance, eliminate confound variance, and reduce error variance. The remainder of this chapter deals with the ways researchers use experimental control to eliminate confound variance and minimize error variance.

Eliminating Confounding

Internal Validity

At the end of every experiment, we would like to have confidence that any differences we observe between the experimental and the control groups resulted from our manipulation of the independent variable rather than from extraneous variables. **Internal validity** is the degree to which a researcher draws accurate conclusions about the effects of the independent variable. An experiment is internally valid when it eliminates all potential sources of confound variance. When an experiment has internal validity, a researcher can confidently conclude that observed differences were due to variation in the independent variable.

To a large extent, internal validity is achieved through experimental control. The logic of experimentation requires that nothing other than the independent variable can differ systematically between the experimental conditions. If something other than the independent variable differs in some systematic way, we say that **confounding** has occurred. When confounding occurs, there is no way to know whether the results were due to the independent variable or to the confound. Confounding is a fatal flaw in experimental designs, one that typically makes the findings worthless. As a result, possible threats to internal validity must be eliminated at all costs.

One well-publicized example of confounding involved the "Pepsi Challenge" (see Huck & Sandler, 1979). The Pepsi Challenge was a taste test in which people were asked to taste two cola beverages and indicate which they preferred. As the test was originally designed, glasses of Pepsi were always marked with a letter M, and glasses of Coca-Cola were marked with a Q. People seemed to prefer Pepsi over Coke in these tests, but a confound was present. Do you see it? The letter on the glass was confounded with the beverage in it. Thus, we don't know for certain whether people's preference was for Pepsi over Coke or for M over Q. As absurd as this possibility may sound, later tests demonstrated that subjects' preferences *were* affected by the letter on the glass. No matter which cola was in which glass, people tended to indicate a preference for the drink marked M over that marked Q.

Before discussing some common threats to the internal validity of experiments, see whether you can find the threat to internal validity in the hypothetical experiment described in the following box.

DEVELOPING YOUR RESEARCH SKILLS

CONFOUNDING: CAN YOU FIND IT?

A researcher was interested in how people's perceptions of others are affected by the presence of a physical handicap. Research suggests that people may rate those with physical disabilities less positively than those without disabilities. Because of the potential implications of this bias for job discrimination against disabled persons, the researcher wanted to see whether subjects exhibited this bias.

Each subject was asked to play the role of an employer who wanted to hire a computer programmer, a job in which physical disability is largely irrelevant. Subjects were shown one of two sets of bogus job application materials prepared in advance by the experimenter. Both sets of application materials included precisely the same information about the applicant's qualifications and background (such as college grades, extracurricular activities, test scores, and so on.) The only difference in the two sets of materials involved the photograph attached to the application. In one picture the applicant was shown seated in a wheelchair, thereby making his disability obvious to subjects. The other photograph did not show that he was disabled; in this picture, only his head and shoulders were shown. Other than the degree to which the applicant's disability was apparent, the content of the two applications was identical in every respect.

In the experiment, 20 subjects saw the photo in which the disability was apparent, and 20 subjects saw the photo in which the applicant did not appear disabled. Subjects were randomly assigned to one of these two experimental conditions. After viewing the application materials, including the photograph, each subject completed a questionnaire on which he or she rated the applicant on several dimensions. For example, subjects were asked how qualified the applicant was for the job, how much they liked the applicant, and whether they would hire him.

1. What was the independent variable in this experiment?

2. What was the dependent variable?

3. The researcher made a critical error in designing this experiment, one that introduced confounding and compromised the internal validity of the study. Can you find the researcher's mistake?

4. How would you design the experiment differently to eliminate this problem?

(Answers to these questions appear at the end of the chapter.)

Threats to Internal Validity

The reason threats to internal validity, such as in the Pepsi Challenge taste test, are so bad is that they introduce alternative rival explanations for the results of a study. Instead of confidently concluding that differences among the conditions are due to the independent variable, the researcher must concede that there are alternative explanations for the results. When this happens, the results are highly suspect, and no one is likely to take them seriously. Although it would be impossible to list all potential threats to internal validity, a few of the more common threats are discussed below.

Biased assignment of subjects to conditions.   We've already discussed one common threat to internal validity. If the experimental conditions were not equated before subjects received the independent variable, the researcher may conclude that the independent variable caused differences between the groups when, in fact, those differences were due to **biased assignment.** Biased assignment of subjects to conditions (which is often referred to as the *selection threat* to internal validity) introduces the possibility that the effects were due to nonequivalent groups rather than to the independent variable. We've seen that this problem is eliminated through simple or matched random assignment or use of within-subjects designs.

This confound poses a problem for research that compares the effects of an independent variable on preexisting groups of subjects. For example, if a researcher were interested in the effects of a particular curricular innovation in elementary schools, he or she may want to compare students in a school that used the innovative curriculum with those in a school that used a traditional curriculum. But, because the students were not randomly assigned to one school or the other, the groups differ in many ways other than in the curriculum being used. As a result, the study possesses no internal validity, and no conclusions can be drawn about the effects of the curriculum.

Experimental confounds.   Ideally, every subject in an experiment should be treated in precisely the same way, except that subjects in different conditions will receive different levels of the independent variable. Of course, it is virtually impossible to treat each subject exactly the same. Even so, it is essential that no *systematic* differences be imposed other than the different levels of the independent variable. When subjects in one experimental condition are treated differently than those in another condition, confounding destroys our ability to identify effects of the independent variable and introduces an alternative rival explanation of the results. The study involving reactions to disabled job applicants provides a good example of an experimental confound, as does the case of the Pepsi Challenge.

Differential attrition.   Attrition refers to the loss of subjects during a study. For example, some subjects may be unwilling to complete the experiment because they find the procedures painful, difficult, objectionable, or embarrassing. In medical research and in some animal studies (but rarely in human behavioral research), attrition may occur because some subjects die.

When attrition occurs in a random fashion and affects all experimental conditions equally, it is only a minor threat to internal validity. However, when the rate of attrition differs across the experimental conditions—a condition known as **differential attrition**—internal validity is weakened. If attrition occurs at a different rate in different conditions, the independent variable may have caused the loss of subjects. The consequence is that the experimental groups are no longer equivalent; differential attrition has destroyed the benefits of random assignment.

For example, suppose we are interested in the effects of physical stressors on intellectual performance. To induce physical stress, subjects in the experimental group will be asked to immerse their right arm to the shoulder in a container of ice water for 15 minutes, a procedure that is painful but not damaging. Subjects in the control condition will put their arms in water that is at room temperature. While their arms are immersed, subjects in both groups will complete a set of mental tasks. For ethical reasons, we must give subjects the choice of whether or not to participate in this study. Let's assume, however, that whereas all of the subjects who were randomly assigned to the room-temperature condition agree to participate, 15% of those assigned to the experimental, ice-water condition decline. Differential attrition has occurred and the two groups are no longer equivalent.

If we assume that subjects who dropped out of the ice-water condition were more fearful than those who remained, then the average subject who remains in the ice-water condition is probably less fearful than the average subject in the room-temperature condition, creating a potential bias. If we find a difference in performance between the two conditions, how do we know whether the difference is due to differences in stress or to differences in the characteristics of the subjects who agreed to participate in the two conditions?

Pretest sensitization. In some experiments, subjects are pretested to obtain a measure of their behavior before receiving the independent variable. Although pretests provide useful baseline data, they have a drawback. Taking a pretest may sensitize subjects to the independent variable so that they react differently to the independent variable than they would have had they not been pretested. When **pretest sensitization** occurs, the researcher may conclude that the independent variable had an effect when, in reality, the effect was a combined result of the pretest and the independent variable.

For example, imagine a teacher has designed a program to raise students' degree of cultural literacy—their knowledge of common facts known by most literate, educated people within a particular culture (for example, what significant event occurred in 1492 or who Thomas Edison was). To test the effectiveness of this program, the teacher administers a pretest of such knowledge to 100 students. Fifty of these students then participate in a 2-week course designed to increase their cultural literacy, whereas the remaining 50 students take another course. Both groups are then tested again, using the same test they completed during the pretest.

Assume the teacher finds that students who took the cultural-literacy course showed a significantly greater increase in knowledge than students in the control group. Was the course responsible for this change? Possibly, but pretest sensitization may also have been involved. When students took the pretest, they undoubtedly encountered questions they couldn't answer. When this material was covered during the course itself, they may have been more attentive to it *because of their experience on the pretest*. As a result, they learned more than they would have had they not taken the pretest. Thus, the pretest sensitized them to the experimental treatment and thereby affected the results of the study.

When researchers are concerned about pretest sensitization, they sometimes design their study so that some subjects take the pretest and other subjects do not. If the subjects who were pretested respond differently in one or more experimental conditions than those who were not pretested, pretest sensitization has occurred.

History. The results of some studies are affected by extraneous events that occur outside the research setting. As a result, the obtained effects are due not to the independent variable itself but to an interaction of the independent variable and **history effects.**

For example, imagine we are interested in the effects of filmed aggression toward women on attitudes toward sexual aggression. Subjects in one group watch a 30-minute movie that contains a realistic depiction of rape, whereas subjects in another group watch a film about wildlife conservation. We then measure both groups' attitudes toward sexual aggression. Now, suppose a female student had been sexually assaulted on campus the week before we conducted the study. It is possible that subjects who viewed the aggressive movie would be reminded of the attack and that their subsequent attitudes would be affected by the *combination* of the film and their thoughts about the campus assault. That is, the movie may have produced a different effect on attitudes given the fact that a real rape had occurred recently. Subjects who watched the wildlife film, however, would not be prompted to think about rape for 30 minutes. Thus, differences we obtain between the two groups could be due to this interaction of history (the real assault) and treatment (the film).

Maturation. In addition to possible outside influences, changes within the subjects themselves can create confounds. If the experiment occurs over a long span of time, for example, developmental **maturation** may occur in which subjects go through age-related changes. If this occurs, we don't know whether the differences we observe between experimental conditions are due to the independent variable or to the independent variable in combination with age-related changes. Obviously, maturation is more likely to be a problem in research involving children.

These by no means exhaust all the factors that can compromise the internal validity of an experiment, but they should give you a feel for unwanted influences that can undermine the results of experimental studies. When critiquing the quality of an experiment, ask yourself, "Did the experimental conditions differ systematically in any way other than the fact that they received different levels of the independent variable?" If so, confounding may have occurred.

Experimenter Expectancies, Demand Characteristics, and Placebo Effects

The validity of researchers' interpretations of the results of a study are also affected by the researchers' and subjects' beliefs about what *should* happen in the experiment. In this section, I'll discuss three potential problems in which people's expectations affect the outcome of an experiment: experimenter expectancies, demand characteristics, and placebo effects.

Experimenter expectancies. Researchers usually have some preconceived idea about how subjects will respond. Indeed, they usually have an explicit hypothesis regarding the results of the study. Unfortunately, experimenters' expectations can distort the results of an experiment by affecting how they interpret subjects' behavior.

A good example of the **experimenter expectancy effect** (sometimes called the **Rosenthal effect**) is provided in a study by Cordaro and Ison (1963). In this experiment, psychology students were taught to classically condition a simple response in planaria (flatworms). Some students were told that the planaria had been previously conditioned and should show a high rate of response. Other students were told that the planaria had not been conditioned; thus they thought their worms would show a low rate of response. In reality, both groups of students worked with identical planaria. Despite the fact that their planaria did not differ in responsiveness, the students who expected responsive planaria recorded 20 times more responses than the students who expected unresponsive planaria!

Did the student experimenters in this study intentionally distort their observations? Perhaps, but it's more likely their observations were affected by their expectations. People's interpretations are often affected by their beliefs and expectations; people often see what they expect to see. Whether such effects involve intentional distortion or an unconscious bias, experimenters' expectancies may affect their perceptions, thereby compromising the validity of an experiment.

Demand characteristics. Subjects' assumptions about the nature of a study can also affect the outcome of research. If you have ever participated in research as a subject, you probably tried to figure out what the study was about and how the researcher expected you to respond.

Demand characteristics are aspects of a study that indicate to subjects how they should behave. Because many people want to be good subjects who do what the experimenter wishes, their behavior is affected by demand characteristics rather than by the independent variable itself. In some cases, experimenters unintentionally communicate their expectations in subtle ways that affect subjects' behavior. In other instances, subjects draw assumptions about the study from the experimental setting and procedure.

A good demonstration of demand characteristics was provided by Orne and Scheibe (1964). These researchers told subjects they were participating in a study of stimulus deprivation. In reality, subjects were not deprived of stimulation at all but simply sat alone in a small, well-lit room for four hours. To create demand characteristics, however, subjects in the experimental group were asked to sign forms that released the researcher from liability if the experimental procedure harmed the subject. They also were shown a "panic button" they could push if they could stand the deprivation no longer. Such cues would likely raise in subjects' minds the possibility that they might have a severe reaction to the study. (Why else would release forms and panic button be needed?) Subjects in the control group were told they were serving as a control group, were not asked to sign release forms, and were not given a panic button. Thus, the experimental setting would not lead control subjects to expect extreme reactions.

As Orne and Scheibe expected, subjects in the experimental group showed more extreme reactions during the deprivation period than subjects in the control group, even though they all underwent *precisely the same* experience of sitting alone for four hours. The only difference between the groups was the presence of demand characteristics that led subjects in the experimental group to expect more severe reactions. Given that early studies of stimulus deprivation were plagued by demand characteristics such as these, Orne and Scheibe concluded that many so-called effects of deprivation were, in fact, the result of demand characteristics rather than of stimulus deprivation per se.

To eliminate demand characteristics, experimenters often conceal the purpose of the experiment from subjects. In addition, they try to eliminate any cues in their own behavior or in the experimental setting that would lead subjects to draw inferences about the hypotheses or about how they should act.

Perhaps the most effective way to eliminate both experimenter expectancy effects and demand characteristics is to use a **double-blind procedure.** With a double-blind procedure, neither the subjects nor the experimenters who interact with them know which experimental condition a subject is in at the time the study is conducted. The experiment is supervised by another researcher, who assigns subjects to conditions and keeps other experimenters "in the dark." This procedure ensures that the experimenters who interact with the subjects will not subtly and unintentionally influence subjects to respond in a particular way.

Placebo effects.   Conceptually related to demand characteristics are placebo effects. A **placebo effect** is a physiological or psychological change that occurs as a result of the mere suggestion that the change will occur. In experiments that test the effects of drugs or therapies, for example, changes in health or behavior may occur because subjects *think* that the treatment will work.

Imagine you are testing the effects of a new drug, Mintovil, on headaches. One way you might design the study would be to administer Mintovil to one group of subjects (the experimental group) but not to another group of subjects (the control group). You could then measure how quickly the subjects' headaches disappear.

Although this may seem to be a reasonable research strategy, this design leaves open the possibility that a placebo effect will occur, thereby jeopardizing internal validity. The experimental conditions differed in two ways; not only did the experimental group receive Mintovil, but they *knew* they were receiving some sort of drug. Subjects in the control group, in contrast, received no drug and knew they had received no drug. If differences are obtained in headache remission for the two groups, we do not know whether the difference is due to Mintovil itself (a true treatment effect) or to the fact that the experimental group received a drug they expected might reduce their headaches (a placebo effect). (If you think this possibility sounds far-fetched, we saw recently that 6.4% of control subjects who received

"Find out who set up this experiment. It seems that half of the patients were given a placebo, and the other half were given a different placebo."

placebo sugar pills in a study of allergy medications reported the "medication" made them drowsy [Janssen, 1993].)

When a placebo effect is possible, researchers use a **placebo control group.** Subjects in a placebo control group are administered an ineffective treatment. For example, in the headache study, a researcher might give the experimental group a pill containing Mintovil and the placebo control group a pill that contains an inactive substance. Both groups would believe they were receiving medicine, but only the experimental group would receive a pharmaceutically active drug. The children who received the aspartame-sweetened beverage in Rosen and his associates' (1988) study of the effects of sugar on behavior were in a placebo control group, as were Schachter and Singer's (1962) subjects who received the saline injection.

The presence of placebo effects can be detected by using both a placebo control group and a true control group in the experimental design. Whereas subjects in the placebo control group receive an inactive substance (the placebo), subjects in the true control group receive no pill and no medicine. If subjects in the placebo control group (who received the inactive substance) improve more than those in the true control group (who received nothing), a placebo effect is operating. If this occurs, the researcher must demonstrate that the experimental group improves more than the placebo control group to conclude that the treatment was effective.

Error Variance

Although a less "fatal" problem than confound variance, error variance creates its own set of difficulties. Error variance decreases the power of an experiment, reducing the researcher's ability to detect effects of the independent variable on the dependent variable. Error variance is seldom eliminated from experimental designs, but researchers try hard to minimize it.

Sources of Error Variance

Recall that error variance is the "static" in an experiment. It results from all of the unsystematic, uncontrolled, and unidentified variables that affect subjects' behavior in large and small ways.

Individual differences.   The most common source of error variance is preexisting individual differences among subjects. When subjects enter an experiment, they already differ in a variety of ways—cognitively, physiologically, emotionally, and behaviorally. As a result of their preexisting differences, even subjects who are in the same experimental condition respond differently to the independent variable, creating error variance.

Of course, nothing can be done to eliminate individual differences among people. One partial solution to this source of error variance, however, is to use a homogeneous sample of subjects. The more alike subjects are, the less error variance is produced by their differences, and the easier it is to detect effects of the independent variable.

This is one reason researchers who use animals as subjects prefer samples composed of littermates. Littermates are genetically similar, are of the same age, and have usually been raised in the same environment. As a result, they differ little among themselves. Similarly, researchers who study human behavior often prefer homogeneous samples. For example, whatever other drawbacks they may have as research subjects, college sophomores at a particular university are often a relatively homogeneous group.

Transient states. In addition to differing on relatively stable dimensions such as those above, subjects differ in terms of *transient states*. At the time of the experiment, some are healthy whereas others are ill; some are tired and others are well rested; some are happy and others are depressed; some are enthusiastic about participating in the study and others resent having to participate. Subjects' current moods, attitudes, and physical conditions can affect their behavior in ways that have nothing to do with the experiment. About all a researcher can do to reduce the impact of these factors is to avoid creating different transient reactions in different subjects during the course of the experiment itself. If the experimenter is friendlier toward some subjects than toward others, for example, error variance will increase.

Environmental factors. Error variance is also affected by differences in the environment in which the study is conducted. For example, subjects who appear for the study drenched to the skin are likely to respond differently than those who sauntered to the experiment under clear skies. External noise may distract some subjects. Collecting data at different times during the day may create extraneous variability in subjects' responses.

To reduce error variance, researchers try to hold the environment as constant as possible as they test different subjects. Of course, little can be done about the weather, and it may not be feasible to conduct the study at only one time each day. However, factors such as laboratory temperature and noise should be held constant. Experimenters try to be sure that the experimental setting is as invariant as possible as different subjects are tested.

Differential treatment. Ideally, researchers should treat every subject within each condition exactly the same in all respects. However, as hard as they may try, experimenters find it difficult to treat all subjects in precisely the same way during the study.

For one thing, the experimenter's mood and health is likely to differ across subjects. As a result, he or she may respond more positively toward some subjects than toward others. The experimenter is also likely to act differently toward different kinds of subjects, such as responding differently toward subjects who are pleasant, attentive, and friendly than toward subjects who are unpleasant, distracted, and belligerent. Even the subjects' physical appearance can affect how he or she is treated by the researcher. Furthermore, the experimenter may inadvertantly modify the procedure slightly, by using slightly different words when giving instructions, for example. Also, male and female subjects may respond differently to male and female experimenters, and vice versa.

Even slight differences in how subjects are treated can introduce error variance into their responses. One solution is to automate the experiment as much as possible, thereby removing the influence of the researcher to some degree. To eliminate the possibility that the experimenter will vary in how he or she treats subjects, many researchers audiotape the instructions for the study, rather than delivering them live. Similarly, animal researchers automate their experiments, using programmed equipment to deliver food, manipulate variables, and measure behavior, thereby minimizing the impact of the human factor on the results.

Measurement error. We saw in Chapter 3 that all behavioral measures contain some degree of measurement error, which contributes to error variance because it causes subjects' scores to vary in unsystematic ways. Researchers should make every effort to use only reliable techniques and should take steps to minimize the influence of factors that create measurement error.

DEVELOPING YOUR RESEARCH SKILLS

TIPS FOR MINIMIZING ERROR VARIANCE

1. Use a homogeneous sample.
2. Aside from differences in the independent variable, treat all subjects precisely the same way at all times.
3. Hold all laboratory conditions (heat, lighting, noise, and so on) constant.
4. Standardize all research procedures.
5. Use only reliable measurement procedures.

Many factors can create extraneous variability in behavioral data. Because the factors that create error variance are spread across all conditions of the design, they do not create confounding or produce problems with internal validity. Rather, they simply add static to the picture produced by the independent variable; they produce unsystematic yet unwanted changes in subjects' scores that can cloud the effects the researcher is studying. After reading Chapter 11, you'll understand more fully why error variance makes it more difficult to detect effects of the independent variable. For now, simply understand what error variance is, the factors that cause it, and how it can be minimized through experimental control.

IN DEPTH

THE SHORTCOMINGS OF EXPERIMENTATION

Because they allow us to determine causal relationships, experimental designs are preferred by many behavioral scientists. However, there are many topics in psychology for which experimental designs are inappropriate. Sometimes, researchers are not interested in cause-and-effect relationships. Survey researchers, for example, often want only to *describe* people's attitudes and aren't interested in *why* people hold the attitudes they do.

In other cases, researchers are interested in causal effects but find it impossible or infeasible to conduct a true experiment. As we've seen, experimentation requires that the researcher be able to control aspects of the research setting carefully. However, researchers are often unwilling or unable to manipulate the variables they study. For example, to do an experiment on the effects of facial deformities on people's self-concepts would require us to randomly assign some people to have their faces disfigured. Likewise, to conduct an experiment on the effects of oxygen deprivation during the birth process on later intellectual performance, we would have to experimentally deprive newborns of oxygen for varying lengths of time. As we saw in Chapter 7, experiments have not been conducted on the effects of smoking on humans because such studies would assign some nonsmokers to smoke heavily.

Despite the fact that experiments can provide clear evidence of causal processes, descriptive and correlational studies, as well as quasi-experimental designs (which we'll examine in Chapter 13), are sometimes more appropriate and useful.

Experimental Control and Generalizability: The Experimenter's Dilemma

We've seen that experimental control involves treating all subjects precisely the same way, with the exception of giving subjects in different conditions different levels of the independent variable. The tighter the experimental control, the more internally valid the experiment will be, and the more internally valid the experiment, the stronger and more definitive are the conclusions we can draw about the causal effects of the independent variables.

However, experimental control is a two-edged sword. Tight experimental control means the researcher has created a highly specific and often artificial situation; the effects of extraneous variables that affect behavior in the real world have been eliminated or held at a constant level. The result is that the more controlled a study is, the more difficult it is to generalize the findings.

Recall that external validity refers to the degree to which the results obtained in one study can be replicated or generalized to other samples, research settings, and procedures. External validity refers to the *generalizability* of the research results to other settings (Campbell & Stanley, 1966).

To some extent, the internal validity and external validity of experiments are inversely related; high internal validity tends to produce lower external validity, and vice versa. The conflict between internal and external validity has been called the **experimenter's dilemma** (Jung, 1971). The more tightly the experimenter controls the experimental setting, the more internally valid are the results, but the lower is the external validity. Thus, researchers face the dilemma of choosing between internal and external validity.

When faced with this dilemma, virtually all experimental psychologists opt in favor of internal validity. After all, if internal validity is weak, then one cannot draw confident conclusions about the effects of the independent variable, and the findings should not be generalized anyway. Furthermore, in experimental research, the goal is seldom to obtain results that generalize to the real world. As we saw in Chapter 1, most research is designed to test hypotheses about the effects of certain variables on behavior. This approach is particularly pervasive in experimental research. Researchers develop tentative hypotheses and then design studies to determine whether those hypotheses are supported by the data. If they are supported, evidence is provided that supports the theory. If they are not supported, the theory is called into question. The goal of experimental research is not to make generalizations but to test them (Mook, 1983).

The purpose of most experiments, then, is not to discover what people do in real-life settings or to create effects that will necessarily generalize to the real world. In fact, the findings of any single experiment should *never* be generalized, no matter how well the study was designed, who its subjects were, or where it was conducted. The results of any particular study are too highly dependent on the specific context in which it was conducted to allow us to generalize its findings.

Rather, the purpose of most experimentation is to test general propositions about the determinants of behavior. If the theory is supported by data, we may then try to generalize the theory, not the results, to other contexts. We determine the generalizability of a theory through replicating experiments in other contexts, with different subjects, and using modified procedures. Replication tells us about the generality of our hypotheses.

Many people do not realize that the artificiality of experiments is often their greatest asset. As Stanovich (1992) noted, "contrary to common belief, the artificiality of scientific experiments is not an accidental oversight. Scientists *deliberately* set up conditions that are unlike those that occur naturally because this is the only way to separate the many inherently correlated variables that determine events in the world" (p. 90). He described several phenomena that would have been impossible to discover under real-world, natural conditions—phenomena ranging from subatomic particles in physics to biofeedback in psychology. Thus, experimental psychologists are usually not concerned with creating conditions in the laboratory that mimic real life in the outside world (what we call **mundane realism**).

They are, however, interested in creating involving and compelling research situations that fully engage the research participants—situations that the subjects regard as "real" (**experimental realism**). When experimental realism is high, subjects get caught up in the context created by the researcher, even though they know they are participating in a study, and even though the context bears little resemblance to situations encountered in everyday life. For example, a researcher interested in small group behavior might have groups of four subjects cooperate on a series of unusual tasks while carefully controlling the amount and type of communication the group members have with each other. Whether the situation resembles real situations in which groups of people interact (mundane realism) is not nearly as important as whether the situation is one in which subjects become fully engaged (experimental realism).

In brief, although important, external validity is not a crucial consideration in most behavioral studies (Mook, 1983). The comment, "But it's not real life" is not a valid criticism of experimental research (Stanovich, 1992).

Summary

1. Of all research designs, only experiments directly allow researchers to provide conclusive evidence regarding causal relationships.

2. In all experiments, the researcher manipulates one or more independent variables to determine their effects on aspects of subjects' behavior (the dependent variable).

3. The logic of the experimental method requires that the various experimental and control groups be equivalent before the independent variable is manipulated.

4. This equivalence is accomplished in one of two ways. In a between-subjects, or randomized groups, design, subjects are randomly assigned to experimental conditions. This ensures that, on the average, subjects in the various conditions are equivalent. Alternatively, in within-subjects, or repeated measures, designs, all subjects serve in all experimental conditions, thereby ensuring their equivalence.

5. A second requirement for experimental research is that nothing other than the independent variable may vary systematically across conditions.

6. When something other than the independent variable differs across groups, confounding occurs. Confounding destroys the internal validity of the experiment, making it difficult, if not impossible, to draw conclusions about the effects of the independent variable. This is the most serious flaw in any experiment.

7. Researchers try to minimize sources of error variance. Error variance is produced by unsystematic differences between subjects within experimental

conditions. Although error variance does not undermine the validity of an experiment, it makes it more difficult to detect effects of the independent variable.

8. Attempts to reduce the error variance in an experiment often lower the study's external validity—the degree to which the results can be generalized. However, the so-called experimenter's dilemma is a problem primarily when the purpose of the experiment is to draw inferences about how people will behave in other settings.

9. Most experiments are designed to test hypotheses about the causes of behavior. If the hypotheses are supported, then they—not the particular results of the study—are generalized.

Key Terms

experiment

independent variable

level

condition

environmental manipulation

confederate

instructional manipulation

invasive manipulation

experimental group

control group

pilot test

manipulation check

dependent variable

simple random assignment

matched random assignment

randomized groups design

between-subjects (or between-groups) design

within-subjects design

repeated measures design

power

order effects

counterbalancing

carryover effects

experimental control

systematic variance

between-groups variance

treatment variance, or primary variance

confound variance, or secondary variance

error variance

within-groups variance

internal validity

confounding

biased assignment

attrition

differential attrition

pretest sensitization

history effects

maturation

experimenter expectancy effect

demand characteristics

double-blind procedure

placebo effect

placebo control group

external validity   mundane realism

experimenter's dilemma   experimental realism

Review Questions

1. What advantage do experiments have over descriptive and correlational studies?

2. A well-designed experiment possesses what three characteristics?

3. Distinguish between qualitative and quantitative levels of an independent variable.

4. Must all experiments include a control group? Explain.

5. Why must researchers ensure that their experimental groups are roughly equivalent before manipulating the independent variable?

6. Explain how a within-subjects design equates the experimental conditions.

7. Discuss the relative advantages and disadvantages of within-subjects designs relative to between-subjects designs.

8. Distinguish between treatment, confound, and error variance.

9. Why is it essential to eliminate sources of confound variance?

10. What is confounding, and what effect does it have on the outcome of an experiment?

11. Discuss the primary factors that reduce internal validity. What can be done to minimize the effects of each of these factors on the outcome of an experiment?

12. What are experimenter expectancy effects, and how do researchers minimize them?

13. How do researchers detect and eliminate placebo effects?

14. What effect does error variance have on the results of an experiment? What can a researcher do to minimize error variance?

15. Discuss the trade-off between internal and external validity. Which is more important? Explain.

Questions for Thought and Discussion

1. Psychology developed primarily as an experimental science. However, during the past 20 to 25 years, nonexperimental methods have become increasingly popular. Why do you think this change has occurred? Do you think an increasing reliance on nonexperimental methods is beneficial or detrimental to the field?

2. Imagine you are interested in the effects of background music on people's performance at work. Design an experiment in which you test the effects of classical music (played at various decibels) on employees' job performance. In designing the study, you will need to decide how many levels of loudness to use, whether to use a control group, how to assign subjects to conditions, how to eliminate confound variance and minimize error variance, and how to measure job performance.

3. The text discusses the trade-off between internal and external validity, known as the *experimenter's dilemma*. Speculate on things a research can do to simultaneously increase internal and external validity, thereby designing a study that ranks high on both.

4. Why is artificiality sometimes an asset when designing an experiment?

Answers to In-Text Problems

Identifying Independent and Dependent Variables (page 181)

1. The independent variable involved generating misspellings of words.

2. The independent variable had two levels.

3. There were two conditions: subjects either did or did not generate two misspellings for each of 13 words.

4. Subjects in the experimental group generated two incorrect spellings of 13 words.

5. Yes, there was a control group; subjects in the control group performed a task unrelated to spelling.

6. The dependent variable was the number of words for which subjects switched from correct to incorrect spellings.

Confounding: Can You Find It? (page 191)

1. The independent variable was the physical disability of the job applicant.

2. The dependent variables involved subjects' ratings of the applicant on several dimensions.

3. The two conditions differed not only in the fact that the applicant appeared to be disabled in one photograph and not in the other but also in the fact that one photograph showed the applicant's whole body, whereas the other photo showed only his head and shoulders. If differences are obtained in subjects' average ratings of the applicant in these two conditions, the researcher will be unable to tell whether the difference was due to the disability variable or to the amount of the applicant's body that was shown. (Perhaps people's ratings of others are affected by whether or not they can

see their bodies.) Thus, an extraneous variable (amount of body shown in the picture) is confounded with the independent variable.

4. One way to correct this problem would be to use full-body pictures of the applicant in both conditions but to show the applicant seated in a wheelchair in the experimental condition and seated in a normal chair in the control condition. In this way, nothing varies between the conditions other than the independent variable.

CHAPTER 10

Experimental Design

People are better able to remember verbal material if they understand what it means. For example, people find it difficult to remember seemingly meaningless sentences such as "the notes were sour because the seams had split." However, once they comprehend the sentence (it refers to a bagpipe), they remember it easily.

Bower, Karlin, and Dueck (1975) were interested in whether comprehension aids memory for pictures as it does for verbal material. These researchers designed an experiment to test the hypothesis that people better remember pictures if they comprehend them than if they don't comprehend them. In this experiment, subjects were shown a series of "droodles." A droodle is a picture that, on first glance, appears meaningless but that has a funny interpretation. An example of a droodle is shown in Figure 10.1. Subjects were assigned randomly to one of two conditions. Half the subjects were given an interpretation of the droodle as they studied each picture; the other half simply studied each picture without being told what it was supposed to be.

After viewing 28 droodles for 10 seconds each, subjects were asked to draw as many droodles as they could remember. Then, one week later, the subjects returned for a recognition test. They were shown 24 sets of three pictures; each set contained one droodle that the subjects had seen the previous week, plus two pictures they had not seen. Subjects rated the three pictures in each set according to how similar each was to a picture they had seen the week before. The two dependent variables in the experiment, then, were the number of droodles the subjects could draw immediately after seeing them and the number of droodles subjects correctly recognized the following week.

The results of this experiment supported the researchers' hypothesis that people better remember pictures if they comprehend them than if they don't

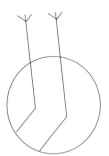

Figure 10.1   Example of a droodle (From "Comprehension and Memory for Pictures" by G. H. Bower, M. B. Karlin, and A. Dueck, 1975, *Memory and Cognition, 3,* p. 217.)

Explanation: What is it? *Answer:* An early bird who caught a very strong worm.

comprehend them. Subjects who had received an interpretation of each droodle accurately recalled significantly more droodles than those who did not receive interpretations. Subjects recalled an average of 70% of the droodles in the interpretation condition but only 51% of the droodles in the no-interpretation condition. We'll return to the droodles study as we discuss basic experimental designs in this chapter.

We'll begin by looking at designs that involve the manipulation of a single independent variable, such as the design of the droodles experiment. Then we'll turn our attention to experimental designs that involve the manipulation of two or more independent variables.

One-Way Designs

Experimental designs involving only one independent variable are called **one-way designs.** The simplest one-way design is a **two-group experimental design,** in which there are only two levels of the independent variable (and thus two conditions). A minimum of two conditions is needed to compare subjects' responses in one experimental condition with those in another condition. Only then can we determine whether the different levels of the independent variable led to differences in subjects' behavior. (A study that had only one condition would not be classified as an experiment at all because no independent variable was manipulated.) The droodles study was a two-group experimental design; subjects in one condition received interpretations of the droodles, whereas subjects in the other condition did not receive interpretations.

Although at least two conditions are necessary in an experiment, experiments often involve more than two levels of the independent variable. For example, in a study designed to examine the effectiveness of weight-loss programs, Mahoney, Moura, and Wade (1973) randomly assigned 53 obese adults to one of five condi-

Self-reward	Self-punishment	Self-reward and self-punishment	Self-monitoring	Control group
6.4	3.7	5.2	0.8	1.4

Figure 10.2   Average pounds lost by subjects in each experimental condition

tions: (1) one group rewarded themselves when they lost weight, (2) another punished themselves when they didn't lose weight, (3) a third group used both self-reward and self-punishment, (4) a fourth group monitored their weight but did not reward or punish themselves, and (5) a control group did not monitor their weight. This study involved a single independent variable that had five levels (the various weight-reduction strategies). (In case you're interested, the results of this study are shown in Figure 10.2. As you can see, self-reward resulted in significantly more weight loss than the other strategies.)

One-way designs come in three basic varieties, each of which we discussed briefly in Chapter 9: the randomized groups design, the matched-subjects design, and the within-subjects or repeated measures design. As we learned earlier, the randomized groups design is a between-subjects design in which subjects are randomly assigned to one of two or more groups. A randomized groups design was used for the droodles experiment described earlier (see Figure 10.3).

We stated in Chapter 9 that matched random assignment is sometimes used to increase the similarity of the experimental groups prior to the manipulation of the independent variable. In a **matched-subjects design,** subjects are matched into blocks on the basis of a variable the researcher believes relevant to the experiment.

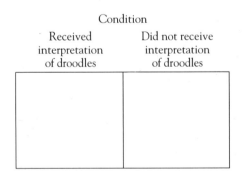

Figure 10.3   A randomized two-group design (From Bower, Karlin, & Dueck, 1975)

Explanation: In a randomized groups design such as this, subjects are randomly assigned to one of the experimental conditions.

Then, subjects in each matched block are assigned randomly to one of the experimental or control conditions.

Recall that, in a repeated measures (or within-subjects) design, each subject serves in all experimental conditions. To redesign the droodles study as a repeated measures design, we would provide interpretations for only *half* the droodles each subject saw, but not for the other half. In this way, each subject would serve in *both* the interpretation and the no-interpretation conditions, and we could see whether subjects remembered more droodles that were accompanied by interpretations than droodles without interpretations.

DEVELOPING YOUR RESEARCH SKILLS

DESIGN YOUR OWN EXPERIMENTS

Following are three research questions. For each, design an experiment in which you manipulate a single independent variable. Your independent variable may have as many conditions as necessary to address the research question.

1. Timms (1980) suggested that if a person who is embarrassed tries to keep him- or herself from blushing, the person may actually blush more than if he or she doesn't try to stop blushing. Design an experiment to determine whether this is true.

2. Design an experiment to determine whether people's reaction times to red stimuli are shorter than to stimuli of other colors.

3. In some studies, subjects are asked to complete a large number of questionnaires over the span of an hour or more. Researchers sometimes worry that completing so many questionnaires may make subjects tired, frustrated, or angry. If so, the process of completing the questionnaires may actually change subjects' moods. Design an experiment to determine whether subjects' moods are affected by completing lengthy questionnaires.

In designing each experiment, did you use a randomized groups, matched-subjects, or repeated measures design? Why? Whichever design you chose for each research question, redesign the experiment using each of the other two kinds of one-way designs. Consider the relative advantages and disadvantages of using each of the designs to answer the research questions.

Posttest and Pretest-Posttest Designs

The three basic one-way experimental designs we've just described are diagrammed in Figure 10.4. Each of these three designs is called a **posttest-only design** because, in each instance, the dependent variable is measured only *after* the experimental manipulation has occurred.

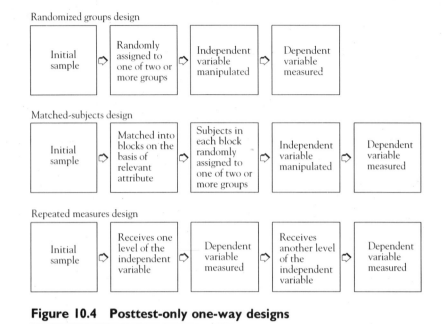

Figure 10.4   Posttest-only one-way designs

In some cases, however, researchers measure the dependent variable twice—once before the independent variable is manipulated and again afterward. Such designs are called **pretest-posttest designs.** Each of the three posttest-only designs shown in Figure 10.4 can be converted to a pretest-posttest design by measuring the dependent variable both before and after manipulating the independent variable. Figure 10.5 shows the pretest-posttest versions of the randomized groups, matched-subjects, and repeated measures designs.

In pretest-posttest designs, subjects are pretested to obtain their scores on the dependent variable at the outset of the study. Pretesting subjects offers three possible advantages over the posttest-only designs. First, by obtaining pretest scores on the dependent variable, the researcher can determine that subjects in the various experimental conditions did not differ with respect to the dependent variable at the beginning of the experiment. In this way, the effectiveness of random or matched assignment can be documented.

Second, by comparing pretest and posttest scores on the dependent variable, researchers can see exactly *how much* the independent variable changed subjects' behavior. Pretests provide useful baseline data for judging the size of the independent variable's effect. (In posttest-only designs, baseline data of this sort is provided by control groups that receive a zero-level of the independent variable.)

Third, pretest-posttest designs are more powerful; that is, they are more likely than posttest-only designs to detect the effects of an independent variable on behavior.

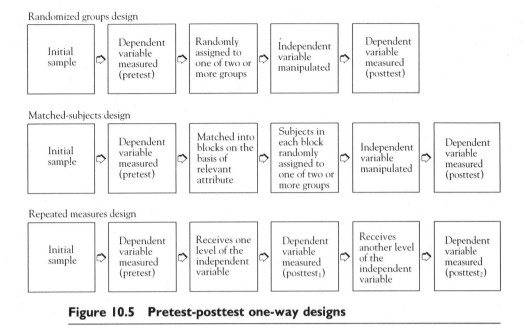

Figure 10.5 Pretest-posttest one-way designs

As we saw in Chapter 9, one possible drawback of using pretests is pretest sensitization. Administering a pretest may sensitize subjects to respond to the independent variable differently than they would have responded had they not been pretested. When subjects are pretested on the dependent variable, researchers sometimes add conditions to their design to look for pretest sensitization effects. For example, half the subjects in each experimental condition could be pretested before receiving the independent variable, whereas the other half would not be pretested. By comparing posttest scores for subjects who were and were not pretested, the researcher could then see whether the pretest had any effects on the results of the experiment.

Although pretest-posttest designs are useful, they are by no means necessary. A posttest-only design provides all the information needed to determine whether the independent variable had an effect on the dependent variable. Assuming that subjects were assigned to conditions in a random fashion or that a repeated measures design was used, posttest differences between conditions indicate that the independent variable had an effect.

Summary

We have identified three basic one-way designs: the randomized groups design, the matched-subjects design, and the repeated measures (or within-subjects) design. Each of these designs can be employed as a posttest-only design or as a pretest-posttest design, depending on the requirements of a particular experiment.

Factorial Designs

With the growth of urban areas during the 1960s, psychologists became interested in the effects of crowding on behavior, emotion, and health. In early work on crowding, researchers assumed that increasing the density of a situation—decreasing the amount of space or increasing the number of people in it—typically leads to negative effects such as aggression and stress. Freedman (1975) questioned this view, proposing that, rather than evoking exclusively negative reactions, high-density situations simply intensify whatever reactions people are experiencing at the time. If people are in an unpleasant situation, increasing density will make their experience even more unpleasant. Feeling crowded during a boring lecture only makes things worse, for example. But if people are enjoying themselves, Freedman predicted, higher density will intensify their positive reactions. The larger the crowd at an enjoyable concert, the more you might enjoy it (within reasonable limits, of course).

Think for a moment about how you might design an experiment to test Freedman's density–intensity hypothesis. According to this hypothesis, people's reactions to social settings are a function of *two* factors: the density of the situation and the pleasantness of people's reactions in it. Thus, testing this hypothesis requires studying the combined effects of two independent variables simultaneously.

The one-way experimental designs we discussed earlier in the chapter would not be particularly useful in this regard. A one-way design allows us to examine the effects of only one independent variable. What is needed is a design that involves two or more variables simultaneously. Such a design, in which two or more independent variables are manipulated, is called a **factorial design**. Often the independent variables are referred to as **factors**. (Do not confuse this use of the term *factor* with the use of the term in *factor analysis*.)

To test his density–intensity hypothesis, Freedman (1975) designed an experiment in which he manipulated two independent variables: the density of the room and the pleasantness of the situation. In his study, subjects delivered a brief speech to a small audience. The audience was instructed to provide the speaker with either positive or negative feedback about the speech. Thus, for subjects in one condition the situation was predominately pleasant, whereas for subjects in the other condition the situation was predominately unpleasant. Freedman also varied the size of the room in which subjects gave their speeches. Some subjects spoke in a large room (150 square feet) and some gave their speeches in a small room (70 square feet). Thus, although audience size was constant in both conditions, the density was higher for some subjects than for others. After giving their speeches and receiving either positive or negative feedback, subjects completed a questionnaire on which they indicated their reactions to the situation, including how much they liked the members of the audience and how willing they were to participate in the study again.

The experimental design for Freedman's experiment is shown in Figure 10.6.

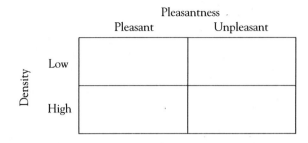

Figure 10.6   A factorial design: Freedman's density–intensity experiment

Explanation: Freedman manipulated two independent variables: the density of the setting (low versus high density) and the pleasantness of the situation (pleasant versus unpleasant). In this design, four conditions reflect all possible combinations of density and pleasantness.

As you can see, two variables were manipulated: density and pleasantness. The four conditions in the study represented the four possible combinations of these two variables. The density–intensity theory predicts that high density will increase positive reactions in the pleasant condition and increase negative reactions in the unpleasant condition. As we'll see, the results of the experiment clearly supported these predictions.

Like the density–intensity theory, many theories stipulate that behavior is a function of two or more variables. Researchers use factorial designs to study the individual and combined effects of two or more factors within a single experiment.

Factorial Nomenclature

To understand factorial designs, you need to become familiar with the nomenclature researchers use to describe the size and structure of such designs. First, just as a one-way design has only one independent variable, a two-way factorial design has two independent variables, a three-way factorial design has three independent variables, and so on. Freedman's test of the density–intensity hypothesis involved a *two-way* factorial design because two independent variables were involved.

The structure of a factorial design is often specified in a way that immediately indicates to a reader how many independent variables were manipulated and how many levels there were of each variable. For example, Freedman's experiment was an example of what researchers call a 2 × 2 (read as "2 by 2") factorial design. The phrase "2 × 2" tells us that the design had two independent variables, each with two levels [see Figure 10.7(a)]. A 3 × 3 factorial design also involves two independent variables, but each variable has three levels [see Figure 10.7(b)]. A 2 × 4 factorial design has two independent variables, one with two levels and one with four levels [see Figure 10.7(c)].

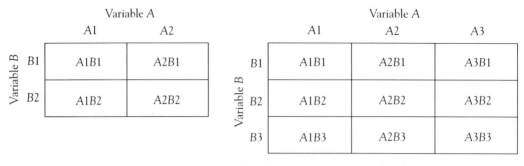

(a) 2×2 design

(b) 3×3 design

(c) 4×2 design

Figure 10.7   Examples of two-way factorial designs

Explanation: (a) A 2 × 2 design has two independent variables, each with two levels, for a total of four conditions. (b) In a 3 × 3 design, there are two independent variables, both of which have three levels. Because there are nine possible combinations of variables *A* and *B*, this design has nine conditions. (c) In this 4 × 2 design, independent variable *A* has four levels and independent variable *B* has two levels, resulting in eight experimental conditions.

So far, our examples have involved two-way factorial designs, that is, designs with two independent variables. However, experiments can have more than two independent variables. For example, a 2 × 2 × 2 design has three independent variables; each of the variables has two levels [see Figure 10.8(a)]. A 2 × 2 × 4 factorial design also has three independent variables; two independent variables have two levels each and the other variable has four levels [see Figure 10.8(b)]. A four-way factorial design, such as a 2 × 2 × 3 × 3 design, would have four independent variables; two would have two levels, and two would have three levels. The size and structure of every factorial design can be described using this system.

We can tell how many experimental conditions a factorial design has simply by multiplying the numbers in a design specification. For example, a 2 × 2 design has four different cells or conditions—that is, four possible combinations of the two

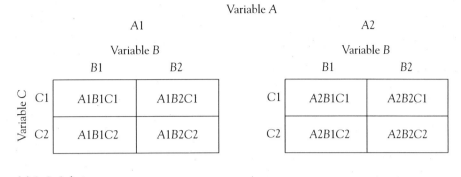

(a) 2×2×2 design

Variable A

A1

Variable B

B1   B2

	B1	B2
C1	A1B1C1	A1B2C1
C2	A1B1C2	A1B2C2

A2

Variable B

B1   B2

	B1	B2
C1	A2B1C1	A2B2C1
C2	A2B1C2	A2B2C2

(b) 2×2×4 design

Figure 10.8   Examples of higher-order designs

Explanation: (a) A three-way design such as this one involves the manipulation of three independent variables: *A*, *B*, and *C*. In a 2 × 2 × 2 design, each of the variables has two levels, resulting in eight conditions. (b) This is a 2 × 2 × 4 (three-way) design. Variables *A* and *B* each have two levels, and variable *C* has four levels. There are 16 possible combinations of the three variables and therefore 16 conditions in the experiment.

independent variables (2 × 2 = 4). A 3 × 4 × 2 design has 24 different experimental conditions (3 × 4 × 2 = 24), and so on.

Assigning Subjects to Conditions

Like the one-way designs we discussed earlier, factorial designs may include randomized groups, matched-subjects, or repeated measures designs. In addition, as we will see, the split-plot or between-within design combines features of the randomized groups and repeated measures designs.

Randomized groups factorial design.   In a randomized groups factorial design (which is also called a completely randomized factorial design) subjects are assigned randomly to one of the possible combinations of the independent variables. In Freedman's (1975) test of the density–intensity hypothesis, subjects were assigned randomly to one of four combinations of density and pleasantness.

Matched factorial design.   As in the matched-subjects one-way design, the matched-subjects factorial design involves first matching subjects into blocks on the basis of some variable that correlates with the dependent variable. There will be as many subjects in each matched block as there are experimental conditions. In a 3 × 2 factorial design, for example, 6 subjects would be matched into each block. Then the subjects in each block are randomly assigned to one of the six experimental conditions. As before, the primary reason for using a matched-subjects design is to more closely equate the subjects in the experimental conditions before introducing the independent variable.

Repeated measures factorial design.   A **repeated measures** (or **within-subjects) factorial design** requires that all subjects participate in every experimental condition. Although repeated measures designs are feasible with small factorial designs (such as a 2 × 2 design), they become unwieldy with larger designs. For example, in a 2 × 2 × 2 × 4 repeated measures factorial design, each subject would serve in 32 different conditions! With such large designs, order and carryover effects can become a problem.

Split-plot factorial design.   Because one-way designs involve a single independent variable, they must involve random assignment, matched subjects, or repeated measures. However, factorial designs involve more than one independent variable, and they can combine features of both randomized groups designs and repeated measures designs in a single experiment. Some independent variables in a factorial experiment may involve random assignment, whereas other variables involve a repeated measure. A design that combines one or more between-subjects variables with one or more within-subjects variables is called a **split-plot factorial design,** or a **between-within design.** (The odd name, *split-plot,* was adopted from agricultural research and actually refers an area of ground that has been subdivided for research purposes.)

To better understand split-plot designs, let's look at a classic study by Walk (1969), who employed a split-plot design to study depth perception in infants using a "visual cliff" apparatus. The visual cliff consists of a clear Plexiglas platform with a checkerboard pattern underneath. On one side of the platform, the checkerboard is directly under the Plexiglas. On the other side of the platform, the checkerboard is farther below the Plexiglas, giving the impression of a sharp drop-off, or cliff. In Walk's experiment, the deep side of the cliff consisted of a checkerboard design five inches below the clear Plexiglas surface. On the shallow side, the checkerboard was directly beneath the glass.

Walk experimentally manipulated the size of the checkerboard pattern. In one condition the pattern consisted of 3/4-inch blocks, and in the other condition in pattern consisted of 1/4-inch blocks. Subjects (who were 6½- to 15-month-old babies) were *randomly assigned* to either the 1/4-inch or 3/4-inch condition as in a randomized groups design. Walk also manipulated a second independent variable as in a repeated measures or within-subjects design; he had each infant tested on the cliff more than once. Each was placed on the board between the deep and shallow sides of the cliff and beckoned by its mother from the shallow side; then the procedure was repeated on the deep side. Thus, each infant served in *both* the shallow and the deep conditions.

This is a split-plot, or between-within, factorial design because one independent variable (size of pattern) involved randomly assigning subjects to conditions, whereas the other independent variable (shallow versus deep side) involved a repeated measure. This design is shown in Figure 10.9.

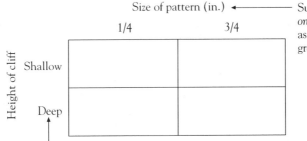

Size of pattern (in.) ← —— Subjects were assigned to *one* of these conditions, as in a randomized groups design.

Subjects served in *both* the shallow and deep conditions, as in a repeated measures design.

Figure 10.9 A split-plot design (After Walk, 1969)

Explanation: In this 2 × 2 split-plot design, one independent variable (size of the block design) was a between-subjects factor in which subjects were assigned randomly to one condition or the other. The other independent variable (height of the visual cliff) was a within-subjects factor. All subjects were tested at both the shallow and the deep sides of the visual cliff.

Main Effects and Interactions

The primary advantage of factorial designs over one-way designs is that they provide information not only about the separate effects of each independent variable but also about the effects of the independent variables when they are combined. That is, assuming we have eliminated all experimental confounds (see Chapter 9), a one-way design allows us to identify only two sources of the total variability we observe in subjects' responses; either the behavioral variability was treatment variance due to the independent variable, or it was error variance. A factorial design allows us to identify other possible sources of the variability we observe in the dependent variable. When we use factorial designs, we can examine whether the variability in scores was due to (1) the individual effects of each independent variable, (2) the combined or interactive effects of the independent variables, or (3) error variance. Thus, factorial designs give researchers a fuller, more complete picture of how behavior is affected by sets of independent variables acting together.

Main effects.   The effect of a single independent variable in a factorial design is called a **main effect**. A main effect reflects the effect of a particular independent variable while ignoring the effects of the other independent variables. When we examine the main effect of a particular independent variable, we pretend for the moment that the other independent variables do not exist. A factorial design will have as many main effects as there are independent variables. For example, because a 2 × 3 design has two independent variables, we can examine two main effects.

In Freedman's (1975) density–intensity experiment, two main effects were tested: the effect of density (ignoring pleasantness) and the effect of pleasantness (ignoring density). To test the main effect of density, Freedman asked whether subjects' responses differed in the high- and low-density conditions (ignoring whether they were in the pleasant or unpleasant condition). Analysis of the data showed no difference between subjects' responses in the low- and high-density conditions—that is, no main effect of density. Thus, *averaging* across the pleasant and unpleasant conditions, Freedman found that subjects' responses in the low- and high-density conditions did not differ significantly. (The means for the low- and high-density conditions were 2.06 and 2.07, respectively.) As Freedman expected, high density by itself had no discernible effect on subjects' reactions.

Not surprisingly, Freedman did find a main effect of the pleasantness variable. Subjects who received positive reactions to their speeches rated the situation as more pleasant (mean rating = 2.12) than those who received negative reactions (mean rating = 2.01). Of course, this main effect is not particularly surprising or interesting, but it serves as a manipulation check by showing that subjects perceived the pleasant situation to be more pleasant than the unpleasant situation.

Interactions.   In addition to providing information about the main effects of each independent variable, a factorial design provides information about interactions between the independent variables. An **interaction** is present when the effect of one independent variable differs across the levels of other independent variables. For example, imagine we conduct a factorial experiment with two independent variables, A and B. If the effect of variable A is different under one level of variable B than it is under another level of variable B, an interaction is present. However, if variable A has the same effect on subjects' responses no matter what level of variable B they received, then no interaction is present.

Consider, for example, what happens if you mix alcohol and certain drugs, such as sedatives. The effect of drinking a given amount of alcohol (variable A) can vary depending on whether you've also taken sleeping pills (variable B). By itself, a strong mixed drink may result in only a mild "buzz." Similarly, taking one or two sleeping pills may make you sleepy, but will have few other effects. However, that same strong drink may create pronounced effects on behavior if you've taken a sleeping pill. And, mixing a strong drink and two or three sleeping pills will produce extreme, potentially fatal, results. Because the effects of a given dose of alcohol depends on how many sleeping pills you've taken, alcohol and sleeping pills *interact* to affect behavior. This is an interaction because the effect of one variable (alcohol) differs depending on the level of the other variable (no pill, one pill, or three pills).

Similarly, the density–intensity hypothesis predicted an *interaction* of density and pleasantness on subjects' reactions. According to the hypothesis, high density should have a different effect on subjects who received positive feedback than on those who received negative feedback. Freedman's data, shown in Figure 10.10, revealed the predicted interaction. High density resulted in *more positive* reactions for subjects in the pleasant condition but in *less positive* reactions for subjects in the unpleasant condition. The effects of density were different under one level of pleasantness than under the other, so an interaction is present. Because the effect of one variable (density) differed under the different levels of the other variable (pleasantness), we say that density and pleasantness *interacted* to affect subjects' responses to the situation.

Higher-Order Designs

The examples of factorial designs we have seen so far were two-way designs that involved two independent variables (such as a 2 × 2, a 2 × 3, or a 3 × 5 factorial design). As we noted earlier, factorial designs often have more than two independent variables.

Increasing the number of independent variables in an experiment increases not only the complexity of the design and statistical analyses but also the complexity of the information the study provides. A two-way design provides information about two main effects and a two-way interaction:

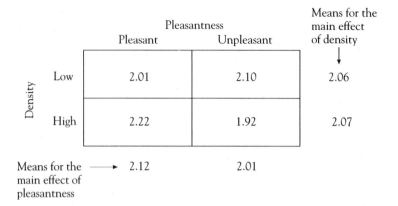

Means for the main effect of pleasantness → 2.12   2.01

Figure 10.10   Effects of density and pleasantness on subjects' liking for other participants in the study (From *Crowding and Behavior* (p. 150) by J. L. Freedman, 1975, San Francisco: W. H. Freeman and Company. Copyright 1975 by J. L. Freedman. Adapted by permission of Jonathan Freedman and the publisher.)

Explanation: These numbers are subjects' average ratings of how much they liked the members of the audience who observed their speeches. Higher numbers indicate greater liking. As the density–intensity hypothesis predicted, high density increased linking more than low density did when the situation was pleasant. However, high density decreased liking more than low density did when the situation was unpleasant. The fact that density had a different effect depending on whether the situation was pleasant or unpleasant indicates the presence of an interaction.

1. Main effect of A
2. Main effect of B
3. Interaction of A by B

A three-way design, such as a 2 ×2 × 2, or a 3 × 2 × 4 design, provides even more information. First, we can examine the effects of each of three independent variables separately:

1. Main effect of A
2. Main effect of B
3. Main effect of C

That is, we can look at the individual effects of each independent variable while ignoring (averaging over) the other two.

Second, a three-way design allows us to look at three two-way interactions— interactions of each pair of independent variables—while ignoring the third independent variable:

4. Interaction of *A* by *B* (while ignoring *C*)

5. Interaction of *A* by *C* (while ignoring *B*)

6. Interaction of *B* by *C* (while ignoring *A*)

Each two-way interaction tells us whether the effect of one independent variable is different at different levels of another independent variable. For example, testing the *B* by *C* interaction tells us whether variable *B* has a different effect on behavior in Condition *C1* than in Condition *C2*.

Third, a three-way factorial design gives us information about the combined effects of all three independent variables:

7. Interaction of *A* by *B* by *C*

If statistical tests show that this three-way interaction is significant, it indicates that the effect of one variable differs depending on which combination of the other two variables we examine. For example, perhaps the effect of variable *A* is different in Condition *B1C1* than in Condition *B1C2*.

Logically, factorial designs can have any number of independent variables and thus any number of conditions. For practical reasons, however, researchers seldom design studies with more than three or four independent variables. For one thing, when a between-subjects design is used, the number of subjects needed for an experiment grows rapidly as we add additional independent variables. For example, a $2 \times 2 \times 2$ factorial design with 15 subjects in each of the 8 conditions could require 120 subjects. Adding a fourth independent variable with two levels (creating a $2 \times 2 \times 2 \times 2$ factorial design) would double the number of subjects required to 240. Adding a fifth independent variable with three levels (making the design a $2 \times 2 \times 2 \times 2 \times 3$ factorial design) would require us to collect and analyze data from 720 subjects!

In addition, as the number of independent variables increases, researchers find it increasingly difficult to draw meaningful interpretations from the data. A two-way interaction is usually easy to interpret, but four- and five-way interactions are quite complex.

Mixed Factorial Designs

Behavioral researchers have long recognized that behavior is a function of both situational factors and an individual's personal characteristics. A full understanding of certain behaviors cannot be achieved without taking both situational and personal factors into account. Put another way, **subject variables** such as sex, age, intelligence, ability, personality, and attitudes moderate or qualify the effects of situational forces on behavior. Not everyone responds in the same manner to the same situation. For example, people's performance on a test is a function not only of the difficulty of the test itself but also of their personal attributes, such as their ability, motivation, and level of test anxiety. A researcher interested in determinants of test performance might want to take into account such personal characteristics (such as subjects' levels of test anxiety) as well as the characteristics of the test itself.

Researchers use a **mixed factorial design** to investigate the combined effects of situational factors and subject variables. In a mixed factorial design, one or more factors involve an independent variable that is *manipulated* by the experimenter, and one or more factors involve preexisting subject variables that are *measured* rather than manipulated.

You need to be aware that the term *mixed factorial design* is used to refer to two quite different designs. Sometimes it is used to refer to designs that include both between-subjects and within-subjects factors—what we have called a split-plot, or between-within, design. Others use it, as we have here, to refer to designs that include both manipulated independent variables and measured subject variables. Because of this confusion, I prefer to call these so-called mixed designs **expericorr** (or **mixed/expericorr**) **designs**. The label *expericorr* is short for experimental–correlational; such designs combine features of an experimental design in which independent variables are manipulated and features of correlational designs in which subject variables are measured.

Uses of mixed designs.   Researchers use mixed/expericorr designs for three reasons. The first is to investigate the generality of an independent variable's effect. Subjects who possess different characteristics often respond to the same situation in quite different ways. Therefore, the effects of certain independent variables may generalize only to subjects with certain characteristics. Mixed/expericorr designs permit researchers to determine whether the effects of a particular independent variable occur for all subjects or only for subjects with certain attributes.

One of the most common uses of mixed designs is to look for differences in how male and female subjects respond to an independent variable. For example, to investigate whether men and women respond differently to success and failure, a researcher might use a 2×3 expericorr design. In this design, one factor would involve a subject variable with two levels, namely gender. The other factor would involve a manipulated independent variable that has three levels: subjects would each take a test and then receive either (1) success feedback, (2) failure feedback, or (3) no feedback. When the data were analyzed, the researcher could examine the main effect of subject gender (whether, overall, men and women differ), the main effect of feedback (whether subjects respond differently to success, failure, and no feedback), and most important, the interaction of gender and feedback (whether men and women respond differently to success, failure, and/or no feedback).

Second, researchers use expericorr designs in an attempt to understand how certain personal characteristics relate to behavior under varying conditions. The emphasis in such studies is on understanding the measured subject variable rather than the manipulated independent variable. For example, a researcher interested in self-esteem might expose persons who were low or high in self-esteem to various experimental conditions. Or a researcher interested in depression might conduct an experiment in which depressed and nondepressed subjects respond to various experimentally manipulated situations. Studying how subjects with different characteristics respond to an experimental manipulation may shed light on that characteristic.

Third, by splitting subjects into groups based on a subject variable, researchers make the subjects within the experimental conditions more homogeneous. Greater homogeneity reduces the error variance (the variability within conditions), thereby increasing the study's sensitivity in detecting effects of the independent variable.

Classifying subjects into groups. When researchers use mixed designs, they typically classify subjects into groups on the basis of the measured subject variable (such as gender or self-esteem), then randomly assign subjects within those groups to levels of the independent variable. For discrete subject variables such as gender and race, it is usually easy to assign subjects into two or more groups.

Sometimes, however, researchers are interested in subject variables that are continuous rather than discrete. For example, a researcher may be interested in how self-esteem moderates reactions to success and failure. Because scores on a measure of self-esteem are continuous, the researcher must decide how to classify subjects into groups. Traditionally, researchers have typically used either the median-split procedure or the extreme groups procedure.

In the **median-split procedure,** the researcher pretests a pool of subjects and identifies the median of the distribution of subjects' scores on the variable of interest (such as self-esteem). You will recall from Chapter 5 that the median is the middle score in a distribution, the score that falls at the 50th percentile. The researcher then classifies subjects with scores below the median as *low* on the variable and those with scores above the median as *high* on the variable. It must be remembered, however, that the designations *low* and *high* are relative to the researcher's sample. All subjects could, in fact, be low or high on the attribute in an absolute sense. In a variation of the median-split procedure, some researchers split their sample into three or more groups, rather than only two.

Alternatively, some researchers prefer the **extreme groups procedure** for classifying subjects into groups. Rather than splitting the sample at the median, the researcher pretests a large number of potential subjects and then selects subjects for the experiment whose scores are unusually low or high on the variable of interest. For example, the researcher may use subjects whose scores fall in the upper and lower 25% of a distribution of self-esteem scores, discarding those with scores in the middle range.

Researchers interested in how independent variables interact with subject variables have traditionally classified subjects into two or more groups using one of these splitting procedures. However, the use of median and extreme group splits has been criticized in the past few years, and many researchers no longer use these approaches. One reason is that classifying subjects into groups on the basis of a measured subject variable often throws away valuable information. When we use subjects' scores on a continuous variable—such as age, self-esteem, or depression—and classify them into only two groups (old versus young, low versus high self-esteem, depressed versus nondepressed), we discard information regarding the true variability in subjects' scores; we've converted a rich set of data into a dichotomy.

Furthermore, recent studies have shown that splitting subjects into groups on the basis of a subject variable, such as self-esteem or anxiety, can lead to biased results. Depending on the nature of the data, the bias sometimes leads researchers to miss effects that were actually present, and at other times it leads researchers to obtain effects that are actually statistical artifacts (Bissonnette, Ickes, Bernstein, & Knowles, 1990; Cohen & Cohen, 1983; Maxwell & Delaney, 1993). In either case, artifically splitting subjects into groups can lead to erroneous conclusions.

Rather than splitting subjects into groups, many researchers now use multiple regression procedures that allow them to analyze the data from mixed/expericorr designs while maintaining the continuous nature of subjects' scores on the measured subject variable (Aiken & West, 1991; Cohen & Cohen, 1983; Kowalski, 1994). The details of such analyses are beyond the scope of this book, but you should be aware that researchers now recognize that median-split and extreme group approaches can be problematic.

BEHAVIORAL RESEARCH CASE STUDY

A MIXED DESIGN: SELF-ESTEEM AND RESPONSES TO EGO THREATS

Baumeister, Heatherton, and Tice (1993) used a mixed/expericorr design to examine how people with low versus high self-esteem respond to threats to their egos. Thirty-five male subjects completed a measure of self-esteem and were classified as low or high in self-esteem on the basis of a median-split procedure.

In a laboratory experiment, the subjects set goals for how well they would perform on a computer video game (Sky Jinks) and wagered money on meeting the goals they had set. As with most wagers, they could make "safe" bets (with the possibility of winning or losing little) or "risky" bets (with the potential to win—and to lose—more). Just before subjects placed their bets, the researcher threatened the egos of half the subjects by remarking that the subject might want to place a safe bet if he were worried he might choke under pressure or didn't "have what it takes" to do well on the game. Thus, this was a 2 by 2 (low versus high self-esteem and ego threat versus no ego threat) mixed factorial design. Self-esteem was a measured subject variable, and ego threat was a manipulated independent variable.

Subjects then made their bets and played the game. The final amount of money won by subjects in each of four conditions is shown in Figure 10.11. Analysis of the data revealed a main effect of self-esteem (low self-esteem subjects won more money on average than half self-esteem subjects), but no main effect of ego threat subjects won roughly the same amount whether or not the researcher threatened their egos).

Most important, the analysis revealed an interaction of self-esteem and ego threat. When subjects' egos had not been threatened, the amount of money won by low and high self-esteem subjects did not differ significantly; highs won an average of $1.40, and lows won an average of $1.29. However, in the presence of an ego threat, subjects with low self-esteem won significantly more money (an average of $2.80) than subjects with high self-esteem (an average of $.25). These data suggest that ego threats may lead people with high self-esteem to set inappropriate, risky goals in an attempt to prove themselves.

	Subject Self-Esteem	
	Low	**High**
No Ego Threat	$1.29	$1.40
Ego Threat	$2.80	$ .25

Figure 10.11   A Mixed Design: Responses of Low and High Self-Esteem People to Ego Threat (From "When Ego Threats Lead to Self-Regulation Failure: Negative Consequences of High Self-Esteem" by R. F. Baumeister, T. F., Heatherton, and D. M. Tice, 1993, *Journal of Personality and Social Psychology, 64,* pp. 141–156.)

Explanation: In this mixed/expericorr study, subjects who scored low versus high in self-esteem were or were not exposed to an ego threat prior to wagering money on their ability to attain certain scores on a computerized game. As the table shows, subjects who were low in self-esteem won slightly more money following an ego threat than when an ego threat had not occurred. In contrast, high self-esteem subjects won significantly less money when their egos were threatened than when they were not threatened.

Cautions in interpreting results of a mixed design.   Researchers must exercise care when interpreting results from mixed designs. Specifically, a researcher can draw causal inferences about only the true independent variables in the experiment—those that were manipulated by the researcher. As always, if effects are obtained for a manipulated independent variable, we can conclude that the independent variable *caused* changes in the dependent variable.

When effects are obtained for the measured subject variable, however, the researcher cannot conclude that the subject variable caused changes in the dependent variable. Because the subject variable is measured rather than manipulated, the results are essentially correlational, and (recall from Chapter 7) we cannot infer causality from a correlation.

If a main effect of the subject variable is obtained, we can conclude that the two groups differed on the dependent variable, but we cannot conclude that the subject variable caused the difference. Rather, we say that the subject variable *moderated* subjects' reactions to the independent variable and that the subject variable is a **moderator variable.** For example, we cannot conclude that high self-esteem caused subjects to make risky bets in the experiment described above (Baumeister et al., 1993). Because people who score low versus high in self-esteem differ in many ways, all we can say is that differences in self-esteem were associated with different responses in the ego threat condition. Or, more technically, self-esteem *moderated* the effects of ego threat on subjects' behavior.

Summary

1. A one-way experimental design is an experiment in which a single independent variable is manipulated. The simplest possible experiment is the two-group experimental design.

2. Researchers use three general versions of the one-way design—the randomized groups design (in which subjects are assigned randomly to two or more groups), the matched-subjects design (in which subjects are first matched into blocks, then randomly assigned to conditions), and the repeated measures design (in which each subject serves in all experimental conditions).

3. Each of these designs may involve a single measurement of the dependent variable after the manipulation of the independent variable, or a pretest and a posttest.

4. In many ways, factorial designs are the mainstay of experimental psychology. The vast majority of experiments involve factorial designs. Factorial designs are experimental designs that include two or more independent variables.

5. There are four general types of factorial design: the randomized groups, matched-subjects, repeated measures, and split-plot (or between-within) factorial designs.

6. Factorial designs provide information not only about the effects of each independent variable (the main effects) but also about the combined effects of the variables.

7. An interaction is present if the effect of one independent variable is different under one level of another independent variable than it is under another level of that variable.

8. Mixed or expericorr factorial designs combine manipulated independent variables and measured subject variables. Such designs are often used to identify subject variables that qualify or moderate the effects of the independent variables.

9. Although researchers using a mixed design sometimes classify subjects into groups using a median-split or extreme groups procedure, other researchers use analyses that allow them to maintain the continuity of the measured subject variable. In either case, causal inferences may be drawn only about the variables in a mixed design that were experimentally manipulated.

Key Terms

one-way design	within-subjects factorial design
two-group experimental design	split-plot factorial design
matched-subjects design	between-within design
posttest-only design	main effect
pretest-posttest design	interaction
pretest sensitization	subject variable
factorial design	mixed factorial design
factor	expericorr (or mixed/expericorr) factorial design
randomized groups factorial design	
completely randomized factorial design	median-split procedure
matched-subjects factorial design	extreme groups procedure
repeated measures factorial design	moderator variable

Review Questions

1. How many conditions are there in the simplest possible experiment?

2. Contrast how subjects are assigned to conditions in a randomized groups, matched-subjects, and repeated measures design.

3. What are the relative advantages and disadvantages of posttest-only versus pretest-posttest experimental designs?

4. Describe a 2 × 3 × 2 factorial design. How many independent variables are involved? How many levels are there of each variable? How many experimental conditions are there?

5. Describe a split-plot factorial design. The split-plot design is a combination of what two other designs?

6. Describe the main effects and interactions that can be tested in (1) a 2×3 factorial design and (2) a $3 \times 3 \times 3$ factorial design.

7. What are mixed/expericorr factorial designs, and why are they used?

CHAPTER 11

Analyzing Experimental Data

Some of my students are puzzled (or, perhaps more accurately, horrified) when they discover that they must learn about *statistics* in a research methods course. More than one student has asked why we talk so much about statistical analyses in my class, considering that entire courses on campus are devoted to statistics. Given that the next two chapters are devoted to statistics, it occurred to me that you may be asking yourself the same question.

Statistical analyses are an integral part of the research process. A person who knew nothing about statistics not only would have difficulty conducting research but also would find it difficult to even understand others' studies and findings. As a result, most seasoned researchers are quite knowledgeable about statistical analyses, although they sometimes consult with statisticians when their research calls for analyses with which they are not already familiar.

Even if you, as a student, have no intention of ever conducting research, a basic knowledge of statistics is essential for understanding most journal articles. If you have ever read research articles published in scientific journals, you likely have encountered an assortment of mysterious analyses—*t*-tests, ANOVAs, MANOVAs, post hoc tests, simple effects tests, and the like—along with an endless stream of seemingly meaningless symbols and numbers, such as "$F(2, 328) = 6.78, p < .01$." If you're like many of my students, you may have skimmed over these parts of the article until you found something that made sense. If nothing else, a knowledge of statistics is necessary to be an informed reader and consumer of scientific knowledge.

Even so, for our purposes here, you do not need a high level of proficiency with all sorts of statistical formulas and calculations. Rather, what you need is an understanding of how statistics work. Thus, we will focus in Chapters 11 and 12 on how experimental data are analyzed from a *conceptual* perspective. Along the way, you will see a few formulas for demonstrational purposes, but the calculational formulas researchers actually use to analyze data will generally take a back seat. At this point, it's more important that you understand how data are analyzed and what the statistical analyses tell us than that you learn to do a variety of analyses; *that's* what statistics courses are for.

An Intuitive Approach to Analysis

After an experiment is conducted, the researcher must analyze the data to determine whether the independent variable had the predicted effect on the dependent variable(s). Did the manipulation of the independent variable cause systematic changes in subjects' responses? Was memory for pictures affected by providing subjects with interpretations of the droodles they saw? Did different patterns of self-reward and self-punishment result in different amounts of weight loss? Was perceived crowding affected by a combination of density and pleasantness?

At the most general level, we can see whether the independent variable had an effect by determining whether the total variance in the data includes any systematic variance due to the manipulation of the independent variable (see Chapter 9). Specifically, the presence of systematic variance in a set of data is determined by comparing the means on the dependent variable for the various experimental groups.

If the independent variable had an effect on the dependent variable, we should find that the means for the experimental conditions differ. Different group averages would suggest that the independent variable had an effect; it created differences in the behavior of subjects in the various conditions and thus resulted in systematic variance. Assuming subjects assigned to the experimental conditions did not differ systematically before the study and no confounds were present, the only thing that could have caused the means to differ at the end of the experiment is the independent variable. However, if the means of the conditions do not differ, no systematic variance is present, and we would conclude the independent variable had no effect.

In the droodles experiment we described in Chapter 10, for example, subjects who were given an interpretation of the droodles recalled an average of 19.6 of the pictures immediately afterward. Subjects in the control group (who received no interpretation) recalled an average of only 14.2 of the pictures (Bower et al., 1975). On the surface, then, inspection of the means for the two experimental conditions indicates that subjects who were given an interpretation of the droodles remembered more pictures than those who were not given an interpretation.

The Problem: Error Variance Can Cause Mean Differences

Unfortunately, this conclusion is not as straightforward as it may appear, and we cannot draw conclusions about the effects of an independent variable simply by looking at the means of the experimental conditions. The difficulty is that the means of the experimental conditions may differ even if the independent variable did *not* have an effect. We discussed one possible cause of such differences in Chapter 9—confound variance. Recall that if something other than the independent variable differs in a systematic fashion between experimental conditions, the differences between the means may be due to this confounding variable rather than to the independent variable.

However, even assuming the researcher successfully eliminates confounding, the means may differ for yet another reason unrelated to the independent variable. Suppose the independent variable did *not* have an effect in the droodles experiment described earlier; that is, providing an interpretation did not enhance subjects' memory for the droodles. What would we expect to find when we calculated the average number of pictures remembered by subjects in the two experimental conditions? Would we expect the mean number of pictures recalled in the two experimental groups to be *exactly* the same? Probably not. Even if the independent variable did not have an effect, it is unlikely that the means would be identical.

To understand this, imagine we randomly assigned subjects to two groups, then showed them droodles while giving interpretations of the droodles to all subjects in *both* groups. Then, we asked subjects to recall as many of the droodles as possible. Would the average number of pictures recalled be exactly the same in both groups even if subjects in both groups received interpretations? Probably not. Even if we created no systematic differences between the two conditions, we would be unlikely to obtain perfectly identical means.

Because of error variance in the data, the average recall of the two groups of subjects is likely to differ slightly even if they are treated the same. You will recall that error variance reflects the random influences of factors that remain unidentified in the study, such as individual differences among subjects and slight variations in how the researcher treats different subjects. These uncontrolled and unidentified variables lead subjects to respond differently whether or not the independent variable has an effect. As a result, the means of experimental groups typically differ even when the independent variable itself did not affect subjects' responses.

But if we expect the means of the experimental conditions to differ somewhat even if the independent variable does *not* have an effect, how can we tell whether the difference between the means of the conditions is due to the independent variable (systematic treatment variance) or due to random differences between the groups (error variance)? How big a difference between the means of our conditions must we observe to conclude that the independent variable has an effect and that the difference between means is not simply due to error variance?

The Solution: Inferential Statistics

The solution to this problem is simple, at least in principle. If we can estimate how much the means of the conditions are expected to differ *even if the independent variable has no effect*, we can then determine whether the difference we observe between the means exceeds this amount. Put another way, we can conclude that the independent variable has an effect when the difference between the means of the experimental conditions is larger than we would expect it to be if the difference is due only to the effects of error variance. We do this by comparing the difference we obtain between experimental conditions with the difference we would expect to obtain based on error variance alone.

Unfortunately, we can never be absolutely certain that the difference we obtain between group means is not just the result of error variance. Even large differences between the means of the groups could be due to error variance rather than to the independent variable. We can, however, specify the *probability* that the difference we observe between the means is due to error variance.

Hypothesis Testing

The Null Hypothesis

Researchers use inferential statistics to determine whether observed differences between the means of the experimental conditions are greater than what would be expected on the basis of error variance alone. If the observed difference between the group means is larger than expected given the amount of error variance in the data, they conclude that the independent variable caused the difference.

To make this determination, researchers statistically test the null hypothesis. The **null hypothesis** states that the independent variable *did not* have an effect on the dependent variable. Of course, this is usually the opposite of the researcher's actual **experimental hypothesis,** which states that the independent variable *did* have an effect. For statistical purposes, however, we test the null hypothesis rather than the experimental hypothesis. The null hypothesis for the droodles experiment was that subjects provided with interpretations of droodles would remember the same number of droodles as those not provided with an interpretation. That is, the null hypothesis says that the mean number of droodles that subjects remembered would be equal in the two experimental conditions.

Based on the results of statistical tests, the researcher will make one of two decisions about the null hypothesis. If analyses of the data show there is a high probability that the null hypothesis is false, the researcher will **reject the null hypothesis** and conclude that the independent variable did indeed have an effect. The researcher will reject the null hypothesis if statistical analyses show that the difference between the means of the experimental groups is larger than would be expected on the basis of how much error variance is in the data.

On the other hand, if the analyses show an unacceptably low probability of the null hypothesis being false, the researcher will **fail to reject the null hypothesis.** Failing to reject the null hypothesis means the researcher will conclude that the independent variable had no effect. This would be the case if the statistical analyses indicated the group means differed about as much as we would expect based on the amount of error variance in the data. Put differently, the researcher will fail to reject the null hypothesis if analyses show a high probability that the difference between the group means reflects nothing more than the influence of error variance.

Notice we say that when the probability of the null hypothesis being false is low, the researcher will *fail to reject* the null hypothesis—not that the researcher would *accept* the null hypothesis. We use this odd terminology because, strictly speaking, we cannot obtain data that allow us to truly accept the null hypothesis as confirmed or verified. Although we can determine that an independent variable probably had an effect on the dependent variable (and thus reject the null hypothesis), we cannot conclusively determine that an independent variable did not have an effect (and thus we cannot accept the null hypothesis).

An analogy may clarify this point. In a murder trial, the defendant is assumed not guilty (a null hypothesis) until the jury becomes convinced by the evidence that the defendant is, in fact, the murderer. If the jury remains unconvinced of the defendant's guilt, it does not necessarily mean the defendant is innocent; it may simply mean there isn't enough conclusive evidence to convict. When this happens, the jury returns a verdict of "not guilty." This verdict does not mean the defendent is innocent; rather, it means only that the current evidence isn't sufficient to pronounce him or her guilty.

Similarly, if we find that the means of our experimental conditions are not different, we cannot logically conclude that the null hypothesis is true (that is, that the independent variable had no effect). We can only conclude that the current evidence isn't sufficient to reject it. Strictly speaking, then, the failure to obtain differences between the means of the experimental conditions leads us to *fail to reject* the null hypothesis rather than to accept it.

Type I and Type II Errors

Figure 11.1 shows the decisions that a researcher may make about the null hypothesis and the outcomes that may result. Four outcomes are possible. First, the researcher may correctly reject the null hypothesis, thereby identifying a true effect of the independent variable. Second, the researcher may correctly fail to reject the

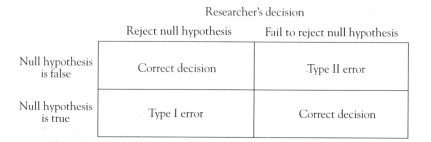

Researcher's decision

	Reject null hypothesis	Fail to reject null hypothesis
Null hypothesis is false	Correct decision	Type II error
Null hypothesis is true	Type I error	Correct decision

Figure 11.1   Statistical decisions and outcomes

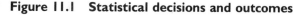

null hypothesis, accurately concluding that the independent variable had no effect. In both cases, a correct conclusion was reached. The other two possible outcomes are the result of two kinds of errors researchers may make when deciding whether to reject the null hypothesis: Type I and Type II errors. A **Type I error** occurs when a researcher erroneously concludes that the null hypothesis is false and, thus, rejects it. More straightforwardly, a Type I error occurs when a researcher concludes that the independent variable had an effect on the dependent variable when, in fact, the observed difference between the means of the experimental conditions was actually due to error variance.

The probability of making a Type I error—of rejecting the null hypothesis when it is true—is called the **alpha level.** As a rule of thumb, researchers set the alpha level at .05: they reject the null hypothesis when there is less than a .05 chance (that is, fewer than 5 chances out of 100) that the difference they obtained between the means of the experimental groups was due to error variance rather than to the independent variable. If statistical analyses indicate there is less than a 5% chance that the difference between the means of our experimental conditions was due to error variance, we reject the null hypothesis, knowing there is only a small chance we were mistaken.

Occasionally, researchers wish to lower their chances of making a Type I error even further and thus set a more stringent criterion for rejecting the null hypothesis. By setting the alpha level at .01 rather than at .05, for example, researchers risk only a 1% chance of making a Type I error.

When we reject the null hypothesis with a low probability of making a Type I error, we refer to the difference between the means as **statistically significant.** A statistically significant finding is one that has a low probability (usually $< .05$) of occurring as a result of error variance alone. We'll return to the important concepts of alpha level and statistical significance later.

On the other hand, the researcher may fail to reject the null hypothesis when, in fact, it is false; this is a **Type II error.** In this case, the researcher concludes that the independent variable did not have an effect when, in fact, it did. Just as the probability of making a Type I error is called alpha, the probability of making a Type II error is called **beta.**

Several factors can increase beta and lead to Type II errors. If the researcher did not measure the dependent variable properly or if the measurement technique was unreliable, he or she might not detect effects of the independent variable that occurred. Mistakes may have been made in collecting, coding, or analyzing the data, or the researcher may have used too few subjects to detect the effects of the independent variable. Excessively high error variance due to unreliable measures, very heterogeneous samples, or poor experimental control can also mask effects of the independent variable and lead to Type II errors. Overall, high beta is associated with low *power*, the ability of a study to detect the effects of an independent variable.

To be sure you understand the difference between Type I and Type II errors, we return to our example of a murder trial. After weighing the evidence, the jury is in the position of having to decide whether or not to reject the null hypothesis of "not guilty." In reaching their verdict, the jury hopes not to make either a Type I or Type II error. In the context of a trial, a Type I error would involve rejecting the null hypothesis (not guilty) when it was true, or convicting an innocent person. A Type II error would involve failing to reject the null hypothesis when it was false— that is, not convicting a defendant who did, in fact, commit murder. Like scientists, jurors are generally more concerned about making a Type I than a Type II error when reaching a verdict: a greater injustice is done if an innocent person is convicted than if a criminal goes free. In fact, jurors are explicitly instructed to convict the defendent (reject the null hypothesis) only if they are convinced "beyond a reasonable doubt" that the defendent is guilty. In essence, using the criterion of "beyond a reasonable doubt" is comparable to setting a relatively stringent alpha level of .01 or .05.

Effect Size

When researchers reject the null hypothesis and conclude that the independent variable had an effect, they often want to know how strong the independent variable's effect was on the dependent variable. They determine this by calculating the **effect size**—the proportion of variability in the dependent variable that was due to the independent variable.

As a proportion, effect size can range from .00, indicating no relationship between the independent variable and the dependent variable, to 1.00, indicating that 100% of the variance in the dependent variable is associated with the independent variable. For example, if we find that our effect size is .47, we know that 47% of the variability in the dependent variable is due to the independent variable.

Several slightly different formulas for calculating effect size exist, and researchers disagree regarding the one that is most useful in all situations. The two most commonly used are called eta-squared and omega-squared.

Summary

In analyzing data collected in experimental research, researchers attempt to determine whether the means of the various experimental conditions differ more than they would if the differences were due only to error variance. If the difference between means is large relative to the error variance, the researcher rejects the null hypothesis and concludes that the independent variable had an effect. The researcher makes this conclusion with the understanding that there is less than a .05 probability he or she has made a Type I error. If the difference in means is no larger than one would expect simply on the basis of the amount of error variance in the data, the researcher fails to reject the null hypothesis and concludes that the independent variable had no effect. When researchers reject the null hypothesis, they often calculate the effect size, which expresses the proportion of variability in the dependent variable associated with the independent variable.

Analysis of Two-Group Experiments: The t-test

Now that you understand the rationale behind inferential statistics, we will look briefly at two statistical tests that are used most often to analyze data collected in experimental research. We will examine *t*-tests in this chapter, and *F*-tests in Chapter 12.

Both analyses are based on the same rationale: the error variance in the data is calculated to provide an estimate of how much the means of the conditions would be expected to differ if the differences were due only to random error variance (and the independent variable had no effect). Then the observed differences between the means are compared with this estimate. If the observed differences between the means are so large, relative to this estimate, that they are highly unlikely to be the result of error variance alone, the null hypothesis is rejected. As we saw, the likelihood of erroneously rejecting the null hypothesis is held at less than whatever alpha level the researcher has stipulated, usually .05.

Conducting a t-test

Although the rationale behind inferential statistics may seem complex and convoluted, conducting a **t-test** to analyze data from a two-group randomized groups experiment is straightforward. In this section, we will walk through the calculation of one kind of *t*-test to demonstrate how the rationale for comparing mean differences to error variance is implemented in practice.

To conduct a *t*-test, we calculate a value for *t* using a simple formula and then see whether this calculated value of *t* exceeds a certain critical value located in a table. If it does, the group means differ by more than what we would expect on the basis of error variance alone. A *t*-test is conducted in the following five steps.

Step 1. Calculate the means of the two groups.

Step 2. Calculate the standard error of the difference between the two means.

Step 3. Find the calculated value of *t*.

Step 4. Find the critical value of *t*.

Step 5. Determine whether the null hypothesis should be rejected by comparing the calculated value of *t* to the critical value of *t*.

Let's examine each of these steps in detail.

Step 1. To test whether the means of two experimental groups are different, we obviously need to know the means. These means will go in the numerator of the formula for a *t*-test. Thus, first we must calculate the means of the two groups, $\bar{x}_1$ and $\bar{x}_2$.

Step 2. To determine whether the means of the two experimental groups differ more than we would expect on the basis of error variance alone, we need an estimate of how much the means would be expected to vary if the difference were due only to error variance. The **standard error of the difference between two means** provides an index of this expected difference.

This quantity is based directly on the amount of error variance in the data. As we saw in Chapter 9, error variance is reflected in the variability *within* the experimental groups. Any variability we observe in the responses of subjects who are in the same experimental condition cannot be due to the independent variable because they all received the *same* level of the independent variable. Rather, this variance reflects extraneous variables, chiefly (1) individual differences in how subjects responded to the independent variable and (2) poor experimental control.

Calculating the standard error of the difference is accomplished in three steps.

2a. First, calculate the variances of the two experimental groups. (You may want to review the section of Chapter 5 that deals with calculating the variance.) The variance for each condition is calculated from this formula:

$$s^2 = \frac{\Sigma x_i^2 - [(\Sigma x_i)^2/n]}{n - 1}$$

Calculate the variance twice, once for each experimental condition.

2b. Then, calculate the pooled variance, s_p^2. This is the average of the variances for the two groups:

$$s_p^2 = \frac{(n_1 - 1)s_1^2 + (n_2 - 1)s_2^2}{n_1 + n_2 - 2}$$

In this formula, n_1 and n_2 are the sample sizes for conditions 1 and 2, and s_1^2 and s_2^2 are the variances of the two conditions calculated in Step 2a.

2c. Finally, take the square root of the pooled variance, which gives you the pooled standard deviation, s_p.

Step 3. Armed with the means of the two groups ($\bar{x}_1$ and $\bar{x}_2$), the pooled standard deviation (s_p), and the sample sizes (n_1 and n_2), we are ready to calculate *t*.

$$t = \frac{\bar{x}_1 - \bar{x}_2}{s_p\sqrt{1/n_1 + 1/n_2}}$$

Step 4. Now we must locate the critical value of *t* in a table designed for that purpose. To find the **critical value** of *t*, we need to know the following two things.

4a. First, we need to calculate the degrees of freedom for the *t*-test. For a two-group randomized design, the degrees of freedom (df) is equal to the number of subjects minus 2 (that is, $n_1 + n_2 - 2$). (Don't concern yourself with what *degrees of freedom* are from a statistical perspective; simply realize we need to take the number of scores into account when conducting inferential statistics, and df is a function of the number of scores.)

4b. Second, we need to specify the alpha level for the test. As we saw earlier, the alpha level is the probability we are willing to accept for making a Type I error—rejecting the null hypothesis when it is true. Usually, researchers set the alpha level at .05.

Taking these two numbers, consult the table in Appendix A-2 to find the critical value of *t*. For example, imagine we have ten subjects in each condition. The degrees of freedom would be $10 + 10 - 2 = 18$. Assuming the alpha level is set at .05, we look down the column marked "1-tailed" until we reach df = 18, where we find that the critical value of *t* is 1.734.

Step 5.   Finally, we compare our calculated value of *t* to the critical value of *t* obtained in the table of *t*-values. If the absolute value of the calculated value of *t* (Step 3) exceeds the critical value of *t* obtained from the table (Step 4), we reject the null hypothesis. The difference between the two means is large enough, relative to the error variance, to conclude that the difference is due to the independent variable and not to error variance alone. As we saw, a difference so large that it is very unlikely to be due to error variance is said to be statistically significant. After finding that the difference between the means is significant, we inspect the means themselves to determine the direction of the obtained effect. By seeing which mean is largest, we can determine the precise effect of the independent variable on whatever we were measuring.

However, if the absolute value of the calculated value of *t* obtained in Step 3 is less than the critical value of *t*, we do not reject the null hypothesis. We conclude that the probability that the difference between the means is due to error variance is unacceptably high. In such cases, the difference between the means is called nonsignificant.

DEVELOPING YOUR RESEARCH SKILLS

COMPUTATIONAL EXAMPLE OF A *t*-TEST

To those of us who are sometimes inclined to overeat, anorexia nervosa is puzzling. The anorexic exercises extreme control over her eating (the majority of anorexics are women) so that she loses a great deal of weight, often to the point that her health is threatened. One theory suggests that anorexics restrict their eating to maintain a sense of control over the world; when everything else in one's life seems out of control, one can always control what and how much one eats. One implication of this theory is that anorexics should respond to a feeling of low control by reducing the amount they eat.

To test this hypothesis, imagine we selected college women who scored high on a measure of anorexic tendencies. We assigned these subjects randomly to one of two experimental conditions. Subjects in one condition were led to experience a sense of having high control, whereas subjects in the other condition experienced a loss of control. Subjects were then given the opportunity to sample sweetened breakfast cereals under the guise of a taste test. The dependent variable is the amount of cereal each subject eats. The number of pieces of cereal for 12 subjects in this study are shown in the following table.

High Control Condition	Low Control Condition
13	3
39	12
42	14
28	11
41	18
58	16

The question to be addressed is whether subjects in the low control condition ate significantly less cereal than subjects in the high control condition. We can conduct a *t*-test on these data by following the five steps we've just outlined.

Step 1. Calculate the means of the two groups.

High control = $\bar{x}_1$ = (13 + 39 + 42 + 28 + 41 + 58)/6 = 36.8

Low control = $\bar{x}_2$ = (3 + 12 + 14 + 11 + 18 + 16)/6 = 12.3

Step 2. 2a. Calculate the variances of the two experimental groups (see Chapter 5 for the calculational formula for the variance).

$$s_1^2 = 228.57 \qquad s_2^2 = 27.47$$

2b. Calculate the pooled variance, using the formula:

$$s_p^2 = \frac{(n_1 - 1)s_1^2 + (n_2 - 1)s_2^2}{n_1 + n_2 - 2}$$

$$= \frac{(6 - 1)(228.57) + (6 - 1)(27.47)}{6 + 6 - 2}$$

$$= \frac{(1142.85) + (137.35)}{10}$$

$$= 128.02$$

$$s_p = \sqrt{128.02} = 11.31$$

Step 3. Solve for the calculated value of t:

$$t = \frac{\bar{x}_1 - \bar{x}_2}{s_p \sqrt{1/n_1 + 1/n_2}}$$

$$= \frac{36.8 - 12.3}{11.31\sqrt{1/6 + 1/6}}$$

$$= \frac{24.5}{11.31\sqrt{.333}}$$

$$= \frac{24.5}{11.31\,(.577)}$$

$$= \frac{24.5}{6.53}$$

$$= 3.75$$

Step 4. Find the critical value of t in Appendix A-2. The degrees of freedom equal 10 ($6 + 6 - 2$), and we'll set the alpha level at .05. Looking down the column for a one-tailed test, we see that the critical value of t is 1.812.

Step 5. Comparing our calculated value of t (3.75) to the critical value (1.812), we see that the calculated value exceeds the critical value. Thus, we conclude that the average amount of cereal eaten in the two conditions differed significantly. The difference between the two means is large enough, relative to the error variance, to conclude that the difference is due to the independent variable and not to error variance. By inspecting the means, we see that subjects in the low control condition (mean = 12.3) ate less cereal than subjects in the high control condition (mean = 36.8).

Back to the Droodles Experiment

To analyze the data from their droodles experiment (see p. 208), Bower and his colleagues conducted a t-test on the number of droodles subjects recalled. When the authors conducted a t-test on these means, they calculated the value of t as 3.43. They then referred to a table of the critical values of t (such as that in Appendix A-2). The degrees of freedom were $n_1 + n_2 - 2$, or $9 + 9 - 2 = 16$. Rather than setting the alpha level at .05, the researchers were more cautious and used an alpha level of .01. (That is, they were willing to risk only a 1-in-100 chance of making a Type I error.) The critical value of t when df = 16 and alpha level = .01 is 2.583. Because the calculated value of t (3.43) was larger than the critical value (2.583), the means differed by more than would be expected if only error variance were operating. Thus, the researchers rejected the null hypothesis that comprehension does not aid memory for pictures, knowing the probability that they made a Type I error was less than 1 in 100. As the authors themselves stated:

> The primary result of interest is that an average of 19.6 pictures out of 28 (70%) were accurately recalled by the label group . . . , whereas only 14.2 pictures (51%) were recalled by the no-label group. . . . The means differ reliably in the predicted direction, $t(16) = 3.43$, $p < .01$. Thus, we have clear confirmation that "picture understanding" enhances picture recall. (Bower et al., 1975, p. 218)

IN DEPTH

DIRECTIONAL AND NONDIRECTIONAL HYPOTHESES

A hypothesis about the outcome of a two-group experiment can be stated in one of two ways. A **directional hypothesis** states which of the two condition means is expected to be larger. That is, the researcher predicts the specific direction of the anticipated effect. A **nondirectional hypothesis** merely states that the two means are expected to differ, but no prediction is ventured regarding which mean will be larger.

When a researcher's prediction is directional, as is most often the case, a **one-tailed** *t*-test is used. Each of the examples we've studied involved one-tailed tests because the direction of the difference between the means was predicted. Because the hypotheses were directional, we used the value for a one-tailed test in the table of *t* values (Appendix A-2). In the droodles experiment, for example, the researchers predicted the number of droodles remembered would be *greater* in the condition in which the droodle was explained than in the control condition. Because this was a directional hypothesis, they used the critical value for a one-tailed *t*-test. Had their hypothesis been nondirectional, a **two-tailed** *t*-test would have been used.

Analyses of Matched-Subjects and Within-Subjects Designs

The procedure we just described for conducting a *t*-test applies to a two-group randomized groups design. A slightly different formula, the **paired t-test,** is used when the experiment involves a matched-subjects or a within-subjects design. The paired *t*-test takes into account the fact that the subjects in the two conditions are similar, if not identical, on an attribute related to the dependent variable. In the matched-subjects design, we randomly assign matched pairs of subjects to the two conditions; in the within-subjects design, the same subjects serve in both conditions.

Either way, each subject in one condition is matched with a subject in the other condition (again, in a within-subjects design the matched subject is the subject him- or herself). As a result of this matching, the matched scores in the two conditions should be correlated. In a matched-subjects design, the matched partners of subjects who score high on the dependent variable in one condition (relative to the other subjects) should score relatively high on the dependent variable in the other condition, and the matched partners of subjects who score low in one condition should tend to score low in the other. Similarly, in a within-subjects design, subjects who score high in one condition should score relatively high in the other condition, and vice versa. Thus, a positive correlation should be obtained between the matched scores in the two conditions.

The paired *t*-test takes advantage of this correlation to reduce the estimate of error variance used to calculate *t*. In essence, we can account for the source of some of the error variance in the data: it comes from individual differences among the subjects. Given that we have matched pairs of subjects, we can use the correlation between the two conditions to estimate the amount of error variance due to these differences. Then we can discard this component of the error variance when we test the difference between the condition means.

Reducing error variance leads to a more *powerful* test of the null hypothesis—one that is more likely to detect the effects of the independent variable than the randomized groups *t*-test. The paired *t*-test is more powerful because we have reduced the size of s_p in the denominator of the formula for *t*; and as s_p gets smaller, the calculated value of *t* gets larger.

We will not go into the formula for the paired *t*-test here. However, a detailed explanation of this test can be found in most introductory statistics books, such as those listed at the end of this chapter.

CONTRIBUTORS TO BEHAVIORAL RESEARCH

STATISTICS IN THE BREWERY: W. S. GOSSET

One might imagine that the important advances in research design and statistics came at the hands of statisticians slaving away in stuffy offices at noted universities. Indeed, many of those who provided the foundation for behavioral science, such as Wilhelm Wundt and Karl Pearson, were academicians. However, many methodological and statistical approaches were developed while solving real-world problems, notably in industry and agriculture.

A case in point involves the work of William Sealy Gosset (1876–1937), whose contributions to research include the *t*-test. Having a background in chemistry and mathematics, Gosset was hired by Guinness Brewery in Dublin, Ireland, in 1899. Among his duties, Gossett investigated how the quality of beer is affected by various raw materials (such as different strains of barley and hops) and by various methods of production (such as variations in brewing temperature).

During 1906–1907, Gosset spent a year in specialized study in London, where he studied under Karl Pearson (see Chapter 7). During this time, Gosset worked on developing solutions to statistical problems he encountered at the brewery. In 1908, he published a paper based on this work that laid out the principles for the *t*-test. Interestingly, he published his work under the pen name Student, and to this day, this test is often referred to as Student's *t*.

Summary

1. Experimental data are analyzed by comparing the difference between the condition means to the amount we would expect the means to differ if the independent variable had no effect on subjects' responses (and the difference was due solely to random error variance).

2. If the means differ more than expected based on the amount of error variance present, researchers reject the null hypothesis and conclude that the independent variable had an effect. If the means do not differ by more than error variance would predict, researchers fail to reject the null hypothesis.

3. Because the decision to reject or fail to reject the null hypothesis is a probabilistic one, researchers may make one or two kinds of errors. A Type I error occurs when the researcher rejects the null hypothesis when it is true; a Type II error occurs when the researcher fails to reject the null hypothesis when it is false.

4. The *t*-test is used to analyze the difference between two means. A value for *t* is calculated by dividing the difference between the means by an estimate of how much the means would be expected to differ on the basis of error variance alone. This calculated value of *t* is then compared to a critical value of *t*. If the calculated value exceeds the critical value, the null hypothesis is rejected.

5. Hypotheses about the outcome of two-group experiments may be directional or nondirectional. Whether the hypothesis is directional or nondirectional has implications for whether the critical value of *t* used in the *t*-test is one-tailed or two-tailed.

Key Terms

null hypothesis	alpha level
experimental hypothesis	statistically significant
reject the null hypotheses	Type II error
fail to reject the null hypothesis	beta
Type I error	effect size

t-test

standard error of the difference
  between two means

critical value of t

directional versus nondirectional
  hypothesis

one-tailed versus two-tailed t-test

paired t-test

Review Questions

1. In analyzing the data from an experiment, why is it not sufficient simply to examine the condition means to see whether they differ?

2. Why do researchers use inferential statistics?

3. Discuss the two decisions a researcher may make about the null hypothesis on the basis of statistical analyses.

4. Differentiate a Type I from a Type II error. In the eyes of most researchers, which of the two is the worse to make?

5. Explain the rationale behind the t-test.

6. Distinguish between one-tailed and two-tailed t-tests.

7. What was W. S. Gosset's contribution to behavioral research?

Exercises

1. This exercise is designed to help you gain experience using the table of the critical values of t in Appendix A-2.

    a. Find the critical value of t for an experiment in which there were 28 subjects, using an alpha level of .05 for a one-tailed test.

    b. Find the critical value of t for an experiment in which there were 28 subjects, using an alpha level of .01 for a one-tailed test.

    c. You will notice that, given the same degrees of freedom, the critical value of t is larger when the alpha level is .01 than when it is .05. Can you figure out why?

2. With the increasing availability of computers, many students now type their class papers using word processors rather than typewriters. Because it is so much easier to edit and change text with word processors, we might expect word-processed papers to be better than those simply typed. To test this hypothesis, imagine we instruct 30 students to write a 10-page term paper. We randomly assign 15 students to type their papers on a typewriter and the other 15 students to type their papers on a word processor. (Let's assume all of the students were at least mediocre typists with some experience on a word processor.) After receiving the students' papers, we then retyped all of the papers to be uniform in appearance (to eliminate the

confound that would occur because typed and word-processed papers *look* different). Then, a professor graded each paper on a 10-point scale. The grades were as follows:

Typed papers	Word-processed papers
6	9
3	4
4	7
7	7
7	6
5	10
7	9
10	8
7	5
4	8
5	7
6	4
3	8
7	7
6	9

Conduct a *t*-test to determine whether the quality of papers written using a word processor was higher than that of papers typed on a typewriter.

Answers to Exercises

1. a. If there are 28 subjects, the degrees of freedom are 26. The critical value of a one-tailed *t*-test with df = 26 and an alpha level of .05 is 1.706.

    b. The critical value for a one-tailed *t*-test with df = 26 and an alpha level of .01 is 2.479.

    c. The critical value of *t* is larger when the alpha level is .01 than .05 because, by setting the alpha level at .01, we require greater certainty that the difference between the condition means was not due to error variance. To achieve this greater certainty, the difference between the means, relative to the error variance, must be greater. Thus, the critical value of *t* is larger.

2. The calculated value of *t* for these data is -2.08, which exceeds the critical value of 1.701 (alpha level = .05, df = 28, one-tailed *t*-test). Thus, the average grade for the papers written on a word processor (mean = 7.2) was significantly higher than the average grade for typed papers (mean = 5.8).

For More Information

Details regarding *t*-tests, including paired *t*-tests, may be found in the following texts.

Statistics for the Behavioral Sciences: A First Course for Students of Psychology and Eduction by F. J. Gravetter and L. B. Wallanu, 1992, St. Paul, MN: West.

Statistics for the Behavioral Sciences by J. Jaccard and M. Becker, 1990, Belmont, CA: Wadsworth.

Application of Statistics in Behavioral Research by R. B. May, M. J. Masson, & M. A. Hunter, 1990, New York: Harper & Row.

CHAPTER 12

The Analysis of Variance

*I*n Chapter 10, we discussed an experiment that investigated the effectiveness of various strategies for losing weight (Mahoney et al., 1973). In this study, obese adults were randomly assigned to one of five conditions: self-reward for losing weight, self-punishment for failing to lose weight, self-reward for losing combined with self-punishment for not losing, self-monitoring of weight (but without rewarding or punishing oneself), and a control condition. At the end of the experiment, the researchers wanted to know whether some conditions were more effective than others in helping subjects lose weight.

Given the data shown in Table 12.1, how would you determine whether some of the weight-reduction strategies were more effective than others in helping subjects lose weight? Clearly the average weight loss was greatest in the self-reward condition than in the other conditions, but as we've seen, we must conduct statistical tests to determine whether the differences among the means are greater than we would expect based on the amount of error variance present in the data.

One possible way to analyze these data would be to conduct 10 *t*-tests, comparing the mean of each experimental group to the mean of every other group: Group 1 versus Group 2, Group 1 versus Group 3, Group 1 versus Group 4, Group 1 versus Group 5, Group 2 versus Group 3, Group 2 versus Group 4, Group 2 versus Group 5, Group 3 versus Group 4, Group 3 versus Group 5, and Group 4 versus Group 5. If you performed all 10 of these *t*-tests, you could tell which means differed significantly from the others and determine whether the strategies differentially affected the amount of weight that subjects lost.

The Problem: Inflated Type I Error

Although we could use several *t*-tests to analyze these data, such an analysis creates a serious problem. Recall that when a researcher sets the alpha level at .05, he or

TABLE 12.1

Average Weight Loss in the Mahoney, Moura, and Wade Study

Group	Condition	Mean pounds lost
1	Self-reward	6.4
2	Self-punishment	3.7
3	Self-reward and self-punishment	5.2
4	Self-monitoring of weight	0.8
5	Control group	1.4

she recognizes that a Type I error will occur on up to 5% of the statistical tests he or she conducts. In other words, 5% of the effects that are statistically significant could actually be the result of error variance rather than the result of the independent variable.

If only one *t*-test is conducted, we have only a 5% chance of making a Type I error. But what if we conduct 10 *t*-tests? or 25? or 100? Although the likelihood of making a Type I error on any particular *t*-test is .05, the overall Type I error becomes compounded as we perform an increasing number of tests. As a result, the more *t*-tests we conduct, the more likely it is that one or more of our significant findings will reflect a Type I error, and the more likely it is we will draw invalid conclusions about our findings.

Imagine we conducted ten *t*-tests to analyze differences between each pair of means from the weight loss data in Table 12.1. The probability of making a Type I error (that is, rejecting the null hypothesis when it is true) on *at least one* of the *t*-tests is approximately .40—that is, 4 out of 10. This is considerably higher than the alpha level of .05 for each individual *t*-test we conducted. [When conducting multiple statistical tests, the probability of making a Type I error can be estimated from the formula $1 - (1 - alpha)^c$, where c equals the number of tests (or comparisons) performed.]

The same problem occurs when we analyze data from factorial designs. Analyzing the interaction from a 3×2 design would require several *t*-tests to test the difference between each pair of means. As a result, we increase the probability of making at least one Type I error during the analysis.

Because Type I error becomes inflated when many *t*-tests are conducted, researchers generally do not use *t*-tests when testing differences among more than two means. When we conduct more than one *t*-test, we increase the risk of committing a Type I error and of concluding that we have a significant effect that is actually due to error variance.

The solution to this problem is **analysis of variance.** Analysis of variance, often abbreviated **ANOVA**, is a statistical procedure used to analyze data from designs that involve more than two conditions. ANOVA analyzes differences between all condition means in an experiment *simultaneously*. Rather than testing the difference between each pair of means as a *t*-test does, ANOVA determines whether *any* of a set of means differs from another using a single statistical test that holds the alpha level at .05 (or whatever level the researcher chooses), regardless of how many group means are involved in the test. For example, rather than conducting 10 *t*-tests among all pairs of 5 means (with the likelihood of a Type I error being .40), ANOVA performs a single, simultaneous test on all condition means with only a .05 chance of making a Type I error.

The Rationale Behind ANOVA

Imagine we conducted an experiment in which we knew the independent variable(s) had *absolutely no effect*. In such a case, we could estimate the amount of error variance in the data in one of two ways: (1) we could calculate the error variance by looking at the variability among the subjects within each of the conditions; (2) we could estimate the error variance based on the differences between the condition means; if we knew the independent variable had no effect (and that there was no confounding), the only source of variability among the condition means would be error variance. In other words, when the independent variable has no effect, the variability among condition means and the variability within groups are two reflections of precisely the same thing—error variance.

However, to the extent the independent variable affected subjects' responses and created differences between the conditions, the variability among condition means should be larger than it would if only error variance were causing the means to differ. Thus, if we find that the variance *between* conditions is markedly greater than the variance *within* conditions, we have evidence that the independent variable caused the difference (again, assuming no confounds).

Analysis of variance is based on a statistic called the **F-test,** which is the ratio of the variance among conditions (between-groups variance) to the variance within conditions (within-groups, or error, variance). The larger the between-groups variance relative to the within-groups variance, the larger is the calculated value of *F*, and the more likely it is that the differences among the condition means reflect true effects of the independent variable rather than error variance. By testing this *F*-ratio, we can estimate the likelihood that the differences between the condition means are due to error variance.

We will devote most of this chapter to exploring how ANOVA works. The purpose here is not so much to show how to conduct an ANOVA as to show how ANOVA operates. In fact, the formulas used are for demonstrational purposes; they show what an ANOVA does, but researchers use other forms of these formulas to actually compute an ANOVA. The computational formulas for ANOVA appear in Appendix B.

How ANOVA Works

Recall that the total variance in a set of experimental data can be broken into two parts: systematic variance (which reflects differences among the experimental conditions) and unsystematic, or error, variance (which reflects differences among subjects within the experimental conditions).

Total variance = Systematic variance + Error variance

In a one-way design with a single independent variable, ANOVA breaks the total variance into just these two components—systematic variance (presumably due to the independent variable) and error variance.

Total Sum of Squares

We learned in Chapter 2 that the sum of squares reflects the total amount of variability in a set of data. We learned also that the total sum of squares is calculated by (1) subtracting the mean from each score, (2) squaring these differences, and (3) adding them up. We used this formula for the **total sum of squares,** which we'll abbreviate SS_{total}:

$$SS_{total} = \Sigma(x_i - \bar{x})^2$$

SS_{total} expresses the total amount of variability in a set of data. ANOVA breaks down, or partitions, this total variability to identify its sources. One part—the sum of squares between groups—involves systematic variance that reflects the influence of the independent variable. The other part—the sum of squares within groups—reflects error variance:

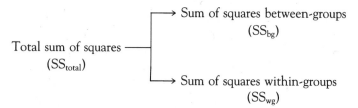

Let's look at these two sources of the total variability more closely.

Sum of Squares Within-Groups

To determine whether differences between condition means reflect only error variance, we need to know how much error variance exists in the data. In an ANOVA, this is estimated by the **sum of squares within-groups** (or SS_{wg}). SS_{wg} is equal to the sum of the sums of squares for each of the experimental groups. In other words, if we calculate the sum of squares (that is, the variability) separately for each experimental group and then add these group sums of squares together, we obtain SS_{wg}.

$$SS_{wg} = \Sigma(x_1 - \bar{x}_1)^2 + \Sigma(x_2 - \bar{x}_2)^2 + \cdots + \Sigma(x_k - \bar{x}_k)^2$$

Think for a moment about what SS_{wg} represents. Because all subjects in a particular condition receive the same level of the independent variable, none of the variability within any of the groups can be due to the independent variable. Thus, when we add the sums of squares across all conditions, SS_{wg} expresses the amount of variability in our data that is *not* due to the independent variable. This, of course, is precisely what error variance is.

As you can see, the size of SS_{wg} increases with the number of conditions. Because we need an index of something like the *average* variance within the experimental conditions, we divide SS_{wg} by $n - k$, where n is the total number of subjects and k is the number of experimental groups. (The quantity, $n - k$, is called the *within-groups degrees of freedom,* or df_{wg}.) By dividing the within-groups sum of squares (SS_{wg}) by the within-group degrees of freedom (df_{wg}), we obtain a quantity know as the **mean square within-groups,** or MS_{wg}.

$$MS_{wg} = SS_{wg}/df_{wg}$$

It should be clear that MS_{wg} provides us with an estimate of the average within-groups, or error, variance. Later we will compare the amount of systematic variance in our data to MS_{wg}.

Sum of Squares Between-Groups

Now that we've estimated the error variance from the variability within the groups, we must calculate the amount of systematic variance in the data. To estimate the systematic variance, ANOVA uses the **sum of squares between-groups** (sometimes called the *sum of squares for treatment*).

The calculation of the sum of squares between-groups (or SS_{bg}) is based on a simple rationale. If the independent variable had no effect, we would expect all the group means to be roughly equal, aside from whatever differences are due to error variance. Because all the means are the same, each condition mean would also be approximately equal to the mean of all the group means (the **grand mean**). However, if the independent variable caused the means of some conditions to be larger or smaller than the means of others, the condition means not only will differ among themselves but also will differ from the grand mean.

Thus, to calculate between-groups variance, we first subtract the grand mean from each of the group means. Small differences indicate the means don't differ very much (and thus the independent variable had little, if any, effect). In contrast, large differences between the condition means and the grand mean indicate large differences between the groups and suggest the independent variable caused the means to differ.

Thus, to obtain SS_{bg}, we (1) subtract the grand mean (GM) from the mean of each group, (2) square these differences, (3) multiply each squared difference by the size of the group, then (4) sum across groups. This can be expressed by the formula

$$SS_{bg} = n_1(\bar{x}_1 - GM)^2 + n_2(\bar{x}_2 - GM)^2 + \cdots + n_k(\bar{x}_k - GM)^2$$

We then divide SS_{bg} by the quantity $k - 1$, where k is the number of group means that went into the calculation of SS_{bg}. The quantity $k - 1$ is called the **between-group degrees of freedom.** When SS_{bg} is divided by its degree of freedom $(k - 1)$, the resulting number is called the **mean square between-groups** (or MS_{bg}), which is our estimate of systematic, or between-groups, variance:

$$MS_{bg} = SS_{bg}/df_{bg}$$

The F-test

We have seen how ANOVA breaks the total variance in subjects' responses into components that reflect within-groups variance and between-groups variance. Because error variance leads the means of the experimental conditions to differ slightly, we expect to find some systematic, between-groups variance even if the independent variables had no effect. Thus, we must test whether the between-groups variance is larger than we would expect based on the amount of within-groups (that is, error) variance in the data.

To do this, we calculate an F-test. To obtain the value of F, we calculate the ratio of between-groups variability to within-groups variability for each effect we are testing. If our study has only one independent variable, we simply divide MS_{bg} by MS_{wg}.

$$F = MS_{bg}/MS_{wg}$$

If the independent variable had no effect, the numerator and denominator of the F-ratio are estimates of the same thing (the amount of error variance), and the value of F will be around 1.00. However, to the extent that the independent variable caused differences among the experimental conditions, systematic variance will be produced and the numerator of F (which contains both systematic and error variance) will be larger than the denominator (which contains error variance only). The only question is *how much* larger the numerator needs to be than the denominator to conclude that the independent variable truly had an effect. We answer this question by locating a critical value of F, just as we did with the t-test.

To find the critical value of F in Appendix A-3, we specify three things: (1) we set the alpha level (usually .05); (2) we calculate the degrees of freedom for the effect we are testing (df_{bg}); (3) we calculate the degrees of freedom for the within-groups variance (df_{wg}). (The calculations for degrees of freedom for various effects are shown in Appendix B.) With these numbers in hand, we can find the critical value of F in the table in Appendix A-3. For example, if we set our alpha level at .05, and the between-groups degrees of freedom is 2 and the within-groups degrees of freedom is 30, the critical value of F is 3.32.

If the value of F we calculate for an effect exceeds the critical value of F obtained from the table, we conclude that at least one of the condition means differs from the others and, thus, that the independent variable had an effect. More formally, if the calculated value of F exceeds the critical value, we *reject the null hypothesis* and conclude that at least one of the condition means differs significantly from another.

If the calculated value of F is less than the critical value, the differences among the group means are no greater than we would expect on the basis of error variance alone. Thus, we fail to reject our null hypothesis and conclude that the independent variable did not have an effect.

In the experiment involving weight loss (Mahoney et al., 1973), the calculated value of F was 4.49. The critical value of F when $df_{bg} = 4$ and $df_{wg} = 48$ is 2.56. Given that the calculated value exceeded the critical value, the authors rejected the null hypothesis and concluded that the five weight-loss strategies were differentially effective.

Extension of ANOVA to Factorial Designs

So far we have seen that, in a one-way ANOVA, we partition the total variability in a set of data into two components: between-groups (systematic) variance and within-groups (error) variance. Put differently, SS_{total} has two sources of variance: SS_{bg} and SS_{wg}.

In factorial designs, such as those we discussed in Chapter 10, the systematic, between-groups portion of the variance can be broken down further into other components to test for the presence of different main effects and interactions. When our design involves more than one independent variable, we can ask whether any systematic variance is related to each of the independent variables, as well as whether systematic variance was produced by interactions among the variables.

Let's consider a two-way factorial design in which we have manipulated two independent variables, which we'll call A and B. (Freedman's density–intensity study of crowding described in Chapter 10 would be a case of such a design.) Using an ANOVA to analyze the data would lead us to break the total variance (SS_{total}) into four parts. Specifically, we could calculate both the sum of squares (SS) and mean square (MS) for:

1. the error variance (SS_{wg} and MS_{wg})
2. the main effect of A (SS_A and MS_A)
3. the main effect of B (SS_B and MS_B)
4. the A × B interaction ($SS_{A \times B}$ and $MS_{A \times B}$)

Together, these four sources of variance would account for all the variability in subjects' responses; that is, $SS_{total} = SS_A + SS_B + SS_{A \times B} + SS_{wg}$.

For example, to calculate SS_A (the systematic variance due to independent variable A), we ignore variable B for the moment and determine how much of the

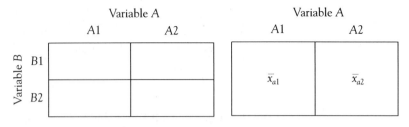

Figure 12.1   Testing the main effect of variable A

Explanation: Imagine we conducted the 2 × 2 factorial experiment shown on the left. When we test for the main effect of variable A, we temporarily ignore the fact that variable B was included in the design, as in the diagram on the right. The calculation for the sum of squares for A (SS_A) is based on the means for Conditions A1 and A2, disregarding variable B.

variance in the dependent variable is associated with A alone. In other words, we disregard the fact that variable B even exists and compute SS_{bg} using just the means for the various conditions of variable A. (See Figure 12.1.)

If the independent variable had no effect, we would expect the means for the various levels of A to be roughly equal to the mean of all of the group means (the grand mean). However, if variable A caused the means of some conditions to be larger than the means of others, the means should differ from the grand mean. Thus, we can calculate the sum of squares for A much as we calculated SS_{bg} earlier:

$$SS_A = n_{a1}(\overline{x}_{a1} - GM)^2 + n_{a2}(\overline{x}_{a2} - GM)^2 + \cdots + n_{aj}(\overline{x}_{aj} - GM)^2$$

Then, by dividing SS_A by the degrees of freedom for A (df_A = number of conditions of A minus 1), we obtain the mean square for A (MS_A), which provides an index of the systematic variance associated with variable A.

The rationale behind testing the main effect of B is the same as that for A. To test the main effect of B, we subtract the grand mean from the mean of each condition of B, ignoring variable A. SS_B is the sum of these squared deviations of the condition means from the grand mean (GM).

$$SS_B = n_{b1}(\overline{x}_{b1} - GM)^2 + n_{b2}(\overline{x}_{b2} - GM)^2 + \cdots + n_{bk}(\overline{x}_{bk} - GM)^2$$

Remember that, in computing SS_B, we ignore variable A, pretending for the moment the only independent variable in the design is variable B (see Figure 12.2). Dividing SS_B by the degrees of freedom for B (the number of conditions for B minus 1), we obtain MS_B, the variance due to B

When analyzing data from a factorial design, we also calculate the amount of systematic variance due to the *interaction* of A and B. As we learned in Chapter 10, an interaction is present if the effects of one independent variable differ as a function of another independent variable.

In an ANOVA, the presence of an interaction is indicated if variance is present in subjects' responses that can't be accounted for by SS_A, SS_B, and SS_{wg}. If

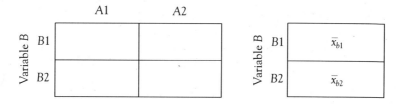

Figure 12.2   Testing the main effect of variable *B*

Explanation: To test the main effect of *B* in the design on the left, ANOVA disregards the presence of *A* (as if the experiment looked like the design on the right). The difference between the mean of *B1* and the mean of *B2* is tested without regard to variable *A*.

no interaction is present, all the variance in subjects' responses can be accounted for by the individual main effects of A and B, as well as error variance (and, thus, $SS_A + SS_B + SS_{wg} = SS_{total}$). However, if the sum of $SS_A + SS_B + SS_{wg}$ is less than SS_{total}, we know the individual main effects of A and B don't account for all the systematic variance in the dependent variable; A and B combine in a nonadditive fashion—that is, they interact. Thus, we can calculate the sum of squares for the interaction by subtracting SS_A, SS_B, and SS_{wg} from SS_{total}. As before, we also calculate $MS_{A \times B}$ to provide the amount of variance due to the $A \times B$ interaction.

In a factorial design, we then calculate a value of F for each main effect and interaction we are testing. For example, in a 2×2 design, we calculate F for the main effect of A by dividing MS_A by MS_{wg}:

$$F_A = MS_A/MS_{wg}$$

We also calculate F for the main effect of B:

$$F_B = MS_B/MS_{wg}$$

To test the interaction, we calculate yet another value of F:

$$F_{A \times B} = MS_{A \times B}/MS_{wg}$$

Each of these calculated values of F is then compared to the critical value of F in a table such as that in Appendix B.

IN DEPTH

CALCULATIONAL FORMULAS FOR ANOVA

The formulas used in the preceding explanation of ANOVA are intended to show conceptually how ANOVA works. When actually calculating an ANOVA, researchers use formulas that, although conceptually identical to those you have just seen, are easier to use. We did not use these calculational formulas in this chapter because, although efficient for calculational purposes, they do not convey as clearly what the various components of ANOVA really reflect. The computational formulas, along with a numerical example, are presented in Appendix B.

Follow-up Tests

When an F-test is statistically significant (that is, when the calculated value of F exceeds the critical value), we know at least one of the group means differs from one of the others. However, because the ANOVA tests all condition means simultaneously, a significant F-test does not always tell us precisely which means differ: perhaps all of the means differ from each other; maybe only one mean differs from the rest; or, some of the means may differ significantly from each other, but not from other means.

The first step in interpreting the results of any experiment is to calculate the means for the significant effects. For example, if the main effect of A is found to be significant, we would calculate the means for the various conditions of A, ignoring variable B. If the main effect of B is significant, we would examine the means for the various conditions of B. If the interaction of A and B is significant, we would calculate the means for all combinations of A and B.

Main effects. If an ANOVA reveals a significant effect for an independent variable that has only two levels, no further statistical tests are necessary. The significant F-test tells us the two means differ significantly, and we can inspect the means to understand the direction and magnitude of the difference between them.

However, if a significant main effect is obtained for an independent variable that has more than two levels, further tests are needed to interpret the finding. Suppose an ANOVA reveals a significant main effect that involves an independent variable that has three levels. The significant main effect indicates that a difference exists between at least two of the three condition means, but it does not indicate which means differ from which.

To identify which means differ significantly, researchers use **follow-up tests,** often called **post hoc tests,** or **multiple comparisons.** Several statistical procedures have been developed for this purpose. Some of the more commonly used are the least significant difference (LSD) test, Tukey's test, Scheffe's test, and Newman–Keuls test. Although differing in specifics, each of these tests is used after a significant F-test to determine precisely which condition means differ.

After obtaining a significant F-test in their study of weight loss, Mahoney and his colleagues used the Newman-Keuls test to determine which weight-loss strategies were more effective. Refer to the means in Table 12.1 as you read their description of the results of this test: "Newman–Keuls comparisons of treatment

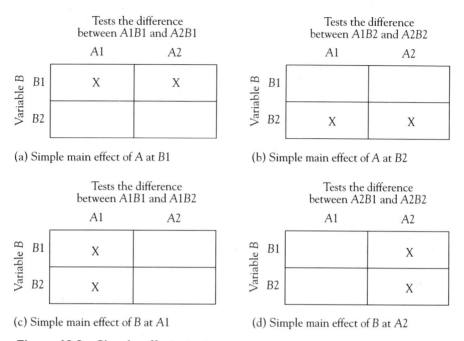

(a) Simple main effect of A at B1

(b) Simple main effect of A at B2

(c) Simple main effect of B at A1

(d) Simple main effect of B at A2

Figure 12.3 Simple effects tests

Explanation: A simple main effect is the effect of one independent variable at only one level of another independent variable. If the interaction in a 2 × 2 design such as this is found to be significant, four possible simple main effects are tested to determine precisely which condition means differ.

means showed that the self-reward S's had lost significantly more pounds than either the self-monitoring ($p < .025$) or the control group ($p < .025$). The self-punishment group did not differ significantly from any other" (1973, p. 406).

Follow-up tests are conducted *only* if the F-test is statistically significant. If the F-test in the ANOVA is not statistically significant, we must conclude that the independent variable had no effect (that is, we fail to reject the null hypothesis) and may not test differences between specific pairs of means.

Interactions. If an interaction is statistically significant, we know the effects of one independent variable differ depending on the level of another independent variable. But again, we must inspect the condition means and conduct additional statistical tests to determine the precise nature of the interaction.

Specifically, when a significant interaction is obtained, we conduct tests of simple main effects. A **simple main effect** is the effect of one independent variable at a particular level of another independent variable. It is, in essence, a *main effect* of the variable but one that occurs *under only one level* of the other variable. If we obtained a significant A × B interaction, we could examine four simple main effects, which are shown in Figure 12.3:

1. The simple main effect of A at B1. (Do the means of Conditions A1 and A2 differ for subjects who received Condition B1?) See Figure 12.3(a).

2. The simple main effect of A at B2. (Do the means of Conditions A1 and A2 differ for subjects who received Condition B2?) See Figure 12.3(b).

3. The simple main effect of B at A1. (Do the means of Conditions B1 and B2 differ for subjects who received Condition A1?) See Figure 12.3(c).

4. The simple main effect of B at A2. (Do the means of Conditions B1 and B2 differ for subjects who received Condition A2?) See Figure 12.3(d).

Testing the simple main effects shows us precisely which condition means within the interaction differ from each other.

CONTRIBUTORS TO BEHAVIORAL RESEARCH

FISHER, EXPERIMENTAL DESIGN, AND THE ANALYSIS OF VARIANCE

No person has contributed more to the design and analysis of experimental research than English biologist Ronald A. Fisher (1890–1962). After early jobs with an investment company and as a public school teacher, Fisher became a statistician for the experimental agricultural station at Rothamsted, England.

Agricultural research relies heavily on experimental designs in which growing conditions are manipulated and their effects on crop quality and yield are assessed. In this context, Fisher developed many statistical approaches that have spread from agriculture to behavioral science, the best known of which is the analysis of variance. In fact, the *F*-test was named for Fisher.

In 1925, Fisher wrote one of the first books on statistical techniques, *Statistical Methods for Research.* Despite the fact that Fisher was a poor writer (someone once said that no student should try to read this book unless he or she had read it before), *Statistical Methods* became a classic in the field. Ten years later, Fisher published *The Design of Experiments,* a landmark in research design. These two books raised the level of sophistication in our understanding of research design and statistical analysis and paved the way for contemporary behavioral science (Kendall, 1970).

Between-Subjects and Within-Subjects ANOVAs

Every example of ANOVA in this chapter involved *between-subjects designs*—experiments in which subjects are randomly assigned to experimental conditions (see Chapter 9). Although the rationale is the same, slightly different computational procedures are used for within-subjects and between-within (or mixed) designs in which each subject serves in more than one experimental condition. Just as we use a paired *t*-test to analyze data from a within-subjects two-group experiment, we use within-subjects ANOVA for multilevel and factorial within-subjects designs, and we use split-plot ANOVA for between-within designs. Like the paired *t*-test, these variations of ANOVA capitalize on the fact that we have repeated measures on each subject to reduce the estimate of error variance, thereby providing a more powerful statistical test. Full details regarding these analyses take us beyond the scope of this book but may be found in most introductory statistics books, such as those listed at the end of Chapter 11.

Multivariate Analysis of Variance

We have discussed the two inferential statistics most often used to analyze differences among means of a single dependent variable: the *t*-test to test differences between two conditions, and the analysis of variance to test differences among more than two conditions.

For reasons that will be clear in a moment, researchers sometimes want to test differences between conditions on several dependent variables simultaneously. Because *t*-tests and ANOVAs cannot do this, researchers turn to multivariate analysis of variance (MANOVA). Whereas an analysis of variance tests differences among the means of two or more conditions on one dependent variable, a **multivariate analysis of variance, or MANOVA,** tests differences between the means of two or more conditions on two or more dependent variables simultaneously.

A reasonable question at this point is, Why would anyone want to test group differences on *several* dependent variables at the same time? Why not simply perform several ANOVAs—one on each dependent variable? Researchers turn to MANOVA rather than ANOVA for the following reasons.

Conceptually Related Dependent Variables

One reason for using MANOVA arises when a researcher has measured several dependent variables, all of which tap into the same general construct. When several dependent variables measure different aspects of the same construct, the researcher may wish to analyze the variables as a set rather than individually.

Suppose you were interested in determining whether a marriage enrichment program improved married couples' satisfaction with their relationships. You conducted an experiment in which couples were randomly assigned to participate for 2 hours in either a structured marriage enrichment activity, an unstructured conversation on a topic of their own choosing, or no activity together. (You should recognize this as a randomized groups design with three conditions; see Chapter 9.) One month after the program, members of each couple were asked to rate their marital satisfaction on 10 dimensions involving satisfaction with finances, communication, ways of dealing with conflict, sexual relations, social life, recreation, and so on.

If you wanted to, you could analyze these data by conducting 10 ANOVAs—one on each dependent variable. However, because all 10 dependent variables reflect various aspects of general marital satisfaction, you might want to know whether the program affected satisfaction *in general* across all the dependent measures. If this were your goal, you might use MANOVA to analyze your data. MANOVA combines the information from all 10 dependent variables into a new composite variable, then analyzes whether subjects' scores on this new composite variable differ among the experimental groups.

Inflation of Type I Error

A second use of MANOVA is to control Type I error. As we saw earlier, the probability of making a Type I error (rejecting the null hypothesis when it is true) increases with the number of statistical tests we perform. For this reason, we conducted one ANOVA rather than many *t*-tests when our experimental design involved more than two conditions (and thus more than two means). Type I error also becomes inflated when we conduct *t*-tests or ANOVAs *on many dependent variables*. The more dependent variables we analyze in a study, the more likely we are to obtain significant differences that are due to Type I error rather than to the independent variable.

To use an extreme case, imagine we conducted a two-group study in which we measured 100 dependent variables, then tested the difference between the two group means on each of these variables with 100 *t*-tests. If we set our alpha level at .05, we could obtain significant *t*-tests on as many as 5 of our dependent variables, even if our independent variable had no effect. Although few researchers use as many as 100 dependent variables in a single study, Type I error increases whenever we analyze more than one dependent variable.

Because MANOVA tests differences among the means of the groups *across all dependent variables simultaneously*, the overall alpha level is held at .05 (or whatever level the researcher chooses), no matter how many dependent variables are tested. Although most researchers don't worry about analyzing a few variables one by one, many use MANOVA to guard against Type I error whenever they analyze many dependent variables.

How MANOVA Works

MANOVA begins by creating a new composite variable that is a weighted sum of the original dependent variables. How this **canonical variable** is mathematically derived need not concern us here. The important thing is that the new canonical variable *includes all the variance in the set of original variables*. Thus, it provides us with a single index of our variable of interest (such as marital satisfaction).

In the second step of the MANOVA, a multivariate version of the *F*-test is performed to determine whether subjects' scores on the canonical variable differ among the experimental conditions. If the multivariate *F*-test is significant, we conclude that the experimental manipulation affected the *set* of dependent variables as a whole. For example, in our study of marriage enrichment, we would conclude that the marriage enrichment workshop created significant differences in the overall satisfaction in the three experimental groups; we would then conduct additional analyses to understand precisely how the groups differed. MANOVA has allowed us to analyze the dependent variables as a set rather than individually.

In cases in which we use MANOVA to limit Type I errors, obtaining a significant multivariate *F*-test allows us to then conduct ANOVAs on each variable separately. Having been assured by the MANOVA that the groups differ significantly on *something*, we may then perform additional analyses without risking an increased chance of Type I error. However, if the MANOVA is not significant, examining the individual dependent variables using ANOVA would run the risk of increasing Type I errors.

BEHAVIORAL RESEARCH CASE STUDY

EFFECTS OF HAVING A DISABLED SIBLING: AN EXAMPLE OF MANOVA

McHale and Gamble (1989) interviewed 62 children between the ages of 8 and 14, half of whom had a younger brother or sister who was mentally retarded. The remaining children had a younger sibling with no disability. Among the data they collected were six ratings relevant to the children's adjustment. They measured each child's self-esteem on four dimensions (academics, social acceptance, conduct, and general self-worth), as well as depression and anxiety.

The researchers conducted a multivariate analysis of variance on these six scores. As explained earlier, the MANOVA tested whether the two groups of children differed on the weighted sum of these six dependent variables (the canonical variable). The MANOVA revealed a significant difference between the two groups, showing that children with disabled siblings had lower overall adjustment scores than those without disabled siblings. In other words, the significant MANOVA showed that the two groups differed on the canonical variable which, remember, involved all six of the variables related to adjustment.

Because the MANOVA was statistically significant, the researchers were permitted to analyze each dependent variable separately using ANOVA. These analyses revealed significant differences between the groups on four of the six dependent variables. Specifically, compared with children without disabled brothers or sisters, children who had a disabled sibling were more depressed, more anxious, and had lower self-esteem relevant to social acceptance and conduct.

Experimental and Nonexperimental Uses of Inferential Statistics

Most of the examples of *t*-tests, ANOVA, and MANOVA we have discussed involved data from true experimental designs in which the researcher randomly assigned subjects to conditions and manipulated one or more independent variables. A *t*-test, ANOVA, or MANOVA was then used to test the differences among the means of the experimental conditions.

Although the *t*-test and analysis of variance were developed in the context of experimental research, they are also widely used to analyze data from nonexperimental studies. In such studies, subjects are not randomly assigned to groups (as in a true experiment) but are categorized into naturally occurring groups. Then, a *t*-test, ANOVA, or MANOVA is used to analyze the differences among the means of these groups. For example, if we want to compare the average depression scores for a group of women and a group of men, we can use a *t*-test, even though the study is not a true experiment.

Butler, Hokanson, and Flynn (1994) obtained a measure of depression for 73 subjects on two different occasions, 5 months apart. On the basis of these two depression scores, they categorized subjects into one of five groups: (1) unremitted depression—subjects who were depressed at both testing times, (2) remitted depression—subjects who were depressed at Time 1 but not at Time 2, (3) new cases—subjects who were nondepressed at Time 1 but fell in the depressed range at Time 2, (4) nonrelapsers—subjects who had once been depressed, but were nondepressed at both Time 1 and Time 2, and (5) never depressed.

The researchers then used MANOVA and ANOVA (as well as Newman–Keuls post hoc tests) to analyze whether these five groups differed in average self-esteem, depression, lability to positive and negative effects, and other measures. Even though this was a nonexperimental design and subjects were classified into groups rather than randomly assigned, ANOVA and MANOVA were appropriate analyses.

Computer Analyses

In the earliest days of behavioral science, researchers conducted all their statistical analyses by hand. Because analyses were time-consuming and cumbersome, researchers understandably relied primarily on relatively simple analytic techniques. The invention of the calculator (first mechanical, then electronic) was a great boon to researchers because it allowed them to perform mathematical operations more quickly and with less error.

However, not until the widespread availability of computers and user-friendly statistical software did the modern age of statistical analysis begin. Analyses that once took many hours (or even days!) to conduct by hand could be performed on a computer in a minute or less. Furthermore, the spread of bigger and faster computers allowed researchers to conduct increasingly complex analyses and test more sophisticated research hypotheses. Thus, over the past 20 years, we have seen an increase in the complexity of the analyses researchers commonly use. For example, prior to 1980, MANOVA—a complex and laborious analysis to perform by hand—was used only rarely; today, its use is quite common.

In the earliest days of the computer, computer programs had to be written from scratch for each new analysis. Researchers either had to be proficient at computer programming or have the resources to hire a programmer to write the programs for them. Gradually, however, statistical software packages were developed that any researcher could use by simply writing a handful of commands to inform the computer how their data were entered and which analyses to conduct.

Today, several software packages exist that can perform most statistical analyses. The statistical software programs used most commonly by behavioral researchers include SPSS^x, SAS, and BMDP. Once the researcher has entered his or her data into the computer and written a short set of commands to instruct the computer what analyses to perform, most analyses take only a few seconds.

Although computers have freed researchers from most hand calculations (occasionally, it is still faster to perform simple analyses by hand than to use the computer), researchers must still understand when to use particular analyses, what requirements must be met for an analysis to be valid, and what the results of a particular analysis tell them about their data. Computers do not at all diminish the importance or necessity of understanding statistics.

Summary

1. Analysis of variance ranks among the most commonly used statistical procedures. When researchers want to compare more than two means, an ANOVA rather than a t-test is used because ANOVA controls the probability of a Type I error.

2. ANOVA partitions the total variability in subjects' responses into between-groups variance and within-groups variance. Then an F-test is conducted to determine whether the between-groups variance exceeds what we would expect based on the amount of within-groups variance in the data.

3. In a one-way design, a single F-test is conducted to test the effects of the lone independent variable. In a factorial design, an F-test is conducted to test each main effect and interaction.

4. For each effect being tested, the calculated value of F (the ratio of MS_{bg}/MS_{wg}) is compared to a critical value of F. If the calculated value exceeds the critical value, we know at least one condition mean differs from the others.

5. If the *F*-tests show that the main effects or interactions are statistically significant, follow-up tests are often needed to elucidate the precise effect of the independent variable. Main effects of independent variables that involve more than two levels require post hoc tests, whereas interactions are decomposed using simple effects tests.

6. Multivariate analysis of variance (MANOVA) is used to test the differences among the means of two or more conditions on a set of dependent variables. MANOVA is used in two general cases: when the dependent variables all measure aspects of the same general construct (and thus lend themselves to analysis as a set), and when the researcher is concerned that performing analyses on several dependent variables will inflate the possibility of a Type I error.

Key Terms

analysis of variance (ANOVA)	follow-up tests
F-test	post hoc tests
total sum of squares (SS_{total})	multiple comparisons
sum of squares within-groups (SS_{wg})	simple main effect
mean square within-groups (MS_{wg})	multivariate analysis of variance
sum of squares between-groups (SS_{bg})	(MANOVA)
grand mean	canonical variable
mean square between-groups (MS_{bg})	

Review Questions

1. Why do researchers use ANOVA rather than *t*-tests to analyze data from experiments that have more than two groups?

2. An ANOVA for a one-way design partitions the total variance in a set of data into two components. What are they?

3. What kind of variance does the sum of squares within-groups (SS_{wg}) reflect?

4. The sum of squares between-groups (SS_{bg}) represents the degree to which the condition means vary around _____.

5. In an experiment with two independent variables, an ANOVA partitions the total variance into four components. What are they?

6. What is the general form of the formula for the *F*-test?

7. Why should the value of *F* be approximately 1.00 when the independent variable had absolutely no effect on subjects' responses?

8. If the calculated value of F is found to be significant for the main effect of an independent variable with more than two levels, what tests does the researcher then conduct? Why are such tests not necessary if the independent variable had only two levels?

9. When are tests of simple main effects used, and what do researchers learn from them?

10. Who developed the rationale and computations for the analysis of variance?

11. When would you use a multivariate analysis of variance?

CHAPTER 13

Quasi-Experimental Designs

To reduce the incidence of fatal traffic accidents, many states have passed laws requiring that passengers in automobiles wear seat belts. Proponents of such laws claim that wearing seat belts significantly decreases the likelihood passengers will be killed or seriously injured in a traffic accident. Opponents of these laws argue that wearing seat belts does not decrease traffic fatalities. Instead, they say, it poses an increased risk because seat belts may trap passengers inside a burning car. Furthermore, they argue that such laws are useless because they are difficult to enforce and few people actually obey them anyway. Who is right? Do laws that require that people wear seat belts actually reduce traffic fatalities?

This question seems simple enough until we consider the kind of research we would need to conduct to show that such laws actually *cause* a decrease in traffic fatalities. To answer such a question would require an experimental design such as those we discussed in Chapters 9 and 10. We would have to randomly assign people to either wear or not wear safety belts for a prolonged period of time, then measure the fatality rate for those two groups.

The problems of doing such a study should be obvious. First, we would find it very difficult both to randomly assign people to wear or not wear seat belts and to ensure that our subjects actually followed our instructions. Second, the incidence of serious traffic accidents is so low, relative to the number of drivers, that we would need a gigantic sample to obtain even a few serious accidents within a reasonable period of time. A third problem is an ethical one: Would we want to randomly assign some people to *not wear seat belts*, with the possibility that we would cause them to be killed or injured if they have an accident? Obviously, it would not be feasible to design a true experiment to determine whether seat belts are effective in reducing traffic injuries and fatalities.

From the earliest days of psychology, behavioral researchers have shown a distinct preference for experimental designs over other approaches to doing research. In experiments we can manipulate the independent variables and carefully control other factors that might affect the outcome of the study, allowing us to draw relatively confident conclusions about whether the independent variable caused changes in the dependent variable.

However, many real-world questions, such as whether seat-belt legislation reduces traffic fatalities, can't always be addressed within the narrow strictures of experimentation. Often, researchers do not have sufficient control over their subjects to randomly assign them to experimental conditions. In other cases, they may be unable or unwilling to manipulate the independent variable of interest. In such instances, researchers often use **quasi-experimental designs.** Unlike true experiments, quasi-experiments do not involve randomly assigning subjects to conditions. Instead, comparisons are made between people in groups that already exist (such as those who live in states with and without seat-belt laws) or within a single group of subjects before and after an experimental treatment has occurred (such as examining injuries before and after a seat-belt law is passed).

Because such designs do not involve random assignment of subjects to conditions, the researcher is not able to determine which subjects will receive the various levels of the independent variable. In fact, in many studies the researcher does not manipulate the independent variable at all; researchers do not have the power to introduce legislation regarding seat-belt use, for example. In such cases, the term **quasi-independent variable** is sometimes used to indicate that the variable was not a true independent variable manipulated by the researcher but instead occurred for other reasons.

The strength of the experimental designs we examined in the preceding few chapters lies in their ability to demonstrate that the independent variables caused changes in the dependent variables. As we saw, experimental designs do this by eliminating alternative explanations for the findings obtained. Experimental designs generally have high internal validity; researchers can conclude that the observed effects were due to the independent variables rather than to other, extraneous factors (see Chapter 9).

Generally speaking, quasi-experimental designs do not possess the same degree of internal validity as experimental designs. Because subjects are not randomly assigned to conditions and the researcher may have no control over the independent variable, potential threats to internal validity are present in most quasi-experiments. Even so, a well-designed quasi-experiment that eliminates as many threats to internal validity as possible can provide strong circumstantial evidence about cause-and-effect relationships.

The quality of a quasi-experimental design depends on how many threats to internal validity it successfully eliminates. Quasi-experimental designs differ in the degree to which they control threats to internal validity. Needless to say, designs that eliminate most of the threats to internal validity are preferable to those that eliminate only a few. In this chapter, we will discuss several basic quasi-experimental designs, beginning with the weakest, least preferable designs in terms of their ability to eliminate threats to internal validity and then moving to stronger quasi-experimental designs.

IN DEPTH

THE INTERNAL VALIDITY CONTINUUM

Researchers draw a sharp distinction between experimental designs (in which the researcher controls both the assignment of subjects to conditions and the independent variable) and quasi-experimental designs (in which the researcher lacks control over one or both of these aspects of the design). However, this distinction should not lead us to hastily conclude that experimental designs are unequivocally superior to quasi-experimental designs. Although this may be true in a very general sense, both experimental and quasi-experimental designs differ widely in terms of their internal validity. Indeed, some quasi-experiments are more internally valid than some true experiments.

A more useful way of conceptualizing research designs is along a continuum of low to high internal validity. Recall from Chapter 9 that *internal validity* refers to the degree to which a researcher draws accurate conclusions about the effects of an independent variable on subjects' responses. At the low validity pole of the continuum are studies that lack the necessary controls to draw any meaningful conclusions about the effects of the independent variable whatsoever. As we move up the continuum, studies have increasingly tighter experimental control and hence higher internal validity. At the high validity pole of the continuum are studies in which exceptional design and tight control allow us to rule out every reasonable alternative explanation for the findings.

There is no point on this continuum at which we can unequivocally draw a line separating studies that are acceptable from the standpoint of internal validity from those that are unacceptable. Virtually all studies—whether experimental or quasi-experimental—possess some potential threats to internal validity. The issue in judging the quality of a study is whether the most serious threats have been eliminated, thereby allowing a reasonable degree of confidence in the conclusions we draw. As we will see, well-designed quasi-experiments can provide rather conclusive evidence regarding the effects of quasi-independent variables on behavior.

Pretest–Posttest Designs

Researchers do not always have the power to assign subjects to experimental conditions. This is particularly true when the research deals with understanding the effects of an intervention on a group of people in the real world. For example, a junior high school may introduce a schoolwide program to educate students about the dangers of drug abuse, and the school board may want to know whether the program is effective in reducing drug use among the students. In this instance, random assignment is impossible because *all* students in the school were exposed to the program. If you were hired as a behavioral researcher to evaluate the effectiveness of this program, what kind of a study would you design?

How NOT to Do a Study: The One-Group Pretest–Posttest Design

One possibility would be to measure student drug use before the antidrug program and again afterward to see whether drug use decreased. Such a design could be portrayed as

$$O1 \quad X \quad O2$$

where O1 is a pretest measure of drug use, X is the introduction of the antidrug program (the quasi-independent variable), and O2 is the posttest measure of drug use one year later. (O stands for *o*bservation.)

It should be apparent that this design, the **one-group pretest–posttest design,** is a very poor research strategy because it fails to eliminate most threats to internal validity. Many other plausible reasons exist to explain any change in drug use we might observe. If you observe a change in students' drug use between O1 and O2, how sure are you that the change was due to the antidrug program as opposed to some other factor?

Many other factors could have contributed to the change. For example, the students may have matured between the pretest and the posttest (maturation effects). Events other than the program may have occurred between O1 and O2 (history effects); perhaps a popular rock musician died of an overdose, the principal started searching students' lockers for drugs, or the local community started a citywide *Just Say No to Drugs* or *DARE* campaign. Another possibility is that the first measurement of drug use (O1) may have started students thinking about drugs, resulting in lower use independent of the antidrug program (testing effect). Extraneous factors such as these may have occurred at the same time as the antidrug education program and may have been responsible for decreased drug use.

In some studies, the internal validity of one-group pretest–posttest designs may also be threatened by **regression to the mean**—the tendency for extreme scores in a distribution to move, or regress, toward the mean of the distribution with repeated testing (Neale & Liebert, 1980). In many studies, subjects are selected because of their extreme scores on some variable of interest. For example, we may want to examine the effects of a drug education program on students who are heavy drug users. Or, perhaps we are examining the effects of a remedial reading program on students who are poor readers. In cases such as this, a researcher may select subjects who have extreme scores on a pretest (of drug use or reading ability, for example), expose them to the quasi-independent variable (the antidrug or reading program), then remeasure them to see whether their scores changed (drug use declined or reading scores improved, for example).

The difficulty with this approach is that when subjects are selected because they have extreme scores on the pretest, their scores may change from pretest to posttest because of a statistical artifact called regression to the mean. As we learned in Chapter 3, all scores contain measurement error that causes subjects' *observed* scores to differ from their *true* scores. Overall, measurement error produces random fluctuations in subjects' scores from one measurement to the next; thus, if we test a sample of subjects twice, subjects' scores are as likely to increase as to decrease from the first to the second test.

However, although the general effect of measurement error on the scores in a distribution is random, the measurement error present in extreme scores tends to bias the scores in an extreme direction—that is, away from the mean. For example, if we select a group of subjects with very low reading scores, these subjects are much more likely to have observed scores that were *deflated* by measurement error (because they were tired or ill, for example) than to have observed scores that were higher than their true scores. When subjects who scored in an extreme fashion on a pretest are retested, many of the factors that contributed to their artificially extreme scores on the pretest are unlikely to be present; for example, students who performed poorly on a pretest of reading ability because they were ill are likely to be healthy at the time of the posttest. As a result, their scores on the posttest are likely to be more moderate than they were on the pretest; that is, their scores are likely to *regress toward the mean* of the distribution. Unfortunately, a one-group pretest–posttest design does not allow us to determine whether changes in subjects' scores are due to the quasi-independent variable or to regression to the mean.

Strictly speaking, the one-group pretest–posttest design is called a **preexperimental design** rather than a quasi-experimental design because it lacks control, has little internal validity, and thereby fails to meet any of the basic requirements for a research design at all. Many alternative explanations of observed changes in subjects' scores can be suggested, undermining our ability to document the effects of the quasi-independent variable itself. As a result, such designs should virtually never be used.

Nonequivalent Control Group Design

One partial solution to the weaknesses of the one-group design is to obtain one or more control groups for comparison purposes. Because we can't randomly assign students to participate or not participate in the antidrug program, a true control group is not possible. However, the design would benefit from adding a *nonequivalent* control group. In a **nonequivalent control group design,** the researcher looks for one or more groups of subjects that appear to be reasonably similar to the group that received the quasi-independent variable. A nonequivalent control group design comes in two varieties, one that involves only a posttest and another that involves both a pretest and a posttest.

Nonequivalent groups posttest-only design.   One option is to measure both groups after one has received the experimental treatment. For example, you could assess drug use among students at the school that used the antidrug program and among students at another, roughly comparable school that did not use drug education. This design, the **nonequivalent groups posttest-only design** (or static group comparison) can be diagrammed like this:

Experimental group: X   O

Nonequivalent control: —   O

Unfortunately, this design also has many weaknesses. Perhaps the most troublesome is that we have no way of knowing whether the two groups were actually similar *before* the experimental group received the treatment. If the two groups differ at time O, we don't know whether the difference was caused by variable X or whether the groups differed even before the experimental group received X (this involves biased assignment of subjects to conditions, or the **selection bias**). Because we have no way of being sure the groups were equivalent before subjects received the quasi-independent variable, the nonequivalent control group posttest-only design is very weak in terms of internal validity and should rarely be used. However, as the following case study shows, such designs can sometimes provide convincing data.

BEHAVIORAL RESEARCH CASE STUDY

NONEQUIVALENT CONTROL GROUP DESIGN: PERCEIVED RESPONSIBILITY AND WELL-BEING AMONG THE AGED

The elderly decline in physical health and psychological functioning after being placed in a nursing home. Langer and Rodin (1976) designed a study to test the hypothesis that a portion of this decline is due to the loss of control the elderly often feel when moved from their own homes to an institutional setting. The subjects in their study were 91 elderly people, from 65 to 90 years old, who lived in a Connecticut nursing home. In designing their study, Langer and Rodin were concerned about the possibility of **experimental contamination.** When subjects in different conditions of a study interact with one another, the possibility exists that they may talk about the study among themselves and that one experimental condition becomes "contaminated" by the other. To minimize the likelihood of contamination, the researchers decided not to randomly assign residents in the nursing home to the two experimental conditions. Rather, they randomly selected two floors in the facility, assigning residents of one floor to one condition and those on the other floor to the other condition. Residents on different floors interacted very little with one another, so this procedure minimized contamination. However, the decision not to randomly assign subjects to conditions made this a quasi-experimental design—specifically, a nonequivalent control group design.

An administrator gave different talks to the residents on the two floors. One speech emphasized the residents' responsibility for themselves and encouraged them to make their own decisions about their lives in the facility; the other emphasized the staff's responsibility for the residents. Thus, one group was made to feel a high sense of responsibility and control, whereas the other group experienced lower responsibility and control. In both cases, the responsibilities and options stressed by the administrator were already available to all residents, so the groups differed chiefly in the degree to which their freedom, responsibility, and choice were explicitly stressed.

The residents were assessed on a number of measures a few weeks after hearing the speech. Compared with the other residents, those who heard the speech that emphasized their personal control and responsibility were more active and alert, happier, and more involved in activities within the nursing home. In addition, the nursing staff rated them as more interested, sociable, self-initiating, and vigorous than the other residents. In fact, follow-up data collected 18 months later showed long-term psychological and physical effects of the intervention, including a lower mortality rate among subjects in the high-responsibility group (Rodin & Langer, 1977).

The implication is, of course, that giving elderly residents greater choice and responsibility *caused* these positive changes. However, in considering these results, we must remember that this was a quasi-experimental design. Not only were subjects not assigned randomly to conditions, but they lived on different floors of the facility. To some extent, subjects in the two groups were cared for by different members of the nursing home staff and lived in different social groups. Perhaps the nursing staff on one floor was more helpful than that on another floor, or social support among the residents was greater on one floor than another. Because of these differences, we cannot eliminate the possibility that the obtained differences between the two groups were due to other variables that differed systematically between the groups.

We should note that most researchers do not view these alternative explanations to Langer and Rodin's findings as particularly plausible. (In fact, their study is highly regarded in the field.) We have no particular reason to suspect that the two floors of the nursing home differed in some way that led to the findings they obtained. Even so, the fact that it is a quasi-experiment should make us less confident of the findings than we might be had a true experimental design been used.

Nonequivalent groups pretest–posttest design.   Some of the weaknesses of the nonequivalent control group design are eliminated by measuring the two groups twice, once before and once after the quasi-independent variable. The **nonequivalent groups pretest–posttest design** can be portrayed as follows:

Experimental group: O1   X   O2

Nonequivalent control: O1   —   O2

This design lets us see whether the two groups scored similarly on the dependent variable (for example, drug use) before the introduction of the treatment at point X. Even if the pretest scores at O1 aren't identical for the two groups, they provide us with baseline information we can use to determine whether the groups *changed* from O1 to O2. If the scores change between the two testing times for the experimental group but *not* for the nonequivalent control group, we have somewhat more confidence that the change was due to the quasi-independent variable.

For example, to evaluate the antidrug program, you might obtain a nonequivalent control group from another junior high school that does not have an antidrug program under way. If drug use changes from pretest to posttest for the experimental group but not for the nonequivalent control group, we might assume the program had an effect.

Even so, the nonequivalent groups pretest–posttest design does not eliminate all threat to internal validity. For example, a **local history effect** may occur. Something may happen to one group that does not happen to the other (Cook & Campbell, 1979). Perhaps some event that occurred in the experimental school but not in the control school affected students' attitudes toward drugs—a popular athlete was kicked off the team for using drugs, for example. If this happens, what appears to be an effect of the antidrug program may actually be due to a local history effect. This confound is sometimes called a **selection-by-history interaction** because a "history" effect occurs in one group but not in the other.

In brief, although the nonequivalent groups design eliminates some threats to internal validity, it doesn't eliminate all of them. Even so, with proper controls and measures, this design can provide useful information about real-world problems.

BEHAVIORAL RESEARCH CASE STUDY

NONEQUIVALENT GROUPS PRETEST–POSTTEST DESIGN: SELF-ESTEEM AND ORGANIZED SPORTS

Children with high self-esteem generally fare better than those with low self-esteem; for example, they tend to be happier, less anxious, and generally better adjusted. In studies designed to identify the sources of high self-esteem in children, researchers have focused primarily on children's experiences in school and within their families. Smoll, Smith, Barnett, and Everett (1993) decided to extend this literature by studying how self-esteem may be affected by the adults who coach children's organized sports. Specifically, they were interested in whether coaches could be trained to treat their players in ways that bolster the players' self-esteem.

The researchers obtained the cooperation of 18 male head coaches of 152 male Little League baseball players in the Seattle area. Rather than assigning coaches and their teams randomly to conditions, the researchers decided to use the 8 teams in one league as the experimental group and the 10 teams from two other leagues as the nonequivalent control group. Although the decision not to use random assignment resulted in a quasi-experimental design, the researchers concluded that this strategy was necessary to prevent information about the training program from being spread from coaches who were in the training group to those who were not.

In looking for possible preexisting differences between the groups, the researchers found that the coaches who had been assigned to the two groups did not differ in average age, years of coaching experience, or socioeconomic level. Nor did the players in the two groups differ in mean age of the players (the average age was 11.4 years). Of course, the two groups may have differed systematically on some variable the researchers did not examine, but at least we have evidence that the coaches and players did not differ on major demographic variables before the study began.

Before the start of the season, a measure of self-esteem was administered to all the players. Then, the 8 coaches in the experimental group underwent a $2\frac{1}{2}$ hour training session designed to help them relate more effectively to child athletes. Among other things, coaches were taught how to use reinforcement and corrective instruction instead of punishment and punitive instruction when working with their players. The coaches in the nonequivalent control group did not participate in such a training session. Immediately after the baseball season ended, players' self-esteem was assessed again.

The results of the study showed that, before the beginning of the season, the average self-esteem score for players in the trained and untrained groups did not differ significantly; the mean self-esteem score was 47.8 for both groups. However, at the end of the season, the self-esteem score of players whose coaches participated in the training program ($M = 47.7$) was significantly higher than that of the players of the untrained coaches ($M = 47.4$).

The effect was even more pronounced when the researchers analyzed the players who had started off with the lowest preseason self-esteem. (Obviously, players who already had high self-esteem were unlikely to change much as a result of how their coaches treated them.) As you can see in Figure 13.1, among boys with initially low-self-esteem, those who played for trained coaches showed a significant increase in self-esteem scores, whereas those who played for untrained coaches did not show a significant change.

These results provide supportive evidence that how coaches treat their players has implications for the players' self-esteem and that coaches can be trained to deal with their team in ways that promote self-esteem. Keep in mind, however, that this was a quasi-experiment in that coaches and players were *not* randomly assigned to the two conditions. Although no differences between the two groups were detected before the start of coaches' training, the design of the study does not completely eliminate the possibility that the groups differed in some other way that was responsible for the results.

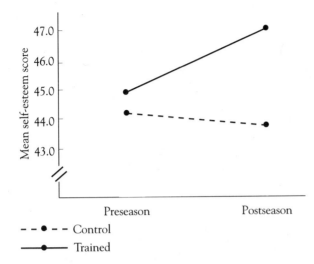

Figure 13.1 Self-esteem scores of low-self-esteem boys who played for trained and untrained coaches (From Smoll et al., 1993)

Explanation: The self-esteem scores of boys who played for trained and untrained coaches did not differ significantly before the Little League season started. However, after the season, the boys whose coaches had received special training scored significantly higher in self-esteem than the boys whose coaches had not received training. In addition, the mean self-esteem score increased significantly for boys who played for trained coaches but remained virtually unchanged for the players of untrained coaches.

Time Series Designs

Some weaknesses of the nonequivalent control group designs are further eliminated by a set of procedures known as time series designs. **Time series designs** measure the dependent variable on several occasions before and on several occasions after the quasi-independent variable occurs. By measuring the target behavior on several occasions, we can further eliminate threats to internal validity.

Simple Interrupted Time Series Design

The **simple interrupted time series design** involves taking several pretest measures before introduction of the independent (or quasi-independent) variable, and then taking several posttest measures afterward. This design can be diagrammed as

O1   O2   O3   O4   X   O5   O6   O7   O8

As you can see, repeated measurements of the dependent variable have been *interrupted* by the occurrence of the quasi-independent variable (X). For example, we could measure drug use every three months for a year before the antidrug program starts, then every three months for a year afterward. If the program had an effect on drug use, we should see a marked change between O4 and O5.

The rationale behind this design is that, by taking multiple measurements both before and after the quasi-independent variable, we can examine the effects of the quasi-independent variable against the backdrop of other changes that may be occurring in the dependent variable. For example, using this design, we should be able to distinguish changes due to aging or maturation from changes due to the quasi-independent variable. If drug use is declining because of changing norms or because the subjects are maturing, we should see gradual changes in drug use from one observation to the next, not just between the first four and the last four observations.

For illustration, compare the two graphs in Figure 13.2. Which of the graphs seems to show that the drug education program lowered drug use? In Figure

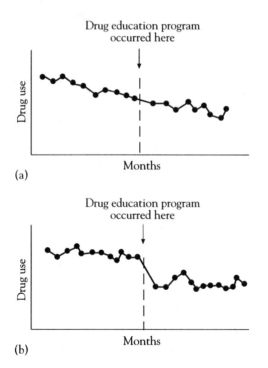

Figure 13.2   Results from a simple interrupted time series design

Explanation: It is difficult to determine from (a) whether the drug education program reduced drug use or whether the lower use after the program was part of a general decline in drug use that started before the program. In contrast, the pattern in (b) is clearer. Because the decrease in drug use occurred immediately after the program, we have greater confidence that the change was due to the program.

Just as Santa suspected, a time series design showed that the month of December is associated with a predictable change in children's behavior.

13.2(a), drug use is lower after the program than before it, but it is unclear whether the decline was associated with the program or was part of a downward pattern that began *before* the initiation of the program. In Figure 13.2(b), on the other hand, the graph shows that a marked decrease in drug use occurred immediately after the program. Although we can't conclude for certain that the program was, in fact, responsible for the change in drug use, the evidence is certainly stronger in 13.2(b) than in 13.2(a).

The central threat to internal validity with a simple interrupted time series design is *contemporary history*. We cannot rule out the possibility that the observed effects were due to another event that occurred *at the same time* as the quasi-independent variable. If a rock star died from drugs or an athlete was barred from the team at about the time that the antidrug program began, we would not know whether the change between O4 and O5 was due to the program or to the contemporaneous outside influence.

BEHAVIORAL RESEARCH CASE STUDY

A SIMPLE INTERRUPTED TIME SERIES DESIGN: THE EFFECTS OF NO-FAULT DIVORCE

Traditionally, for a married couple to obtain a divorce, one member of the couple had to accuse the other of failing to meet the obligations of the marriage contract (by claiming infidelity or mental cruelty, for example). In the past 25 years, many states have passed no-fault divorce laws in which a couple can end a marriage simply by agreeing to, without one partner having to sue the other.

Critics maintain that no-fault divorce laws make it too easy to obtain a divorce and have contributed to the rising number of divorces in this country. To examine this question, Mazur-Hart and Berman (1977) used an interrupted time series analysis to study the effects of the passing of a no-fault divorce law in Nebraska in 1972.

Mazur-Hart and Berman obtained the number of divorces in Nebraska from 1969 to 1974. As in all interrupted time series analyses, these years were interrupted by the introduction of the quasi-independent variable (the new no-fault divorce law). Their results are shown in Figure 13.3. This figure shows the number of divorces per month for each of the six years of the study, as well as the point at which the new law went into effect.

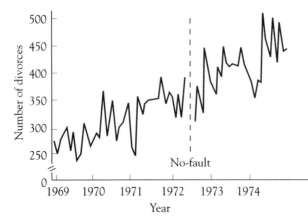

Figure 13.3   Effects of no-fault divorce laws on the number of divorces
(From "Changing from Fault to No-Fault Divorce: An Interrupted Time Series Analysis" by S. F. Mazur-Hart and J. J. Berman, 1977, *Journal of Applied Social Psychology, 7,* p. 306.)

Explanation: This graph shows the results of an interrupted time series analysis of divorce rates before and after the Nebraska no-fault divorce law. Although the divorce rate rose after the law went into effect, the increase was clearly part of a general upward trend that started before the law went into effect. Thus, the law appears not to have affected the divorce rate.

On first glance, one might be tempted to conclude that divorces did increase after the law was passed. The number of divorces was greater in 1973 and 1974 than in 1969, 1970, and 1971. However, if you look closely, you can see that the divorce rate was increasing even *before* the new law was passed; there is an upward slope to the data for 1969–1972. The data for 1973–1974 continues this upward trend, but there is no evidence that the number of divorces increased an unusual amount after the law went into effect. In fact, statistical analyses showed that there was no discontinuity in the slope of the line after the introduction of the law. As the authors concluded, "during the period of time studied divorces did systematically increase but . . . the intervention of no-fault divorce had no discernible effect on that increase."

This study demonstrates one advantage of a time series design over designs that compare only two groups or only two points in time. Had the researchers used a simple pretest–posttest design and analyzed data for only 1971 and 1973 (the years before and after the new law), they probably would have concluded that the law increased the divorce rate. By taking several measures before and after the law went into effect, they were able to tell that the increase in divorces after the new legislation was part of an upward trend that had begun at least three years before the law went into effect.

Interrupted Time Series with a Reversal

In special instances, the influence of extraneous factors may be discounted by observing what happens to behavior when the quasi-independent variable or treatment is first introduced, then removed. The *interrupted time series design with a reversal* may be portrayed like this:

O1 O2 O3 O4 X O5 O6 O7 O8 −X O9 O10 O11 O12

You can think of this as two interrupted time series designs in succession. The first examines the effects of the quasi-independent variable (X) on changes in the target behavior (O). As before, we can see whether X is associated with an unusual increase or decrease in the dependent variable (O) between O4 and O5. Then, after X has been in place for a while, we can remove it (at point −X) and observe what happens to O. Under some circumstances, we would expect the behavior to return to its pre-X level.

If this occurs, we are more confident that X produced the observed changes. It would be unlikely that some external, historical influence occurred with X, then disappeared when X was removed. Such an effect is logically possible, but in most instances it is unlikely.

To further increase our confidence that the quasi-independent variable, and not outside historical events, created the observed changes at X and −X, we could then *reintroduce* the independent variable, observe its effects, and then remove it a second time. This is known as an *interrupted time series design with multiple replications* and can be diagrammed as follows:

O1   O2   O3   X   O4   O5   O6   −X   O7   O8   O9   X   O10   O11   O12   −X   O13   O14   O15

Quasi-experimental designs in which the variable of interest is introduced and then removed have three major limitations. The primary one is that researchers often do not have the power to remove the quasi-independent variable—to repeal new seat-belt laws or no-fault divorce laws, for example. Second, the effects of some quasi-independent variables remain even after the variable itself is removed. For example, the effects of a communitywide program to reduce racial prejudice should linger even after the program itself is discontinued. Third, the removal of a quasi-independent variable may produce changes that are not due to the effects of the variable per se. For example, if we were interested in the effects of a new incentive system on employee morale, removing work incentives might dampen morale because the employees would be angry about having the system removed (Cook & Campbell, 1979).

Control Group Interrupted Time Series Design

So far, we have discussed time series designs that measure a single group of subjects before and after the quasi-independent variable. Adding comparison groups strengthens these designs by eliminating additional threats to internal validity. By measuring more than one group on several occasions, only one of which receives the quasi-independent variable, we can minimize the plausibility of certain alternative interpretations of the results. For example, we could perform an interrupted time series analysis on the group that received the quasi-independent variable and on a nonequivalent control group that did not receive the quasi-independent variable:

Experimental: O1   O2   O3   O4   X   O5   O6   O7   O8
Nonequivalent control: O1   O2   O3   O4   —   O5   O6   O7   O8

This design helps us rule out certain history effects. If both groups experience the same outside events but a change is observed only for the experimental group, we can be more certain (though not positive) that the change was due to X rather than to an outside influence. Of course, local history effects are possible in which the experimental group experiences extraneous events that the nonequivalent control group does not.

"Patched-up" Quasi-Experimental Designs

In most instances where researchers use quasi-experimental designs, they do not have the necessary control over the environment to structure the research setting precisely as they would like. In many cases, quasi-experimentation involves a pragmatic approach to research—one that attempts to collect the most meaningful data under circumstances than are often less than ideal (Condray, 1986). The best quasi-experiments are those in which the researcher uses whatever procedures are available to devise a reasonable test of the research hypotheses. Thus, rather than adhering blindly to one particular design, quasi-experimentalists creatively "patch up" basic designs to provide the most meaningful and convincing data possible.

For example, researchers often not only measure the effects of the quasi-independent variable on the outcome behavior but also assess the *processes* assumed to mediate their relationship. Given the absence of random assignment, simply showing that a particular quasi-independent variable was associated with changes in the dependent variable may not convince us that the quasi-independent variable caused the dependent variable to change. However, if the researcher can also demonstrate that the quasi-independent variable was associated with changes in processes assumed to mediate the change in the dependent variable, more confidence is warranted.

For example, rather than simply measuring students' drug use to evaluate the effects of a school's antidrug campaign, a researcher might also measure other variables that should mediate changes in drug use, such as students' knowledge about and attitudes toward drugs. Unlike some extraneous events (such as searches of students' lockers by school authorities), the program should affect not only drug use but also knowledge and attitudes. Thus, if changes in knowledge and attitudes are observed at the experimental school (but not at a nonequivalent control school), the researcher has more confidence that the antidrug program, and not other factors, produced the change.

By patching up basic quasi-experimental designs with additional quasi-independent variables, comparison groups, and dependent measures, researchers increase their confidence in the inferences they draw about the causal link between the quasi-independent and dependent variables. Such patched-up designs are inelegant and may not conform to any formal design shown in research methods books, but they epitomize the way scientists can structure their collection of data to draw the most accurate conclusions possible (Condray, 1986). And they show that researchers should never hesitate to invent creative strategies for analyzing whatever problem is at hand.

Evaluating Quasi-Experimental Designs

For many years, most behavioral scientists held a well-entrenched bias against quasi-experimental designs. For many, the tightly controlled experiment was the benchmark of behavioral research, and anything less than a true experiment was regarded with suspicion. Most contemporary behavioral researchers tend not to share this bias against quasi-experimentation, recognizing that the limitations of quasi-experimental designs are compensated by some notable advantages.

The first advantage is a pragmatic one. True experimentation—that involving random assignment and researcher-manipulated independent variables—is limited in the questions it can address. We often want to study the effects of certain variables on behavior but are unable or unwilling to conduct a true experiment that will allow unequivocal conclusions about causality. Faced with the limitations of the true experiment, we have a choice. We can abandon the topic, leaving potentially important questions unanswered, or we can conduct quasi-experimental research that provides us with tentative answers. Without quasi-experimental research, we would have no way of addressing many important questions.

Second, to suggest that quasi-experimental designs are inherently invalid is fallacious. As we saw earlier, studies fall along a continuum of internal validity. Although no one doubts that studies high in internal validity are to be preferred over those low in internal validity, alternative explanations may be raised about the results of experiments and quasi-experiments alike. In many instances, we must be satisfied with making well-informed decisions on the basis of the best available evidence, while acknowledging that a certain degree of uncertainty exists. Although all science involves a mixture of objective methods and human judgment, the role of judgment is perhaps more pronounced in quasi-experimental research (Condray, 1986).

Third, our confidence in the conclusions we draw from empirical research comes from two sources. When we conduct experiments, we have confidence in our findings because our study was tightly designed, eliminating most threats to internal validity. Even when a particular study cannot eliminate all threats to internal validity, however, we can increase our confidence on the basis of the results of accumulated evidence that demonstrates the same general effect. Thus, rather than reaching conclusions on the basis of a single study, researchers often piece together many strands of information accumulated by a variety of methods, much the way Sherlock Holmes would piece together evidence in breaking a case (Condray, 1986). So, although the results of a single quasi-experimental investigation of an antidrug program at one school may be open to criticism, demonstrating the effects of the program at 10 schools gives us considerable confidence in concluding that the program was effective.

Because our confidence about causal relationships increases as we integrate many diverse pieces of evidence, quasi-experimentation is enhanced by **critical multiplism** (Shadish, Cook, & Houts, 1986). The critical multiplist perspective argues that researchers should critically consider many ways of obtaining evidence relevant to a particular hypothesis, then employ several different approaches in the same study. In quasi-experimental research, no single research approach can yield unequivocal conclusions. However, evidence from multiple approaches may converge to yield conclusions that are as concrete as those obtained in experimental research. Like a game of chess in which each piece has its strengths and weaknesses and in which no piece can win the game alone, quasi-experimentation requires the coordination of several different pieces of research strategy (Shadish et al., 1986). Although any single piece of evidence may be suspect, the accumulated results may be quite convincing.

Thus, do not be misled into thinking that the data provided by quasi-experimental designs are worthless. Rather, we must generally interpret such data with greater caution. Quasi-experimentation provides an important set of research strategies for the behavioral researcher.

IN DEPTH

EVALUATING QUASI-EXPERIMENTATION

One way to evaluate the usefulness of quasi-experimental research is to consider what is required to establish that a particular variable *causes* changes in behavior. As we discussed earlier, to infer causality, we must be able to show that:

1. The presumed causal variable preceded the effect in time.
2. The cause and the effect covary.
3. All other alternative explanations of the results are eliminated through randomization or experimental control.

Quasi-experimental designs meet the first two criteria. First, even if we did not experimentally manipulate the quasi-independent variable, we usually know when it occurred. Thus, we can establish that the presumed cause preceded the presumed effect. Second, it is easy to determine whether two variables covary. A variety of statistical techniques, including correlation and ANOVA, allow us to demonstrate that variables are related to one another. Covariance can be demonstrated just as easily whether the research design is correlational, experimental, or quasi-experimental. Thus a quasi-experimental design is as strong on this count as any other design.

The primary weakness in quasi-experimental designs is the degree to which they eliminate the effects of extraneous variables on the results. Such designs seldom allow random assignment or control over extraneous variables. As a result, we can never rule out all alternative rival explanations of the findings. As we have seen, however, a well-designed quasi-experiment that eliminates as many threats to internal validity as possible can provide important, convincing information. Furthermore, evidence accumulated from a number of studies can lead to relatively clear-cut conclusions.

Conducting Quasi-Experimental Research

Quasi-experimental designs are used most commonly in the context of program evaluation research. Recall that program evaluation uses research methods to assess the effects of programs on behavior. A program is any intervention designed to influence behavior. For example, a program may involve a new educational intervention designed to raise students' achievement test scores, a new law intended to increase seat-belt use, an incentive program designed to increase employee morale, a marketing campaign implemented to affect the public's image of a company, or a training program for Little League coaches.

Although program evaluations often contribute to basic knowledge about human behavior, their primary goal is usually to provide information to those who must make decisions about the target programs. Often, the primary audience for a program evaluation is not the scientific community (as is the case with basic research) but decision makers such as government administrators, legislators, school boards, and company executives. Such individuals need information about program effectiveness to determine whether program goals are being met, to decide whether to continue certain programs, to consider how programs might be improved, and to allocate money and other resources to programs.

In some instances, program evaluators use true experimental designs to assess program effectiveness. Sometimes, they are able to randomly assign people to one program or another and have control over the implementation of the program (which is, in essence, the independent variable). In educational settings, for example, new curricula and teaching methods are often tested using true experimental designs.

More commonly, however, program evaluators have little or no control over the programs they evaluate. When evaluating the effects of new legislation, such as the effects of no-fault divorce or seat-belt laws, researchers cannot use random assignment or control the independent variable. In industrial settings, researchers have little control over new policies regarding employees. Even so, companies often want to know whether new programs and policies reduce absenteeism, increase morale, or bolster productivity. By necessity, then, program evaluation involves the use of quasi-experimental designs, and increasing numbers of behavioral researchers are using quasi-experimental methods to provide valuable information to decision makers.

Summary

1. Many important research questions are not answered easily using true experimental designs. Quasi-experimental designs are used when researchers cannot control the assignment of subjects to conditions or cannot manipulate the independent variable. Instead, comparisons are made

between people in groups that already exist or within one or more existing groups of subjects before and after a quasi-independent variable has occurred.

2. The quality of a quasi-experimental design depends on its ability to minimize threats to internal validity.

3. One-group pretest–posttest designs possess little internal validity and should seldom be used.

4. In the nonequivalent control group designs, an experimental group that receives the quasi-independent variable is compared with a nonequivalent comparison group that does not receive the quasi-independent variable. The effectiveness of this design depends on the degree to which the groups can be assumed to be equivalent and the degree to which local history effects can be discounted.

5. In time series designs, one or more groups are measured on several occasions, both before and after the quasi-experimental variable is introduced.

6. Although quasi-experimental designs do not allow the same degree of certainty about cause-and-effect relationships as an experiment does, a well-designed quasi-experiment can provide convincing circumstantial evidence regarding the effects of one variable on another.

Key Terms

quasi-experimental design

quasi-independent variable

one-group pretest–posttest design

regression to the mean

preexperimental design

nonequivalent groups posttest-only design

selection bias

experimental contamination

nonequivalent groups pretest–posttest design

local history effect

selection-by-history interaction

time series design

simple interrupted time series design

critical multiplism

Review Questions

1. How do quasi-experimental designs differ from true experiments?

2. Under what sets of circumstances would a researcher use a quasi-experimental rather than an experimental design?

3. Why should researchers almost never use the one-group pretest–posttest design?

4. What threats to internal validity are present when the nonequivalent control group posttest-only design is used? Which threats are eliminated by the pretest–posttest version of this design?

5. Explain the rationale behind time series designs.

6. Describe the simple interrupted time series design. Discuss how the interrupted time series design with a reversal and the interrupted time series design with multiple replications improves on the simple interrupted time series design.

7. Why does quasi-experimentation sometimes require the use of "patched-up" designs?

8. Discuss the philosophy of critical multiplism as it applies to quasi-experimental research.

9. What three criteria must be met to establish that one variable causes changes in behavior? Which of these criteria are met by quasi-experimental designs? Which of these criteria are not met, and why?

10. Why do program evaluators rely heavily on quasi-experimental designs in their work?

Questions for Thought and Discussion

1. Although quasi-experimental designs are widely accepted in behavioral science, some researchers are troubled by the fact that the evidence provided by quasi-experiments is seldom as conclusive as that provided by true experiments. Imagine you are trying to convince a dubious experimentalist of the merits of quasi-experimental research. What arguments would you use to convince him or her of its value?

2. Imagine that your town or city has increased its nighttime police patrols to reduce crime. Design two quasi-experiments to determine whether this intervention has been effective, one that uses some variation of a nonequivalent control group design and one that uses some variation of a time series design. For each design, discuss the possible threats to interval validity, as well as ways in which the design could be patched up to provide more conclusive evidence.

CHAPTER 14

Single-Case Research

When I describe the results of a particular study to my students, they sometimes respond to the findings by pointing out exceptions. "That study can't be right," they object. "I have a friend (brother, aunt, roommate) who does just the opposite." For example, if I tell my class that first-born children tend to be more achievement-oriented than later-born children, I can count on some student saying, "No way. I'm the third-born in my family, and I'm much more achievement-oriented than my older brothers." If I mention a study showing that anxiety causes people to prefer to be with other people, someone may retort, "But my roommate withdraws from people when she's anxious."

What such responses indicate is that many people do not understand the probabilistic nature of behavioral science. Our research uncovers generalities and trends, but we can almost always find exceptions to the general pattern. Overall, achievement motivation declines slightly with birth order, but not every firstborn child is more achievement-oriented than his or her younger siblings. Overall, people tend to seek out the company of other people when they are anxious or afraid, but some people prefer to be left alone when they are upset.

Behavioral science is not unique in this regard. Many principles and findings of all sciences are probabilities. When medical researchers claim that smoking causes lung cancer, they do not mean *every person* who smokes will get cancer. Rather, they mean more people in a group of smokers will get lung cancer than in an equivalent group of nonsmokers. Smoking and cancer are related in a probabilistic fashion, but there will always be exceptions to the general finding—like the old man who has smoked three packs a day since he was 16 yet is in perfect health (Stanovich, 1992). But exceptions such as these do not violate the general principle: overall, people who smoke are more likely to get cancer than people who don't smoke.

Although specific exceptions do not invalidate the findings of a particular study, these apparent contradictions between general principles and specific cases raise an important point for researchers to consider. Whenever we obtain a general finding based on a large number of subjects, we must recognize that the effect we obtained is unlikely to be true of everybody in the world or even of every subject in the sample under study. We may find large differences between the average responses of subjects in various experimental conditions, for example, even if the independent variable affected the behavior of only some of our subjects. This point has led some to suggest that researchers should pay more attention to the behavior of individual subjects.

Since the earliest days of behavioral science, researchers have debated the merits of a nomothetic versus idiographic approach to understanding behavior. Most researchers view the scientific enterprise as inherently **nomothetic,** seeking to establish general principles and broad generalizations that apply across individuals. However, as we have seen, these general principles do not always apply to everyone.

As a result, some researchers have argued that the nomothetic approach must be accompanied by an **idiographic** perspective (see, for example, Allport, 1961). Idiographic research seeks to describe, analyze, and compare the behavior of *individual* subjects. According to proponents of the idiographic approach, behavioral scientists should focus not only on general trends—the behavior of the "average" subject—but also on the unique behaviors of specific individuals.

An emphasis on the study of single organisms has been championed by two quite different groups of behavioral researchers with different interests and orientations. On one hand, some experimental psychologists interested in basic psychological processes have advocated the use of single-subject, or single-case, experimental designs. As we will see, these are designs in which researchers manipulate independent variables and exercise strong experimental control over extraneous variables, then analyze the behavior of *individual subjects* rather than grouped data.

On the other hand, other researchers have advocated the use of case studies in which the behavior and personality of a single individual or group are described in detail. Unlike single-subject experiments, case studies usually involve uncontrolled impressionistic descriptions rather than controlled experimentation. Case studies have been used most widely in clinical psychology, psychiatry, and other fields that specialize in the treatment of individual problems.

CONTRIBUTORS TO BEHAVIORAL RESEARCH

SINGLE-CASE RESEARCHERS

Single-case research—whether single-subject experiments or case studies—has had a long and distinguished history in behavioral science. In fact, in the early days of behavioral science, it was common practice to study only one or a few subjects. Only after the 1930s did researchers begin to rely on larger sample sizes, as most researchers do today (Boring, 1954; Robinson & Foster, 1979).

Many advances in behavioral science came from the study of single individuals in controlled experimental settings. Ebbinghaus, who began the scientific study of memory, conducted his studies on a single individual—himself. Stratton, an early researcher in perception, also used himself as a subject as he studied the effects of wearing glasses that reversed the world from left to right and top to bottom. (He soon learned to function quite normally in his reversed and inverted environment.) Many seminal ideas regarding conditioning were discovered and tested in single-subject experiments—notably, those of both Pavlov and Skinner. Many advances in psychophysiology, such as Sperry's (1975) work on split-brain patients, have come from the study of individuals undergoing brain surgery.

Case studies, often taken from clinical practice, have also contributed to the development of ideas in behavioral science. Kraepelin, who developed an early classification system of mental disorders that was the forerunner of the psychiatric system still used today, based his system on case studies (Garmezy, 1982). Most of the seminal ideas of Freud, Jung, Adler, and other early personality theorists were based on case studies. In developmental psychology, Piaget used case studies of children in developing his influential ideas about cognitive development.

Thus, although single-case research is less common than research that involves groups of subjects, such studies have had a long and distinguished tradition in behavioral science.

Despite the fact that many noted behavioral researchers have used single-case approaches, single-subject research has a mixed reputation in contemporary psychology. Some researchers insist that research involving the study of individuals is essential for the advancement of behavioral science, whereas other researchers see such approaches as having limited usefulness. In this chapter, we explore the rationale behind these two varieties of single-case research, along with the advantages and limitations of each.

Single-Subject Experimental Designs

In each of the experimental and quasi-experimental designs we have discussed so far, researchers assess the effects of variables on behavior by comparing the average responses of two or more groups of subjects. In these designs, the unit of analysis is always grouped data. In fact, in analyzing the data obtained from these designs, information about the responses of individual participants is usually ignored.

Group designs, such as those we have been discussing, reflect the most common approach to research in behavioral science. Most experiments and quasi-experiments conducted by behavioral scientists involve group designs. Even so, group designs have their critics, some as notable as the late B. F. Skinner, who offer an alternative approach to experimental research.

In the **single-subject experimental design,** the unit of analysis is not the experimental group, as in group designs, but the individual participant. Often, more than one subject participates in the experiment (typically three to eight), but each subject's responses are analyzed separately and the data from individual subjects are rarely averaged. Because averages are not used, the data from single-subject experiments cannot be analyzed using inferential statistics such as *t*-tests and *F*-tests.

At first, the single-subject approach may strike you as an odd, if not ineffective, way to conduct and analyze behavioral research. However, before you pass judgment, let's examine several criticisms of group experiments and how they may be resolved by using single-subject designs.

Criticisms of Group Designs and Analyses

Proponents of single-subject designs have suggested that group experimental designs fail to adequately handle three research issues—error variance, generality, and reliability.

Error variance.   We saw earlier that all data contain error variance—the results of unidentified factors that affect subjects' responses in an unsystematic fashion. We also learned that researchers must minimize error variance because error variance masks the effects of the independent variable (see Chapter 9 for a review).

Group experimental designs, such as those we've been discussing, provide two partial solutions to the problem of error variance. First, although the responses of any particular subject are contaminated by error variance in unknown ways, *averaging* the responses of several subjects should provide a more accurate estimate of the typical effect of the independent variable. In essence, many idiosyncratic sources of error variance cancel each other out when we calculate a group mean. Presumably, then, the mean for a group of subjects is a better estimate of the typical subject's response to the independent variable than the score of any particular subject.

Second, by using groups of subjects, we can estimate the amount of error variance in our data. This is what we did when we calculated the denominator of *t*-tests and *F*-tests (see Chapters 11 and 12). With this estimate, we can test whether the differences among the means of the groups are greater than we would expect if the differences were due only to error variance. Indeed, the purpose of using inferential statistics is to separate error variance from systematic variance to determine whether the differences among the group means are likely due to the independent variable or only to error variance.

Although group data provide these two benefits, proponents of single-subject designs criticize the way group designs and inferential statistics handle error variance. They argue that, first, much of the error variance in group data does not reflect variability in behavior per se but is *created* by the group design itself; and second, researchers who use group designs accept the presence of error variance too blithely.

As we noted earlier, much of the error variance in a set of data is due to individual differences among the subjects. However, in one sense, this **intersubject variance** is *not* the kind of variability that behavioral researchers are usually trying to understand and explain. Error variance resulting from individual differences among subjects is an artificial creation of the fact that, in group designs, we pool the responses of many subjects.

Single-subject researchers emphasize the importance of studying **intrasubject variance**—variability in *an individual's* behavior when he or she is in the same situation on different occasions. This is true behavioral variability that demands our attention. What we typically call error variance is, in one sense, partly a product of individual differences rather than real variations in a subject's behavior.

Because data are not aggregated across subjects in single-subject research, individual differences do not contribute to error variance. Error variance in a single-subject design shows up when a particular participant responds differently under various administrations of the same experimental condition.

Most researchers who use group designs ignore the fact that their data contain a considerable amount of error variance, as long as they obtain a significant effect of the independent variable. For single-subject researchers, ignoring error variance is tantamount to being content with sloppy experimental design and one's own ignorance (Sidman, 1960). After all, error variance is the result of factors that have remained unidentified and uncontrolled by the researcher. Proponents of single-subject designs maintain that, rather than accepting error variance, researchers should design studies in a way that allows them to seek out its causes and eliminate them. Through tighter and tighter experimental control, more and more intrasubject error variance can be eliminated. And in the process, we can learn more and more about the factors that influence behavior.

Generality. In the eyes of researchers who use group designs, averaging across subjects serves an important purpose. By pooling the scores of several participants, researchers minimize the impact of the idiosyncratic responses of any particular subject. It is their hope that by doing so they can identify the general, overall effect of the independent variable, an effect that should generalize to most subjects most of the time.

In contrast, single-subject researchers argue that the data from group designs do not permit us to identify the general effect of the independent variable, as many researchers suppose. Rather than reflecting the typical effect of the independent variable on the average subject, results from group designs represent an average of many individuals' responses that may not accurately portray the response of *any* particular subject. I read recently, for example, that Americans are having an average of 2.1 children. Although we all understand what this statistic tells us about childbearing in this country, it clearly does not reflect any family I know!

Given that group averages may not represent any particular subject's responses, attempts to generalize from overall group results may be misleading. Put differently, group means may have no counterpart in the behavior of individual subjects

(Sidman, 1960). This point is demonstrated in the accompanying box, "How Group Designs Misled Us About Learning Curves."

In addition, exclusive reliance on group summary statistics may obscure the fact that the independent variable affected the behavior of some subjects but had no effect (or even opposite effects) on other subjects. Researchers who use group designs rarely examine their raw data to see how many subjects showed the effect and whether some subjects showed effects contrary to the general trend.

Reliability. A third criticism of group designs is that, in most cases, they demonstrate the effect of the independent variable a single time, and no attempt is made to determine whether the observed effect is reliable—that is, whether it can be obtained again. Of course, researchers may replicate their and others' findings in later studies, but replication *within a single experiment* is rare.

When possible, single-subject experiments replicate the effects of the independent variable in two ways. As you will see, some designs introduce an independent variable, remove it, then reintroduce it. This procedure involves **intrasubject replication**—replicating the effects of the independent variable with a single subject.

In addition, most single-subject research involves more than one subject, typically three to eight. Studying the effects of the independent variable on more than one subject involves **intersubject replication.** Through intersubject replication, the researcher can determine whether the effects obtained for one subject generalize to other subjects. Keep in mind that even though multiple subjects are used, their data are examined individually. In this way, researchers can see whether all subjects responded similarly to the independent variable. That is, unlike group experimental designs, single-subject designs allow the generality of one's hypothesis to be assessed through replication on a case-by-case basis.

IN DEPTH

HOW GROUP DESIGNS MISLED US ABOUT LEARNING CURVES

On certain kinds of tasks, learning is an all-or-none process (Estes, 1964). During early stages of learning, people thrash around in a trial-and-error fashion. However, once they hit upon the correct answer or solution, they subsequently give the correct response every time. Thus, their performance jumps from *incorrect* to *correct* in a single trial.

The performance of a single subject on an all-or-none learning task can be graphed as in Figure 14.1. This subject got the answer wrong for seven trials, then hit upon the correct response on the eighth trial. Of course, after obtaining the correct answer, the subject got it right on all subsequent trials.

Different subjects will hit upon the correct response on different trials. Some will get it right on the first trial, some on the second trial, some on the third trial, and

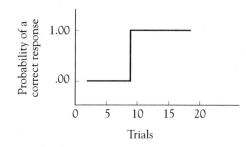

Figure 14.1

so on. In light of this variation, think what would happen if we averaged the responses of a large number of subjects on a learning task such as this. What would the graph of the data look like? Rather than showing the all-or-none pattern we see for each subject, the graph of the averaged group data will show a smooth curve, like that in Figure 14.2.

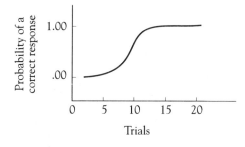

Figure 14.2

On the average, the probability of getting the correct response starts low, then gradually increases until virtually every subject obtains the correct answer on every trial. However, using group data obscures the fact that at the level of the individual subject, the learning curve was discontinuous rather than smooth. In fact, the results from the averaged, group data *do not reflect the behavior of any subject.* In instances such as this, group data can be quite misleading, whereas single-subject designs show the true pattern.

Basic Single-Subject Designs

In this section, we examine the three basic single-subjects designs: the ABA, multiple-I, and multiple baseline designs.

ABA designs.   The most common single-subject research designs involve variations of what is known as the **ABA design.** The researcher who uses these designs attempts to demonstrate that an independent variable affects behavior, first by showing that the variable causes a target behavior to occur, then by showing that removal of the variable causes the behavior to cease. For obvious reasons, these are sometimes called **reversal designs.**

In ABA designs, the subject is first observed in the absence of the independent variable (the baseline or control condition). Many measures of behavior are taken during this phase to establish an adequate baseline for comparison. Then, after the target behavior is seen to be relatively stable, a level of the independent variable is introduced and the behavior is observed again. If the independent variable influences behavior, we should see a change in behavior from the baseline to the treatment period. (In many ways, the ABA design can be regarded as an interrupted time series design performed on a single subject.)

However, even if behavior changes when the independent variable is introduced, the researcher should not be too hasty to conclude that the effect was caused by the independent variable. Just as in the time series designs we discussed in Chapter 13, some other event occurring at the same time as the treatment could have produced the observed effect. To reduce this possibility, the independent variable is then withdrawn. If the independent variable is, in fact, maintaining the behavior, the behavior may return to its baseline level. The researcher can further increase his or her confidence that the observed behavioral changes were due to the independent variable by replicating the study on other subjects.

The design just described is an example of an ABA design, the simplest single-subject design. In this design, A represents a baseline period in which the independent variable is not present, and B represents an experimental period. So, the ABA design involves a baseline period (A), followed by introduction of a level of the independent variable (B), followed by the reversal period in which the independent variable is removed (A). Many variations and elaborations of the basic ABA design are possible. To increase confidence that the changes in behavior were due to the independent variable, a researcher may decide to introduce the same level of the independent variable a second time. This design would be labeled an ABAB design.

Deitz (1977) used an ABAB design to examine the effects of teacher reinforcement on the disruptive behavior of a retarded student in a special education class. To reduce the frequency with which this student disrupted class by talking out loud, the teacher made a contract with the student, saying that she would spend 15 minutes with him after class (something he valued) if he talked aloud 3 times or less. Baseline data showed that, before the treatment program started, the student talked aloud between 30 and 40 times per day. The reinforcement program was then begun, and the rate of disruptive behavior dropped quickly to ten outbursts, then to three or fewer (see Figure 14.3). When the reinforcement program was withdrawn, the number of outbursts increased, although not to their original level.

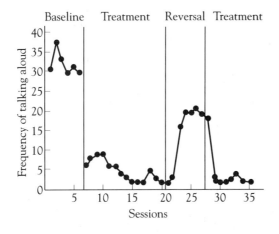

Figure 14.3 Decreasing disruptive behavior

Explanation: During the 6 days of baseline recording, this student engaged in a high level of disruptive behavior, talking aloud at least 30 times each class period. When the teacher promised to give the student special attention if he didn't disrupt, the number of disruptions dropped to less than three per session. However, when the teacher stopped the program (the reversal phase), disruptions increased to approximately 20 per session. When the treatment was again implemented, disruptions were nearly eliminated. The pattern of results across the four phases of this ABAB design demonstrate that the teacher's treatment program successfully controlled the student's disruptive behavior.

Then, when it was reinstated, the student virtually stopped disrupting class. These data provide rather convincing evidence that the intervention was successful in modifying the student's behavior.

Logically, a researcher could reintroduce and then remove a level of the independent variable again and again, as in an ABABABA or ABABABABA design. Each successive intrasubject replication of the effect increases our confidence that the independent variable is causing the observed effects.

In many instances, however, the independent variable produces *permanent* changes in subjects' behavior, changes that do not reverse when the independent variable is removed. When this happens, a single subject's data do not unequivocally show whether the initial change was due to the independent variable or to some extraneous variable that occurred at the same time. However, if the same pattern is obtained for other subjects, we have considerable confidence that the observed effects were due to the independent variable.

Multiple-I designs. ABA-type designs compare behavior in the absence of the independent variable (during A) with behavior in the presence of a nonzero level of an independent variable (during B). However, other single-subject designs test differences among *levels* of an independent variable. Single-subject designs that present varying nonzero levels of the independent variable are called **multiple-I designs.**

In one such design, the **ABC design,** the researcher obtains a baseline (A), then introduces one level of the independent variable (B) for a certain period of time. Then, this level is removed and another level of the independent variable is introduced (C). Of course, we could continue this procedure to create an ABCDEFG . . . design.

Often, researchers insert a baseline period between each successive introduction of a level of the independent variable, resulting in an ABACA design. After obtaining a baseline (A), the researcher introduces one level of the independent variable (B), then withdraws it as in an ABA design. Then, a second level of the independent variable is introduced (C), then withdrawn (A). We could continue to manipulate the independent variable by introducing new levels of it, returning to baseline each time.

Such designs are commonly used in research that investigates the effects of drugs on behavior. Subjects are given different dosages of a drug, with baseline periods occurring between the successive dosages. In one such study, Dworkin, Bimle, and Miyauchi (1989) tested the effects of cocaine on how rats react to punished and nonpunished responding. Over several days, four different dosages of cocaine were administered to five pairs of rats, with baseline sessions scheduled between each administration of the drug. While under the influence of the drug, one rat in each pair received punishment, whereas the other did not. We'll return to the results of this experiment in a moment.

Multiple baseline designs.   As noted earlier, the effects of an independent variable do not always disappear when the variable is removed. For example, if a clinical psychologist teaches a client a new way to cope with stress, it is difficult to "unteach" it. When this is so, how can we be sure the obtained effects are due to the independent variable as opposed to some extraneous factor? One way is to use a multiple baseline design. In a **multiple baseline design,** two or more behaviors are studied simultaneously. After obtaining baseline data on all behaviors, levels of an independent variable are introduced that are hypothesized to affect *only one of the behaviors.* In this way, the selective effects of a variable on a specific behavior can be documented.

By measuring several behaviors, the researcher can show that the independent variable caused the target behavior to change but did not affect other behaviors. If the effects of the independent variable can be shown to be specific to certain behaviors, the researcher has increased confidence that the obtained effects were, in fact, due to the independent variable.

Data from Single-Subject Designs

As we noted earlier, researchers who use single-subject designs resist analyzing their results in the forms of means, standard deviations, and other descriptive statistics based on group data. Furthermore, because they object to averaging data across subjects, those who use such designs do not use statistics such as t-tests and F-tests to test whether the differences between experimental conditions are statistically significant.

The preferred method of presenting the data from single-subject designs is with graphs that show the results individually for each subject. Rather than testing the significance of the experimental effects, single-subject researchers employ **graphic analysis** (also known simply as **visual inspection**).

Put simply, the single-subject researcher judges whether or not the independent variable affected behavior by visually inspecting graphs of the data for individual subjects. If the behavioral changes are pronounced enough to be discerned through a visual inspection of such graphs, the researcher concludes that the independent variable affected the subject's behavior. If the pattern is not clear enough to conclude that a behavioral change occurred, the researcher concludes that the independent variable did not have an effect.

Ideally, the researcher would like to obtain results like those shown in Figure 14.4. As you can see in this ABA design, the behavior was relatively stable during the baseline period, changed quickly when the independent variable was introduced, and then returned immediately to baseline when the independent variable was removed.

Unfortunately, the results are not always this clear-cut. Look, for example, at the data in Figure 14.5. During the baseline period, the subject's responses were fluctuating somewhat. Thus, it is difficult to tell whether the independent variable

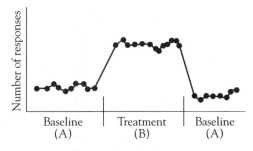

Figure 14.4   Results from an ABA design—1

Explanation: In this ABA design, the effect of the independent variable is clear-cut. The number of responses increased sharply when the treatment was introduced, then returned to baseline when it was withdrawn.

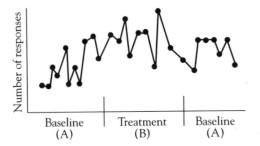

Figure 14.5   Results from an ABA design—II

Explanation: In this ABA design, whether the independent variable affected the number of responses is unclear. Because responding was not stable during the baseline (A), it is difficult to determine the extent to which responding changed when the treatment was introduced (B). In addition, responding did not return to the baseline level when the treatment was withdrawn.

caused a change in behavior during the treatment period, or whether the observed change was a random fluctuation, such as those that occurred during baseline. (This is why single-subject researchers try to establish a stable baseline before introducing the independent variable.) Furthermore, when the independent variable was removed, the subject's behavior changed but did not return to the original baseline level. Did the independent variable cause changes in behavior? In the case of Figure 14.5, the answer to this question is uncertain.

Figure 14.6 shows the results from two subjects in the study of the effects of cocaine on rats' reactions to punishment described earlier (Dworkin et al., 1989). In this study, graphic analysis revealed marked differences in how subjects in the punished and nonpunished conditions responded under different dosages of cocaine. Furthermore, inspection of the graphs for the other subjects in the study revealed exactly the same pattern, thereby providing converging evidence of the effects of various doses of cocaine on punished and nonpunished responding.

Compared to the complexities of inferential statistics, graphic analysis may appear astonishingly straightforward and simple. However, many researchers are disturbed by the looseness of using visual inspection to assess whether or not an independent variable influenced behavior; eyeballing, they argue, is not sufficiently sensitive or objective as a means of data analysis. Specifically, many researchers criticize graphic analysis because of the ambiguity of the criteria for determining whether or not an effect of the independent variable was obtained. How big an effect is *big enough?*

Proponents of single-subject research counter that, on the contrary, visual inspection is *preferable* to inferential statistics. Because graphic analysis is admittedly a relatively insensitive way to examine data, only the strongest effects will be accepted as real (Kazdin, 1982). This is in contrast to group data, in which very weak effects may be found to be statistically significant.

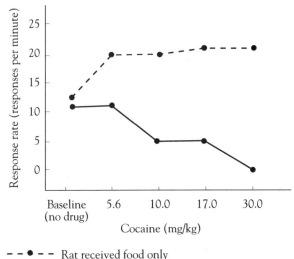

‑ ‑ •‑ ‑ ‑ Rat received food only
———•——— Rat received food and shock

Figure 14.6   Effects of varying dosages of cocaine on punished and nonpunished responding (Adapted from "Differential Effects of Pentobarbital and Cocaine on Punished and Nonpunished Responding" by S. I. Dworkin, C. Bimle, and T. Miyauchi, 1989, *Journal of the Experimental Analysis of Behavior, 51,* p. 182. Used with permission of the Society for the Experimental Analysis of Behavior.)

Explanation: This graph shows the behavior of two rats in the Dworkin, Bimle, and Miyauchi study. One rat received only food when it pressed a bar (nonpunished); the other rat received food and shock (punished). The graph shows that increasing dosages of cocaine had quite different effects on the response rates for these two animals. Increasing dosages resulted in increased responding for the nonpunished rat, but in decreased responding for the punished rat. Dworkin and his colleagues replicated this pattern on four other pairs of rats, thereby demonstrating the intersubject generalizability of their findings.

Uses of Single-Subject Designs

During the earliest days of psychology, single-subject research was the preferred research strategy. As we've seen, many of the founders of behavioral science—Weber, Wundt, Pavlov, Thorndike, Ebbinghaus, and others—relied heavily on single-subject approaches.

Today, the use of single-subject designs is closely wedded to the study of operant conditioning. Single-subject designs have been used to study operant processes in both humans and nonhumans, including rats, pigeons, mice, dogs, fish, monkeys, and cats. Single-subject designs have been widely used to study the effects of various schedules of reinforcement and punishment on behavior. In fact, virtually the entire research literature involving schedules of reinforcement is based on single-subject designs. Furthermore, most of Skinner's influential research on operant conditioning involved single-subject designs. Single-subject designs are also used by researchers who study psychophysiological processes, as well as by those who study sensation and perception.

In applied research, single-subject designs have been used most frequently to study the effects of behavior modification—techniques for changing problem behaviors based on the principles of operant conditioning. Such designs have been used extensively, for example, in the context of therapy to study the effects of behavior modification on phenomena as diverse as bed-wetting, delinquency, catatonic schizophrenia, aggression, depression, self-injurious behavior, and shyness (Jones, 1993; Kazdin, 1982). Single-subject research has also been used in industrial settings (to study the effects of various treatments on a worker's performance, for example) and in schools (to study the effects of token economies on learning).

Finally, single-subject designs are sometimes used for demonstrational purposes, simply to show that a particular behavioral effect can be obtained. For example, developmental psychologists have been interested in whether young children can be taught to use memory strategies to help them remember better. Using a single-subject design to show that five preschool children learned to use memory strategies would demonstrate that young children can, in fact, learn such strategies. The causal inferences one can draw from such demonstrations are often weak and the effects are of questionable generalizability, but such studies can provide indirect, anecdotal evidence that particular effects can be obtained.

BEHAVIORAL RESEARCH CASE STUDY

A SINGLE-SUBJECT EXPERIMENT: TREATMENT OF STUTTERING

Among the most effective treatments for stuttering are procedures that teach stutterers to consciously regulate their breathing as they speak. Wagaman, Miltenberger, and Arndorfer (1993) used a single-subject design to test a simplified variation of such a program on 8 children ranging in age from 6 to 10 years.

The study occurred in three phases consisting of baseline, treatment, and posttreatment. (You should recognize this as an ABA design.) To obtain a baseline measure of stuttering, the researchers audiotaped the children talking to their parents. The researchers then counted the number of words the children spoke, as well as the number of times they stuttered. Using these two numbers, the researchers calculated the percentage of words stuttered by each child. Analyses showed that interrater reliability was acceptably high on these measures; two researchers agreed in identifying stuttering 86% of the time.

In the treatment phase of the study, the children were taught how to regulate their breathing so that they would breath deeply and slowly through their mouths as they spoke. The children practiced speaking while holding their fingertips in front of their mouths to assure that they were, in fact, exhaling as they talked. They also

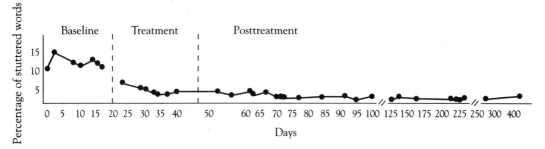

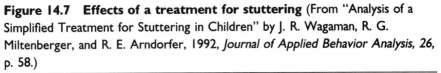

Figure 14.7 Effects of a treatment for stuttering (From "Analysis of a Simplified Treatment for Stuttering in Children" by J. R. Wagaman, R. G. Miltenberger, and R. E. Arndorfer, 1992, *Journal of Applied Behavior Analysis, 26,* p. 58.)

Explanation: This graph shows the percentage of words on which Jake stuttered during the baseline, treatment, and posttreatment phases. His initial rate of stuttering during baseline was over 10%, but it dropped quickly to less than 5% after treatment started. After treatment stopped, Jake's rate of stuttering remained less than 3% for the remainder of the study.

learned to stop immediately each time they stuttered, then consciously implement the breathing pattern they had learned. Parents were also taught these techniques so they could practice them with their children. Conversations between the children and their parents were audiotaped at the beginning of each treatment session, and the rate of stuttering was calculated. Treatment occurred in 45 to 60-minute sessions three times a week until the child stuttered on less than 3% of his or her words (normal speakers stutter less than 3% of the time). After the rate of stuttering had dropped below 3% for a particular child, treatment was discontinued for that subject. However, posttreatment measures of stuttering were taken regularly for over a year to be sure the effects of treatment were maintained over a long period of time.

In the article describing this study, Wagaman et al. (1993) presented graphs showing the percentage of stuttered words separately for each of the eight children across the course of the study. The data for each of the eight subjects showed precisely the same pattern; Figure 14.7 shows the data for one of the children (Jake). During baseline, Jake stuttered on over 10% of his words. When the treatment began, his rate of stuttering dropped sharply to less than 3% and stayed at this low rate for at least a year after treatment was discontinued. Given that the pattern of data was identical for all eight subjects, this single-subject study provides convincing evidence that this treatment is effective in permanantly reducing stuttering to normal levels.

Critique of Single-Subject Designs

Well-designed single-subject experiments can provide convincing evidence about the causal effects of independent variables on behavior. They have been used quite effectively in the study of many phenomena, particularly the study of basic learning processes.

However, despite the argument that the results of single-subject studies are more generalizable than the results of group designs, single-subject experiments do not inherently possess greater external validity. Generalizability depends heavily on the manner in which subjects are selected. Even when strong experimental effects are obtained across all subjects in a single-subject experiment, these effects may still be limited to others who are like those subjects. It is certainly true, however, that single-subject designs permit researchers to see how well the effects of the independent variable generalize across subjects in a way rarely possible with group designs.

Importantly, one reason that single-subject experiments are often used by animal researchers is that the results obtained on one subject are more likely to generalize to other potential subjects than is the case in research with humans. This is because the animals used for laboratory research (mostly rats, mice, pigeons, and rabbits) are partially or fully inbred, thereby minimizing genetic variation. Furthermore, the subjects used in a particular study are usually of the same age, were raised in the same controlled environment, are fed the same food, then are tested under identical conditions. As a result, all possible subjects are "clones or near-clones, both with respect to genetics and experiential history" (Deneberg, 1982, p. 21). Thus, unlike human research, in which the individual participants differ greatly (and in which one subject's response may or may not resemble another's), the responses of only two or three subjects in experimental laboratory research may be representative of many.

One limitation of single-subject designs is that they are not well suited for studying *interactions* among variables. Although one could logically test a subject under all possible combinations of the levels of two or more independent variables, such studies are often difficult to implement (see Kratochwill, 1978).

Finally, ethical issues sometimes arise when ABA designs are used to assess the effectiveness of clinical interventions. Is it ethical to withdraw a potentially helpful treatment from a troubled client to assure the researcher that the treatment was, in fact, effective? For example, we might be hesitant to withdraw the treatment introduced to reduce depression in a suicidal patient simply to convince ourselves that the treatment did, in fact, ameliorate the client's depression.

Case Study Research

We now turn our attention to a very different kind of single-case research—the case study. A **case study** is a detailed study of a single individual, group, or event. Within behavioral research, case studies have been most closely associated with clinical psychology, psychiatry, and other applied fields, where they are used to describe noteworthy cases of psychopathology or treatment. For example, a psychotherapist may describe the case of a client who is a sociopath or detail the therapist's efforts to use a particular treatment approach on a client who is afraid of thunderstorms. Similarly, psychobiographers have conducted psychological case studies of famous people, such as Jesus, Lincoln, and van Gogh (see Runyan, 1982).

Although case studies of individuals are most common, researchers sometimes perform case studies of *groups*. For example, in his attempt to understand why groups sometimes make bad decisions, Janis (1982) conducted case studies of several political and military decision-making groups. Within educational research, studies are sometimes made of exemplary schools, with an eye toward understanding why these particular schools are so good (U. S. Department of Education, 1991). A great deal of social anthropology involves case studies of non-Western social groups, and ethologists have conducted case studies of troupes of baboons, chimpanzees, gorillas, and other nonhuman animals.

The "data" for case studies can come from a variety of sources, including observation, interviews, questionnaires, news reports, and archival records (such as diaries, minutes of meetings, or school records). Typically, the researcher pulls the available information together into a narrative description of the person, group, or event. In some instances, the researcher's subjective impressions are supplemented by objective measures (such as measures of personality or behavior). The available information is then interpreted to explain how and why the behavior (individual or group) under study occurred, and conclusions, solutions, decisions, or recommendations are offered (Bromley, 1986).

Uses of the Case Study Method

Although used far less often by researchers than the other approaches we have examined, the case study method has at least three uses in behavioral research.

As a source of insights and ideas. Perhaps the most important use of case studies is as a source of ideas in the early stages of investigating a topic. (Recall that doing an intensive case study was recommended as one approach to obtaining research ideas in Chapter 1.) Studying a few particular individuals in detail can provide a wealth of ideas for future investigation.

In fact, many seminal ideas in behavioral science emerged from intensive case studies of individuals or groups. For example, Freud's ideas emerged from his case studies of clients who came to him for therapy, and Piaget's ground-breaking work on cognitive development was based on the case studies he performed on his own children. Within social psychology, Janis's case studies of high-level decision-making groups paved the way for his theory of Groupthink, and Festinger's case study of a group who predicted the end of the world led to the theory of cognitive dissonance.

To describe rare phenomena.   Some behavioral phenomena occur so rarely that researchers are unlikely to obtain a large number of subjects displaying the phenomenon for study. For example, if we were interested in the psychology of presidential assassins, we would be limited to case studies of the few people who have killed or tried to kill U.S. presidents (Weisz & Taylor, 1969). Similarly, studies of mass murderers require a case study approach. Luria (1968) used a case study approach to describe the life of a man who had nearly perfect memory—another rare phenomenon. The literature in psychology and psychiatry contains many case studies of people with unusual psychological problems or abilities, such as multiple personalities, phobic reactions to dead birds, and "photographic memories."

Neuropsychologists, psychophysiologists, and neurologists sometimes conduct case studies of people who—because of unusual injuries, diseases, or surgeries—have sustained damage to their nervous systems. Although they would never purposefully damage people's brains or spinal cords, researchers sometimes take advantage of unusual opportunities to study the effects of brain trauma on personality and behavior.

As illustrative anecdotes.   Real, concrete examples often have more power than abstract statements of general principles. Researchers and teachers alike often use case studies to illustrate general principles to other researchers and to students. Although this use of case studies may seem of minor importance in behavioral science, we should remember that scientists must often convince others of the usefulness of their findings. Supplementing "hard" empirical data with illustrative case studies may be valuable in this regard. Such case studies can never be offered as "proof" of a scientist's assertion, but they can be used to provide concrete, easy-to-remember examples of abstract concepts and processes.

Limitations of the Case Study Approach

Although the case study approach has its uses, it also has noteworthy limitations as a scientific method.

Failure to control extraneous variables.   First, case studies are virtually useless in providing evidence to test behavioral theories or psychological treatments. Because case studies deal with the informal observation of isolated events that occur in an uncontrolled fashion and without comparison information, researchers are unable to assess the viability of alternative explanations of their observations. No matter how plausible are the explanations offered for the individual's behavior or for the effectiveness of a given treatment, alternative explanations cannot be ruled out.

Too often, however, people use case studies as evidence for the accuracy of a particular explanation or for the effectiveness of a particular intervention. Recently, I heard on the radio that a particular member of Congress had spoken out against the president's plan to require a waiting period for the purchase of hand-guns, claiming such legislation was bound to be ineffective. His reasoning was based on the case of Washington, D.C., a city that has relatively strict handgun controls yet a very high murder rate. Clearly, he argued, the case of Washington shows that gun controls do not reduce violent crime. Can you see the problem with this argument?

His argument is based on case study evidence about a single city rather than on scientific data, and we have absolutely no way of knowing what the effect of handgun control is on the murder rate in Washington, D. C. Perhaps the murder rate would be *even higher* if there were no controls on the purchase of guns. For that matter, it's logically possible that the rate would be lower if there was no gun control. The point is, without relevant comparison information and control over other variables associated with murder (such as poverty and drug use), no conclusions about the effects of handgun control are possible from such case study evidence.

Observer biases. Most case studies rely on the observations of a single researcher. In behavioral science, the researcher is most likely to be the subject's psychotherapist. In light of this relationship, we often have no way of determining the reliability or validity of the researchers' observations or interpretations. In addition, because the researcher–observer often has a stake in the outcome of the investigation (such as whether a therapeutic procedure works), we must worry about self-fulfilling prophecies and demand characteristics (see Chapter 9).

BEHAVIORAL RESEARCH CASE STUDY

A CASE STUDY OF A CASE STUDY

Case study approaches to research have commonly been used to describe particular cases of psychopathology or to document the effects of specific psychotherapeutic approaches. In many instances, case studies may be the only way to collect information about unusual phenomena.

Consider, for example, the case of Jeffrey, a 28-year-old Israeli who developed posttraumatic stress disorder (PTSD) in the aftermath of a terrorist attack that left him seriously burned and disabled. PTSD is a prolonged psychological reaction to highly traumatic events and is characterized by anxiety, irritability, withdrawal, insomnia, confusion, depression, and other signs of severe stress. Jeffrey's case was quite severe; he had stopped working, had isolated himself from family and friends, and was depressed and withdrawn.

In their case study of Jeffrey, Bar-Yoseph and Witztum (1992) first described Jeffrey's psychological and behavioral reactions to the attack that nearly killed both him and his father three years earlier. They then presented their approach to helping Jeffrey overcome his problems through psychotherapy.

In the first phase of therapy, the primary goal was to establish a therapeutic relationship with Jeffrey. Because he was so depressed, withdrawn, and pessimistic about the prospect of getting better, the therapists proceeded slowly and carefully, focusing initially on only one of his problems (insomnia) rather than on all of them at once. Interestingly, because his symptoms did not emerge until a year after the attack (such a delay is common in PTSD), he continually refused to acknowledge that his problems were caused by the attack itself.

After Jeffrey saw that he was improving, therapy entered a second phase. Week by week, the therapists encouraged Jeffrey to take up one activity that his physical injuries, depression, and apathy had led him to abandon after the attack. Thus, for the first time in three years, he began to mow the yard, go shopping, play soccer, and go to the library.

In the third phase of therapy, the therapists helped Jeffrey take yet another step toward psychological recovery: returning to full-time work. Although he had difficulty relating to his co-workers, he found he was again able to face the daily stresses of the working world. Even so, he continued to agonize over the fact that his life was not the way it had been before his problems began. As a result, he viewed the positive changes that had occurred as a result of therapy as simply not good enough.

Along the way, Jeffrey continued to deny that the terrorist attack was the cause of his difficulties. For whatever reason, he found it too threatening to acknowledge he was unable to cope with this particular misfortune. Believing it was essential for Jeffrey to see the connection between the attack and his problems, the therapists tried a number of approaches to show him the link. However, Jeffrey found such efforts too upsetting and insisted that the therapists stop. The therapists finally concluded it was not in Jeffrey's best interests to force the issue further, and Jeffrey terminated treatment. Periodic follow-ups showed that, even three years later, Jeffrey had maintained the improvements he made during therapy, and he continued to get better.

After describing Jeffrey's case, Bar-Yoseph and Witztum (1992) discussed its implications for understanding and treating PTSD. As we've seen, the conclusions that can be drawn from such studies are tenuous at best. Yet, a carefully documented case study can provide other psychotherapists with novel approaches for their own practice as well as generate hypotheses to be investigated using controlled research strategies.

Summary

1. Single-case research comes in two basic varieties—single-subject designs and case studies—both of which can be traced to the earliest days of behavioral science.

2. Single-subject experimental designs investigate the effects of independent variables on individual research participants. Unlike group designs, in which data are averaged across subjects for analysis, each subject's responses are analyzed separately, and the data from individual subjects are not averaged.

3. The most common single-subject designs, variations of the ABA design, involve a baseline period, followed by a period in which the independent variable is introduced; then, the independent variable is withdrawn. More complex designs may involve several successive periods in which the independent variable is reintroduced, then withdrawn.

4. In multiple-I designs, several levels of the independent variable are administered in succession, often with a baseline period between each administration.

5. Multiple baseline designs allow researchers to document that the effects of the independent variable are specific to particular behaviors. Such designs involve the simultaneous study of two or more behaviors, only one of which is hypothesized to be affected by the independent variable.

6. Because averages are not used, the data from single-subject experiments cannot be analyzed using inferential statistics. Rather, effects of the independent variable on behavior are detected through graphic analysis.

7. A case study is a detailed, descriptive study of a single individual, group, or event. The case is described in detail, and conclusions, solutions, or recommendations are offered.

8. Case studies rarely allow a high degree of confidence in the researcher's interpretations of the data, because extraneous variables are never controlled and the biases of the researcher may influence his or her observations to a greater extent than in other kinds of research. Even so, case studies are useful in generating new ideas, studying rare phenomena, and serving as illustrative anecdotes.

Key Terms

nomothetic approach	ABA design
idiographic approach	reversal design
group design	multiple-I design
single-subject experimental design	ABC design
intersubject variance	multiple baseline design
intrasubject variance	graphic analysis
intrasubject replication	visual inspection
intersubject replication	case study

Review Questions

1. Distinguish between nomothetic and idiographic approaches to research.

2. Discuss the common criticisms of group designs leveled by proponents of single-subject designs.

3. What is the rationale behind the ABA design?

4. Can single-subject designs be used to test among various levels of an independent variable (as in a one-way group design)?

5. When are multiple baseline designs typically used?

6. How do single-subject researchers analyze their data?

7. Discuss the advantages and disadvantages of single-subject designs relative to group designs.

8. Why are behavioral scientists reluctant to trust case studies as a means of testing hypotheses?

9. What are some reasons that researchers use case studies?

Questions for Thought and Discussion

1. Single-subject designs are controversial. Many researchers argue that they are the preferred method of experimental research, but others reject them as being of limited usefulness. How researchers feel about single-subject designs appears to stem, in part, from their personal areas of expertise. Single-subject designs lend themselves well to certain areas of investigation, whereas they are difficult, if not impossible, to use in other areas. What do you see as some topics in behavioral science for which single-subject designs might be most useful? What are some topics for which such designs would be difficult or impossible to use, and why? Are there topics for which group and single-subject designs would be equally appropriate?

2. Which side of the controversy regarding single-subject designs do you find most convincing? What is your position regarding single-subject designs?

3. Locate a published experiment that used a group design, and redesign it using a single-subject approach. Remember that many group designs do not convert easily to single-subject designs.

4. Conduct a case study of someone you know (you could even use yourself). Select a choice the person has made (whom to date or marry, where to attend school, what career to pursue), and gather as much information as possible to help to *explain* why the person made the choice he or she did. For example, you could delve into factors such as the person's background, previous experiences, personality, relationships, and situational pressures. (Don't rely too heavily on the reasons the person gives; people don't always

know why they do things). Write a brief report explaining the person's decision in light of these factors.

5. After writing the case study in Question 4, critically evaluate it. How certain are you that your observations and interpretations are valid? Can you generate alternative, equally plausible explanations?

CHAPTER 15

Ethical Issues in Behavioral Research

Imagine you are a student in an introductory psychology course. One of the course requirements is that you participate in research being conducted by faculty in the psychology department. When the list of available studies is posted, you sign up for a study titled "Decision Making."

When you report to a laboratory in the psychology building, you are met by a researcher who tells you that the study in which you will participate involves how people make decisions. You will work with two other research participants on a set of problems, then complete questionnaires about your reactions to the task. The study sounds innocuous and mildly interesting, so you agree to participate.

You and the other two participants then work together on a set of difficult problems. As the three of you reach agreement on an answer to each problem, you give your team's answer to the researcher. After your group has answered all the problems, the researcher says that, if you wish, he'll tell you how well your group performed on the problems. The three of you agree, so the researcher gives you a score sheet that shows that your group scored in the bottom 10% of all groups he has tested. Nine out of every 10 groups of subjects performed better than your group! Not surprisingly, you're somewhat deflated by this feedback.

Then, to make things worse, one of the other subjects off-handedly remarks to the researcher that the group's poor performance was mostly *your* fault. Now, you're not only depressed about the group's performance but embarrassed and angry as well. The researcher, clearly uneasy about the other subject's accusation, quickly escorts you to another room where you complete a questionnaire on which you give your reaction to the problem-solving task and the other two participants.

When you finish the questionnaire, the researcher says, "Before you go, let me tell you more about the study you just completed. The study was *not*, as I told you earlier, about decision making. Rather, we are interested in how people respond when they are blamed for a group's failure by other members of the group." The researcher goes on to tell you that your group did *not* really perform poorly on the decision problems; in fact, he did not even score your group's solutions. You were assigned randomly to the failure condition of the experiment, so you were told your group had performed very poorly. Furthermore, the other two subjects were not subjects at all but confederates—accomplices of the researcher—who were instructed to blame you for the group's failure.

This example, which is similar to some studies in psychology, raises a number of ethical questions. Was it ethical:

- for you to be required to participate in a study to fulfill a course requirement?
- for the researcher to mislead you regarding the purpose of the study? (After all, your agreement to participate in the experiment was based on false information about its purpose.)
- for you to be led to think that the other participants were subjects, when they were actually confederates?
- for the researcher to lie about your performance on the decision-making test, telling you that your group performed very poorly?
- for the confederate to blame you for the group's failure, making you feel bad?

In brief, you were lied to and humiliated as part of a study in which you had little choice but to participate. As a subject who participated in this study, how would you feel about how you were treated? As an outsider, how do you evaluate the ethics of this study? Should people be required to participate in research? Is it acceptable to mislead and deceive subjects if necessary to obtain needed information? How much distress, psychological or physical, may researchers cause subjects in a study?

Behavioral scientists have wrestled with ethical questions such as these for many years. In this chapter, we'll examine many of the ethical issues that behavioral researchers address each time they design and conduct a study.

Approaches to Ethical Decisions

Most ethical issues in research arise because behavioral scientists have two sets of obligations that sometimes conflict. On the one hand, the behavioral researcher's job is to provide information that enhances our understanding of behavioral processes and leads to the improvement of human or animal welfare. This obligation requires that scientists pursue research they believe will be useful in extending knowledge or solving problems. On the other hand, behavioral scientists also have an obligation to protect the rights and welfare of the people and animals who participate in their research.

When these two obligations coincide, few ethical issues arise. However, when the researcher's obligations to science and society conflict with obligations to protect the rights and welfare of research participants, the researcher faces an ethical dilemma.

The first step in understanding ethical issues in research is to recognize that well-meaning people may disagree—sometimes strongly—about the ethics of particular research procedures. Not only do people disagree over specific research practices, but they often disagree over the fundamental ethical principles that should be used to make ethical decisions. Ethical conflicts often reach an impasse because of basic disagreements regarding how ethical decisions should be made and, indeed, whether they can be made at all.

People tend to adopt one of three general approaches to resolving ethical issues about research. These three approaches differ in terms of the criteria people use to make decisions regarding right and wrong (Schlenker & Forsyth, 1977). An individual operating from a **deontological** position maintains that ethics must be judged in light of a universal moral code. Certain actions are inherently unethical and should never be performed, regardless of the circumstances. A researcher who operates from a deontological perspective might argue, for example, that lying is immoral in all situations regardless of the consequences, and thus that deception in research is always unethical.

In contrast, **ethical skepticism** asserts that concrete and inviolate moral codes such as those proclaimed by the deontologist cannot be formulated. Given the diversity of opinions regarding ethical issues and the absence of consensus on ethical standards, skeptics resist those who claim to have an inside route to moral truth. Skepticism does not deny that ethical principles are important, only that ethical rules are arbitrary and relative to culture and time. According to ethical skepticism, ethical decisions must be a matter of the individual's conscience: one should do what one thinks is right and refrain from doing what one thinks is wrong. The final arbiter on ethical questions is the individual him- or herself. Thus, a skeptic would claim that research ethics cannot be imposed from the outside but are a matter of the individual researcher's conscience.

The third approach to ethical decisions is **utilitarian,** one that maintains that judgments regarding the ethics of a particular action depend on the consequences of that action. An individual operating from a utilitarian perspective argues that the potential benefits of a particular action should be weighed against the potential costs. If the benefits are sufficiently large relative to the costs, the action is ethically permissible. Researchers who operate from this perspective base decisions regarding whether a particular research procedure is ethical on the benefits and costs associated with using the procedure. As we will discuss below, the official guidelines for research enforced by the federal government and most professional organizations (including the American Psychological Association) are essentially utilitarian.

People with different ethical ideologies often have a great deal of difficulty agreeing on which research procedures are permissible and which are not. As you can see, these debates involve not only the ethics of particular research practices, such as deception, but also disagreements about the fundamental principles that should guide ethical decisions. Thus, we should not be surprised that well-meaning people sometimes disagree about the acceptability of certain research methods.

IN DEPTH

WHAT IS YOUR ETHICAL IDEOLOGY?

To what extent do you agree or disagree with the following statements?

1. Weighing the potential benefits of research against its potential harm to participants could lead to sacrificing the participants' welfare and hence is wrong.

2. Scientific concerns sometimes justify potential harm to research participants.

3. If a researcher can foresee any type of harm, no matter how small, he or she should not conduct the study.

4. What is ethical varies from one situation and society to the next.

5. Lying to participants about the nature of a study is always wrong, irrespective of the type of study or the amount of information to be gained.

6. It is possible to develop codes of ethics that can be applied without exception to all psychological research.

A deontologist would agree with statements 1, 3, 5, and 6 and disagree with statements 2 and 4. A skeptic would agree with statement 4 and disagree strongly with statements 5 and 6. How a skeptic would respond to statements 1, 2, and 3 would depend on his or her personal ethics. A utilitarian would agree with statements 2, 4, and 6, and disagree with statements 1, 3, and 5.

From Schlenker, B. R., & Forsyth, D. R., 1977, *Journal of Experimental Social Psychology.* Reprinted with permission of Barry R. Schlenker and Academic Press.

Basic Ethical Guidelines

Whatever their personal feelings about such matters, behavioral researchers are bound by two sets of ethical guidelines. The first involves principles formulated by professional organizations, such as the American Psychological Association (APA). The APA's *Ethical Principles of Psychologists and Code of Content* sets forth ethical standards that psychologists must follow in all areas of professional life, including therapy, evaluation, teaching, and research (*Ethical Principles,* 1992). To help researchers make sound decisions regarding ethical issues, the APA has also published a set of guidelines for research that involves human participants, as well as regulations for the use and care of nonhuman animals in research. In addition, the division of the APA for specialists in developmental psychology has set standards for research involving children.

Behavioral researchers are also bound by regulations set forth by the federal government. Concerned about the rights of research participants, the surgeon general of the United States issued a directive in 1966 that required certain kinds of research to be reviewed to ensure the welfare of human research participants. Since then, a series of federal laws has been passed to protect the rights and welfare of humans and animals who participate in research.

The official approach to research ethics in both the APA principles and federal regulations is essentially a utilitarian or pragmatic one. Rather than specifying a rigid set of dos and don'ts, these guidelines require that researchers weigh potential benefits of the research against its potential costs and risks. Thus, in determining whether to conduct a piece of research, researchers must consider the likely benefits and costs of a particular study. Weighing the pros and cons of a study is called a **cost–benefit analysis.**

Potential Benefits

Behavioral research has five potential benefits that should be considered when a cost–benefit analysis is conducted.

Basic knowledge. The most obvious benefit of research is that it enhances our understanding of behavioral processes. Of course, studies differ in the degree to which they are expected to enhance knowledge. In a cost–benefit analysis, greater potential risks and costs are considered permissible when the contribution of the research is expected to be high.

Improvement of research or assessment techniques. Some research is conducted to improve the techniques researchers use to measure and study behavior. The benefit of such research is not to extend knowledge directly but to improve the research enterprise itself. Of course, such research has an indirect effect on knowledge by providing more reliable, valid, useful, or efficient research methods.

Practical outcomes. Some studies provide practical benefits by directly improving human or animal welfare. For example, research in clinical psychology may improve the quality of psychological assessment and treatment, studies of educational processes may enhance learning in schools, tests of experimental drugs may lead to improved drug therapy, and investigations of prejudice may reduce racial tensions.

Benefits for researchers. Those who conduct research usually stand to gain from their research activities. First, research serves an important educational function. Through conducting research, students gain firsthand knowledge about the research process and about the topic they are studying. Indeed, students are often required to conduct research for class projects, senior research, master's theses, and doctoral dissertations. Fully trained scientists also benefit from research. Not only does it fulfill an educational function for them as it does for students, but many researchers must conduct research to maintain their jobs and advance in their careers.

Benefits for research participants.   The people who participate in research may also benefit from their participation. Such benefits are most obvious in clinical research in which subjects receive experimental therapies that help them with a particular problem. Research participation also can serve an educational function, as subjects learn about behavioral science and its methods. Finally, some studies may, in fact, be enjoyable to participants.

Potential Costs

Benefits such as these must be balanced against potential risks and costs of the research. Some of these costs are relatively minor. For example, research participants invest a certain amount of time and effort into a study; their time and effort should not be squandered on research that has limited value.

More serious are risks to participants' mental or physical welfare. Sometimes, in the course of a study, participants may suffer social discomfort, threats to their self-esteem, stress, boredom, anxiety, pain, or other aversive states. Participants may also suffer if the confidentiality of their data is compromised and others learn about their responses. Most serious are studies in which human and nonhuman animals are exposed to conditions that may threaten their health or lives. We'll return to these kinds of costs and how we protect subjects against them in a moment.

In addition to costs to the research participants, research has other costs. Conducting research costs money in terms of salaries, equipment, and supplies, and researchers must determine whether their research is justified financially. In addition, some research practices may be detrimental to the profession or to society at large. For example, the use of deception may promote a climate of distrust toward behavioral research.

Balancing Benefits and Costs

The issue facing the researcher, then, is whether the benefits expected from a particular study are sufficient to warrant the expected costs. A study with only limited benefits warrants only minimal costs and risks, whereas a study that may make a potentially important contribution may permit greater costs.

Of course, the researcher may not be the most objective judge of the merits of his or her own research. For this reason, federal guidelines require that research be approved by an Institutional Review Board.

The Institutional Review Board

Many years ago, decisions regarding research ethics were left to the conscience of the individual investigator. However, after several cases in which the welfare of human and nonhuman subjects was compromised (most of these cases were in medical rather than psychological research), the United States government ordered that all research involving human participants be reviewed by an **Institutional Review Board (IRB)** at the investigator's institution. All institutions that receive federal funds (which includes virtually every college and university in the United States) must have an IRB that reviews research conducted with human participants.

To ensure maximum protection for subjects, an institution's IRB must have a minimum of five members who come from a variety of both scientific and nonscientific disciplines. In addition, at least one member of the IRB must be a member of the community who is not associated with the institution in any way.

Researchers who use human participants must submit a written proposal to their institution's IRB for approval. This proposal describes the purpose of the research, the procedures that will be used, and the potential risks to research participants. Although the IRB may exempt certain pieces of research, most research involving human participants should be submitted for consideration. Research cannot be conducted without prior approval of the institution's IRB.

Six issues dominate the discussion of ethical issues in research that involves human participants (and, thus, the discussions of the IRB): lack of informed consent, invasion of privacy, coercion to participate, potential physical or mental harm, deception, and violation of confidentiality. In the following sections, we discuss each of these issues.

The Principle of Informed Consent

One of the primary ways of ensuring that subjects' rights are protected is to obtain their informed consent prior to participating in a study. As the term implies, **informed consent** involves informing the research participant of the nature of the study and obtaining his or her explicit agreement to participate. Obtaining informed consent not only ensures that researchers do not violate people's privacy, it also ensures that prospective research participants are given enough information about the nature of a study to make a reasoned decision regarding whether they want to participate.

Obtaining Informed Consent

The accepted general principal governing informed consent states:

> Using language that is reasonably understandable to participants, psychologists inform participants of the nature of the research; they inform participants that they are free to participate or to decline to participate or to withdraw from the research; they explain the foreseeable consequences of declining or withdrawing; they inform participants of significant factors that may be expected to influence their willingness to participate (such as risks, discomforts, adverse effects, or limitations on confidentiality) . . .; and they explain other aspects about which the prospective participants inquire. (*Ethical Principles*, 1992, p. 1608)

Note that this principle does not require that the investigator divulge everything about the study. However, researchers are required to inform subjects about features of the research that might influence their willingness to participate. Thus, a researcher may withhold the hypotheses of the study, but he or she cannot fail to tell participants that they will experience pain or discomfort. Whenever a researcher chooses to be less than fully candid with a subject, he or she is obligated to later inform the subject of all relevant details.

To document that informed consent was obtained, an **informed consent form** is typically used. This form provides the required information about the study and must be signed by the subject or by the subject's legally authorized representative (such as the parents if the subjects are children). A copy of the form must be given to the person who signs it. In some cases, informed consent may be given orally but only if a witness is present to attest that informed consent occurred.

Problems with Obtaining Informed Consent

Although few would quarrel in principle with the notion that subjects should be informed about a study and be allowed to choose whether or not to participate, certain considerations either may make researchers hesitant to use informed consent or may preclude informed consent altogether.

Compromising the validity of the study. The most common difficulty arises when fully informing participants about a study would compromise the validity of the data. People often act quite differently when they are under scrutiny than when they don't think they are being observed. Furthermore, divulging the nature of the study may sensitize subjects to aspects of their behavior of which they are not normally aware. It would be fruitless, for example, for a researcher to tell subjects, "This is a study of nonverbal behavior. During the next 5 minutes, researchers will be rating your expression, gestures, body position, and movement. Please act naturally." Thus, researchers sometimes wish to observe people without revealing to the participants that they are being observed, or at least without telling them what aspect of their behavior is being studied.

Subjects who are incompetent to give informed consent.   Certain classes of people are unable to give valid consent. Children, for example, are neither cognitively nor legally able to make such informed decisions. Similarly, individuals who are mentally retarded or who are out of touch with reality (such as psychotics) cannot be expected to give informed consent. When one's research calls for participants who cannot provide valid consent, consent must be obtained from the parent or legal guardian of the participant.

Ludicrous cases of informed consent.   Some uses of informed consent would be ludicrous because obtaining participants' consent would pose a greater burden than not obtaining it. For a researcher who was counting the number of people riding in cars that passed a particular intersection, obtaining informed consent would be both impossible and unnecessary.

Federal guidelines permit certain, limited kinds of research to be conducted without obtaining informed consent: (1) if the research involves no more than minimal risk to participants; (2) if the waiver of informed consent will not adversely affect the rights and welfare of subjects; and (3) if the research could not feasibly be carried out if informed consent were required. For example, a researcher observing patterns of seating on public buses would probably not be required to obtain participants' informed consent. Because the risk to participants is minimal, failure to obtain their consent would not adversely affect their welfare and rights, and the research could not be carried out if people riding buses were informed in advance that their choice of seats was being observed.

Invasion of Privacy

The right to privacy is a person's right to decide "when, where, to whom, and to what extent his or her attitudes, beliefs, and behavior will be revealed" to others (Singleton, Straits, Straits, & McAllister, 1988, p. 454). The APA does not offer explicit guidelines regarding **invasion of privacy,** noting only that "the ethical investigator will assume responsibility for undertaking a study involving covert investigation in private situations only after very careful consideration and consultation" (American Psychological Association, 1982, p. 39). Thus, the circumstances under which researchers may collect data without participants' knowledge is left to the investigator to judge.

Most researchers believe that research involving the observation of people in *public places* (shopping or eating, for example) does not constitute invasion of privacy. However, if people are to be observed under circumstances in which they reasonably expect privacy, invasion of privacy may be an issue.

DEVELOPING YOUR RESEARCH SKILLS

YOU BE THE JUDGE: WHAT CONSTITUTES INVASION OF PRIVACY?

In your opinion, which, if any, of these actual studies constitute an unethical invasion of privacy?

- Men using a public restroom are observed surreptitiously by a researcher hidden in a toilet stall, who records the time they take to urinate (Middlemist, Knowles, & Matter, 1976).

- A researcher pretends to be a lookout for gay men having sex in a public restroom. On the basis of the men's car license plates, the researcher tracks down the subjects through the Department of Motor Vehicles. Then, under the guise of another study, he interviews them in their homes (Humphreys, 1975).

- Researchers covertly film people who strip the parts from seemingly abandoned cars (Zimbardo, 1969).

- Subjects waiting for an experiment are videotaped without their prior knowledge or consent. However, they are given the option of erasing the tapes if they do not want their tapes to be used for research purposes (Ickes, 1982).

- Shoppers in a drugstore are exposed to a shoplifting confederate, and their reactions are observed (Gelfand, Hartmann, Walder, & Page, 1973).

- Researchers hide under dormitory beds and eavesdrop on college students' conversations (Henle & Hubbell, 1938).

What criteria did you use to decide which, if any, of these studies were acceptable to you?

Freedom from Coercion to Participate

All ethical guidelines insist that potential subjects must not be coerced into participating in research. *Coercion* occurs when subjects agree to participate because of real or implied pressure from an individual who has authority or influence over them. The most common example involves cases in which professors require that their students serve as research subjects. Other examples include employees in business and industry who are asked to participate in research by their employers, military personnel who are required to serve as subjects, prisoners who are asked to volunteer for research, and clients who are asked to provide data by their therapists or physicians. What all these classes of subjects have in common is that they may believe, correctly or incorrectly, that refusing to participate will have negative consequences for them—receiving a lower course grade, having one's job in jeopardy, getting reprimands from one's superiors, or simply displeasing an important person.

The APA's *Ethical Principles* states that researchers must respect an individual's freedom to decline to participate in research or to discontinue participation at any time. Furthermore, to ensure that subjects are not indirectly coerced by offering exceptionally high inducements, the guidelines state that researchers cannot "offer excessive or inappropriate financial or other inducements to obtain research participants, particularly when it might tend to coerce participation" (*Ethical Principles*, 1992, Principle 6.14). Furthermore, "when research participation is a course requirement or opportunity for extra credit, the prospective participant is given the choice of equitable alternative activities" (*Ethical Principles*, 1992, Principle 6.11d). Thus, when university and college students are required to participate in research, they must be given the option of fulfilling the requirement in an alternative fashion, such as by writing a paper that would require as much time and effort as serving as a research subject.

Minimizing Physical and Mental Stress

Most behavioral research is innocuous. However, because many important topics in behavioral science involve how people or animals respond to unpleasant physical or psychological events, it is important that we understand the effects of unpleasant events such as stress, failure, fear, and pain. Researchers find it difficult to study such topics if they are prevented from exposing their subjects to at least small amounts of physical or mental stress. But how much discomfort may a researcher inflict on participants?

At the extremes, most people tend to agree regarding the amount of discomfort that is permissible. For example, most people agree that an experiment that leads subjects to think they are dying is highly unethical. One study did just that by injecting subjects, without their knowledge, with a drug that caused them to stop breathing temporarily (Campbell, Sanderson, & Laverty, 1964). On the other hand, few people object to studies that involve only minimal risk. **Minimal risk** is "risk that is no greater in probability and severity than that ordinarily encountered in daily life or during the performance of routine physical or psychological examinations or tests" (*Official IRB Guidebook*, 1986).

Between these extremes, however, considerable controversy arises regarding the amount of physical and mental distress to be permitted in research. In large part, the final decision must be left to the individual investigator and the IRB at his or her institution. The decision is often based on a cost–benefit analysis of the research. Research procedures that cause stress or pain may be allowed only if the potential benefits of the research are extensive and only if the subject volunteers to participate after being fully informed of the possible risks.

Deception in Research

Perhaps no research practice has evoked as much controversy among behavioral researchers as **deception.** Thirty years ago, methodological deception was rare, but the use of deception increased dramatically during the 1960s (Christensen, 1988). Although some areas of behavioral research use deception rarely, if at all, it is common in other areas. A survey of 691 studies in social psychology—the area in which deception is most common—showed that, of articles published in leading journals between 1965 and 1979, 58% used some form of deception technique (Gross & Fleming, 1982).

Behavioral scientists use deception for a number of reasons. The most common one is to prevent subjects from learning the true purpose of a study so their behavior will not be artificially affected. Other uses include:

- presenting subjects with a false purpose of the study
- using an experimental confederate who poses as another subject or as an uninvolved bystander
- providing false feedback to subjects
- presenting two related studies as unrelated
- giving incorrect information regarding stimulus materials

In each instance, researchers use deception because they believe it is necessary for studying the topic of interest.

Objections to Deception

Many objections have been raised regarding the use of deception; these can be classified roughly into two basic categories. The most obvious objection is a strictly ethical one: lying and deceit are immoral and reprehensible acts, even when they are used for good purposes such as research. Baumrind (1971) argued, for example, that "fundamental moral principles of reciprocity and justice are violated" when research psychologists use deception. She added that "scientific ends, however laudable they may be, do not themselves justify the use of means that in ordinary transactions would be regarded as reprehensible" (p. 890). This objection is obviously a deontological one, based on the violation of moral rules.

The second objection is pragmatic. Even if deception can be justified on the grounds that it leads to positive outcomes (the utilitarian perspective), it may lead to undesirable consequences. For example, because of widespread deception, research participants may enter research studies already suspicious of what the researcher tells them. In addition, subjects who learn they have been deceived may come to distrust behavioral scientists and the research process in general, undermining the public's trust in psychology and related fields.

Although the first objection is a purely ethical one for which there is no objective resolution, the second concern has been examined empirically. Several studies have tested how research participants react when they learn they have been deceived by the researcher. In most studies that assessed reactions to deception, the vast majority of subjects (usually over 90%) say they realize that deception is sometimes necessary for methodological reasons and report positive feelings about their participation in the study. Even Milgram (1963), who has been soundly criticized for his use of deception, found that less than 2% of his subjects reported having negative feelings about their participation in his experiment on obedience. (See the box, "The Milgram Experiments.")

In general, as long as they are informed about details of the study afterward, subjects appear not to mind being misled for good reasons (Christensen, 1988). Research participants do not seem to regard deception in research settings in the same way they view lying in everyday life. Instead, they view it as a necessary aspect of certain research (Smith & Richardson, 1983). In fact, research shows that, assuming they are properly debriefed, subjects report *more* positive reactions to their participation and higher ratings of a study's scientific value if the study included deception (Smith & Richardson, 1983; Straits, Wuebben, & Majka, 1972). Findings such as these should not be taken to suggest that deception is necessarily an acceptable practice; however, they do show that, when properly handled, deception per se need not have negative consequences for research participants.

Both APA and federal guidelines state that researchers should use not use deception unless they have determined that the use of deception is justified by the research's possible scientific, educational, or applied value and that the research could not feasibly be conducted without the use of deception. Importantly, researchers are never justified in deceiving subjects about aspects of the study that might affect their willingness to participate. In the process of obtaining participants' informed consent, the researcher must accurately inform participants regarding possible risks, discomfort, or unpleasant experiences.

Debriefing

Whenever deception is used, participants must be informed "as early as it is feasible" (*Ethical Principles*, 1992, Principle 6.15c). Subjects usually are debriefed immediately after they participate, but occasionally researchers wait until the entire study is over and all the data have been collected.

A good **debriefing** accomplishes four goals. First, the debriefing clarifies the nature of the study for participants. Although the researcher may have withheld certain information at the beginning of the study, the participant should be more fully informed after it is over. This does not require that the researcher give a lecture regarding the area of research: only that the participant leave the study with a sense of what was being studied and how his or her participation contributed to knowledge in an area.

Occasionally, subjects are angered or embarrassed when they find they were fooled by the researcher. Of course, the more smug a researcher is about the deception, the more likely the subject is to react negatively. Thus, researchers should be sure to explain the reasons for the deception, express their apologies for misleading the subject, and allow the participant to express his or her feelings about being deceived.

The second goal of debriefing is to remove any stress or other negative consequences. For example, if subjects were provided with false feedback about their performance on a test, the deception should be explained. In cases in which subjects have been led to perform embarrassing or socially undesirable actions, researchers must be sure that participants leave with no bad feelings about what they have done.

A third goal of the debriefing is for the researcher to obtain subjects' reactions to the study itself. Often, if carefully probed, participants will reveal that they didn't understand part of the instructions, were suspicious about aspects of the procedure, were disturbed by the study, or had heard about the study from other people. Such revelations may require modifications in the procedure.

The fourth goal of a debriefing is more intangible. Subjects should leave the study feeling good about their participation. Researchers should convey their genuine appreciation for subjects' time and cooperation and give subjects the sense that their participation was important.

Confidentiality

The information obtained about research participants in the course of a study is confidential. *Confidentiality* means that such information may be used only for purposes of the research and may not be divulged to others. When others have access to participants' data, their privacy is invaded.

Admittedly, in most behavioral research, participants would experience no adverse consequences if confidentiality were broken and others obtained access to their data. In some cases, however, the information collected during a study may be quite sensitive, and disclosure would undoubtedly have negative repercussions for the participant. For example, issues of confidentiality have been paramount among health psychologists who study persons who have tested positively for HIV or AIDS (Rosnow, Rotheram-Borus, Ceci, Blanck, & Koocher, 1993).

The easiest way to maintain confidentiality is to ensure that subjects' responses are *anonymous*. If no information is collected that can be used to identify the subject, confidentiality will not be a problem. In many instances, however, researchers need to know the identity of a research participant. For example, they may need to collate data collected in two different research sessions. To do so, they must know which subjects' data is which.

Several practices are used to solve this problem. Sometimes subjects are given codes to use on their data that allow researchers to connect their data without divulging their identities. In cases in which the data are in no way potentially sensitive or embarrassing, names may be collected. In such cases, however, researchers should remove all information that might identify a subject after the identifying information is no longer needed.

THE MILGRAM EXPERIMENTS

Perhaps no research has been the center of as much ethical debate as Stanley Milgram's (1963) studies of obedience to authority. Milgram was interested in factors that affect the degree to which people obey an authority's orders, even when those orders lead them to harm another person. To examine this question, he tested subjects' reactions to an experimenter who ordered them to harm another subject.

The Study

Subjects were recruited by mail to participate in a study of memory and learning. Upon arriving at a laboratory at Yale University, the subject met an experimenter and another subject who was participating in the same experimental session.

The experiment was described as a test of the effects of punishment on learning. Based on a drawing, one subject was assigned the role of teacher and the other subject was assigned the role of learner. The teacher watched as the learner was strapped into a chair and fitted with an electrode on his wrist. The teacher was then taken to an adjoining room and seated in front of an imposing shock generator that would deliver shocks to the other subject. The shock generator had a row of 30 switches, each of which was marked with a voltage level, beginning with 15 volts and proceeding in 15-volt increments to 450 volts.

The experimenter told the teacher to read the learner a list of word pairs, such as *blue–box* and *wild–duck*. After reading the list, the teacher would test the learner's memory by giving him the first word in each pair. The learner was then to give the second word in the pair. If the learner remembered the word correctly, the teacher was to go to the next word on the list. However, if the learner remembered the word incorrectly, the teacher was to deliver a shock by pressing one of the switches. The teacher was to start with the switch marked *15 volts*, then increase the voltage one level each time the learner missed a word.

Once the study was under way, the learner began to make a number of errors. At first, the learner didn't react to the shocks, but as the voltage increased, he began to object. When the learner received 120 volts, he simply complained that the shocks were painful. As the voltage increased, the learner first asked and then demanded that the experimenter stop the study. However, the experimenter told the teacher that "the experiment requires that you continue." With increasingly strong shocks, the learner began to yell, then pound on the wall, and, after 300 volts, scream in anguish. Most of the teachers were reluctant to continue, but the experimenter insisted that the subject continue with the experimental procedure. After 330 volts, the learner stopped responding altogether; the teacher was left to imagine that the subject had fainted or, worse, died. Even then, the experimenter instructed the teacher to treat no response as a wrong answer and to deliver the next shock.

As you probably know (or have guessed), the learner was in fact a confederate of the experimenter and received no shocks. The real subjects, of course, thought they were actually shocking another person. Even so, 65% of the subjects delivered all 30 shocks—up to 450 volts—even though the learner had protested, then fallen silent. This level of obedience was entirely unexpected and attests both to the power of authority figures to lead people to perform harmful actions and to the compliance of research subjects.

The Ethical Issues

Milgram's research raised a number of ethical issues and stimulated an intense debate on research ethics that continues today. Milgram's study raised virtually every ethical question that can be raised.

- Subjects were misled about the purpose of the study.
- A confederate posed as another subject.
- Subjects were led to believe they were shocking another person.
- Subjects were led to perform a behavior that, in retrospect, may have been very disturbing to them.
- Subjects experienced considerable stress as the experiment continued. They sweated, trembled, stuttered, swore, and laughed nervously as they delivered increasingly intense shocks.
- Subjects' attempts to withdraw from the study were discouraged by the experimenter's insistence that they continue.

What is your reaction to Milgram's experiment? Did Milgram violate basic ethical principles in this research?

Common Courtesy

A few years ago I conducted an informal survey of students who had participated in research as part of their course in introductory psychology. In this survey, I asked what problems they had encountered in their participation. The vast majority of their responses did not involve violations of basic ethical principles involving coercion, harm, deception, or violation of confidentiality. Rather, their major complaints had to do with how they were treated *as people* during the course of the study. Their chief complaints were that: (1) the researcher failed to show up or was late; (2) the researcher was not adequately prepared; (3) the researcher was cold, abrupt, or downright rude; and (4) the researcher failed to show appreciation for the subject.

Aside from the formal guidelines, ethical research requires a large dose of common courtesy. The people who participate in research are contributing their time and energy, often without compensation, to your research. They deserve the utmost in common courtesy.

Ethics in Research with Animals

The *Ethical Principles* contain standards regarding the ethical treatment of animals, and the APA has published a more detailed discussion of these issues in *Guidelines for Ethical Conduct in the Care and Use of Animals*. These guidelines are noticeably less detailed than those involving human subjects, but they are no less explicit regarding the importance of treating nonhuman animals in a humane and ethical fashion.

These guidelines stipulate that all research using nonhuman animals be monitored closely by a person experienced in the care and use of laboratory animals, and a veterinarian must be available for consultation. Furthermore, all personnel, including students, involved in animal research must be familiar with these guidelines and adequately trained regarding the use and care of animals. Thus, if you should become involved with such research, you are obligated to aquaint yourself with these guidelines and abide by them at all times.

The facilities in which laboratory animals are housed are closely regulated by the National Institutes of Health, as well as federal, state, and local laws. Obviously, animals must be housed under humane and healthful conditions. The facilities should be inspected by a veterinarian at least twice a year.

Advocates of animal rights are most concerned, of course, about the experimental procedures to which the animals are subjected during research. APA guidelines direct researchers to "make reasonable efforts to minimize the discomfort, infection, illness, and pain of animal subjects," and require that the investigator justify the use of all procedures that involve more than momentary or slight pain to the animal: "A procedure subjecting animals to pain, stress, or privation is used only when an alternative procedure is unavailable and the goal is justified by its prospective scientific, educational, or applied value" (*Ethical Principles,* 1992, p. 1609, Standard 6.20). Procedures that involve more than minimal pain or distress require strong justification.

The APA regulations also provide guidelines for the use of surgical procedures, the study of animals in field settings, the use of animals for educational (as opposed to research) purposes, and the disposition of animals at the end of the study.

IN DEPTH

BEHAVIORAL RESEARCH AND ANIMAL RIGHTS

During the 1980s, several animal rights organizations were formed to protest the use of animals for research purposes. Although the protests were aimed initially at medical researchers, behavioral researchers have also been accused of misusing and mistreating the animals they use in their research. Some animal rights groups have simply pressured researchers to treat animals more humanely, whereas others have demanded that the practice of using animals in research be stopped entirely. (Members of some such groups have even burglarized animal research laboratories and released the animals.)

Like most ethical issues in research, debates involving the use of animals in research arise because of the competing pressures to advance knowledge and improve welfare on the one hand and to protect animals on the other. Undoubtedly, animals occasionally have been mistreated, either by being housed under inhumane conditions or by being subjected to unnecessary pain or distress during the research itself. However, researchers who conduct research on animals argue that such unfortunate abuses should not blind us to the value of behavioral research that uses animal subjects.

In the address he delivered upon receiving the APA's Award for Distinguished Professional Contributions, Neal Miller (1985) chronicled the significant contributions of animal research. In defending the use of animals in behavioral research, Miller noted that animal research has contributed to the rehabilitation of neuromuscular disorders, to understanding and reducing stress and pain, to developing drugs for the treatment of various human and animal problems, to exploring processes involved in substance abuse, to improving memory deficits in the elderly, to improving the survival rate for premature infants, and to developing behavioral approaches in psychotherapy. Miller's list involves only the contributions of *behavioral* research and does not include the many advances in medicine and other fields that have also come about through the use of animals.

To some animal rights activists, the benefits of the research are beside the point. They argue that, like people, nonhuman animals have certain moral rights and that humans have no right to subject nonhuman animals to pain, stress, and often death for their own purposes.

In an ideal world, we would be able to solve problems of human suffering without using animals in research. But in our less than perfect world, most behavioral researchers subscribe to the utilitarian view that the potential benefits of most animal research outweigh its potential costs.

Scientific Misconduct

In addition to adhering to principles governing the treatment of human and animal subjects, behavioral researchers are bound by general ethical principles involving the conduct of scientific research. Such principles are not specific to behavioral research but apply to all scientists regardless of their discipline. Most scientific organizations have set ethical standards for their members to guard against **scientific misconduct.**

The National Academy of Sciences identifies three major categories of ethical problems in science. The first category involves the most serious and blatant forms of scientific dishonesty, such as fabrication, falsification, and plagiarism. The APA *Ethical Principles* also address these issues, stating that researchers must not fabricate data or report false results. Furthermore, if they discover significant errors in their findings or analyses, researchers are obligated to take steps to correct such errors. Likewise, researchers do not plagiarize others' work, presenting "substantial portions or elements of another's work or data as their own. . . ." (*Ethical Principles*, 1992, Standard 6.22).

A recent study of graduate students and faculty members in chemistry, civil engineering, microbiology, and sociology found that between 6% and 9% of the 4000 respondents reported direct knowledge of faculty members who had plagiarized or falsified their data. Among graduate students, between 10% and 20% (depending on the discipline) reported that their student peers had falsified data, and over 30% of the faculty reported knowledge of student plagiarism (Swazey, Anderson, & Lewis, 1993).

Although not rampant, such abuses are disturbingly common. Most behavioral scientists agree with former director of the National Science Foundation, Walter Massey, who observed that "Few things are more damaging to the scientific enterprise than falsehoods—be they the result of error, self-deception, sloppiness, and haste, or, in the worst case, dishonesty" (Massey, 1992). Because science relies so heavily on honesty and is so severely damaged by dishonesty, the penalties for scientific misconduct, whether by professional researchers or by students, are severe.

A second category of ethical abuses involve questionable research practices that, although not constituting scientific misconduct per se, are problematic. For example, researchers should take credit for work only in proportion to their true contribution. This issue sometimes arises when researchers must decide whom to include as authors on research articles or papers, and in what order to list them (authors are usually listed in descending order of their scientific or professional contributions to the project). Problems of "ownership" can occur in both directions: in some cases, researchers have failed to properly acknowledge the contributions of other people, whereas in other cases, researchers have awarded authorship to people who didn't contribute substantially to the project (such as their boss or a colleague who lent them a piece of equipment).

Other ethically questionable research practices include misusing research funds for other purposes, failing to report data inconsistent with one's own views, and failing to make one's data available to other competent professionals who wish to verify the researcher's conclusions by reanalyzing the data. In the study described earlier, the reported incidence of these questionable practices was also disturbingly

*"They discovered that your research is fraudulent,
so your grant will be funded in counterfeit bills."*

Copyright © 1990 by Sidney Harris, *American Scientist* Magazine.

high. For example, 15% of the respondents reported knowing researchers who did not present data that were inconsistent with their own previous research.

Finally, some ethical problems in research involves behavior that is not unique to scientific investigation: sexual harassment (of research assistants or research participants), abuse of power, discrimination, or failure to follow government regulations. Not surprisingly, such unethical behaviors occur in science as they do in all human endeavors (Swazey et al., 1993).

By and large, the guidelines discussed in this chapter provide only a framework for making ethical decisions about research practices. Rather than specifying a universal code of dos and don'ts, they present the principles by which researchers should resolve ethical issues. No unequivocal criteria exist by which researchers can decide how much stress is too much, when deception is and is not appropriate, or whether data may be collected without subjects' knowledge in a particular study. As a result, knowledge of APA principles and federal regulations must be accompanied by a good dose of common sense.

Summary

1. Ethical issues arise in virtually every study of human or animal behavior. Usually the issues are minor ones, but often they involve the fundamental conflict between the scientific search for knowledge and the welfare of research participants.

2. Researchers sometimes disagree not only regarding the ethicality of specific research practices but also regarding how ethical decisions should be made. Researchers operating from the deontological, skeptical, and utilitarian perspectives use very different standards for judging the ethical acceptability of research procedures.

3. Professional organizations and the federal government have provided regulations for the protection of human and animal subjects.

4. Six issues must be considered when human participants are used: informed consent, invasion of privacy, coercion to participate, potential physical or psychological harm, deception, and confidentiality. Although APA and federal guidelines provide general guidance regarding these issues, in the last analysis, individual researchers must weigh the potential benefits of their research against its potential costs.

5. Federal regulations require an Institutional Review Board (IRB) at an investigator's institution to approve research involving humans to protect research participants.

6. Professional and governmental regulations also govern the use and care of nonhuman animals in research.

7. Scientific misconduct involves behaviors that compromise the integrity of the scientific enterprise, including dishonesty (fabrication, falsification, and plagiarism), questionable research practices, and otherwise unethical behavior (such as sexual harassment and misuse of power).

Key Terms

deontology	informed consent form
ethical skepticism	invasion of privacy
utilitarianism	minimal risk
cost–benefit analysis	deception
Institutional Review Board (IRB)	debriefing
informed consent	scientific misconduct

Review Questions

1. Distinguish between deontology, skepticism, and utilitarianism as approaches to making decisions.

2. Which of these three ethical philosophies comes closest to the official ethical guidelines expressed by federal regulatory agencies and the American Psychological Association?

3. What factors should be considered when doing a cost–benefit analysis of a proposed study?

4. What is the purpose of the Institutional Review Board?

5. According to the principle of informed consent, what must subjects be told before soliciting their agreement to participate in a study?

6. When is it not necessary to obtain informed consent?

7. In general, how much mental or physical risk is permissible in research?

8. Why do researchers use deception?

9. What are some methods researchers use to maintain the confidentiality of subjects' responses?

10. Describe the Milgram (1963) study and discuss the ethical issues it raised.

11. What are the basic ethical principles that animal researchers must follow?

12. What are some examples of scientific misconduct?

Questions For Thought and Discussion

1. In your view, when is deception permissible in research?

2. Milgram conducted his experiments on obedience before it became the practice to have all research scrutinized by an Institutional Review Board. Imagine, however, that Milgram had submitted his research to an IRB of which you were a member. What ethical issues would you raise as a member of the board? Would you have voted to approve Milgram's research? In thinking about this, keep in mind that, before the study was conducted, no one expected subjects to obey the researcher as strongly as they did (see Schlenker & Forsyth, 1977).

3. To gain practice writing an informed consent form, write one for the Milgram study described in this chapter.

CHAPTER 16

Scientific Writing

As a system for enhancing knowledge, science requires that investigators share their findings with the rest of the scientific community. Only if one's findings are made public can knowledge accumulate as researchers build on and refine one another's work. As we discussed in Chapter 1, a defining characteristic of science is that, over the long haul, it is self-correcting; but self-correction can occur only if research findings are widely disseminated. To this end, informing others of the outcome of one's work is a critical part of the research process.

In this chapter, we will examine how researchers distribute their work—to other scientists, to students, and to the general public. Because the effective communication of one's research nearly always involves writing, much of this chapter will be devoted to scientific writing. We will discuss criteria for good scientific writing and help you improve your own writing skills. We will also examine the guidelines behavioral researchers use to prepare their research reports, a system of rules known as APA style. To begin, however, we'll take a look at the three main routes by which behavioral scientists disseminate their research to others.

How Scientific Findings Are Disseminated

Researchers disseminate the results of their investigations in three ways: journal publications, presentations at professional meetings, and personal contact.

Journal Publication

Journal publication is the primary route by which research findings are disseminated to the scientific community. Scientific journals serve not only as a means of communication among researchers (most researchers subscribe to one or more journals in their fields) but also as the basis for the permanent storage of research findings in library collections.

Before most journals will publish a research paper, it must undergo the process of **peer review.** In peer review, a paper is evaluated by other scientists who have expertise in the topic under investigation. Although various journals use slightly different systems of peer review, the general process is as follows.

1. The author submits copies of his or her paper to the editor of a relevant journal. (The editor's name and address typically appear on the inside front cover of the journal.) Authors are permitted to submit a particular piece of work to only one journal at a time.

2. The editor then sends a copy of the paper to two or more peer reviewers known to be experts in the area of the paper. Each of the reviewers reads and evaluates the paper, addressing its conceptualization, methodology, analyses, and implications. Each reviewer decides whether the paper, considered in its entirety, warrants publication in the journal.

3. The reviewers then send written reviews, typically a page or two in length, to the journal editor, along with their recommendations regarding whether the paper should be published.

4. Having received the reviewers' comments, suggestions, and recommendations, the editor considers their input and usually reads the paper him- or herself. The editor then makes one of four editorial decisions. First, he or she may decide to publish the paper as is. Editors rarely make this decision, however; even if the paper is exceptional, the reviewers virtually always suggest ways in which it can be improved. Second, the editor may accept the paper for publication contingent on the author making certain changes and clarifications. Third, the editor may decide *not* to accept the paper for publication in the journal but will ask the authors to revise the paper in line with the reviewers' recommendations and resubmit it for reconsideration. Editors make this decision when they think the paper has potential merit but see too many problems to warrant publication in its original form. The fourth decision an editor may make is to reject the paper, with no opportunity for the author to resubmit the paper to that particular journal. However, once the manuscript is rejected, the author may submit it for consideration at another journal.

The most common editorial decision is the fourth one—rejection. In the leading journals in behavioral science, between 70% and 90% of the submitted manuscripts are rejected for publication (*Summary Report of Journal Operations,* 1993). Even if they are ultimately accepted for publication, most submitted papers undergo one or more rounds of reviews and revisions before they are published. In all, from the initial submission of the paper to final publication, the process typically takes a year or two.

Presentations at Professional Meetings

The second route by which scientific findings are distributed is through presentations at professional meetings. Most behavioral researchers belong to one or more professional organizations (such as the American Psychological Association, the American Psychological Society, the American Educational Research Association, the Psychonomic Society), regional organizations (such as the Southeastern, Midwestern, and Western Psychological Associations), and a number of other groups that cater to specific areas of behavioral science (such as psychophysiology, law and psychology, social psychology, health psychology, and so on). Most of these organizations hold annual meetings at which researchers present their latest work.

In most instances, researchers who wish to present their research submit a short proposal that is peer reviewed by other researchers. However, the acceptance rate for professional meetings is much higher than that for journal publication.

Depending on the specific organization and on the researcher's preference, the presentation of a paper at a professional meeting can take one of two forms. The traditional manner involves a verbal presentation to an audience. Typically, papers on related topics are included in the same *paper session,* in which each speaker has 15 or 20 minutes to present his or her research and answer questions from the audience.

A second mode of presentation is the poster session. In a poster session, researchers display summaries of their research on poster boards, then stand beside their posters to answer questions and discuss their work with interested persons. (These poster sessions somewhat resemble the format of a science fair.) Although some researchers view poster sessions as somewhat less professional than verbal presentations, many prefer poster sessions. Not only do more people typically attend a particular poster session than a paper session (thus, the research gets wider exposure), but poster sessions allow more one-on-one interactions between researchers.

Personal Contact

A great deal of communication among scientists occurs through informal channels, such as personal contact. After researchers have been actively involved in an area of investigation for a few years, they get to know others who are interested in the same topic. Not only do they talk with one another at professional meetings, sharing their latest ideas and findings, but they often send prepublication drafts of their latest papers to each other and may even collaborate on research projects. In the last few years, computer electronic mail (e-mail) has facilitated researchers' ability to stay in regular contact with one another.

This network of researchers from around the world, which has been called the hidden university, is an important channel of scientific communication that allows researchers to stay informed regarding the latest advances in their fields. Researchers who are linked in these informal networks often become aware of advances in their fields a year or more before those advances are published in scientific journals.

Elements of Good Scientific Writing

Good writing skills are essential for researchers. No matter how insightful, creative, or well-designed particular studies may be, they are unlikely to have an impact on behavioral science if researchers do not convey their ideas and findings in a clear, accurate, and engaging manner. Unfortunately, good writing cannot be taught as easily as experimental design or the calculation of a correlation coefficient. It develops only through conscious attention to the details of good writing, coupled with practice and feedback from others.

You cannot learn to be an effective writer from the next few pages, but you can find some suggestions that will set you on the way toward developing your own writing skills. Specifically, this section will focus on the importance of organization, clarity, and conciseness and offer you hints on how to achieve them.

Organization

The first prerequisite for clear writing is *organization*, or the order in which one's ideas are expressed. The general organization of research reports in behavioral science is dictated by guidelines established by the American Psychological Association. Among other things, these guidelines stipulate the order in which sections of a paper must appear. In light of these guidelines (which we will examine in detail later in this chapter), you will have few problems with the general organization of a research paper.

Problems are more likely to arise in the organization of ideas *within* sections of the paper. If the order in which ideas are expressed is faulty, readers are likely to become confused. Someone once said that good writing is like a good road map; the writer should take the reader from point A to point B—from beginning to end—in the straightest possible route, without backtracking, without detours, and without getting the reader lost along the way. To do this, you must present your ideas in an orderly and logical progression. One thought should follow from and build on another in a manner that will be easily grasped by the reader.

Before you start writing, make a rough outline of the major points you wish to express. This doesn't necessarily need to be one of those detailed, multilevel outlines you learned to make in school; just a list of major points will usually suffice. Be sure the major points in your outline progress in an orderly fashion. Starting with an outline may alert you to the fact that your ideas do not flow coherently or that you need to add certain points to make them progress more smoothly.

As you write, be sure transitions between one idea and another are clear. If you move from one idea to another too abruptly, the reader may miss the connection between them and lose your train of thought. Pay particular attention to the transitions from one paragraph to another. Often, you'll need to write transition sentences that explicitly lead the reader from one paragraph to the next.

Clarity

Perhaps the fundamental requirement of scientific writing is *clarity*. Unlike some forms of fiction in which vagueness enhances the reader's experience, the goal of scientific writing is to communicate information. It is essential, then, that the information be conveyed in a clear, articulate, and unclouded manner.

This is a very difficult task, however. You don't have to read many articles published in scientific journals to know that not all scientific writers express themselves clearly. Often, writers find it difficult to step outside themselves and imagine how a reader will interpret their words. Even so, clarity must be a writer's first and foremost goal.

Two primary factors contribute to the clarity of one's writing: sentence construction and word choice.

Sentence construction.   The best way to enhance the clarity of your writing is to pay close attention to how you construct your sentences; awkwardly constructed sentences distract and confuse the reader. First, state your ideas in the most explicit and straightforward manner possible. One way to do this is to avoid the passive voice. For example, compare the following sentences:

> The subjects were told by the experimenter to press the button when they were finished (passive voice).

> The experimenter told the subjects to press the button when they finished (active voice).

I think you can see that the second sentence, which is written in the active voice, is the better of the two.

Second, avoid overly complicated sentences. Be *economical* in the phrases you use. For example, the sentence "There were several different subjects who had not previously been told what their IQ scores were" is terribly convoluted. It can be streamlined to "Several subjects did not know their IQ scores." (In a moment, I'll share with you one method I use for identifying awkwardly constructed sentences in my own writing.)

Word choice.   A second way to enhance the clarity of your writing is to choose your words carefully. Choose words that convey *precisely* the idea you wish to express. "Say what you mean and mean what you say" is the scientific writer's dictum.

In everyday language, we often use words in ways that are discrepant from their true dictionary definition. For example, we tend to use *theory* and *hypothesis* interchangeably in everyday language, but they mean different things to researchers.

Calvin and Hobbes   by Bill Watterson

Similarly, people talk informally about seeing a therapist or counselor, but psychologists draw a distinctions between therapists and counselors. Can you identify the problem in this sentence?

> Many psychologists feel that the conflict between psychology and psychiatry is based on fundamental differences in their theoretical assumptions.

In everyday language, we loosely interchange *feel* for *believe*; in this sentence, *feel* is the wrong choice.

Use specific terms. When expressing quantity, avoid loose approximations such as *most* and *very few*. Be careful with words, such as *significant*, that can be interpreted in two ways (*important* versus *statistically significant*). Use verbs that convey precisely what you mean. The sentence "Smith *argued* that earlier designs were flawed" connotes greater animosity on Smith's part than does the sentence "Smith *suggested* that earlier designs were flawed." Use the most accurate word. It would be impossible to identify all the pitfalls of poor word choice; just remember to consider your words carefully to be sure you "say what you mean."

Finally, avoid excessive jargon. As in every discipline, psychology has a specialized vocabulary for the constructs it studies, such as operant conditioning, cognitive dissonance, and preoperational stage—constructs without which behavioral scientists would find communication difficult. However, refrain from using jargon when a more common word exists that conveys the desired meaning. In other words, don't be like Calvin in the above cartoon; don't use jargon when everyday language will do the job.

Conciseness

A third important consideration in scientific writing is *conciseness*; say what you are going to say as economically as possible. Like you, readers are busy people. Think how you feel when you must read a 26-page journal article that could have conveyed all of its points in only 15 pages. Have mercy on your readers! Conciseness is also important for practical reasons. Scientific journals publish a limited number of pages each year, so papers that are unnecessarily long rob the field of badly needed journal space.

However, do not use conciseness as an excuse for skimpy writing. Research papers *must* contain all necessary information. Ideas must be fully developed, methods must be described in detail, results must be examined carefully, and so on. The advice to "be concise" should be interpreted as an admonition to include only the necessary information and to express it as succinctly (yet clearly) as possible.

DEVELOPING YOUR RESEARCH SKILLS

WHAT'S WRONG WITH THESE SENTENCES?

Like all writers, scientists are expected to use words and grammar correctly to convey their ideas. Each of the following sentences contains one or more common writing or grammatical errors. Can you spot them?

1. Since this finding was first obtained on male subjects, several researchers have questioned its generalizability.

   Error: The preferred meaning of *since* is "between a particular past time and the present," and it should not be used as a synonym for *because*. In this example, the meaning of *since* is ambiguous—does it mean *because* or *in the time since?*

2. This phenomena has been widely studied.

   Error: *Phenomena* is plural; the singular form is *phenomenon.*

3. While most researchers have found a direct relationship between incentives and performance, some studies have obtained a curvilinear relationship.

   Error: *While* should be used to mean *during the same time as*. The proper word here is *whereas* or *although.*

4. Twenty females were used as subjects.

   Error: APA style specifies that *female* (and *male*) are to be used as adjectives, not as nouns. As such, they must modify a noun (female students, female employees, for example).

5. After assigning subjects to conditions, subjects in the experimental group completed the first questionnaire.

   Error: The phrase *after assigning subjects to conditions* is a dangling modifier that has no referent in the sentence (this implies that subjects assigned subjects to conditions). One possible remedy would be to write, "After the experimenter assigned subjects to conditions, subjects in the experimental group completed the first questionnaire."

6. The data was analyzed with a *t*-test.

   Error: *Data* is plural; *datum* is singular. Thus, the sentence should be, "The data *were* analyzed . . ."

7. It is hypothesized that shy subjects will participate less fully in the group discussion.

   Error: As a pronoun, *it* must refer to some noun. In this sentence, *it* has no referent. The sentence could be rewritten in a number of ways, such as:

   "This study tested the hypothesis that . . ."

   "The hypothesis tested in this study was that . . ."

   "On the basis of previous research, one would expect that . . ."

8. When a person is in a manic state, they often have delusions of grandeur.

   Error: Pronouns must agree in *number* with their corresponding nouns. In this case, *person* is singular but *they* is plural. The sentence could be rewritten in one of two ways:

   When people are in a manic state, they often have delusions of grandeur. (The noun and pronoun are both plural.)

   When a person is in a manic state, he or she often has delusions of grandeur. (The noun and pronoun are both singular.)

Proofreading and Rewriting

Good writers are *rewriters*. Writers whose first draft is ready for public distribution are extremely rare, if they exist at all. Most researchers revise their papers several times before they allow anyone else to see them (unlike the students I've known who hand in their first draft!).

When you reread your own writing, do so with a critical eye. Have you included everything necessary to make your points effectively? Is the paper organized? Are ideas presented in a logical and orderly progression, and are the transitions between them clear? Is the writing clear and concise? Have you used precise vocabulary throughout?

When you proofread your paper, *read it aloud*. I often imagine that I am a television newscaster and that my paper is the script of a documentary I am narrating. If you feel silly pretending to be a newscaster, simply read your paper aloud and listen carefully to how it sounds. Reading a paper aloud is the best way I know to spot awkward constructions. Sentences that look fine on paper often sound stilted or convoluted when spoken.

Allow yourself enough time to write and revise your paper, then to set it aside for a few days. After a period away from the paper, I am always able to see weaknesses I had missed earlier. Many researchers also seek feedback from colleagues and students. They ask others to critique a polished draft of the paper. Typically, other people will find areas of confusion, awkwardness, poor logic, and other problems. If you ask for others' feedback, be prepared to accept their criticisms and suggestions graciously. After all, that's what you asked them to give you! Whatever tactics you use, proofread and revise your writing several times until it reads smoothly from beginning to end.

Using Nonsexist Language

Consider for a moment the following sentence: "The therapist who owns his own practice is as much a businessman as a psychologist." Many people regard such writing as unacceptable because it involves sexist language—language that reinforces sexism by treating men and women differently. In the sentence above, the use of *he* and *businessman* seems to imply that all therapists are men.

In the 1970s, the American Psychological Association was one of several organizations and publishers to adopt guidelines for the use of **gender-neutral** (or **nonsexist**) **language.** Using gender-neutral language is important for two reasons. First, careless use of gender-related language may promote sexism. For example, consider the sentence "Fifty fraternity men and 50 sorority girls were recruited to serve in the study." The use of the nonparallel phrase *men* and *girls* reinforces stereotypes about, and status differences between, men and women. Second, sexist language can create ambiguity. For example, does the sentence "Policemen experience a great deal of job-related stress" refer only to police*men* or to both male and female police officers?

The APA discusses many variations of sexist language and offers suggestions on how to use gender-neutral substitutes in your writing (American Psychological Association, 1994, pp. 54–56). Here we'll discuss three of the most common cases of sexist language.

Generic Pronouns

Historically, writers have used generic pronouns such as *he, him,* and *his* to refer to both men and women, as in the sentence "Every citizen should exercise his right to vote." However, the use of generic masculine pronouns to refer to people of both sexes is problematic on two counts.

First, using masculine pronouns can create ambiguity and confusion. Consider the sentence "After each subject completed his questionnaire, he was debriefed." Were the subjects described here both men and women or men only? Second, many have argued that the use of generic masculine pronouns is inherently male centered and sexist (see Pearson, 1985). What is the possible justification, they ask, for using masculine pronouns to refer to both sexes?

Writers deal with the problem of generic pronouns in one of two ways. One way is to use phrases that include both pronouns, as in *he or she* or *his or her*; "After each subject completed his or her questionnaire, he or she was debriefed." However, the endless repetition of *he or she* in a paper can become tiresome. A second, preferred way to avoid sexist language is to use plural nouns and pronouns; the plural form of generic pronouns, such as they, them, and theirs are gender-free: "After subjects completed their questionnaires, they were debriefed." Incidentally, APA style discourages use of the form *he/she* (with a slash) to refer to both sexes.

The Word Man

Similar problems arise when the word *man* and its variations (mankind, the average man, manpower, businessman, policeman, mailman, and so on) are used to refer to both men and women. Not only do man-linked words foster confusion, but we also need to ask ourselves why we use words such as *policeman* to refer to female police officers.

In most instances, other gender-neutral words can be substituted for man-linked words. For example, terms such as *police officer, letter carrier, chairperson, fire fighter,* and *supervisor* are preferable to *policeman, mailman, chairman, fireman,* and *foreman*. Not only are such gender-neutral terms sometimes more descriptive than the man-linked version (the term *fire fighter* more clearly expresses the nature of the job than does *fireman*), but using gender-neutral language avoids the absurdity of reading about policemen who go home at lunchtime each day to breast-feed their babies.

Nonequivalent Forms

Other instances of sexist language involve words that are not used equivalently for women and men. The earlier example involving "fraternity men and sorority girls" is an example of this inequity. Furthermore, some words that *seem* structurally equivalent for men and women have different connotations. For example, a person who *mothered* a child did something quite different from the person who *fathered* a child. If caretaking behavior is meant, gender-neutral words such as *parenting* or *nurturing* are preferred over *mothering*. Avoid words such as *coed* that have no equivalent form for the other gender (what is a *male coed* called?).

IN DEPTH

SEXIST LANGUAGE: DOES IT REALLY MATTER?

Some writers object to being forced to use nonsexist language. Some argue that so-called sexist language is really unnecessary because everyone knows *he* refers to both men and women and *mankind* includes everybody. Others point out that nonsexist language leads to awkwardly constructed sentences and distorts the English language.

At one level, the arguments for and against nonsexist language are philosophical or political. Should we write in ways that discourage sexism and promote egalitarianism? At another level, however, the debate regarding nonsexist language can be examined empirically. Several researchers have investigated the effects of sexist and nonsexist language on readers' comprehension.

Kidd (1971) examined the question of whether readers interpret the word *man* to refer to everyone as opponents of nonsexist language maintain. In her study, subjects read sentences that used either the word *man* or a variation, then answered questions in which they identified the gender of the person referred to in each sentence. Although the word *man* was used in the generic sense, subjects interpreted it to refer specifically to men 86% of the time. If you want to demonstrate this effect on your own, ask 10 people to draw a *caveman* and see how many opt to draw a cave*woman*. People do not assume that *man* refers to everybody.

In another study, Stericker (1981) studied the effects of gender-relevant pronouns on students' attitudes toward jobs. Subjects read descriptions of several jobs (such as lawyer, interior decorator, high school teacher). In these descriptions, Stericker manipulated whether the job descriptions used *he, he or she,* or *they.* Her results showed that female subjects were more interested in the jobs when *he or she* was used in the description than when only *he* was used but that male subjects' preferences were unaffected by which pronoun was used.

In brief, studies have shown that whether writers use sexist or gender-neutral language *does* make a difference in the inferences readers draw (see Adams & Ware, 1989; Pearson, 1985). In the eyes of most readers, *man, he,* and other masculine pronouns are not generic, gender-neutral designations that refer to men and women equally.

APA Style

In 1929, the American Psychological Association adopted a set of guidelines regarding the preparation of research reports. This first set of guidelines, which was only seven pages long, was subsequently revised and expanded several times. The most recent edition of these guidelines—the *Publication Manual of the American Psychological Association* (4th edition)—was published in 1994 and runs more than 300 pages.

Most journals that publish behavioral research—not only in psychology but also in other areas such as education and communication—require that manuscripts conform to **APA style**. In addition, most colleges and universities insist that students use APA style when they write theses and dissertations, and many professors ask that their students write class papers in APA style. Thus, a basic knowledge of APA style is an essential part of the behavioral researcher's toolbox.

The guidelines in the *Publication Manual* serve three purposes. First, many of the guidelines are intended to help authors write more effectively. Thus, the manual includes discussions of grammar, clarity, word usage, punctuation, and so on. Second, some of the guidelines are designed to make published research articles uniform in certain respects. For example, the manual specifies the sections that every paper must include, the style of reference citations, and the composition of tables and figures. When writers conform to a single style, readers are spared the distraction of a variety of idiosyncratic styles that may detract from the content of the paper itself. Third, some of the guidelines are designed to facilitate the conversion of manuscripts typed on typewriters or word processors into printed journal articles. Certain style conventions assist the editors, proofreaders, and typesetters who prepare manuscripts for publication.

The APA *Publication Manual* specifies the parts that every research report must have, as well as the order in which they appear. Generally speaking, a research paper should have a minimum of seven sections:

Title page

Abstract

Introduction

Method

Results

Discussion

References

Papers additionally may have sections for author notes, footnotes, tables, figures, and/or appendixes, all of which appear at the end of the typed manuscript. Each of these sections is discussed briefly in the following pages.

Title Page

The title page of a research paper should include four pieces of information: the title, the authors' names, the authors' affiliation, and a running head.

The title should state the central topic of the paper clearly yet concisely. As much as possible, it should mention the major variables under investigation. Titles of research reports are generally less than 15 words long. The title is centered near the top of the first page of the manuscript.

Good titles

Effects of caffeine on the acoustic startle response

Parenting styles and children's ability to delay gratification

Probability of relapse after recovery from an episode of depression

Poor titles

A study of memory

Effects of feedback, anxiety, cuing, and gender on semantic and episodic memory under two conditions of threat: A test of competing theories

In the examples of poor titles, the first is not sufficiently descriptive, and the phrase "A study of" is unnecessary; the second title is too long and involved.

Directly beneath the title are the author's name and affiliation. Most authors use their first name, middle initial, and last name. The affiliation identifies the institution where the researcher is employed (or is a student).

At the top of the title page is the running head, an abbreviated form of the title. For example, the title "Effects of social exclusion on dysphoric emotions" could be reduced to "Effects of exclusion." When an article is typeset for publication, the running head appears at the top of every other page of the printed article.

Abstract

The second page of a manuscript consists of the **abstract**, a brief summary of the content of the paper. The abstract should describe, in approximately 120 words:

- the problem under investigation
- the subjects used in the study
- the research procedures
- the findings
- the conclusions or implications of the study

Because this is a great deal of information to convey in so few words, many researchers find it difficult to write an accurate and concise abstract that is coherent and readable. In some ways, the abstract is the single most important part of a journal article. Most readers decide whether or not to read an article on the basis of its abstract. Furthermore, the abstract is published in *Psychological Abstracts* and is retrieved by many computerized literature search services, such as *PsycLit*. Although the abstract is usually the last part of a paper to be written, it is by no means the least important section.

Introduction

The body of a research report begins on page 3 of the manuscript. The title of the paper is repeated at the top of page 3, followed by the introduction itself (the heading *Introduction* does not appear, however).

The introduction describes for the reader the problem under investigation and presents a background context in which the problem can be understood. The author discusses aspects of the existing research literature that pertain to the study. This by no means involves an exhaustive review of all research that has been conducted on the topic; rather, the introduction should selectively review previous work that deals specifically with the topic under investigation.

When reviewing previous research, write in the past tense. Not only does it make sense to use past tense to write about research that has already been conducted ("Smith's findings *showed* the same pattern"), but writing in the present tense often leads to awkward sentences in which deceased persons seem to speak from the grave to make claims in the present ("Freud suggests that childhood memories may be repressed"). (Throughout the paper, but particularly in the introduction, you will cite previous research conducted by others. We'll return later to how one cites previous studies using APA style.)

After addressing the problem and previous research, discuss the purpose and rationale of your research. Typically, this is done by stating explicit hypotheses that were examined in the study.

The introduction should proceed in an organized and orderly fashion. You are presenting, systematically and logically, the conceptual background that provides a rationale for your particular study. In essence, you are building a case for why your study was conducted and what you expected to find.

After writing the introduction, ask yourself:

- Did I adequately orient the reader to the purpose of the study?
- Did I review the literature adequately, using appropriate, accurate, and complete citations?
- Did I deal with both theoretical and empirical issues relevant to the topic?
- Did I clearly state the research question or hypothesis?

Method

The method section describes precisely how the study was conducted. A well-written method allows readers to judge the adequacy of the procedures used and provides a context for them to interpret the findings. A complete description of the method is essential so readers may assess what a study does and does not demonstrate. The method section also allows other researchers to replicate the study if they wish. Thus, the method should describe, as concisely and as clearly as possible, precisely how the study was conducted.

The method is subdivided into three sections, labeled Participants, Apparatus (or Materials), and Procedure. The Participants and Procedure sections are nearly always included, but the Apparatus or Materials section is optional.

Participants.   The participants section describes the subjects and how they were selected. If human participants were used, researchers typically report the number, sex, and age of the subjects, along with their general demographic characteristics. In many cases, the manner in which the subjects were obtained is also included. If nonhuman animals were used, researchers report the number, genus, species, and strain, as well as their sex and age. Often, relevant information regarding the housing, nutrition, and other treatment of the animals is included as well.

Apparatus or materials. If special equipment or materials were used in the study, they are described in a section labeled *Apparatus* or *Materials*. For example, sophisticated equipment for presenting stimuli or measuring responses should be described, as well as special instruments or inventories. This section is optional, however, and may be omitted if no special apparatus or materials were used.

Procedure.   The procedure section describes, in a step-by-step fashion, precisely how the study was conducted. Included here is information regarding experimental manipulations, instructions to the subjects, and all experimental procedures.

After writing the method, ask yourself:

- Did I describe the method adequately and clearly, including all information that would be needed for another investigator to replicate the study?
- Did I fully identify the subjects who participated?
- Did I describe the apparatus and materials fully?
- Did I report fully on the research procedure in a step-by-step fashion?

Results

The results section reports the statistical analyses of the data obtained in the study. Generally, writers begin by reporting the most important results, then work their way to secondary findings. Researchers are obligated to describe all relevant results, even those that are contrary to their predictions. However, you should not feel compelled to include every piece of data obtained in the study. Most researchers collect and analyze more data than needed to make their points. However, you are not permitted to selectively present only those data that support your hypothesis!

When reporting the results of statistical tests, such as *t*-tests or *F*-tests, include information about the kind of analysis that was conducted, the degrees of freedom for the test, the calculated value of the statistic, and an indication of its significance or nonsignificance. If an experimental design was involved, also include the means and standard deviations for the effect. (Because it is difficult to type the conventional symbol for the mean, $\bar{x}$, on a typewriter, the symbol $\underline{M}$ is used for the mean.) The results of statistical analyses are typically separated from the rest of the sentence by commas, as in the following sentence.

A $\underline{t}$-test revealed that subjects exposed to uncontrollable noise made more errors ($\underline{M}$ = 7.5, $\underline{SD}$ = 2.14) than subjects who were exposed to controllable noise ($\underline{M}$ = 4.3, $\underline{SD}$ = 2.10), $\underline{t}$(39) = 4.77, $\underline{p}$ < .05.

Note that this sentence includes the name of the analysis, the condition means and standard deviations, the degrees of freedom (39), the calculated value of t (4.77), and the significance level of the test (.05).

When you need to report a large amount of data—many correlations or means, for example—consider putting some of the data in tables or in figures (graphs). APA style requires that tables and figures be appended to the end of the manuscript, with a statement in the body of the paper indicating where the table or figure should appear when the article is printed. Tables and figures are often useful, but they should be used only when the results are too complex to describe in the text itself. Furthermore, avoid repeating the same data in both the text and a table or figure. Remember to be economical.

The results should be reported as objectively as possible with minimal interpretation, elaboration, or discussion. The material included in the results section should involve what your data showed, *not* your interpretation of the data.

After writing the results, ask yourself:

- Did I clearly describe how the data were analyzed?

- Did I include all results that bear on the original purpose of the study?

- Did I include all necessary information when reporting statistical tests?

- Did I describe the findings objectively, with minimal interpretation and discussion?

Discussion

Having described the results, you are free in the discussion to interpret, evaluate, and discuss your findings. As a first step, discuss the results in terms of the original purpose or hypothesis of the study. Most researchers begin the discussion with a statement of the central findings and how they relate to the hypotheses under investigation. They then move on to discuss other major findings in the study.

In your discussion, integrate your results with existing theory and previous findings, referencing others' work where appropriate. Note inconsistencies between your results and those of other researchers, and mention qualifications and limitations of your study. However, do not feel compelled to dwell on every possible weakness or flaw in your research. All studies have shortcomings; it is usually sufficient simply to note yours in passing.

After writing the discussion, ask yourself:

- Did I state clearly what I believe are the major contributions of my research?

- Did I integrate my findings with both theory and previous research, citing others' work where appropriate?

- Did I note possible qualifications and limitations of my findings?

References

Throughout the text of the paper, you will cite previous work that is relevant to your study. APA guidelines specify the form that such references should take.

Citations in the text of the paper.   If you are like most students, you have probably learned to use footnotes to cite others' work. Rather than using footnotes, APA style uses the *author–date system* in which others' work is cited by inserting the last name of the author and the year of publication at the appropriate point in the text. The book you are reading uses the author–date system.

The author–date system allows you to cite a reference in one of two ways. In the first, the author's last name, followed by the date of publication in parentheses, is included as part of the sentence, as shown in the following examples.

Jones (1990) showed that subjects . . .

In a recent review of the literature, Jones (1990) concluded . . .

This finding was replicated by Jones (1990).

If the work being cited has two authors, cite both names each time.

Jones and Williams (1990) showed . . .

In a recent review of the literature, Jones and Williams (1990) concluded . . .

If the work has more than two authors but fewer than six, cite all authors the *first* time you use the reference. Then, if the reference is cited again, include only the first author, followed by *et al.* and the year:

Jones, Williams, Smith, Cutlip, Miller, and Bell (1990) showed that subjects who . . . (first citation)

Jones et al. (1990) revealed . . . (subsequent citations)

The second way of citing references in the text is to place the authors' last names, along with the year of publication, within parentheses at the appropriate point.

Several studies have obtained similar results (Jones & Smith, 1990).

If several works are cited in this fashion, alphabetize them by the last name of the first author and separate them by semicolons.

The effects of stress on decision making have been investigated in several studies (Anderson, 1987; Cohen & Bourne, 1978; Smith, Havert, & Menken, 1980; Williams, 1974).

The reference list.   All references cited in the text must appear in a reference list that begins on a new page immediately after the discussion section. References are listed in alphabetical order by the first author's last name. The APA *Publication Manual* presents 77 variations of reference style, depending on whether the work being referenced is a book, journal article, newspaper article, dissertation, film, or whatever. However, the vast majority of citations are to journal articles, books, book chapters, and papers presented at professional meetings, so I'll limit my examples to these four types of references.

The reference to a *journal article* includes, in this order:

1. Author's last name(s) and initials
2. Year of publication (in parentheses)
3. Title of the article, with only the first word of the title capitalized (with the exception of words that follow colons, which are also capitalized)
4. Name of the journal (All important words in the title are capitalized, and the title is underlined; words underlined in a manuscript will be typeset in italic.)
5. Volume number of the journal (underlined)
6. Page numbers of the article

> Smith, M. B. (1980). The effects of research methods courses on student depression. Journal of Cruelty to Students, 15, 67–78.

> Smith, M. B., Jones, H. H., & Long, I. M. (1988). The relative impact of t-tests and F-tests on student mental health. American Journal of Unfair Teaching, 7, 235–240.

Note that the first line of each reference is indented five spaces.

References to *books* include, in this order:

1. Author's last name(s) and initial(s)
2. Year of publication (in parentheses)
3. Title of the book (only the first word of the title is capitalized, and the title is underlined)
4. City and state in which the book was published (followed by a colon)
5. Name of the publisher

> Leary, M. R. (1995). Introduction to behavioral research methods (2nd ed.). Pacific Grove, CA: Brooks/Cole.

References to a *book chapter* in an edited volume include, in this order:

1. Author's last name(s) and initial(s)
2. Year of publication (in parentheses)
3. Title of the chapter
4. The word "In," followed by the initial(s) and last name(s) of the editor(s) of the book, with "Eds." in parentheses
5. Title of the book (only the first word of the title is capitalized, and the title is underlined)

6. Page numbers of the chapter in parentheses

7. City and state in which the book was published (followed by a colon)

8. Name of the publisher

> Smith, K. L. (1992). Techniques for inducing statistical terror. In J. Jones & V. Smith (Eds.), <u>A manual for the sadistic teacher</u> (pp. 45–67). Baltimore: Neurosis Press.

References to a *paper presented at a professional meeting* include, in this order:

1. Author's last name(s) and initial(s)

2. Year and month in which the paper was presented (in parentheses)

3. Title of the paper (underlined)

4. Phrase "Paper presented at the meeting of . . ." following by the name of the organization

5. City and state in which the meeting occurred

> Wilson, H. K., & Miller, F. M. (1988, April). <u>Research methods, existential philosophy, schizophrenia, and the fear of death.</u> Paper presented at the meeting of the Society for Undergraduate Teaching, Dallas, TX.

Optional Sections

In addition to the title page, abstract, introduction, method, results, discussion, and references, which are required in all research reports, most papers include one or more of the following sections.

Author notes. Often, a page labeled *Author Notes* directly follows the references. In the author notes, the author(s) thanks those who helped with the study, acknowledges grants and other financial support for the research, and gives an address where he or she may be contacted for additional information or for copies of the paper. Although the author notes are inserted at the end of a typed manuscript, they typically appear at the bottom of the first page of the published article.

Footnotes. In APA style, footnotes are used only rarely. They are used to present ancillary information and are typed at the end of the paper. In the published article, however, they appear at the bottom of the page on which the footnote superscript appears.

Tables and figures. As noted above, tables and figures are often used to present results. A table is a arrangement of words or numbers in columns and rows; a figure is any type of illustration, such as a graph, photograph, or drawing. The APA

Publication Manual provides extensive instructions regarding how tables and figures should be prepared. In the typed manuscript they appear at the end of the paper; in the published article, they are inserted at the point indicated in the text.

Appendixes.   Appendixes are rarely included in published journal articles. Occasionally, however, authors wish to include detailed information that does not easily fit into the text itself. If so, the appendix appears at the end of the manuscript and at the end of the article.

Headings, Spacing, Pagination, and Numbers

Headings.   With the exception of the introduction, each section we have discussed is labeled. For the other major sections of the paper—abstract, method, results, discussion, and references— the heading is centered in the middle of the page. For subsections of these major sections (such as the subsections for participants, apparatus, and procedure), a side heading is used. A side heading is typed flush with the left margin and is underlined. For example, the headings for the method section typically look like this:

Method←Major heading centered

Participants←Secondary sections use side headings

Apparatus

Procedure

The title and abstract appear on the first two pages of every manuscript. The introduction then begins on page 3. The method section does *not* start on a new page but begins directly after the introduction. Similarly, the results and discussion sections begin immediately after the method and results sections, respectively. Thus, the text begins with the introduction on page 3, but the next three sections do not start on new pages. However, the references, author notes, footnotes, tables, figures, and appendixes each begin on a new page.

Spacing.   Research reports written in APA style are *double-spaced* from start to finish—no single spacing or triple spacing is permitted. Set your typewriter or word processor on double spacing and leave it there.

Pagination.   Pages are numbered in the upper right corner, starting with the title page as page 1. In APA style, a *short title*, consisting of the first two or three words of the title, is also typed in the upper right corner of each page, just above the page number. Often, the pages of a manuscript become separated during the editorial and publication process; this short title allows the editor or typesetter to identify which pages go with which manuscript. This short title should not be confused with the running head, which appears only at the top of the title page.

Numbers.   In APA style, whole numbers less than 10 are generally expressed with words (The data for two subjects were omitted from the analysis), whereas numbers 10 and above are expressed with numerals (Of the 20 subjects who agreed to participate, 10 were women). However, numbers that begin a sentence must be expressed in words (Twenty rats served as subjects). Furthermore, numbers that precede units of measurement should always be expressed in numerals (The temperature was 72 degrees), as should numbers that represent time, dates, ages, and sample sizes (2 weeks; November 29, 1954; 5-year-olds; $n = 7$).

Sample Manuscript

To the new researcher, APA style is complex and confusing; indeed, few veteran researchers are familiar with every detail in the APA *Publication Manual*. Even so, the guidelines contained in this manual are designed to enhance effective communication among researchers, and behavioral researchers are expected to be familiar with the basics of APA style.

What follows is an example of a short research report prepared according to APA style. This represents a typewritten manuscript that an author might submit for publication; the published article would, of course, look very different. I've annotated this manuscript to point out some of the basic guidelines discussed in this chapter.

Running head: HINDSIGHT DISTORTION

Hindsight Distortion and the 1980 Presidential Election

Mark R. Leary

Wake Forest University

The title page includes the title, the author's name, and the author's institutional affiliation. At the top is the running head—the short title that appears at the top of each page of a published article. The "short title" and page number are typed in the upper right corner of each page.

Abstract

The tendency for people to overestimate the degree to which they expected past events to occur was examined in the context of the 1980 presidential election. Previous research has concluded that distorted hindsight occurs because people have difficulty reconstructing prior probabilities for an event after it has occurred. However, the possible mediation of motivational factors, specifically self-esteem and self-presentation, has not been adequately examined. Two hundred seventy-five subjects were asked either before or after the 1980 presidential election, and under public or private response conditions, to predict the outcome of the election (preelection) or to indicate what they would have predicted the outcome to be had they been asked before the election (postelection). In addition, subjects were classified as being either high or low in ego involvement regarding knowledge of politics. Results showed clear evidence of hindsight distortion: Subjects asked after the election said they would have predicted an outcome closer to the results of the election than those asked before, but there was no evidence of mediation by self-esteem or self-presentation concerns.

The abstract appears on page 2 and summarizes the study in approximately 120 to 150 words. The first line of the abstract is not indented.

Hindsight Distortion and the 1980 Presidential Election

The introduction starts on Page 3, with the title of the paper centered at the top of the page. The text begins immediately (one double-space) below the title.

Although the magnitude of Ronald Reagan's victory over Jimmy Carter in the 1980 presidential election took all but professional political observers by surprise, a great deal of postelection commentary focused retrospectively on preelection signs that a Republican victory was in the works (see "Carter Post-Mortem," 1980). The tone of many of these analyses suggested that the writers were not, after all, particularly surprised by Carter's defeat and that the election outcome was easily understandable in terms of certain critical events during the Carter administration, particularly during the campaign itself. These commentaries make one forget that the election was too close to call until the last few days of the campaign, and appear to reflect the general tendency for people retrospectively to overestimate the degree to which they could have predicted certain events.

The paper starts with a general introduction to the topic under investigation—distorted hindsight—followed by a brief review of previous research on this topic. The reference to "Carter Post-Mortem" is the citation style for a newspaper or magazine article that has no author listed.

Research has repeatedly demonstrated that people overestimate the prior probability of events they believe have occurred. For example, Fischhoff (1975b) asked subjects to read about a historical incident and estimate how likely various outcomes had been at the time the incident occurred.

The preceding sentence contains a reference citation that uses the author—date format. In this instance, the author's name is incorporated into the sentence. The date following "Fischhoff" has the letter *b* attached (1975b) because the reference list contains two articles by Fischhoff that were published in 1975. Note that the review of previous studies is written in past tense.

Subjects who knew the outcome of the event considered that outcome to have been more probable than subjects who did not know the outcome. Even when subjects were instructed to respond as if they did not know the actual outcome of the event, they were unable to ignore this information and continued to overestimate the prior probabilities of events they believed had occurred (Fischhoff & Beyth, 1975).

In the preceding sentence, the reference citation appears in parentheses.

More recently, Fischhoff (1977) and Wood (1978) showed that people also overestimate the degree to which they had known answers to questions of fact, even when warned of potential bias in their responses and admonished to be as accurate as possible in recalling what they had known before being told the correct answer.

In attempting to explain the occurrence of distorted hindsight, also known as the "I-knew-it-all-along" effect, Fischhoff (1975a, 1975b) suggested that once they know the outcome of an event, people find it difficult to reconstruct what they actually knew before the event. By reasoning backward from the event to its possible causes, people may see relationships among factors that were not obvious before the event took place. Factors clearly associated with the event are recalled more easily, whereas factors unrelated to the observed outcome are less salient.

Conflicting information that does not fit into the reconstruction of the causes of the event is either ignored or reinterpreted in light of what has subsequently happened.

The possibility exists, however, that distorted hindsight may arise due to motivational, rather than informational, processes. First, people may retrospectively claim they "knew it would happen" to enhance their self-esteem. The conclusion that one was adequately intelligent, perceptive, or farsighted to anticipate an event may rightfully result in a more positive self-evaluation. Such an effect would be more likely among people who take pride in their knowledge of such events because the failure to predict accurately would be more threatening to their self-image (Walster, 1967).

Alternatively, people may distort their public statements regarding the event as a self-presentation strategy (Goffman, 1959; Schlenker, 1980), expecting to gain social rewards by demonstrating their perceptiveness to others.

In this sentence, the two reference citations that appear in parentheses are in alphabetical order.

Fischhoff (1977) and Wood (1978) dismissed a self-presentation explanation of the hindsight phenomenon because distorted hindsight has been obtained despite nonevaluative instructions that deemphasized subjects' performance, admonitions to work hard to recall predictions accurately, and warnings to beware of potential hindsight distortion in one's responses. However, previous studies have not completely eliminated factors that may motivate subjects to claim they knew more than they actually did for self-presentational purposes. If distorted hindsight were obtained even when subjects' responses were entirely private and anonymous, thus affording them no opportunity to impress others with their perceptiveness, we would have a stronger case for dismissing self-presentation as a mediating factor.

In an initial test of these motivational hypotheses, Leary (1981) asked subjects to predict the score of a football game (pregame) or to state what they would have predicted the score to be had they been asked before the game (postgame). Subjects responded either publicly or privately and were asked the degree to which their knowledge of football was important to them. Consistent with Fischhoff's information-processing hypothesis, subjects asked after the game said they would have predicted a score that was significantly closer to the actual score than subjects who made predictions before the game, but this was not qualified by ego involvement in sports knowledge or response publicness, demonstrating that distorted hindsight may occur in the absence of motivational effects.

The final paragraph of the introduction states the objectives of the study.

In the present study, the role of information processing, self-esteem, and self-presentation factors in distorted hindsight were reexamined while attempting to increase the strength of the motivational factors studied by Leary (1981). An attempt was made to reduce the plausibility of alternative explanations for previous results by making subjects' responses more anonymous in the private response condition than was possible in the milling throng of a football game, devising a better measure of ego involvement in knowledge of the target event, and utilizing a potentially more involving event (the 1980 presidential election).

> The method begins immediately following the end of the introduction, with the heading "Method" centered on the page. The subheadings for participants and procedure appear as side heads. Because no specialized materials or apparatus were used in this study, an apparatus/materials section is not included.

Method

Participants

Subjects were 134 male and 141 female university students between the ages of 18 and 22. They were randomly assigned to experimental conditions before the start of the study.

> The number, sex, and age of the subjects are given. Numbers 10 and above are expressed in numerals.

Procedure

Subjects were contacted in their living quarters on either the Monday before or the Wednesday after the 1980 presidential election and asked to participate in an election survey. In the public response condition, subjects were asked to sign their names on the questionnaires, complete them as the experimenter watched, then return them directly to him or her. In the private response condition, subjects were asked not to sign their names, were assured that their responses would be completely anonymous, completed the questionnaires out of sight of the experimenter, and returned them to the experimenter in a sealed envelope.

The first two questions were designed to ascertain the degree to which subjects' knowledge of politics was important to their self-esteem. Ego involvement in knowledge of a topic appears to be a joint function of how knowledgeable individuals believe themselves to be regarding the topic and how important they consider such knowledge to be. Thus, subjects answered questions to assess these two factors on 12-point Likert scales. Their responses on these items were later multiplied and the product taken as an index of ego involvement in knowledge of politics.

Subjects were then asked to indicate the percentage of the popular vote that they believed each of the three major candidates (Anderson, Carter, and Reagan) would receive in the election (preelection condition) or the percentage they would have predicted the candidates would receive had they been asked before the election (postelection condition). Subjects were told that their estimates for the three candidates should add to 100%.

The method provides sufficient detail for other investigators to replicate the study if they wish. The results begin immediately after the method.

Results

Subjects' responses to the items assessing self-reported knowledge about the election and the importance they placed on such knowledge were multiplied, and subjects were classified as either low or high in ego involvement regarding knowledge of politics (median = 71). The ego-involvement factor was then entered with timing (before or after election) and response publicness (public or private) into a $2 \times 2 \times 2$ ANOVA for each candidate.

A median split procedure was used to classify subjects as low or high in ego involvement regarding politics. To do this, subjects' scores on the measure of ego involvement in politics were ranked. Subjects with scores above the median were classified as high in ego involvement and those with scores below the median were classified as low in ego involvement.

Because one factor in this design—ego involvement—was a subject variable, whereas the other two factors were manipulated, this is an example of the mixed/expericorr design we discussed in Chapter 10. Note that the analyses were described very explicitly.

Only a main effect of timing, $\underline{F}(1, 267) = 4.89$, $\underline{p} < .03$, was obtained on subjects' estimates of the percentage of votes Ronald Reagan would obtain in the election. Examination of means (see Table 1) reveals that, consistent with past research, subjects who knew the outcome of the election said they would have predicted an outcome significantly closer to the actual outcome than subjects who made their predictions before the election. Like the media, subjects asked before the election underestimated how well Reagan would perform; those asked after the election revised their "predictions" upward. No effects of response publicness or ego involvement were obtained, either singly or in interaction with other variables.

Insert Table 1 about here

This statement designates where the table is to be placed when the article is typeset for publication. In the manuscript itself, however, the table appears at the end of the paper.

Both a main effect of timing, $F(1, 267) = 11.86$, $p < .001$, and a main effect of

ego involvement in knowledge of politics, $F(1, 267) = 7.71$, $p < .01$, were obtained

on estimates of the percentage of the vote John Anderson would receive.

Note that in describing the results of the F-tests, the degrees of
freedom, the calculated value of F, and the probability level are
included. The means appear in the table.

First, subjects asked before the election (see Table 1) greatly overestimated how

well Anderson would do, whereas those asked afterward, although still too high,

were significantly closer to the actual outcome, again demonstrating hindsight

distortion. Second, the main effect of ego involvement showed that subjects

classified as high in ego involvement in knowledgeability of politics ($M = 10.8$)

were significantly more accurate in assessing Anderson's vote-getting power than

those low in ego involvement ($M = 13.6$).

No effects of the independent or subject variables were obtained on subjects'

estimates of how well Carter would perform in the election. Examination of means

(see Table 1) for the pre- and postelection conditions reveals why. Subjects'

preelection estimates of the percentage of votes Carter would obtain were quite

close to the percentage Carter actually received. Hindsight distortion cannot occur

when people's preevent predictions are accurate.

The discussion begins immediately after the results.

Discussion

Consistent with previous research, subjects' postelection recall of how well

they had expected the candidates to fare in the election was closer to the actual results of the election than subjects' preelection estimates. Yet, despite clear evidence of hindsight distortion, no evidence of mediation by either self-esteem or self-presentation motives was obtained.

The discussion begins with a general statement of the study's findings.

Thus the present results are consistent with those obtained previously that supported an information-processing explanation of distorted hindsight (Fischhoff, 1975b, 1977; Fischhoff & Beyth, 1975; Leary, 1981; Wood, 1978). Subjects' knowledge of the election outcome appears to have hindered their cognitive reconstruction of the information that was actually available prior to the election. Subjects asked after the election seemed to believe, if not that they had foreseen the outcome, at least that their preelection expectancies were less discrepant from the election results than they really were.

Although postelection recall was distorted toward the actual election results, postelection estimates were still somewhat discrepant from the final vote. This suggests that certain factors constrained the degree of hindsight distortion that occurred. A priori predictions may serve as an anchor that prevents people from claiming post facto that they had made a perfectly accurate prediction. Although one's initial expectancies cannot be perfectly reconstructed after an outcome is known, enough information is available to hold postevent recall in check. Subjects appeared unable to recall accurately their preelection predictions, but they knew, for example, that few people had expected Reagan to do as well as 51% of the vote and thus could not, in retrospect, claim that they had known he would do that well.

The paper concludes with recommendations for future research.

Given the ubiquitousness of distorted hindsight, additional research is needed that examines the conditions under which it does and does not occur, as well as the behavioral consequences of overestimating one's accuracy in judging events. For example, attributions of blame are often predicted on the belief that the consequences of certain decisions and actions were potentially foreseeable (Shaw & Sulzer, 1964). As a result, distorted hindsight may lead individuals to unjustifiably blame others for failing to see what was "foreseeable" only in retrospect (Fischhoff, 1975a). Similarly, given that disconfirmed expectancies and observed incongruences often serve to facilitate learning and adjustment, the failure to be surprised by certain occurrences may interfere with experience-based learning and lead people to underestimate what may be learned from the past (Fischhoff, 1975a, 1977). In short, the "Monday morning quarterback" in us all warrants future research attention.

The references begin on a new page. Like the rest of the manuscript, the references are double-spaced.

References

Carter post-mortem: Debate hurt, but it wasn't only cause of defeat. (1980, November 9). The New York Times, pp. 1, 18.

This is the reference format for a newspaper article with no author listed.

Fischhoff, B. (1975a, April). The silly certainty of hindsight. Psychology Today, pp. 71–76.

This is the reference format for a magazine article.

Fischhoff, B. (1975b). Hindsight is not equal to foresight: The effect of outcome knowledge on judgment under uncertainty. Journal of Experimental Psychology: Human Perception and Performance, 1, 288–299.

Fischhoff, B. (1977). Perceived informativeness of facts. Journal of Experimental Psychology: Human Perception and Performance, 3, 349–358.

This reference for a journal article includes the author's name, the year of publication (in parentheses), the title of the article, the name of the journal (underlined), the volume number (underlined), and the page numbers.

Fischhoff, B., & Beyth, R. (1975). "I knew it would happen"--Remembered probability of once-future things. Organizational Behavior and Human Performance, 13, 1–16.

Goffman, E. (1959). The presentation of self in everyday life. Garden City, NY: Doubleday.

This reference to a book includes the author's name, the year of publication, the title (underlined), the city of publication, and the publisher.

Leary, M. R. (1981). The distorted nature of hindsight. Journal of Social Psychology, 15, 25–29.

Schlenker, B. R. (1980). Impression management: The self-concept, social identity, and interpersonal relations. Pacific Grove, CA: Brooks/Cole.

Shaw, M. E., & Sulzer, J. L. (1964). An empirical test of Heider's levels in attribution of responsibility. Journal of Abnormal and Social Psychology, 69, 39–46.

Walster, E. (1967). Second-guessing important events. Human Relations, 20, 239–249.

Wood, G. (1978). The knew-it-all-along effect. Journal of Experimental Psychology: Human Perception and Performance, 4, 345–353.

Author Notes

This is an edited and revised version of an article that was published in Personality and Social Psychology Bulletin. At the time the experiment was conducted, the author was at Denison University. The author thanks the members of Psychology 201 who helped with the study. Requests for reprints should be sent to Mark R. Leary, Department of Psychology, Wake Forest University, Winston-Salem, NC 27109.

The author notes report information about the execution of the study, express acknowledgments, and provide an address where the author may be reached. Although they are typed on a separate page at the end of the manuscript, in a published article the author's notes appear at the bottom of the first page.

Table 1

Pre- and Postelection Estimates of the Percentage of the Vote Obtained by

Each Candidate

Candidate	Preelection	Postelection	Actual percentage
Reagan	44.3	46.6	51.0
Anderson	14.1	10.5	7.0
Carter	41.7	42.9	41.0

Note. The differences between the preelection means and the postelection means

are significant for Reagan and Anderson, but not for Carter.

Tables appear at the end of the manuscript. The table number and
title are typed flush left and underlined; then, the table itself is typed
as shown. Authors often add a Note to explain aspects of the
information included in the table.

Key Terms

peer review   APA style

gender-neutral language   abstract

Review Questions

1. What are the three primary ways scientists share their work with the scientific community?

2. When an author submits a manuscript to a journal, by what general process is the decision made whether or not to publish the paper?

3. What are the three central characteristics of good writing?

4. Why do authors avoid using sexist language?

5. List in order the major sections of all research papers.

6. What is the purpose of the introduction of a paper?

7. What information should be included in the method section of a paper?

8. When presenting the results of statistical analyses, what information should be presented?

9. Show the proper form (APA style) for the reference citation to (a) a journal article and (b) a book.

Statistical Tables

Table of Random Numbers

54	83	80	53	90	50	90	46	47	12	62	68	30	91	21	01	37	36	20	95	56	44
36	85	49	83	47	89	46	28	59	02	87	98	10	47	22	67	27	33	13	60	56	74
60	98	76	53	02	01	82	77	45	12	68	13	09	20	73	07	92	53	45	42	88	00
62	79	39	83	88	02	60	92	82	00	76	30	77	98	45	00	97	78	16	71	80	25
43	32	31	21	10	50	42	16	85	20	74	29	64	72	59	58	96	30	73	85	50	54
04	06	78	46	48	03	45	42	29	96	84	39	43	11	45	33	29	98	73	24	85	16
88	92	41	05	15	27	96	28	95	35	89	35	37	97	32	63	45	83	48	12	13	86
77	55	21	12	47	48	36	64	45	52	23	47	98	27	08	63	26	05	45	12	02	89
66	56	61	47	78	76	79	71	47	80	14	78	01	33	00	87	07	02	71	28	22	87
07	52	33	33	62	64	27	52	21	08	39	74	15	66	41	04	93	20	49	23	83	91
91	56	78	63	85	29	88	09	97	30	55	53	68	48	85	52	90	80	11	88	29	84
02	71	28	22	87	97	19	42	21	03	50	39	80	61	30	80	12	75	84	32	76	33
15	50	42	16	66	78	90	11	23	45	52	62	69	79	86	96	03	13	19	82	22	93
64	65	33	97	30	74	07	40	84	27	60	94	31	93	76	97	31	47	65	23	98	32
66	00	19	89	62	32	37	74	85	50	78	76	20	87	25	94	03	46	77	47	97	32
53	88	67	43	29	16	24	91	62	49	04	17	76	79	81	18	41	15	88	62	62	28
23	89	00	30	81	69	80	17	50	48	85	68	27	33	93	45	99	79	48	60	02	82
78	32	26	30	92	41	33	82	88	50	08	53	43	51	78	88	83	77	67	98	07	35
57	84	36	18	38	52	30	76	32	85	42	93	87	61	95	04	53	18	34	29	23	23
58	20	13	24	27	27	19	39	57	30	56	82	24	06	89	96	38	30	58	74	14	95
13	39	15	65	09	20	71	01	53	11	40	99	63	36	39	43	82	77	37	40	23	29
89	62	56	22	12	56	34	46	73	32	50	91	48	19	54	54	07	31	05	60	35	89
95	01	61	16	96	94	44	43	80	69	84	95	14	93	57	48	61	36	15	26	65	10
87	07	15	56	09	36	90	74	78	28	97	82	45	36	11	82	02	13	72	70	13	45
14	65	89	78	52	33	02	05	97	32	13	07	47	21	51	61	44	38	68	01	25	04
63	25	42	44	14	27	77	78	56	91	39	37	19	60	17	99	68	76	14	16	24	34
89	40	87	73	19	90	15	27	68	93	76	95	45	41	41	34	37	92	68	60	27	37
91	71	57	46	17	64	98	17	15	64	36	83	22	97	58	80	97	45	39	90	83	96
19	55	28	47	72	56	17	10	51	31	30	43	15	46	41	38	66	23	62	46	42	46
16	67	20	88	26	82	94	22	57	52	91	24	92	31	38	98	32	62	09	76	88	39
26	55	42	12	15	77	06	08	55	86	68	56	74	06	23	01	35	16	20	58	61	93
07	41	37	55	67	62	77	83	26	25	49	35	18	09	18	92	30	76	44	89	66	22
49	97	63	88	58	07	94	08	07	83	59	99	67	35	95	83	67	28	71	67	04	77
63	41	65	82	12	58	31	76	14	02	36	32	82	30	84	67	13	98	14	90	07	44
46	49	86	69	62	09	45	07	66	69	82	10	06	85	64	37	24	50	37	76	66	13
07	83	36	27	20	35	63	17	32	08	93	87	51	18	01	75	72	46	28	88	34	86
14	08	64	69	40	98	03	39	03	21	82	36	96	19	15	20	06	62	19	90	80	37
63	33	98	17	10	72	17	96	96	03	97	00	07	26	74	63	47	73	73	11	62	78
47	37	57	04	14	46	07	06	86	67	96	68	35	80	34	17	75	33	63	57	25	90
08	84	98	27	72	48	10	48	84	30	28	24	74	96	78	40	41	74	45	41	40	51
03	91	76	37	27	35	31	42	97	76	41	66	30	17	20	92	00	01	01	58	72	05
46	42	60	16	64	82	85	99	15	81	74	16	61	42	71	40	30	17	79	71	37	49
57	68	54	54	74	25	07	47	34	88	15	95	89	79	26	15	19	36	55	22	37	10

Critical Values of t

1-tailed		0.25	0.1	0.05	0.025	0.01	0.005	0.001	0.0005
2-tailed		0.5	0.2	0.1	0.05	0.02	0.01	0.002	0.001
df	1	1.000	3.078	6.314	12.706	31.821	63.657	318.31	636.62
	2	0.816	1.886	2.920	4.303	6.965	9.925	22.327	31.598
	3	.765	1.638	2.353	3.182	4.541	5.841	10.214	12.924
	4	.741	1.533	2.132	2.776	3.747	4.604	7.173	8.610
	5	0.727	1.476	2.015	2.571	3.365	4.032	5.893	6.869
	6	.718	1.440	1.943	2.447	3.143	3.707	5.208	5.959
	7	.711	1.415	1.895	2.365	2.998	3.499	4.785	5.408
	8	.706	1.397	1.860	2.306	2.896	3.355	4.501	5.041
	9	.703	1.383	1.833	2.262	2.821	3.250	4.297	4.781
	10	0.700	1.372	1.812	2.228	2.764	3.169	4.144	4.587
	11	.697	1.363	1.796	2.201	2.718	3.106	4.025	4.437
	12	.695	1.356	1.782	2.179	2.681	3.055	3.930	4.318
	13	.694	1.350	1.771	2.160	2.650	3.012	3.852	4.221
	14	.692	1.345	1.761	2.145	2.624	2.977	3.787	4.140
	15	0.691	1.341	1.753	2.131	2.602	2.947	3.733	4.073
	16	.690	1.337	1.746	2.120	2.583	2.921	3.686	4.015
	17	.689	1.333	1.740	2.110	2.567	2.898	3.646	3.965
	18	.688	1.330	1.734	2.101	2.552	2.878	3.610	3.922
	19	.688	1.328	1.729	2.093	2.539	2.861	3.579	3.883
	20	0.687	1.325	1.725	2.086	2.528	2.845	3.552	3.850
	21	.686	1.323	1.721	2.080	2.518	2.831	3.527	3.819
	22	.686	1.321	1.717	2.074	2.508	2.819	3.505	3.792
	23	.685	1.319	1.714	2.069	2.500	2.807	3.485	3.767
	24	.685	1.318	1.711	2.064	2.492	2.797	3.467	3.745
	25	0.684	1.316	1.708	2.060	2.485	2.787	3.450	3.725
	26	.684	1.315	1.706	2.056	2.479	2.779	3.435	3.707
	27	.684	1.314	1.703	2.052	2.473	2.771	3.421	3.690
	28	.683	1.313	1.701	2.048	2.467	2.763	3.408	3.674
	29	.683	1.311	1.699	2.045	2.462	2.756	3.396	3.659
	30	0.683	1.310	1.697	2.042	2.457	2.750	3.385	3.646
	40	.681	1.303	1.684	2.021	2.423	2.704	3.307	3.551
	60	.679	1.296	1.671	2.000	2.390	2.660	3.232	3.460
	120	.677	1.289	1.658	1.980	2.358	2.617	3.160	3.373
	∞	.674	1.282	1.645	1.960	2.326	2.576	3.090	3.291

Note: From Table 12 of *Biometrika Tables for Statisticians* (Vol. 1, ed. 1) by E. S. Pearson and H. O. Hartley, London: Cambridge University Press, 1966, p. 146. Adapted by permission of the publisher and the Biometrika Trustees.

Critical Values of F

Values of F (for alpha level = .05)

df associated with the numerator (df_{bg})

df associated with the denominator (df_{wg})

	1	2	3	4	5	6	7	8	9	10	12	15	20	24	30	40	60	120	∞
1	161.4	199.5	215.7	224.6	230.2	234.0	236.8	238.9	240.5	241.9	243.9	245.9	248.0	249.1	250.1	251.1	252.2	253.3	254.3
2	18.51	19.00	19.16	19.25	19.30	19.33	19.35	19.37	19.38	19.40	19.41	19.43	19.45	19.45	19.46	19.47	19.48	19.49	19.50
3	10.13	9.55	9.28	9.12	9.01	8.94	8.89	8.85	8.81	8.79	8.74	8.70	8.66	8.64	8.62	8.59	8.57	8.55	8.53
4	7.71	6.94	6.59	6.39	6.26	6.16	6.09	6.04	6.00	5.96	5.91	5.86	5.80	5.77	5.75	5.72	5.69	5.66	5.63
5	6.61	5.79	5.41	5.19	5.05	4.95	4.88	4.82	4.77	4.74	4.68	4.62	4.56	4.53	4.50	4.46	4.43	4.40	4.36
6	5.99	5.14	4.76	4.53	4.39	4.28	4.21	4.15	4.10	4.06	4.00	3.94	3.87	3.84	3.81	3.77	3.74	3.70	3.67
7	5.59	4.74	4.35	4.12	3.97	3.87	3.79	3.73	3.68	3.64	3.57	3.51	3.44	3.41	3.38	3.34	3.30	3.27	3.23
8	5.32	4.46	4.07	3.84	3.69	3.58	3.50	3.44	3.39	3.35	3.28	3.22	3.15	3.12	3.08	3.04	3.01	2.97	2.93
9	5.12	4.26	3.86	3.63	3.48	3.37	3.29	3.23	3.18	3.14	3.07	3.01	2.94	2.90	2.86	2.83	2.79	2.75	2.71
10	4.96	4.10	3.71	3.48	3.33	3.22	3.14	3.07	3.02	2.98	2.91	2.85	2.77	2.74	2.70	2.66	2.62	2.58	2.54
11	4.84	3.98	3.59	3.36	3.20	3.09	3.01	2.95	2.90	2.85	2.79	2.72	2.65	2.61	2.57	2.53	2.49	2.45	2.40
12	4.75	3.89	3.49	3.26	3.11	3.00	2.91	2.85	2.80	2.75	2.69	2.62	2.54	2.51	2.47	2.43	2.38	2.34	2.30
13	4.67	3.81	3.41	3.18	3.03	2.92	2.83	2.77	2.71	2.67	2.60	2.53	2.46	2.42	2.38	2.34	2.30	2.25	2.21
14	4.60	3.74	3.34	3.11	2.96	2.85	2.76	2.70	2.65	2.60	2.53	2.46	2.39	2.35	2.31	2.27	2.22	2.18	2.13
15	4.54	3.68	3.29	3.06	2.90	2.79	2.71	2.64	2.59	2.54	2.48	2.40	2.33	2.29	2.25	2.20	2.16	2.11	2.07
16	4.49	3.63	3.24	3.01	2.85	2.74	2.66	2.59	2.54	2.49	2.42	2.35	2.28	2.24	2.19	2.15	2.11	2.06	2.01
17	4.45	3.59	3.20	2.96	2.81	2.70	2.61	2.55	2.49	2.45	2.38	2.31	2.23	2.19	2.15	2.10	2.06	2.01	1.96
18	4.41	3.55	3.16	2.93	2.77	2.66	2.58	2.51	2.46	2.41	2.34	2.27	2.19	2.15	2.11	2.06	2.02	1.97	1.92
19	4.38	3.52	3.13	2.90	2.74	2.63	2.54	2.48	2.42	2.38	2.31	2.23	2.16	2.11	2.07	2.03	1.98	1.93	1.88
20	4.35	3.49	3.10	2.87	2.71	2.60	2.51	2.45	2.39	2.35	2.28	2.20	2.12	2.08	2.04	1.99	1.95	1.90	1.84
21	4.32	3.47	3.07	2.84	2.68	2.57	2.49	2.42	2.37	2.32	2.25	2.18	2.10	2.05	2.01	1.96	1.92	1.87	1.81
22	4.30	3.44	3.05	2.82	2.66	2.55	2.46	2.40	2.34	2.30	2.23	2.15	2.07	2.03	1.98	1.94	1.89	1.84	1.78
23	4.28	3.42	3.03	2.80	2.64	2.53	2.44	2.37	2.32	2.27	2.20	2.13	2.05	2.01	1.96	1.91	1.86	1.81	1.76
24	4.26	3.40	3.01	2.78	2.62	2.51	2.42	2.36	2.30	2.25	2.18	2.11	2.03	1.98	1.94	1.89	1.84	1.79	1.73
25	4.24	3.39	2.99	2.76	2.60	2.49	2.40	2.34	2.28	2.24	2.16	2.09	2.01	1.96	1.92	1.87	1.82	1.77	1.71
26	4.23	3.37	2.98	2.74	2.59	2.47	2.39	2.32	2.27	2.22	2.15	2.07	1.99	1.95	1.90	1.85	1.80	1.75	1.69
27	4.21	3.35	2.96	2.73	2.57	2.46	2.37	2.31	2.25	2.20	2.13	2.06	1.97	1.93	1.88	1.84	1.79	1.73	1.67
28	4.20	3.34	2.95	2.71	2.56	2.45	2.36	2.29	2.24	2.19	2.12	2.04	1.96	1.91	1.87	1.82	1.77	1.71	1.65
29	4.18	3.33	2.93	2.70	2.55	2.43	2.35	2.28	2.22	2.18	2.10	2.03	1.94	1.90	1.85	1.81	1.75	1.70	1.64
30	4.17	3.32	2.92	2.69	2.53	2.42	2.33	2.27	2.21	2.16	2.09	2.01	1.93	1.89	1.84	1.79	1.74	1.68	1.62
40	4.08	3.23	2.84	2.61	2.45	2.34	2.25	2.18	2.12	2.08	2.00	1.92	1.84	1.79	1.74	1.69	1.64	1.58	1.51
60	4.00	3.15	2.76	2.53	2.37	2.25	2.17	2.10	2.04	1.99	1.92	1.84	1.75	1.70	1.65	1.59	1.53	1.47	1.39
120	3.92	3.07	2.68	2.45	2.29	2.17	2.09	2.02	1.96	1.91	1.83	1.75	1.66	1.61	1.55	1.50	1.43	1.35	1.25
∞	3.84	3.00	2.60	2.37	2.21	2.10	2.01	1.94	1.88	1.83	1.75	1.67	1.57	1.52	1.46	1.39	1.32	1.22	1.00

APPENDIX A-3 (Continued)

Critical Values of F

Values of F (for alpha level = .01)

df associated with the numerator (df_{bg})

df_{wg}	1	2	3	4	5	6	7	8	9	10	12	15	20	24	30	40	60	120	∞
1	4052	4999.5	5403	5625	5764	5859	5928	5981	6022	6056	6106	6157	6209	6235	6261	6287	6313	6339	6366
2	98.50	99.00	99.17	99.25	99.30	99.33	99.36	99.37	99.39	99.40	99.42	99.43	99.45	99.46	99.47	99.47	99.48	99.49	99.50
3	34.12	30.82	29.46	28.71	28.24	27.91	27.67	27.49	27.35	27.23	27.05	26.87	26.69	26.60	26.50	26.41	26.32	26.22	26.13
4	21.20	18.00	16.69	15.98	15.52	15.21	14.98	14.80	14.66	14.55	14.37	14.20	14.02	13.93	13.84	13.75	13.65	13.56	13.46
5	16.26	13.27	12.06	11.39	10.97	10.67	10.46	10.29	10.16	10.05	9.89	9.72	9.55	9.47	9.38	9.29	9.20	9.11	9.02
6	13.75	10.92	9.78	9.15	8.75	8.47	8.26	8.10	7.98	7.87	7.72	7.56	7.40	7.31	7.23	7.14	7.06	6.97	6.88
7	12.25	9.55	8.45	7.85	7.46	7.19	6.99	6.84	6.72	6.62	6.47	6.31	6.16	6.07	5.99	5.91	5.82	5.74	5.65
8	11.26	8.65	7.59	7.01	6.63	6.37	6.18	6.03	5.91	5.81	5.67	5.52	5.36	5.28	5.20	5.12	5.03	4.95	4.86
9	10.56	8.02	6.99	6.42	6.06	5.80	5.61	5.47	5.35	5.26	5.11	4.96	4.81	4.73	4.65	4.57	4.48	4.40	4.31
10	10.04	7.56	6.55	5.99	5.64	5.39	5.20	5.06	4.94	4.85	4.71	4.56	4.41	4.33	4.25	4.17	4.08	4.00	3.91
11	9.65	7.21	6.22	5.67	5.32	5.07	4.89	4.74	4.63	4.54	4.40	4.25	4.10	4.02	3.94	3.86	3.78	3.69	3.60
12	9.33	6.93	5.95	5.41	5.06	4.82	4.64	4.50	4.39	4.30	4.16	4.01	3.86	3.78	3.70	3.62	3.54	3.45	3.36
13	9.07	6.70	5.74	5.21	4.86	4.62	4.44	4.30	4.19	4.10	3.96	3.82	3.66	3.59	3.51	3.43	3.34	3.25	3.17
14	8.86	6.51	5.56	5.04	4.69	4.46	4.28	4.14	4.03	3.94	3.80	3.66	3.51	3.43	3.35	3.27	3.18	3.09	3.00
15	8.68	6.36	5.42	4.89	4.56	4.32	4.14	4.00	3.89	3.80	3.67	3.52	3.37	3.29	3.21	3.13	3.05	2.96	2.87
16	8.53	6.23	5.29	4.77	4.44	4.20	4.03	3.89	3.78	3.69	3.55	3.41	3.26	3.18	3.10	3.02	2.93	2.84	2.75
17	8.40	6.11	5.18	4.67	4.34	4.10	3.93	3.79	3.68	3.59	3.46	3.31	3.16	3.08	3.00	2.92	2.83	2.75	2.65
18	8.29	6.01	5.09	4.58	4.25	4.01	3.84	3.71	3.60	3.51	3.37	3.23	3.08	3.00	2.92	2.84	2.75	2.66	2.57
19	8.18	5.93	5.01	4.50	4.17	3.94	3.77	3.63	3.52	3.43	3.30	3.15	3.00	2.92	2.84	2.76	2.67	2.58	2.49
20	8.10	5.85	4.94	4.43	4.10	3.87	3.70	3.56	3.46	3.37	3.23	3.09	2.94	2.86	2.78	2.69	2.61	2.52	2.42
21	8.02	5.78	4.87	4.37	4.04	3.81	3.64	3.51	3.40	3.31	3.17	3.03	2.88	2.80	2.72	2.64	2.55	2.46	2.36
22	7.95	5.72	4.82	4.31	3.99	3.76	3.59	3.45	3.35	3.26	3.12	2.98	2.83	2.75	2.67	2.58	2.50	2.40	2.31
23	7.88	5.66	4.76	4.26	3.94	3.71	3.54	3.41	3.30	3.21	3.07	2.93	2.78	2.70	2.62	2.54	2.45	2.35	2.26
24	7.82	5.61	4.72	4.22	3.90	3.67	3.50	3.36	3.26	3.17	3.03	2.89	2.74	2.66	2.58	2.49	2.40	2.31	2.21
25	7.77	5.57	4.68	4.18	3.85	3.63	3.46	3.32	3.22	3.13	2.99	2.85	2.70	2.62	2.54	2.45	2.36	2.27	2.17
26	7.72	5.53	4.64	4.14	3.82	3.59	3.42	3.29	3.18	3.09	2.96	2.81	2.66	2.58	2.50	2.42	2.33	2.23	2.13
27	7.68	5.49	4.60	4.11	3.78	3.56	3.39	3.26	3.15	3.06	2.93	2.78	2.63	2.55	2.47	2.38	2.29	2.20	2.10
28	7.64	5.45	4.57	4.07	3.75	3.53	3.36	3.23	3.12	3.03	2.90	2.75	2.60	2.52	2.44	2.35	2.26	2.17	2.06
29	7.60	5.42	4.54	4.04	3.73	3.50	3.33	3.20	3.09	3.00	2.87	2.73	2.57	2.49	2.41	2.33	2.23	2.14	2.03
30	7.56	5.39	4.51	4.02	3.70	3.47	3.30	3.17	3.07	2.98	2.84	2.70	2.55	2.47	2.39	2.30	2.21	2.11	2.01
40	7.31	5.18	4.31	3.83	3.51	3.29	3.12	2.99	2.89	2.80	2.66	2.52	2.37	2.29	2.20	2.11	2.02	1.92	1.80
60	7.08	4.98	4.13	3.65	3.34	3.12	2.95	2.82	2.72	2.63	2.50	2.35	2.20	2.12	2.03	1.94	1.84	1.73	1.60
120	6.85	4.79	3.95	3.48	3.17	2.96	2.79	2.66	2.56	2.47	2.34	2.19	2.03	1.95	1.86	1.76	1.66	1.53	1.38
∞	6.63	4.61	3.78	3.32	3.02	2.80	2.64	2.51	2.41	2.32	2.18	2.04	1.88	1.79	1.70	1.59	1.47	1.32	1.00

df associated with the denominator (df_{wg})

Note: From Table 18 of Biometrika Tables for Statisticians [Vol. 1, ed. 1] by E. S. Pearson and H. O. Hartley, London: Cambridge University Press, 1966, pp. 171–173.

Computational Formulas for ANOVA

Appendix B-1

Calculational Formulas for a One-Way ANOVA

The demonstrational formulas for one-way ANOVA presented in Chapter 12 help to convey the rationale behind ANOVA, but they are unwieldy for computational purposes. Appendix B-1 presents the calculational formulas for performing a one-way ANOVA on data from a between-groups (completely randomized) design.

The data used in this example are from a hypothetical study of the effects of physical appearance on liking. In this study, subjects listened to another subject talk about him- or herself over an intercom for 5 minutes. Subjects were led to believe that the person they listened to was either very attractive, moderately attractive, or unattractive. To manipulate perceived attractiveness, the researcher gave each subject a Polaroid photograph that was supposedly a picture of the other subject. In reality, the pictures were prepared in advance and were *not* of the person who talked over the intercom.

After listening to the other person, subjects rated how much they liked him or her on a 7-point scale (where 1 = disliked greatly and 7 = liked greatly). Six subjects participated in each of the three conditions. The ratings for the 18 subjects are shown below.

Attractive picture	*Unattractive picture*	*Neutral picture*
7	4	5
5	3	6
5	4	6
6	4	4
4	3	5
6	5	5

Step 1.   For each condition, compute

1. The sum of all of the scores in each condition (Σx)

2. The mean of the condition ($\bar{x}$)

3. The sum of the squared scores (Σx^2)

4. The sum of squares ($\Sigma x^2 - [(\Sigma x)^2/n]$)

You'll find it useful to enter these quantities into a table such as the following:

	Attractive picture	*Unattractive picture*	*Neutral picture*
Σx	33	23	31
$\bar{x}$	5.5	3.8	5.2
Σx^2	187	91	163
SS	5.50	2.83	2.83

Steps 2–4 calculate the within-groups portion of the variance.

Step 2. Compute SS_{wg}—the sum of the SS of each condition:

$$SS_{wg} = SS_{a1} + SS_{a2} + SS_{a3}$$
$$= 5.50 + 2.83 + 2.83$$
$$= 11.16$$

Step 3. Compute df_{wg}:

$$df_{wg} = N - k, \quad \text{where } N = \text{total number of subjects and}$$
$$k = \text{number of conditions}$$

$$= 18 - 3$$
$$= 15$$

Step 4. Compute MS_{wg}:

$$MS_{wg} = SS_{wg}/df_{wg}$$
$$= 11.16/15$$
$$= .744$$

Set MS_{wg} aside momentarily as you calculate SS_{bg}.

Steps 5–7 calculate the between-groups portion of the variance.

Step 5. Compute SS_{bg}:

$$SS_{bg} = \frac{(\Sigma x_{a1})^2 + (\Sigma x_{a2})^2 + \cdots + (\Sigma x_{ak})^2}{n} - \frac{(\Sigma x)^2}{N}$$

$$= \frac{(33)^2 + (23)^2 + (31)^2}{6} - \frac{(33 + 23 + 31)^2}{18}$$

$$= \frac{1089 + 529 + 961}{6} - \frac{(87)^2}{18}$$

$$= 429.83 - 420.50$$
$$= 9.33$$

Step 6. Compute df_{bg}:

$$df_{bg} = k - 1, \quad \text{where } k = \text{number of conditions}$$
$$= 3 - 1$$
$$= 2$$

Step 7. Compute MS_{bg}:

$$MS_{bg} = SS_{bg}/df_{bg}$$
$$= 9.33/2$$
$$= 4.67$$

Step 8. Compute the calculated value of F:

$$F = MS_{bg}/MS_{wg}$$
$$= 4.67/.744$$
$$= 6.28$$

Step 9. Determine the critical value of F using Appendix A-3. For example, the critical value of F when $df_{bg} = 2$, $df_{wg} = 15$, and alpha $= .05$ is 3.68.

Step 10. If the calculated value of F (Step 8) is equal to or greater than the critical value of F (Step 9), we reject the null hypothesis and conclude that at least one mean differed from the others. In our example, 6.28 was greater than 3.68. Thus, we reject the null hypothesis and conclude that at least one mean differed from the others. Looking at the means, we see that subjects who received attractive pictures liked the other person most ($\bar{x} = 5.5$), those who received moderately attractive photos were second ($\bar{x} = 5.2$), and those who received unattractive pictures liked the other person least ($\bar{x} = 3.8$). We would need to conduct post hoc tests to determine which means differed significantly (see Chapter 12).

If the calculated value of F (Step 8) is less than the critical value (Step 9), we fail to reject the null hypothesis and conclude that the independent variable had no effect on subjects' responses.

Appendix B-2

Calculational Formulas for a Two-Way Factorial ANOVA

The conceptual rationale and demonstrational formulas for factorial analysis of variance are discussed in Chapter 12. The demonstrational formulas in Chapter 12 help to convey what each aspect of factorial ANOVA reflects, but they are unwieldy for computational purposes. Appendix B-2 presents the calculational formulas for performing factorial ANOVA on data from a between-groups factorial design.

The data are from a hypothetical study of the effects of audience size and composition on speech disfluencies, such as stuttering and hesitations. Twenty subjects told the study of Goldilocks and the Three Bears to a group of elementary school children or to a group of adults. Some subjects spoke to an audience of 5; others spoke to an audience of 20. This was a 2 × 2 factorial design, the two independent variables being audience composition (children versus adults) and audience size (5 versus 20). The dependent variable was the number of speech disfluencies—stutters, stammers, misspeaking, and the like—that the subject displayed while telling the story.

The data were as follows:

		B AUDIENCE SIZE	
		Small (b_1)	Large (b_2)
Children (a_1)		3	7
		1	2
		2	5
		5	3
A AUDIENCE COMPOSITION		4	4
Adults (a_2)		3	13
		8	9
		4	11
		2	8
		6	12

Step 1. For each condition (each combination of a and b), compute:

1. The sum of all of the scores in each condition (Σx)
2. The mean of the condition ($\bar{x}$)
3. The sum of the squared scores (Σx^2)
4. The sum of squares ($\Sigma x^2 - [(\Sigma x)^2/n]$)

You'll find it useful to enter these quantities into a table such as that given below:

		B	
		b_1	b_2
a_1	Σx	15	21
	$\bar{x}$	3.0	4.2
	Σx^2	55	103
	SS	10	14.8
A			
a_2	Σx	23	53
	$\bar{x}$	4.6	10.6
	Σx^2	129	579
	SS	23.2	17.2

Also, calculate $\Sigma(\Sigma x)^2/N$—the square of the sum of the condition totals divided by the total number of subjects:

$$\Sigma(\Sigma x)^2/N = (15 + 21 + 23 + 53)^2/20$$
$$= (112)^2/20$$
$$= 12544/20$$
$$= 627.2$$

This quantity appears in several of the formulas below.

Steps 2–4 compute the within-groups portion of the variance.

Step 2.   Compute SS_{wg}:

$$SS_{wg} = SS_{a1b1} + SS_{a1b2} + SS_{a2b1} + SS_{a2b2}$$
$$= 10 + 14.8 + 23.2 + 17.2$$
$$= 65.2$$

Step 3.   Compute df_{wg}:

$$df_{wg} = (j \times k)(n - 1), \qquad \text{where } j = \text{levels of } A$$
$$k = \text{levels of } B$$
$$n = \text{subjects per condition}$$

$$= (2 \times 2)(5 - 1)$$
$$= 16$$

Step 4.   Compute MS_{wg}:

$$MS_{wg} = SS_{wg}/df_{wg}$$
$$= 65.2/16$$
$$= 4.075$$

Set MS_{wg} aside for a moment. You will use it in the denominator of the F-tests you perform to test the main effects and interaction below.

Steps 5–8 calculate the main effect of A.

Step 5.   Compute SS_A:

$$SS_A = \frac{(\Sigma x_{a1b1} + \Sigma x_{a1b2})^2 + (\Sigma x_{a2b1} + \Sigma x_{a2b2})^2}{(n)(k)} - \frac{[\Sigma(\Sigma x)]^2}{N}$$

$$= \frac{(15 + 21)^2 + (23 + 53)^2}{(5)(2)} - 627.2$$

$$= \frac{(36)^2 + (76)^2}{10} - 627.2$$

$$= \frac{1296 + 5776}{10} - 627.2$$

$$= 707.2 - 627.2$$
$$= 80.0$$

Step 6.   Compute df_A:

$$df_A = j - 1, \qquad \text{where } j = \text{levels of } A$$
$$= 2 - 1$$
$$= 1$$

Step 7. Compute MS_A:

$MS_A = SS_A/df_A$

$\qquad = 80.0/1$

$\qquad = 80.0$

Step 8. Compute F_A:

$F_A = MS_A/MS_{wg}$

$\qquad = 80.0/4.075$

$\qquad = 19.63$

Step 9. Determine the critical value of F using Appendix A-3. The critical value of F (alpha level $= .05$) when $df_A = 1$ and $df_{wg} = 16$ is 4.49.

Step 10. If the calculated value of F (Step 8) is equal to or greater than the critical value of F (Step 9), we reject the null hypothesis and conclude that at least one mean differed from the others. In our example, 19.63 was greater than 4.49, so we reject the null hypothesis and conclude that a_1 differed from a_2. To interpret the effect, we would inspect the means of a_1 and a_2 (averaging across the levels of B). When we do this, we find that subjects who spoke to adults ($\bar{x} = 7.6$) emitted significantly more disfluencies than those who spoke to children ($\bar{x} = 3.6$).

If the calculated value of F (Step 8) is less than the critical value (Step 9), we fail to reject the null hypothesis and conclude that the independent variable had no effect on subjects' responses.

Steps 11–14 calculate the main effect of B.

Step 11. Compute SS_B:

$$SS_B = \frac{(\Sigma x_{a1b1} + \Sigma x_{a2b1})^2 + (\Sigma x_{a1b2} + \Sigma x_{a2b2})^2}{(n)(j)} - \frac{[\Sigma(\Sigma x)]^2}{N}$$

$$= \frac{(15 + 23)^2 + (21 + 53)^2}{(5)(2)} - 627.2$$

$$= \frac{(38)^2 + (74)^2}{10} - 627.2$$

$$= \frac{1444 + 5476}{10} - 627.2$$

$$= 692 - 627.2$$

$$= 64.8$$

Step 12.   Compute df_B:

$$df_B = k - 1 \qquad \text{where } k = \text{levels of } B$$
$$= 2 - 1$$
$$= 1$$

Step 13.   Compute MS_B:

$$MS_B = SS_B/df_B$$
$$= 64.8/1$$
$$= 64.8$$

Step 14.   Computer F_B:

$$F_B = MS_B/MS_{wg}$$
$$= 64.8/4.075$$
$$= 15.90$$

Step 15.   Determine the critical value of F using Appendix A-3. The critical value of $F(1, 16) = 4.49$.

Step 16.   If the calculated value of F (Step 14) is equal to or greater than the critical value of F (Step 15), we reject the null hypothesis and conclude that at least one mean differed from the others. In our example, 15.90 was greater than 4.49, so the main effect of B—audience size—was significant. Looking at the means for b_1 and b_2 (averaged across levels of A), we find that subjects emitted more speech disfluencies when they spoke to large audiences than when they spoke to small audiences; the means for the large and small audiences were 7.4 and 3.8, respectively.

    If the calculated value of F (Step 14) is less than the critical value (Step 15), we fail to reject the null hypothesis and conclude that the independent variable had no effect on subjects' responses.

Steps 17–23 calculate the A × B interaction.   The simplest way to obtain $SS_{A \times B}$ is by subtraction. If we subtract SS_A and SS_B from SS_{bg} (the sum of squares between-groups), we get $SS_{A \times B}$.

Step 17. Compute SS_{bg}:

$$SS_{bg} = \frac{(\Sigma x_{a1b1})^2 + (\Sigma x_{a1b2})^2 + (\Sigma x_{a2b1})^2 + (\Sigma x_{a2b2})^2}{n} - \frac{\Sigma(\Sigma x)^2}{N}$$

$$= \frac{(15)^2 + (21)^2 + (23)^2 + (53)^2}{5} - 627.2$$

$$= \frac{225 + 441 + 529 + 2809}{5} - 627.2$$

$$= 800.8 - 627.2$$

$$= 173.6$$

Step 18. Compute $SS_{A \times B}$:

$$SS_{A \times B} = SS_{bg} - SS_A - SS_B$$

$$= 173.6 - 80.0 - 64.8$$

$$= 28.8$$

Step 19. Compute $df_{A \times B}$:

$$df_{A \times B} = (j - 1)(k - 1)$$

$$= (2 - 1)(2 - 1)$$

$$= (1)(1)$$

$$= 1$$

Step 20. Compute $MS_{A \times B}$:

$$MS_{A \times B} = SS_{A \times B}/df_{A \times B}$$

$$= 28.8/1$$

$$= 28.8$$

Step 21. Compute $F_{A \times B}$:

$$F_{A \times B} = MS_{A \times B}/MS_{wg}$$

$$= 28.8/4.075$$

$$= 7.07$$

Step 22. Determine the critical value of F using Appendix A-3. We've seen already that for $F(1, 16)$, the critical value is 4.49.

Step 23. If the calculated value of F (Step 21) is equal to or greater than the critical value of F (Step 22), we reject the null hypothesis and conclude that at least one mean differed from the others. In our example, 7.07 was greater than 4.49, so we conclude that the $A \times B$ interaction was significant.

Looking at the means we calculated in Step 1, we see that subjects who spoke to a large audience of adults emitted a somewhat greater number of speech disfluencies than those in the other three conditions.

Audience composition	Audience size	
	Small	Large
Children	3.0	4.2
Adults	4.6	10.6

To determine precisely which means differed from one another, we would conduct tests of simple main effects.

If the calculated value of F (Step 21) is less than the critical value (Step 22), we fail to reject the null hypothesis and conclude that variables A and B (audience composition and size) did not interact.

Glossary

ABA design   A single-subject design in which baseline data are obtained (A), the independent variable is introduced and behavior is measured again (B), then the independent variable is withdrawn and behavior is observed a third time (A)

ABC design   a multiple-I single-subject design that contains a baseline period (A), followed by the introduction of one level of the independent variable (B), followed by the introduction of another level of the independent variable (C)

abstract   a brief summary of an article, presentation, or research report

acquiescence response style   the tendency for some people to agree with statements regardless of their content

alpha level   the maximum probability that researcher is willing to make a Type I error; typically, the alpha level is set at .05

analysis of variance (ANOVA)   an inferential statistical procedure used to test differences between means

APA style   guidelines set forth by the American Psychological Association for preparing research reports; these guidelines may be found in the *Publication Manual of the American Psychological Association* (4th ed.)

applied research   research aimed toward solving real-world problems or improving the quality of life

a priori prediction   a prediction made about the outcome of a study before data are collected

archival research   research in which data are analyzed from existing records, such as census reports, court records, or personal letters

attrition   the loss of subjects during a study

bar graph   a graph of data on which the variable on the *x*-axis is measured on a nominal or ordinal scale of measurement; because the *x*-variable is not continuous, the bars do not touch one another

basic research   research aimed toward basic understanding without regard for whether that understanding will be immediately applicable to solving real-world problems

behavioral coding system   a procedure for converting observed behaviors to numerical data for purposes of analysis

behavioral measure   the direct observation of a particular behavior

beta   the probability of committing a Type II error

between-groups design   an experimental design in which each subject serves in only one condition of the experiment

between-groups variance   the portion of the total variance in a set of scores that reflects systematic differences between the experimental groups

between-subjects design   an experimental design in which each subject serves in only one experimental condition

between-within design   an experimental design that combines one or more between-subjects factors with one or more within-subjects factors; a split-plot design

biased assignment   a threat to internal validity that occurs when subjects are assigned to conditions in a nonrandom manner, producing systematic differences among conditions prior to introduction of the independent variable

canonical correlation   a multivariate statistic that expresses the relationship between two sets of variables

canonical variable   a composite variable that is calculated by summing two or more dependent variables that have been weighted according to their ability to differentiate among groups of subjects

carryover effects   a situation in within-subjects designs in which the effects of one level of the independent variable are still present when another level of the independent variable is introduced

case study   a detailed, descriptive study of a individual, group, or event

checklist   a tally sheet used to record attributes of the subject and whether particular behaviors were observed

class interval   a subset of a range of scores; in a grouped frequency distribution, the number of subjects who fall into each class interval is shown

cluster sampling   a sampling procedure in which the researcher first samples clusters or groups of participants, then samples participants from the selected clusters

coefficient of determination   the square of the correlation coefficient; indicates the proportion of variance in one variable that can be accounted for by the other variable

completely randomized factorial design   an experimental design in which subjects are randomly assigned to experimental conditions

conceptual definition   an abstract, dictionary-type definition

concurrent validity a form of criterion-related validity that reflects the extent to which a measure allows a researcher to distinguish between respondents at the time the measure is taken

condition one level of an independent variable

confederate an accomplice of an experimenter whom subjects assume to be another subject or an uninvolved bystander

confounding a condition that exists when something other than the independent variable differs systematically among the experimental conditions

confound variance the portion of the total variance in a set of scores that is due to extraneous variables that differ systematically between the experimental groups; also called **secondary variance**

construct validity the degree to which a measure of a particular construct correlates as expected with measures of related constructs

content analysis procedures used to convert textual written or spoken information to more manageable data relevant to the researcher's goals

contrived observation the observation of behavior in settings that have been arranged specifically for observing and recording behavior

control group subjects who receive a zero level of the independent variable

convenience sample a nonprobability sample that includes whatever subjects happen to be readily available

convergent validity documenting the validity of a measure by showing that it correlates appropriately with measures of related constructs

converging operations measuring a particular behavior or construct using several different measurement approaches

correlational research research designed to examine the nature of the relationship between two naturally occurring variables

correlation coefficient an index of the direction and magnitude of the relationship between two variables; the value of a correlation coefficient ranges from -1.00 to $+1.00$

cost–benefit analysis a method of making decisions in which the potential costs and risks of a study are weighed against its likely benefits

counterbalancing a procedure used in within-subjects designs in which different subjects receive the levels of the independent variable in different orders; counterbalancing is used to avoid systematic order effects

criterion-related validity the extent to which a measure allows a researcher to distinguish among respondents on the basis of some behavioral criterion

criterion variable the variable being predicted in a regression analysis; the dependent, or outcome, variable

critical multiplism   the philosophy that researchers should use many ways of obtaining evidence regarding a particular hypothesis rather than relying on a single approach

critical value   the minimum value of a statistic (such as t or F) at which the results would be considered statistically significant

Cronbach's alpha coefficient   an index of interitem reliability

cross-lagged panel correlational design   a research design in which two variables are measured at two points in time and correlations between the variables across time are examined

debriefing   the procedure through which research participants are told about the nature of a study after it is completed

deception   the practice of misleading or lying to subjects for research purposes

deduction   the process of reasoning from a general proposition to a specific implication of that proposition; for example, hypotheses are often deduced from theories

demand characteristics   aspects of a study that indicate to subjects how they are expected to respond

dependent variable   the response measured in a study; typically a measure of subjects' thoughts, feelings, behavior, or physiological reactions

descriptive research   research designed to describe the behavior, thoughts, or feelings of a group of subjects

descriptive statistics   numbers that summarize and describe the behavior of subjects in a study; the mean and standard deviation are examples of descriptive statistics

diary methodology   a method of data collection in which subjects keep a daily record of their behavior, thoughts, or feelings

differential attrition   the loss of subjects during a study in a manner such that the loss is not randomly distributed across experimental conditions

directional hypothesis   a prediction that explicitly states the direction of a hypothesized effect; for example, which of two condition means will be larger

discriminant validity   documenting the validity of a measure by showing that it does not correlate with measures of conceptually unrelated constructs

disguised observation   observing subjects' behavior without their knowledge

double-blind procedure   the practice of concealing the purpose and hypotheses of a study both from the participants and from the researchers who have direct contact with the participants.

economic sample   a sample that provides a reasonable degree of accuracy at a reasonable cost in terms of money, time, and effort

effect size   the strength of the relationship between two or more variables, usually expressed as the proportion of variance in one variable than can be accounted for by another variable

empiricism   the practice of relying on observation to draw conclusions about the world

environmental manipulation   an independent variable that involves the experimental modification of the subject's physical or social environment

epsem design   a sampling procedure in which all cases in the population have an equal probability of being chosen for the sample; epsem stands for *equal-probability selection method*

error of estimation   the degree to which data obtained from a sample are expected to deviate from the population as a whole; also called the **margin of error**

error variance   that portion of the total variance in a set of data that remains unaccounted for after systematic variance is removed; variance unrelated to the variables under investigation in a study; also called **within-groups variance**

evaluation research   see **program evaluation**

expericorr design   an experimental design that includes one or more manipulated independent variables and one or more preexisting subject variables that are measured rather than manipulated; a mixed factorial design

experiment   a study in which the researcher assigns subjects to conditions and manipulates at least one independent variable

experimental contamination   a situation that occurs when subjects in one experimental condition are indirectly affected by the independent variable in another experimental condition because they interacted with subjects in the other condition

experimental control   the practice of eliminating or holding constant extraneous variables that might affect the outcome of an experiment

experimental group   subjects who receive a nonzero level of the independent variable

experimental hypothesis   the hypothesis that the independent variable did have an effect; equivalently, the hypothesis that the means of the various experimental conditions will differ from one another

experimental realism   a research setting that subjects find psychologically involving and compelling

experimental research   research designed to test whether certain variables cause changes in behavior, thoughts, or feelings

experimenter expectancy effect   the influence of the researcher's hypotheses on the outcome of a study; also called the **Rosenthal effect**

experimenter's dilemma   the fact that, generally speaking, the greater the internal validity of an experiment, the lower its external validity, and vice versa

external validity   the degree to which the results obtained in one study can be replicated or generalized to other samples, research settings, and procedures

extreme groups procedure   creating two groups of subjects with unusually low or unusually high scores on a particular variable

face validity   the extent to which a measurement procedure appears to measure what it is suppose to measure

factor   (1) in experimental designs, an independent variable; (2) in factor analysis, the underlying dimension that is assumed to account for observed relationships among variables

factor analysis   a class of multivariate statistical techniques used to identify the underlying dimensions (factors) that account for the observed relationships among a set of measured variables

factorial design   an experimental design in which two or more independent variables are manipulated

factor loading   in factor analysis, the correlation between a variable and a factor

factor matrix   a table that shows the results of a factor analysis; in this matrix, the rows are variables and the columns are factors

failing to reject the null hypothesis   concluding on the basis of statistical evidence that the null hypothesis is true—that the independent variable did not have an effect

falsifiability   the requirement that a hypothesis must be capable of being falsified

follow-up tests   inferential statistics that are used after a significant F-test to determine which means differ from which; so called **post hoc tests** or **multiple comparisons**

frequency   the number of subjects who obtained a particular score

frequency distribution   a table that shows the number of subjects who obtained each possible score on a measure

frequency polygon   see **line graph**

F-test   an inferential statistical procedure used to test for differences among condition means; the F-test is used in ANOVA

gender-neutral language   language that treats men and women equitably

grand mean   the mean of all of the condition means in an experiment

graphic analysis   in single-subject research, the visual inspection of graphs of the data to determine whether or not the independent variable affected the subject's behavior; also called visual inspection

group design   an experimental design in which several subjects serve in each condition of the design and the data are analyzed by examining the average responses of subjects in these conditions

grouped frequency distribution   a table that indicates the number of subjects who obtained each of a range of scores

halo bias the tendency for observers' ratings of a subject to be distorted by their overall evaluation of the subject

histogram a form of bar graph

history effects changes in subjects' responses between pretest and posttest that are due to an outside, extraneous influence rather than to the independent variable

hypothesis a proposition that follows logically from a theory; also, a prediction regarding the outcome of a study

hypothetical construct an entity that cannot be directly observed but is inferred on the basis of observable evidence; intelligence, status, and anxiety are examples of hypothetical constructs

idiographic approach research that describes, analyzes, or compares the behavior of individual subjects

independent variable in an experiment, the variable that is varied or manipulated by the researcher to assess its effects on subjects' behavior

induction the process of reasoning from specific instances to a general proposition about those instances; for example, hypotheses are sometimes induced from observed facts

inferential statistics mathematical analyses that allow researchers to draw conclusions regarding the reliability and generalizability of their data; t-tests and F-tests are inferential statistics

informed consent the practice of informing participants regarding the nature of their participation in a study and obtaining their explicit consent to participate

informed consent form a form that describes the nature of subjects' participation in a study (including all possible risks) and provides a place for subjects to indicate their willingness to participate

Institutional Review Board (IRB) a committee mandated by federal regulations that must evaluate the ethics of research conducted at institutions that receive federal funding

instructional manipulation an independent variable that is varied through verbal information provided to subjects

interaction the combined effect of two or more independent variables such that the effect of one independent variable differs across the levels of the other independent variable(s)

interbehavior latency the time that expires between the performance of two behaviors

interitem reliability the consistency of respondents' scores on a set of conceptually related items; the degree to which a set of items that ostensibly measure the same construct are intercorrelated

internal validity the degree to which a researcher draws accurate conclusions about the effects of an independent variable

interquartile range   the interval or range from the first to the third quartile; the range of the middle 50% of a distribution of scores

interrater reliability   the degree to which the observations of two independent raters or observers agree; also called interjudge or interobserver reliability

interrupted time series design   a study in which the dependent variable is measured several times, the independent variable is introduced, and then the dependent variable is measured several more times

intersubject replication   in single-subject research, the attempt to document the generalizability of an experimental effect by demonstrating the effect on other participants

interval scale   a measure on which equal distances between scores represent equal differences in the property being measured

interview   a method of data collection in which the researcher asks questions and the subject responds orally

interview schedule   the series of questions and accompanying response formats that guides an interviewer's line of questioning during an interview

intrasubject replication   in single-subject research, the attempt to repeatedly demonstrate an experimental effect on a single participant by alternatively introducing and withdrawing the independent variable

invasion of privacy   violation of research participants' rights to determine how, when, or where they will be studied

invasive manipulation   an independent variable that directly alters the participant's body, such as surgical procedures or the administration of chemical substances

item-total correlation   the correlation between respondents' scores on one item from a scale and the sum of their responses on the remaining items; an index of **interitem reliability**

knowledgeable informant   someone who knows a subject well enough to report on his or her behavior

latency   the amount of time that elapses between a particular event and a behavior

level   one value of an independent variable

linear regression analysis   a statistical procedure in which an equation is developed to predict scores on one variable from scores on another variable

line graph   a graph in which the means for various groups are plotted and connected by a line

local history effect   a threat to internal validity in which some extraneous event happens to one experimental group that does not happen to the other group(s)

main effect   the effect of a particular independent variable, ignoring the effects of other independent variables in the experiment

manipulation check   a measure that documents whether an independent variable was manipulated successfully

margin of error   see **error of estimation**

matched random assignment   a procedure for assigning subjects to experimental conditions in which subjects are first matched into homogeneous blocks, then subjects within each block are assigned randomly to conditions

matched-subjects design   an experimental design in which subjects are matched into homogeneous blocks, and subjects in each block are randomly assigned to the experimental conditions

matched-subjects factorial design   a factorial design in which subjects are first matched into homogeneous blocks, then randomly assigned to experimental conditions

maturation   changes in subjects' responses between pretest and posttest due to the passage of time rather than to the independent variable; aging, fatigue, and hunger may produce maturation effects, for example

mean   the mathematical average of a set of scores; the sum of a set of scores divided by the number of scores

mean square between-groups   a measure of between-groups variance calculated by dividing the sum of squares between-groups by the between-groups degrees of freedom

mean square within-groups   the average variance within experimental conditions; the sum of squares within-groups divided by the degrees of freedom within-groups

measure of strength of association   a statistic that expresses the degree to which two or more variables are related

measurement error   the deviation of a subject's observed score from its true score

measures of central tendency   descriptive statistics that convey information about the average or most typical score in a distribution; the mean, median, and mode are measures of central tendency

measures of variability   descriptive statistics that convey information about the spread or variability of a set of data; the range, variance, and standard deviation are measures of variability

median   the score that falls at the 50th percentile in a rank-ordered distribution; the middle score in a distribution

median-split procedure   assigning subjects to two groups depending on whether their scores on a particular variable fall below or above the median of that variable

meta-analysis   a statistical procedure used to analyze and integrate the results from many individual studies

minimal risk   risk to research participants that is no greater than they would be likely to encounter in daily life or during routine physical or psychological examinations

mixed factorial design   (1) an experimental design that includes one or more manipulated independent variables and one or more preexisting subject variables that are measured rather than manipulated; an expericorr design; (2) the term is also used by some researchers to refer to a between-within design

mode   the most frequent score in a distribution

moderator variable   a variable that qualifies or moderates the effects of another variable on behavior

multiple baseline design   a single-subject design in which two or more behaviors are studied simultaneously

multiple comparisons   inferential statistics used after a significant *F*-test to determine which means differ from which; also called **post hoc tests** or **follow-up tests**

multiple correlation coefficient   the correlation between one variable and a set of other variables

multiple-I design   a single-subject design in which levels of an independent variable are introduced one at a time

multiple regression analysis   a statistical procedure in which an equation is derived by which one variable (the criterion variable) can be predicted from a set of other variables (the predictor variables)

multistage sampling   a variation of cluster sampling in which large clusters of subjects are sampled, followed by smaller clusters from within the larger clusters, followed by still smaller clusters, until subjects are sampled from the small clusters

multivariate analysis of variance (MANOVA)   a statistical procedure that simultaneously tests differences among the means of two or more groups on two or more dependent variables

mundane realism   a research setting that recreates situations encountered in the real world

narrative record   a full description of a subject's behavior

naturalistic observation   observation of ongoing behavior as it occurs naturally with no intrusion or intervention by the researcher

naysaying   the tendency for some subjects to disagree with questions on questionnaires or in interviews regardless of the question content

negative correlation   an inverse relationship between two variables such that subjects with high scores on one variable tend to have low scores on the other variable, and vice versa

negatively skewed distribution   a distribution in which there are more high scores than low scores

nominal scale   a measure on which the numbers assigned to subjects' characteristics are merely labels; subject gender is on a nominal scale, for example

nomothetic approach   research that seeks to establish general principles and broad generalizations

nondirectional hypothesis   a prediction that does not express the direction of a hypothesized effect, for example which of two condition means will be larger

nonequivalent groups posttest-only design   a quasi-experimental design in which preexisting groups are studied—one that has received the quasi-independent variable and one or more others that have not

nonequivalent groups pretest–posttest design   a quasi-experimental design in which preexisting groups are tested—one that has received the quasi-independent variable and one that has not; each group is tested twice, once before and once after one group receives the quasi-independent variable

nonprobability sample   a sample selected in such a way that the likelihood of any member of the population being chosen for the sample cannot be determined

normal distribution   a distribution of scores that rises to a rounded peak in the center with symmetrical tails descending to the left and right of the center

null finding   obtaining no significant differences among condition means; concluding that the independent variable did not have an effect

null hypothesis   the hypothesis that the independent variable will not have an effect; equivalently, the hypothesis that the means of the various experimental conditions will not differ

one-group pretest–posttest design   a preexperimental design in which one group of subjects is tested both before and after a quasi-independent variable has occurred; because it fails to control for nearly all threats to internal validity, this design should rarely be used

one-tailed test   a statistic (such as *t*) used to test a directional hypothesis

one-way design   an experimental design with a single independent variable

operational definition   a definition that defines a construct by specifying precisely how it is measured or manipulated in a particular study

operationism   the philosophy that says that only operational definitions may be used in science

order effects   an effect on behavior produced by the specific order in which levels of the independent variable are administered in a within-subjects design

ordinal scale   a measure on which the numbers assigned to subjects' responses reflect the rank order of subjects from highest to lowest

outlier   an extreme score; typically, scores that fall further than ±3 standard deviations from the mean are considered outliers

paired *t*-test   a *t*-test performed on a repeated measures two-group design

partial correlation   the correlation between two variables with the influence of one or more other variables removed

participant observation   a method of data collection in which the researcher engages in the same activities as the subjects he or she is observing

path analysis   a statistical technique that tests the plausibility of various explanations of the relationships among a set of correlated variables

Pearson correlation coefficient   the most commonly used measure of correlation

peer review   the process of having research evaluated by other scientists to determine its suitability for publication, presentation, or funding

perfect correlation   a correlation of -1.00 or $+1.00$, indicating that two variables are so closely related that one can be perfectly predicted from the other

physiological measure   a measure of bodily activity; in behavioral research, physiological measures generally are used to assess processes within the nervous system

pilot test   a preliminary test of the effectiveness of an independent variable prior to conducting an experiment

placebo control group   subjects who receive an ineffective treatment; used to identify and control for **placebo effects**

placebo effect   a physiological or psychological change that occurs as a result of mere suggestion that the change will occur

positive correlation   a direct relationship between two variables such that subjects with high scores on one variable also tend to have high scores on the other variable, and low scorers on one variable also tend to score low on the other

positively skewed distribution   a distribution in which there are more low scores than high scores

post hoc explanation   an explanation offered for a set of findings after the data are collected and analyzed

post hoc tests   inferential statistics used after a significant *F*-test to determine which means differ; also called **follow-up tests** or **multiple comparisons**

posttest-only design   an experiment in which subjects' responses are measured only once—after introduction of the independent variable

power   the degree to which a research design is sensitive to the effects of the independent variable; powerful designs are able to detect effects of the independent variable more easily than less powerful designs

predictive validity   a form of criterion-related validity that reflects the extent to which a measure allows a researcher to distinguish between respondents at some time in the future

predictor variables   in a regression analysis, the variables that are used to predict scores on the criterion or dependent variable

preexperimental design   a design that lacks the necessary controls to minimize threats to internal validity; typically, preexperimental designs do not involve adequate control or comparison groups

pretest–posttest design   an experiment in which subjects' responses are measured twice—once before and once after introduction of the independent variable

pretest sensitization   the situation that occurs when being pretested affects subjects' responses on the posttest

primary variance   that portion of the total variance in a set of scores that is due to the independent variable; also called **treatment variance**

probability sample   a sample selected in such a way that the likelihood of any individual in the population being selected can be specified

program evaluation   the use of behavioral research methods to assess the effects of programs on behavior; also called **evaluation research**

pseudoscience   claims of knowledge that are couched in the trappings of science but that violate the central criteria of scientific investigation, such as systematic empiricism, public verification, and testability

psychometrics   the field devoted to the study of psychological measurement; experts in this field are known as *psychometricians*

purposive sample   a sample selected on the basis of the researcher's judgment regarding the "best" subjects to select for research purposes

quartile   when a set of scores is split into four equal parts, the point at the upper limit of each quarter of scores

quasi-experimental design   a research design in which the researcher cannot assign subjects to conditions and/or manipulate the independent variable; instead, comparisons are made between groups that already exist or within a single group before and after a quasi-experimental treatment has occurred

quasi-independent variable   the independent variable in a quasi-experimental design; the designator *quasi*-independent is used when the variable was not manipulated by the researcher

questionnaire   a method of data collection in which subjects respond to written questions or statements

quota sample   a sample selected to include specified proportions of certain kinds of subjects

randomized groups design   an experimental design in which each subject is randomly assigned to serve in only one condition of the experiment; a **between-groups design**

range   a measure of variability equal to the difference between the largest and smallest scores in a set of data

ratio scale   a measure on which scores possess all the characteristics of real numbers

raw data matrix a table of the original data collected on a sample of subjects; in this table, each subject is represented by a row and each dependent variable is represented by a column

reaction time the time that elapses between a particular stimulus and a subject's response

reactive measure the measure of a behavior that is affected by subjects' knowledge that they are being observed

regression coefficient the slope of a regression line

regression constant the y-intercept in a regression equation; the value of y when $x = 0$

regression equation an equation from which one can predict scores on one variable from one or more other variables

regression to the mean the tendency for subjects who are selected on the basis of their extreme scores on some measure to obtain less extreme scores when they are retested

rejecting the null hypothesis concluding on the basis of the statistical evidence that the null hypothesis is false—concluding that the independent variable did have an effect

relative frequency distribution a table that indicates the proportion of subjects who fell in each class interval

reliability the consistency or dependability of a measurement procedure

repeated measures design an experimental design in which each subject serves in more than one condition of the experiment; a **within-subjects design**

repeated measures factorial design an experimental design involving two or more independent variables in which each subject serves in every condition of the design; also called a **within-subjects factorial design**

representative sample a sample from which one can draw accurate, unbiased estimates of the characteristics of a larger population

response format the manner in which respondents indicate their answers to questions

restricted range the condition that exists when a set of scores fall in only a narrow range due to the homogeneity of the subjects on the attribute being measured

reversal design a single-subject experimental design in which the effects of an independent variable are examined by introducing the independent variable, and then withdrawing it; the ABA design is the simplest example of a reversal design

Rosenthal effect see **experimenter expectancy effect**

sample a subset of a population; the group of subjects who are selected to participate in a research study

sampling   the process by which a sample is chosen from a population to participate in a research study

sampling error   the difference between the data obtained on a sample and the data that would have been obtained if the entire population had been studied

sampling frame   a listing of the members of a population

scatterplot   a graphical representation of subjects' scores on two variables; the values of one variable are plotted on the *x*-axis and those of the other variable are plotted on the *y*-axis

scientific misconduct   behavior that violates basic ethical principles of scientific investigation

secondary variance   that portion of the total variance in a set of scores that is due to extraneous variables that differ systematically between the experimental groups; also called **confound variance**

selection bias   a threat to internal validity involving experimental groups that are not equivalent before the manipulation of the independent or quasi-independent variable

selection-by-history interaction   see **local history effect**

self-report measure   a measure on which subjects provide information about themselves—on a questionnaire or in an interview, for example

simple frequency distribution   a table that indicates the number of subjects who obtained each score

simple interrupted time series design   a quasi-experimental design in which subjects are tested on many occasions—several before and several after the introduction of the quasi-independent variable

simple main effect   the effect of one independent variable at a particular level of another independent variable

simple random assignment   placing subjects in experimental conditions in such a way that every subject has an equal chance of being placed in any condition

simple random sample   a sample selected in such a way that every possible sample of the desired size has the same chance of being selected from the population

single-subject design   an experimental design in which the unit of analysis is the individual participant rather than the experimental group; also called a single-case design

social desirability response bias   the tendency for some people to distort their responses in a manner that portrays them in a positive light

split-half reliability   the correlation between respondents' scores on two halves of a single instrument; an index of **interitem reliability**

split-plot factorial design   an experimental design that combines one or more between-subjects factors with one or more within-subjects factors; also called a **between-within design**

standard deviation a measure of variability equal to the square root of the variance

statistical notation a system of letters and symbols used to convey statistical operations mathematically

statistical significance a finding that is very unlikely to be due to error variance

strategy of strong inference the strategy of designing research in such a way that it tests the relative viability of two or more competing theories

stratified random sampling a sampling procedure in which the population is divided into strata, then subjects are sampled randomly from each stratum

stratum a subset of a population that shares a certain characteristic; for example, a population could be divided into the strata of men and women

subject variable a personal characteristic of research participants, such as age, self-esteem, or extraversion

sum of squares the sum of the squared deviations of subjects' scores from the mean

sum of squares between-groups the total variance in a set of scores associated with the independent variable; the sum of the squared differences between each condition mean and the grand mean

sum of squares within-groups the sum of the variances of the scores within particular experimental conditions

systematic sampling a sampling procedure in which every *n*th name is selected from a list

systematic variance that portion of the total variance in a set of scores that is related in an orderly, predictable fashion to the variables the researcher is investigating

table of random numbers a table containing numbers that occur in a random order; such a table appears in Appendix A-1

task completion time the amount of time a subject takes to complete a task

test–retest reliability the consistency of respondents' scores on a measure across time

theory a set of propositions that attempts to specify the interrelationships among a set of constructs

time series design a class of quasi-experimental designs in which subjects are tested on many occasions—several before and several after the introduction of the quasi-independent variable

total mean square the variance of a set of data; the sum of squares divided by its degrees of freedom

total sum of squares the total variability in a set of data; calculated by subtracting the mean from each score, squaring these differences, and summing them

total variance the total sum of squares divided by $n - 1$

treatment variance that portion of the total variance in a set of scores that is due to the independent variable; also called **primary variance**

triangulation see **converging operations**

true score the hypothetical score a subject would have obtained if the attribute being measured could be measured without error

t-test an inferential statistical procedure used to test the difference between two means

two-group experimental design an experiment with two conditions; the smallest possible experiment

two-tailed test a statistic (such as t) used to test a nondirectional hypothesis

Type I error erroneously rejecting the null hypothesis; concluding that an independent variable had an effect when, in fact, it did not

Type II error erroneously failing to reject the null hypothesis; concluding that the independent variable did not have an effect when, in fact, it did

undisguised observation observing subjects with their knowledge

unobtrusive measure a dependent variable that can be measured without affecting subjects' responses

validity the extent to which a measurement procedure actually measures what it is intended to measure

variance a numerical index of the variability in a set of data

within-groups variance the variability among scores within a particular experimental condition; see also **error variance**

within-subjects design an experimental design in which each subject serves in more than one condition of the experiment; a **repeated measures design**

within-subjects factorial design an experimental design involving two or more independent variables in which each subject serves in every condition of the design; also called a **repeated measures factorial design**

z-score an indication of how much a particular subject's score varies from the mean in terms of standard deviations; also called a standard score

References

Abramson, L. Y., Seligman, M. E. P., & Teasdale, J. D. (1978). Learned helplessness in humans: Critique and reformulation. *Journal of Abnormal Psychology, 87,* 49–74.

Adams, K. L., & Ware, N. C. (1989). Sexism and the English language: The linguistic implications of being a woman. In J. Freeman (Ed.), *Women: A feminist perspective* (pp. 470–484). Mountain View, CA: Mayfield.

Aiken, L. S., & West, S. G. (1991). *Multiple regression: Testing and interpreting interactions.* Newbury Park, CA: Sage.

Allport, G. W. (1961). *Pattern and growth in personality.* New York: Holt, Rinehart & Winston.

American Psychological Association. (1982). *Ethical principles in the conduct of research with human participants.* Washington, DC: Author.

American Psychological Association. (1994). *Publication manual of the American Psychological Association* (4th ed.). Washington, DC: Author.

American Psychological Association. (1985). *Guidelines for ethical conduct in the care and use of animals.* Washington, DC: Author.

Anderson, C. A. (1989). Temperature and aggression: Ubiquitous effects of heat on occurrence of human violence. *Psychological Bulletin, 106,* 74–96.

Asendorpf, J. (1990). The expression of shyness and embarrassment. In W. R. Crozier (Ed.), *Shyness and embarrassment* (pp. 87–118). Cambridge: Cambridge University Press.

Ayala, F. J., & Black, B. (1993). Science and the courts. *American Scientist, 81,* 230–239.

Bales, R. F. (1970). *Personality and interpersonal behavior.* New York: Holt, Rinehart & Winston.

Bar-Yoseph, T. L., & Witztum, E. (1992). Using strategic psychotherapy: A case study of chronic PTSD after a terrorist attack. *Journal of Contemporary Psychotherapy, 22,* 263–276.

Baron, R. A., & Bell, P. A. (1976). Aggression and heat: The influence of ambient temperature, negative affect, and a cooling drink on physical aggression. *Journal of Personality and Social Psychology, 33,* 245–255.

Baumeister, R. F., Heatherton, T. F., & Tice, D. M. (1993). When ego threats lead to self-regulation failure: Negative consequences of high self-esteem. *Journal of Personality and Social Psychology, 64,* 141–156.

Baumrind, D. (1971). Principles of ethical conduct in the treatment of subjects: Reactions to the draft report of the committee on ethical standards in psychological research. *American Psychologist, 26,* 887–896.

Bell, C. R. (1962). Personality characteristics of volunteers for psychological studies. *British Journal of Social and Clinical Psychology, 1,* 81–95.

Berelson, B. (1952). *Content analysis in communication research.* New York: Free Press.

Bissonnette, V., Ickes, W., Bernstein, I., & Knowles, E. (1990). Personality moderating variables: A warning about statistical artifact and a comparison of analytic techniques. *Journal of Personality, 58,* 567–587.

Boring, E. G. (1954). The nature and history of experimental control. *American Journal of Psychology, 67,* 573–589.

Bower, G. H., Karlin, M. B., & Dueck, A. (1975). Comprehension and memory for pictures. *Memory and Cognition, 3,* 216–220.

Braginsky, B., & Braginsky, D. (1967). Schizophrenic patients in the psychiatric interview: An experimental study of their effectiveness at manipulation. *Journal of Consulting Psychology, 30,* 295–300.

Braginsky, B. M., Braginsky, D. D., & Ring, K. (1982). *Methods of madness: The mental hospital as a last resort.* Lanham, MD: University Press of America.

Bringmann, W. (1979). Wundt's lab: "humble . . . but functioning" (letter to the editor). *APA Monitor* (Sept/Oct), p. 13.

Bromley, D. B. (1986). *The case-study method in psychology and related disciplines.* Chichester: Wiley.

Brown, A. S. (1988). Encountering misspellings and spelling performance: Why wrong isn't right. *Journal of Educational Psychology, 80,* 488–494.

Bryan, J. H., & Test, M. A. (1967). Models and helping: Naturalistic studies in aiding behavior. *Journal of Personality and Social Psychology, 6,* 400–407.

Butler, A. C., Hokanson, J. E., & Flynn, H. A. (1994). A comparison of self-esteem lability and low trait self-esteem as vulnerability factors for depression. *Journal of Personality and Social Psychology, 66,* 166–177.

Campbell, D., Sanderson, R. E., & Laverty, S. G. (1964). Characteristics of a conditioned response in human subjects during extinction trials following a single traumatic conditioning trial. *Journal of Abnormal and Social Psychology, 68,* 627–639.

Campbell, D. T., & Stanley, J. C. (1966). *Experimental and quasi-experimental designs for research.* Skokie, IL: Rand McNally.

Campbell, P. B. (1983). The impact of societal biases on research methods. In B. L. Richardson & J. Wirtenberg (Eds.), *Sex role research* (pp. 197–214). New York: Praeger.

Carlson, R. (1971). Where is the person in personality research? *Psychological Bulletin, 75,* 203–219.

Chassin, L., Pillow, D. R., Curran, P. J., Molina, B. S. G., & Barrera, Jr., M. (1993). Relation of parental alcoholism to early adolescent substance use: A test of three mediating mechanisms. *Journal of Abnormal Psychology, 102,* 3–19.

Cheek, J. M. (1982). Aggregation, moderator variables, and the validity of personality tests: A peer-rating study. *Journal of Personality and Social Psychology, 43,* 1254–1269.

Chevalier-Skolnikoff, S., & Liska, J. (1993). Tool use by wild and captive elephants. *Animal Behavior, 46,* 209–219.

Christensen, L. (1988). Deception in psychological research: When is its use justified? *Personality and Social Psychology Bulletin, 14,* 664–675.

Cialdini, R. B., Vincent, J. E., Lewis, S. K., Catalan, J., Wheeler, D., & Darby, B. L. (1975). Reciprocal concessions procedure for inducing compliance: The door-in-the-face technique. *Journal of Personality and Social Psychology, 31,* 206–215.

Cochran, W. G., Mosteller, F., & Tukey, J. W. (1953). Statistical problems in the Kinsey report. *Journal of the American Statistical Association, 48,* 673–716.

Cohen, J. (1977). *Statistical power analysis for the behavioral sciences* (Rev. ed.). New York: Academic Press.

Cohen, J., & Cohen, P. (1983). *Applied multiple regression/correlation analysis for the behavioral sciences* (2nd ed.). Hillsdale, NJ: Erlbaum.

Condray, D. S. (1986). Quasi-experimental analysis: A mixture of methods and judgment. In W. M. K. Trochim (Ed.), *Advances in quasi-experimental design and analysis* (pp. 9–28). San Francisco: Jossey-Bass.

Cook, T. D., & Campbell, D. T. (1979). *Quasi-experimentation.* Boston: Houghton Mifflin.

Cooper, H. (1990). Meta-analysis and the integrative research review. In C. Hendrick & M. S. Clark (Eds.), *Reseach methods in personality and social psychology.* Newbury Park, CA: Sage.

Cooper, W. H. (1981). Ubiquitious halo. *Psychological Bulletin, 90,* 218–244.

Cordaro, L., & Ison, J. R. (1963). Psychology of the scientist: X. Observer bias in classical conditioning of the planaria. *Psychological Reports, 13,* 787–789.

Cowles, M. (1989). *Statistics in psychology: An historical perspective.* Hillsdale, NJ: Erlbaum.

Cronbach, L. J. (1970). *Essentials of psychological testing* (3rd ed.). New York: Harper & Row.

Cronbach, L. J., & Meehl, P. E. (1955). Construct validity in psychological tests. *Psychological Bulletin, 52,* 281–302.

Deitz, S. M. (1977). An anlysis of programming DRL schedules in educational settings. *Behaviour Research and Therapy, 15,* 103–111.

Denenberg, V. H. (1982). Comparative psychology and single-subject research. In A. E. Kazdin & A. H. Tuma (Eds.), *Single-case research designs* (pp. 19–31). San Francisco: Jossey-Bass.

Dworkin, S. I., Bimle, C., & Miyauchi, T. (1989). Differential effects of pentobarbital and cocaine on punished and nonpunished responding. *Journal of the Experimental Analysis of Behavior, 51,* 173–184.

Eagly, A. H., & Johnson, B. T. (1990). Gender and leadership style. *Psychological Bulletin, 108,* 233–256.

Eron, L. D., Huesmann, L. R., Lefkowitz, M. M., & Walder, L. O. (1972). Does television violence cause aggression? *American Psychologist, 27,* 253–263.

Estes, W. K. (1964). All-or-none processes in learning and retention. *American Psychologist, 19,* 16–25.

Ethical Principles of Psychologists and Code of Conduct. (1992). *American Psychologist, 47,* 1597–1611.

Festinger, L., Riecken, H. W., & Schachter, S. (1956). *When prophecy fails.* Minneapolis: University of Minnesota Press.

Feyerabend, P. K. (1965). Problems of empiricism. In R. Colodny (Ed.), *Beyond the edge of certainty.* Englewood Cliffs, NJ: Prentice-Hall.

Fiedler, F. E. (1967). *A theory of leadership effectiveness.* New York: McGraw-Hill.

Fontana, A. F., & Gessner, T. (1969). Patients' goals and the manifestation of psychopathology. *Journal of Consulting and Clinical Psychology, 33,* 247–253.

Freedman, J. L. (1975). *Crowding and behavior.* San Francisco: W. H. Freeman.

Garmezy, N. (1982). The case for the single case in research. In A. E. Kazdin & A. H. Tuma (Eds.), *Single-case research designs* (pp. 5–17). San Francisco: Jossey-Bass.

Gelfand, D. M., Hartmann, D. P., Walder, P., & Page, B. (1973). Who reports shoplifters: A field-experimental study. *Journal of Personality and Social Psychology, 25,* 276–285.

Glass, G. V. (1976). Primary, secondary, and meta-analysis of research. *Educational Researcher, 5,* 3–8.

Gottschalk, L. A., Uliana, R., & Gilbert, R. (1988). Presidential candidates and cognitive impairment measured from behavior in campaign debates. *Public Administration Review, 48,* 613–618.

Grady, K. E. (1981). Sex bias in research design. *Psychology of Women Quarterly, 5,* 628–636.

Gross, A. E., & Fleming, I. (1982). Twenty years of deception in social psychology. *Personality and Social Psychology Bulletin, 8,* 402–408.

Hansel, C. E. M. (1980). *ESP and parapsychology: A critical re-evaluation.* Buffalo, NY: Prometheus Books.

Hart, E. A., Leary, M. R., & Rejeski, W. J. (1989). The measurement of social physique anxiety. *Journal of Sport and Exercise Psychology, 11,* 94–104.

Hempel, C. G. (1966). *Philosophy of natural science.* Englewood Cliffs, NJ: Prentice-Hall.

Henle, M., & Hubbell, M. B. (1938). "Egocentricity" in adult conversation. *Journal of Social Psychology, 9,* 227–234.

Hilliard, R. B. (1993). Single-case methodology in psychotherapy process and outcome research. *Journal of Consulting and Clinical Psychology, 61,* 373–380.

Hite, S. (1987). *Women and love.* New York: Knopf.

Horner, J. R. (1990). *Digging dinosaurs.* New York: Harper & Row.

Huck, S. W., & Sandler, H. M. (1979). *Rival hypotheses: Alternative explanations of data-based conclusions.* New York: Harper & Row.

Huff, D. (1954). *How to lie with statistics.* New York: Norton.

Humphreys, L. (1975). *Tearoom trade: Impersonal sex in public places.* Chicago: Aldine.

Hunt, M. (1974). *Sexual behavior in the 1970s.* Chicago: Playboy Press.

Hyde, J. S., Fennema, E., & Lamon, S. J. (1990). Gender differences in mathematics performance: A meta-analysis. *Psychological Bulletin, 107,* 139–155.

Ickes, W. (1982). A basic paradigm for the study of personality, roles, and social behavior. In W. Ickes & E. S. Knowles (Eds.), *Personality, roles, and social behavior* (pp. 305–341). New York: Springer-Verlag.

Ickes, W., Bissonnette, V., Garcia, S., & Stinson, L. L. (1990). Implementing and using the dyadic interaction paradigm. In C. Hendrick & M. S. Clark (Eds.), *Research methods in personality and social psychology* (pp. 16–44). Newbury Park, CA: Sage.

Janis, I. L. (1982). *Groupthink.* Boston: Houghton Mifflin.

Jones, E. E. (1993). Introduction to special section: Single-case research in psychotherapy. *Journal of Consulting and Clinical Psychology, 61,* 371–372.

Jung, J. (1971). *The experimenter's dilemma.* New York: Harper & Row.

Kaplan, R. M. (1982). Nader's raid on the testing industry. *American Psychologist, 37,* 15–23.

Kazdin, A. E. (1982). *Single-case research designs.* New York: Oxford.

Kendall, M. G. (1970). Ronald Aylmer Fisher, 1890–1962. In E. S. Pearson & M. G. Kendall (Eds.), *Studies in the history of probability and statistics* (pp. 439–453). London: Griffin.

Keppel, G. (1982). *Design and analysis: A researcher's handbook.* Englewood Cliffs, NJ: Prentice-Hall.

Kidd, V. (1971). A study of the images produced through the use of the male pronoun as the generic. *Moments in Contemporary Rhetoric and Communication, 1,* 25–30.

Kinsey, A. C., Pomeroy, W. B., & Martin, C. E. (1948). *Sexual behavior in the human male.* Philadelphia: Saunders.

Kinsey, A. C., Pomeroy, W. B., Martin, C. E., & Gebhard, P. H. (1953). *Sexual behavior in the human female.* Philadelphia: Saunders.

Kirby, D. (1977). The methods and methodological problems of sex research. In J. S. DeLora & C. A. B. Warren (Eds.), *Understanding sexual interaction.* Boston: Houghton Mifflin.

Kneip R. C., Delamater, A. M., Ismond, T., Milford, C., Salvia, L., & Schwartz, D. (1993). Self- and spouse ratings of anger and hostility as predictors of coronary heart disease. *Health Psychology, 12,* 301–307.

Kowalski, R. M. (1994). *Teaching the appropriate approach to the analysis of mixed experimental designs.* Manuscript under review, Western Carolina University.

Kramer, A. F., Coyne, J. T., & Strayer, D. L. (1993). Cognitive function at high altitude. *Human Factors, 35,* 329–344.

Kratochwill, T. R. (1978). *Single subject research.* New York: Academic Press.

Kuhn, T. S. (1962). *The structure of scientific revolutions.* Chicago: University of Chicago Press.

Langer, E. J., & Rodin, J. (1976). The effects of choice and enhanced personal responsibility for the aged: A field experiment in an institutional setting. *Journal of Personality and Social Psychology, 34,* 191–198.

Leary, M. R., & Meadows, S. (1991). Predictors, elicitors, and concomitants to social blushing. *Journal of Personality and Social Psychology, 60,* 254–262.

Leary, M. R., & Miller, R. S. (1986). *Social psychology and dysfunctional behavior.* New York: Springer-Verlag.

Levesque, R. J. R. (1993). The romantic experience of adolescents in satisfying love relationships. *Journal of Youth and Adolescence, 22,* 219–251.

Levin, I., & Stokes, J. P. (1986). An examination of the relation of individual difference variables to loneliness. *Journal of Personality, 54,* 717–733.

Lewinsohn, P. M., Hops, H., Roberts, R. E., Seeley, J. R., & Andrews, J. A. (1993). Adolescent psychopathology: I. Prevalence and incidence of depression and other *DSM-III-R* disorders in high school students. *Journal of Abnormal Psychology, 102,* 133–144.

Luria, A. R. (1968). *The mind of a mnemonist.* New York: Basic Books.

Mahoney, M. J., Moura, N. G. M., & Wade, T. C. (1973). Relative efficacy of self-reward, self-punishment, and self-monitoring techniques for weight loss. *Journal of Consulting and Clinical Psychology, 40,* 404–407.

Massey, W. (1992). *National Science Foundation Annual Report 1991.* Washington, DC: National Science Foundation.

Masters, W. H., & Johnson, V. (1966). *Human sexual response.* Boston: Little, Brown.

Maxwell, S. E., Camp, C. J., & Avery, R. D. (1981). Measures of strength of association: A comparative examination. *Journal of Applied Psychology, 66,* 525–534.

Maxwell, S. E., & Delaney, H. D. (1993). Bivariate median splits and spurious statistical significance. *Psychological Bulletin, 113,* 181–190.

Mazur-Hart, S. F., & Berman, J. J. (1977). Changing from fault to no-fault divorce: An interrupted time series analysis. *Journal of Applied Social Psychology, 7,* 300–312.

McCall, R. (1988). Science and the press. *American Psychologist, 43,* 87–94.

McClelland, D. C., Atkinson, J. W., Clark, R. A., & Lowell, E. L. (1953). *The achievement motive.* New York: Appleton-Century-Crofts.

McCrae, R. R., & Costa, P. T., Jr. (1987). Validation of the five-factor model of personality across instruments and observers. *Journal of Personality and Social Psychology, 52,* 81–90.

McHale, S. M., & Gamble, W. C. (1989). Sibling relationships of children with disabled and nondisabled brothers and sisters. *Developmental Psychology, 25,* 421–429.

Middlemist, R. D., Knowles, E. S., & Matter, C. F. (1976). Personal space invasion in the lavatory: Suggestive evidence for arousal. *Journal of Personality and Social Psychology, 35,* 541–546.

Milgram, S. (1963). Behavioral study of obedience. *Journal of Abnormal and Social Psychology, 67,* 371–378.

Miller, N. E. (1985). The value of behavioral research on animals. *American Psychologist, 40,* 423–440.

Minium, E. (1978). *Statistical reasoning in psychology and education* (2nd ed.). New York: Wiley.

Mischel, W. (1968). *Personality and assessment.* New York: Wiley.

Mook, D. G. (1983). In defense of external invalidity. *American Psychologist, 38,* 379–387.

Moscowitz, D. S. (1986). Comparison of self-reports, reports by knowledgeable informants, and behavioral observation data. *Journal of Personality, 54,* 294–317.

Murray, H. A. (1938). *Explorations in personality.* Oxford, England: Oxford University Press.

Neale, J. M., & Liebert, R. M. (1980). *Science and behavior.* Englewood Cliffs, NJ: Prentice-Hall.

Nisbett, R. E., & Wilson, T. D. (1977). Telling more than we can know: Verbal reports on mental processes. *Psychological Review, 84,* 231–259.

Nunnally, J. C. (1978). *Psychometric theory* (2nd ed.). New York: McGraw-Hill.

Official IRB guidebook. (1986). The President's Commission for the Study of Ethical Problems in Medicine and Biomedical and Behavioral Research. Washington, DC: Government Printing Office.

Orbach, I., Kedem, P., Gorchover, O., Apter, A., & Tyano, S. (1993). Fear of death in suicidal and nonsuicidal adolescents. *Journal of Abnormal Psychology, 102,* 553–558.

Orne, M. T., & Scheibe, K. E. (1964). The contribution of nondeprivation factors in the production of sensory deprivation effects: The psychology of the "panic button." *Journal of Abnormal and Social Psychology, 68,* 3–12.

Pearson, E. S., & Kendall, M. G. (1970). *Studies in the history of statistics and probability.* London: Griffin.

Pearson, J. C. (1985). *Gender and communication.* Dubuque, IA: William C. Brown.

Pennebaker, J. W. (1990). *Opening up: The healing power of confiding in others.* New York: Morrow.

Pennebaker, J. W., Kiecolt-Glaser, J. K., & Glaser, R. (1988). Disclosure of traumas and immune function: Health implications for psychotherapy. *Journal of Consulting and Clinical Psychology, 56,* 239–245.

Piaget, J. (1951). *Play, dreams, and imitation in childhood* (trans. C. Gattegno & F. M. Hodgson). New York: Norton.

Piliavin, I. M., Rodin, J., & Piliavin, J. A. (1969). Good Samaritanism: An underground phenomenon? *Journal of Personality and Social Psychology, 13,* 289–299.

Platt, J. R. (1964). Strong inference. *Science, 146,* 347–353.

Popper, K. R. (1959). *The logic of scientific discovery.* New York: Basic Books.

Prussia, G. E., Kinicki, A. J., & Bracker, J. S. (1993). Psychological and behavioral consequences of job loss: A covariance structure analysis using Weiner's (1985) attribution model. *Journal of Applied Psychology, 78,* 382–394.

Radner, D., & Radner, M. (1982). *Science and unreason.* Belmont, CA: Wadsworth.

Reardon, P., & Prescott, S. (1977). Sex as reported in a recent sample of psychological research. *Psychology of Women Quarterly, 2,* 57–61.

Reis, H. T., & Wheeler, L. (1991). Studying social interaction with the Rochester Interaction Record. In M. P. Zanna (Ed.), *Advances in experimental social psychology* (Vol. 24, pp. 270–318). San Diego: Academic Press.

Robinson, P. W., & Foster, D. F. (1979). *Experimental psychology: A small-N approach.* New York: Harper & Row.

Rodin, J., & Langer, E. J. (1977). Long-term effects of a control-relevant intervention with the institutionalized aged. *Journal of Personality and Social Psychology, 35,* 897–902.

Rosen, K. S., & Rothbaum, F. (1993). Quality of parental caregiving and security of attachment. *Developmental Psychology, 29,* 358–367.

Rosen, L. A., Booth, S. R., Bender, M. E., McGrath, M. L., Sorrell, S., & Drabman, R. S. (1988). Effects of sugar (sucrose) on children's behavior. *Journal of Consulting and Clinical Psychology, 56,* 583–589.

Rosenberg, M. (1965). *Society and the adolescent self-esteem.* Princeton, NJ: Princeton University Press.

Rosengren, K. E. (1981). *Advances in content analysis.* Newbury Park, CA: Sage.

Rosnow, R. L., Rotheram-Borus, M. J., Ceci, S. J., Blanck, P. D., & Koocher, G. P. (1993). The institutional review board as a mirror of scientific and ethical standards. *American Psychologist, 48,* 821–826.

Runyan, W. M. (1982). *Life histories and psychobiography: Explorations in theory and method.* New York: Oxford University Press.

Sawyer, H. G. (1961). *The meaning of numbers.* Speech before the American Association of Advertising Agencies, as cited in E. J. Webb, D. T.

Campbell, R. D. Schwartz, & L. Sechrest, *Unobtrusive measures* (1966). Skokie, IL: Rand McNally.

Scarr, S., Webber, P. L., Weinberg, R. A., & Wittig, M. A. (1981). Personality resemblance among adolescents and their parents in biologically related and adoptive families. *Journal of Personality and Social Psychology, 40,* 885–898.

Schachter, S., & Singer, J. (1962). Cognitive social and physiological determinants of emotional state. *Psychological Review, 65,* 379–399.

Scheier, M. F., & Carver, C. S. (1985). Dispositional optimism and physical well-being: The influence of generalized outcome expectancies on health. *Journal of Personality, 55,* 169–210.

Schlenker, B. R., & Forsyth, D. R. (1977). On the ethics of psychological research. *Journal of Experimental Social Psychology, 13,* 369–396.

Schuman, H., & Kalton, G. (1985). Survey methods. In G. Lindzey & E. Aronson (Eds.), *Handbook of social psychology* (3rd ed., Vol. 1). New York: Random House.

Sedikides, C. (1993). Assessment, enhancement, and verification determinants of the self-evaluation process. *Journal of Personality and Social Psychology, 65,* 317–38.

Shadish, W. R., Cook, T. D., & Houts, A. C. (1986). Quasi-experimentation in a critical multiplist mode. In W. M. K. Trochim (Ed.), *Advances in quasi-experimental design and analysis* (pp. 29–46). San Francisco: Jossey-Bass.

Sidman, M. (1960). *Tactics of scientific research.* New York: Basic Books.

Simonton, D. K. (1988). Presidential style: Personality, biography, and performance. *Journal of Personality and Social Psychology, 55,* 928–936.

Singleton, Jr., R., Straits, B. C., Straits, M. M., & McAllister, R. J. (1988). *Approaches to social research.* New York: Oxford University Press.

Smith, S. S., & Richardson, D. (1983). Amelioration of deception and harm in psychological research: The important role of debriefing. *Journal of Personality and Social Psychology, 44,* 1075–1082.

Smoll, F. L., Smith, R. R., Barnett, N. P., & Everett, J. J. (1993). Enhancement of children's self-esteem through social support training for youth sport coaches. *Journal of Applied Psychology, 78,* 602–610.

Sperry, R. W. (1975). Lateral specialization in the surgically separated hemispheres. In B. Milner (Ed.), *Hemisperic specialization and interaction.* Cambridge: MIT Press.

Stanovich, K. E. (1992). *How to think straight about psychology.* Chicago: Scott, Foresman.

Steinberg, L., Fegley, S., & Dornbush, S. M. (1993). Negative impact of part-time work on adolescent adjustment: Evidence from a longitudinal study. *Developmental Psychology, 29,* 171–180.

Stericker, A. (1981). Does this "he or she" business really make a difference?

The effect of masculine pronouns as generics on job attitudes. *Sex Roles, 7,* 637–641.

Stigler, S. M. (1986). *The history of statistics.* Cambridge, MA: Belknap Press.

Stiles, W. B. (1978). Verbal response modes and dimensions of interpersonal roles: A method of discourse analysis. *Journal of Personality and Social Psychology, 36,* 693–703.

Straits, B. C., Wuebben, P. L., & Majka, T. J. (1972). Influences on subjects' perceptions of experimental research situation. *Sociometry, 35,* 499–518.

Summary report of journal operations, 1992. (1993). *American Psychologist, 48,* 829.

Swazey, J. P., Anderson, M. S., & Lewis, K. S. (1993). Ethical problems in academic research. *American Scientist, 81,* 542–553.

Terkel, J., & Rosenblatt, J. S. (1968). Maternal behavior induced by maternal blood plasma injected into virgin rats. *Journal of Comparative and Physiological Psychology, 65,* 479–482.

Timms, M. W. H. (1980). Treatment of chronic blushing by paradoxical intention. *Behavioral Psychotherapy, 8,* 59–61.

Underwood, B. J. (1957). *Psychological research.* New York: Appleton-Century-Crofts.

U.S. Department of Education. (1991). *Effective compensatory education sourcebook* (Vol. 5). Washington, DC: Government Printing Office.

U.S. Department of Health and Human Services. (1983). *Code of federal regulations pertaining to the protection of human subjects.* Washington, DC: Government Printing Office.

Viney, L. L. (1983). The assessment of psychological states through content analysis of verbal communications. *Psychological Bulletin, 94,* 542–563.

von Daniken, E. (1970). *Chariots of the Gods?* New York: Bantam.

Wagaman, J. R., Miltenberger, R. G., & Arndorfer, R. E. (1993). Analysis of a simplified treatment for stuttering in children. *Journal of Applied Behavior Analysis, 26,* 53–61.

Walk, R. D. (1969). Two types of depth discrimination by the human infant with five inches of visual depth. *Psychonomic Society, 14,* 251–255.

Watson, C. G. (1972). A comparison of the ethical self-presentations of schizophrenics, prisoners, and normals. *Journal of Clinical Psychology, 28,* 479–483.

Watson, R. I. (1978). *The great psychologists* (4th ed.). Philadelphia: Lippincott.

Weber, R. P. (1990). *Basic content analysis* (2nd ed.). Newbury Park, CA: Sage.

Weick, K. E. (1968). Systematic observational methods. In G. Lindzey & E. Aronson (Eds.), *The handbook of social psychology* (2nd ed., Vol. 2., pp. 357–451). Reading, MA: Addison-Wesley.

Weisz, A. E., & Taylor, R. L. (1969). American Presidential assassinations. *Diseases of the Nervous System, 30,* 659–668.

Wheeler, L., Reis, H., & Nezlek, J. (1983). Loneliness, social interaction, and sex roles. *Journal of Personality and Social Psychology, 45,* 943–953.

Wundt, W. (1874). *Principles of physiological psychology.* Leipzig: Engelmann.

Zeskind, P. S., Parter-Pierce, S., & Barr, R. G. (1993). Rhythmic organization of the sound of infant crying. *Developmental Psychobiology, 26,* 321–333.

Zimbardo, P. G. (1969). The human choice: Individuating reason, and order versus deindividuation, impulse, and chaos. In W. J. Arnold & D. Levine (Eds.), *Nebraska symposium on motivation,* 1969. Lincoln, NE: University of Nebraska Press.

Name Index

Abramson, L. Y., 13
Adams, K. L., 344
Aiken, L. S., 226
Anderson, M. S., 330, 331
Anderson, C. A., 41
Andrews, J. A., 21
Apter, A., 103
Arndorfer, R. E., 302, 303
Asendorpf, J., 78
Atkinson, J. W., 130
Avery, R. D., 43
Ayala, F. J., 14, 19

Bales, R. F., 51, 78, 80
Bar-Yoseph, T. L., 307, 308
Barnett, N. P., 275, 277
Baron, R. A., 40, 41, 42
Barr, R. G., 79
Barrera, Jr., M., 167
Baumeister, R. F., 226, 227, 228
Baumrind, D., 323
Bell, C. R., 130
Bell, P. A., 40, 41, 42
Bender, M. E., 186, 198
Berelson, B., 88
Berman, J. J., 280
Bernstein, I., 226
Bimle, C., 298, 300, 301
Binet, A., 49, 50, 63
Bissonnette, V., 76, 226
Black, B., 14, 19
Blanck, P. D., 325
Booth, S. R., 186, 198
Boring, E. G., 290

Bower, G. H., 208, 209, 210, 243
Bracker, J. S., 43, 44
Braginsky, B. M., 72, 90
Braginsky, D., 72, 90
Bringmann, W., 6
Bromley, D. B., 305
Brown, A. S., 181
Bryan, J. H., 78
Butler, A. C., 264

Camp, C. J., 43
Campbell, D., 322
Campbell, D. T., 165, 202, 282
Carlson, R., 130
Carver, C. S., 41, 42
Catalan, J., 175, 176
Cattell, J. M., 7
Ceci, S. J., 325
Chassin, L., 167
Cheek, J. M., 51
Chevalier-Skolnikoff, S., 73
Christensen, L., 323
Clark, R. A., 130
Cochran, W. G., 127
Cohen, J., 44, 148, 226
Cohen, P., 226
Condray, D. S., 283, 284
Cook, T. D., 165, 282, 284, 285
Cooper, H., 45
Cooper, W. H., 87
Cordaro, L., 195
Costa, Jr., P. T., 171

Cowles, M., 146
Coyne, J. T., 78
Cronbach, L. J., 61, 64, 65
Curran, P. J., 167

Darby, B. L., 175, 176
Darwin, C., 145
Deitz, S. M., 296
Delamater, A. M., 22
Delaney, H. D., 226
Denenberg, V. H., 304
Dornbusch, S. M., 23
Drabman, R. S., 186, 198
Dueck, A., 208, 209, 210, 243
Dworkin, S. I., 298, 300, 301

Eagley, A. H., 46
Eron, L. D., 165
Estes, W. K., 294
Everett, J. J., 275, 277

Fegley, S., 23
Fennema, E., 46
Festinger, L., 73, 75, 305
Feyerabend, P. K., 19
Fiedler, F. E., 10
Fisher, R. A., 260
Fleming, I., 323
Flynn, H. A., 264
Fontana, A. F., 90
Forsyth, D. R., 314, 315
Fossey, D., 73
Foster, D. F., 290
Freedman, J. L., 214, 215, 218, 220, 222, 255
Freud, S., 13, 305

Subject Index

TO THE OWNER OF THIS BOOK:

I hope that you have found *Introduction to Behavioral Research Methods*, Second Edition, useful. So that this book can be improved in a future edition, would you take the time to complete this sheet and return it? Thank you.

School and address: _____

Department: _____

Instructor's name: _____

1. What I like most about this book is: _____

_____

_____

2. What I like least about this book is: _____

_____

_____

3. My general reaction to this book is: _____

_____

4. The name of the course in which I used this book is: _____

_____

5. Were all of the chapters of the book assigned for you to read? _____

    If not, which ones weren't? _____

  6. In the space below, or on a separate sheet of paper, please write specific suggestions for improving this book and anything else you'd care to share about your experience in using the book.

_____

_____

_____

_____

_____

Optional:

Your name: _____ Date: _____

May Brooks/Cole quote you, either in promotion for *Introduction to Behavioral Research Methods*, Second Edition, or in future publishing ventures?

Yes: _____ No: _____

Sincerely,

Mark R. Leary

FOLD HERE

NO POSTAGE
NECESSARY
IF MAILED
IN THE
UNITED STATES

BUSINESS REPLY MAIL
FIRST CLASS   PERMIT NO. 358   PACIFIC GROVE, CA

POSTAGE WILL BE PAID BY ADDRESSEE

ATT: *Mark R. Leary* _____

Brooks/Cole Publishing Company
511 Forest Lodge Road
Pacific Grove, California 93950-9968

FOLD HERE